The Formation of Islam

Religion and Society in the Near East, 600–1800

Jonathan Berkey's book surveys the religious history of the peoples of the Near East from roughly 600 to 1800 CE. The opening chapter examines the religious scene in the Near East in late antiquity, and the religious traditions which preceded Islam. Subsequent chapters investigate Islam's first century and the beginnings of its own traditions, the 'classical' period from the accession of the ʿAbbasids to the rise of the Buyid amirs, and thereafter the emergence of new forms of Islam in the middle period. Throughout, close attention is paid to the experiences of Jews and Christians, as well as Muslims. The book stresses that Islam did not appear all at once, but emerged slowly, as part of a prolonged process whereby it was differentiated from other religious traditions and, indeed, that much that we take as characteristic of Islam is in fact the product of the medieval period. This book has been written for students and for all those with an interest in the emergence and evolution of Islam.

Jonathan P. Berkey is Associate Professor of History at Davidson College. His publications include *Popular Preaching and Religious Authority in the Medieval Islamic Near East* (2001).

THEMES IN ISLAMIC HISTORY comprises a range of titles exploring different aspects of Islamic history, society and culture by leading scholars in the field. Books are thematic in approach, offering a comprehensive and accessible over-view of the subject. Generally, surveys treat Islamic history from its origins to the demise of the Ottoman empire, although some offer a more developed analysis of a particular period, or project into the present, depending on the subject-matter. All the books are written to interpret and illuminate the past, as gateways to a deeper understanding of Islamic civilization and its peoples.

Editorial adviser: Patricia Crone, *Institute for Advanced Study, Princeton*

Already published:
Chase F. Robinson *Islamic Historiography*
0 521 62081 3 hardback
0 521 62936 5 paperback

To Vivien

The Formation of Islam

Religion and Society in the Near East, 600–1800

JONATHAN P. BERKEY
Davidson College

CAMBRIDGE
UNIVERSITY PRESS

CAMBRIDGE
UNIVERSITY PRESS

University Printing House, Cambridge CB2 8BS,United Kingdom

Published in the United States of America by Cambridge University Press, New York

Cambridge University Press is part of the University of Cambridge.

It furthers the University s mission by disseminating knowledge in the pursuit of education, learning and research at the highest international levels of excellence.

www.cambridge.org
Information on this title: www.cambridge.org/9780521582148

First published 2003
10th printing 2014

Printed in the United Kingdom by Clays, St Ives plc.

A catalogue record for this publication is available from the British Library.

National Library of Australia Cataloguing in Publication data
Berkey, Jonathan Porter.
The formation of Islam : religion and society in the Near
East, 600-1800.
Bibliography.
ISBN 0-521-58214-8 (hbk.) – ISBN 0-521-58813-8 (pbk.)
1. Islam – History.   I. Title. (Series: Themes in Islamic
history; 2).
297.09

ISBN 978-0-521-58214-8 Hardback
ISBN 978-0-521-58813-3 Paperback

Contents

Preface

This book constitutes an attempt to describe and understand the slow emergence of a distinctively Islamic tradition over the centuries which followed the death of that tradition's founder, Muhammad ibn ʿAbdallah, in 632 CE. It is not a narrative history, although its analytical approach is (I hope) historical. I have cast the central questions as those of religious identity and authority. The question of what it means to be a Muslim requires, I believe, a dynamic answer. Had the question been posed to Muhammad, his answer (if indeed he would have understood the question) would have been quite different than that of a jurist in Baghdad in the ninth century, or of a Sufi mystic in Cairo in the fifteenth. From a historical perspective, no answer is better than any other, and none has any value except against the background of the larger historical factors that produced it. In the multicultural Near East, those factors have always included faith traditions other than Islam, and so I have tried throughout to give some account of the complex ties which, from the very first, have bound Muslim identities to those of Jews, Christians, and others.

The target audience for this book is quite broad, and therefore the target is, paradoxically, perhaps more difficult to strike squarely than with, say, a scholarly monograph of the usual sort, or a conventional introduction to "Islam". It is hoped that the book will serve students, both graduates and undergraduates, and also an interested lay public, as an introduction to the historical origins and development of the Islamic tradition. At the same time, I have tried to write it in such a way that specialists may also find it of use. I have, therefore, made decisions regarding editorial matters such as transliteration and footnoting with an eye on the whole target rather than any one portion of it. I have not shied away from using foreign (mostly Arabic) terms; on the other hand, those terms are transliterated in a simplified fashion, omitting most of the diacritical marks that are standard in scholarly writing, and a glossary is provided for the convenience of non-Arabic speakers. For non-specialists, this may remove a source of visual distraction and confusion; specialists, by contrast, should have no difficulty recognizing the indicated Arabic terms. The footnotes I have used for disparate purposes: both to indicate the particular sources from which I have taken information or ideas, and also to suggest to the interested reader places where she or he might be able to pick up and pursue further the thread of an argument touched on necessarily briefly here. The scope of this book's topic is enormous, and so it has been impractical to cite every relevant work; the notes should be viewed as a launching pad for further investigation. With (again) an eye on the audience, I have in citations privileged secondary literature over primary sources, and tried to cite material in English wherever possible. For the sake of simplicity and familiarity, I have throughout the book given dates according to the Western rather than the Islamic calendar.

Finally I come to the matter of thanks. Over the course, not simply of writing this book, but of two decades of thinking seriously about the Islamic world, I have incurred a variety of purely scholarly debts, to individuals I have known and with whom I have studied, and to others whom I have never met. Some of those will be apparent from the notes – the curious will easily discern there the names of those scholars whose writings on various topics of Islamic history have most significantly influenced my own. More immediately, I have the privilege of thanking those who contributed directly and (not always) knowingly to the writing of this book, by reading portions of it, answering queries, offering suggestions, passing on publications of their own. They include Robert Berkey, Sonja Brentjes, David Frankfurter, Matthew Gordon, Oleg Grabar, Emil Homerin, Lawrence Fine, Keith Lewinstein, Christopher Melchert, Megan Reid, Daniella Talmon-Heller, Christopher Taylor, and Cynthia Villagomez. Joe Gutekanst, of the Interlibrary Loan department at the Davidson College library, was as central a figure in the writing of this book as Ibn ʿAbbas was to the transmission of prophetic traditions – the cognoscenti will be able to appreciate fully my debt to him. I don't know whether it is a good thing to say of editors that they are patient, but Marigold Acland of the Cambridge University Press has been not only patient but helpful and encouraging, which is far more important. A number of people read and commented upon the entire manuscript, including my Davidson colleagues Robert Williams and Scott Denham, and also a perceptive anonymous reader for the Cambridge University Press. Patricia Crone began her association with this manuscript as an anonymous reader, but eventually I learned her name, and from her I have learned more about Islamic history than an Associate Professor would normally care to admit. Paul Cobb owed me nothing beyond a friendship cultivated on long car rides over to a seminar in Chapel Hill, but repaid that meager debt generously with his time, constructive comments, and unfailing enthusiasm.

To my family, whose patience and understanding and support have been essential during the five years in which I have been actively working on this project, I will simply paraphrase the old spiritual: "Done at last! Done at last! Thank God Almighty, I'm done at last!"

Glossary

This glossary is provided for the convenience of readers unfamiliar with Arabic. Many of these terms or phrases have complex or multiple meanings; those stressed here correspond to the sense in which they are used in this book. Fuller definitions of most of these terms can be found in the *Encyclopaedia of Islam*, second edition (*EI²*).

ahbar: a Koranic term used in conjunction with *rabbaniyun*, indicating Jewish religious authorities (i.e., rabbis)

ahl al-bayt: literally, "the people of the house," i.e., the family of the Prophet

ahl al-dhimma: see *dhimmi*

ᶜalim: scholar, the singular of *ᶜulamaᵓ*

amir: literally, "commander"; a title commonly used among the military rulers of the Middle Period

ashab al-hadith: the partisans of hadith, i.e., those who stressed hadith as a source of juristic authority

ashab al-raᵓy: those who championed the use of human reason in fashioning the law

ashraf: see *sharif*

atabeg: a military tutor or guardian, a title common among the military regimes of the Middle Period

baba: a Turkish and Persian honorific meaning father, and sometimes used to refer to respected Sufi dervishes

bakkaᵓun: literally, "those who weep," used especially for a group of early Muslim ascetics and penitents

baraka: blessing, and more particularly a spiritual power commonly associated with certain pious individuals or activities

bidᶜa: innovation, the opposite of *sunna*

daᶜwa: a call or summoning, used to refer to the missionary activity of various religio-political movements

dawla: literally, a "turning," including a turn or change of rulers, which by extension came to refer to a dynasty such as the ᶜAbbasids

dhikr: remembrance, as in the act of remembering the name of God, used to refer to one of the most common Sufi activities

dhimmi: one of the *ahl al-dhimma*, the "people of the covenant of protection," i.e., non-Muslims living under the protection of Muslim regimes

diwan: a list or register, as of names; specifically, a list of those in the early Islamic polity entitled to a share of the wealth taken as booty during the early conquests

*fana*ʾ: annihilation, a term used by the Sufis to describe their ecstatic spiritual state

faqih (pl. *fuqaha*ʾ): a jurist, a scholar of the law

faqir (pl. *fuqara*ʾ): poor, a term used to identify a Sufi

fard ʿayn: a legal obligation incumbent on individual Muslims

fard kifaya: a legal obligation incumbent on the community of Muslims as a whole

fatwa: a legal opinion issued by a competent jurist

fiqh: the science of Islamic jurisprudence

fitna: literally, a "temptation," used to refer to a series of civil wars which threatened the unity of the Islamic polity in its early years

futuwwa: literally, "the qualities of young men," used to refer to a variety of mostly urban fraternal organizations

ghazi: a holy warrior

ghazw: a military expedition or raid

ghulat: literally, "extremists," used especially of those Shiʿis accused of espousing heretical doctrines

hadith: reports about the words of deeds of Muhammad and his companions

hajj: the Muslim pilgrimage to holy sites in and around Mecca

hakam: an arbiter of disputes in pre-Islamic Arabia

halqa (pl. *halaq*): literally, a "circle," as in a teaching circle, consisting of a teacher and his students

hanif (pl. *hunafa*ʾ): one who follows the true monotheistic religion, sometimes used to refer to pre-Islamic Arabian monotheists

hanifiyya: the religion of the *hunafa*ʾ

hijra: the "flight" of Muhammad and his companions from Mecca to Yathrib/Medina, which event marks the founding of the first Muslim community and the start of the Muslim calendar

hisba: either (1) the Koranic injunction to "order what is good and forbid what is wrong," or (2) the office of the *muhtasib*

hiyal: "tricks" developed by the jurists to circumvent some of the more restrictive doctrines of Islamic law, especially in the area of commercial practice

hujja: literally "proof," used by Ismaʿilis to refer to an authoritative figure in the religious hierarchy

ijaza: the authorization issued by an author or scholar to a pupil allowing the pupil to transmit a text on his authority

*ijma*ʿ: the consensus of the community, or of the scholars of the law, one of the principal foundations or sources of Islamic law *ijtihad*: literally "exertion," used by the jurists to refer to the process of determining valid legal judgments from the various sources of the law, and thus the opposite of *taqlid*

ʿilm: knowledge, and especially religious knowledge, that is, the content of the religious sciences

imam: a prayer leader; but also a term for the leader of the community, used especially by the Shiʿis to refer to those members of the Prophet's family whom they recognize as their rightful leader

isnad: a chains of authorities, linking a student through his teacher and his teacher's teachers back to the author or source of a text (especially a hadith)

israʾiliyyat: stories and traditions concerning Biblical figures who are mentioned in the Koran which supplemented and contextualized the sparse Koranic narratives, but which many ulama later looked upon with suspicion

ittihad: a complex theological term which some Sufis used to indicate spiritual "union" with God

jahiliyya: the "time of ignorance" before the coming of Islam

jamaʿa: "group," that is, the collectivity of Muslims

jihad: struggle, that is, in the path of God, including a particular form of that struggle, "holy war"

jinn: a category of daemonic beings or spirits, mentioned by the Koran

jizya: a head tax or poll tax, to which non-Muslims living under Muslim rule are normally subject

Kaʿba: the pre-Islamic shrine at Mecca, which Muslim tradition associates with Abraham

khalifa: the caliph, or leader of the Sunni Muslim community; more precisely, the *khalifat rasul allah*, or "deputy of the prophet of God" or in more controversial language, as the holder of the office has been called at certain times, the *khalifat allah*, the "deputy of God"

khanqah: a Sufi convent or monastery

khariji: literally, "one who goes out"; the term refers to a member of the earliest major Islamic sectarian group

khirqa: the patched and tattered cloak symbolizing the Sufi mystic's poverty

khushdashiyya: the special bond of loyalty among the Mamluk soldiers and their patrons

khutba: a formal sermon delivered to Muslim congregations at noon on Fridays

maʿrifa: knowledge, and specifically the intuitive knowledge of mystical insight, and distinct therefore from *ʿilm*

madhhab (pl. *madhahib*): literally, "way," that is, one of the recognized Sunni schools of law

madrasa: a college or school in which Islamic law was the principal subject of instruction

mahdi: literally "one who is rightly-guided [by God]," the term came to have messianic overtones and referred to the awaited savior who would restore justice and return the community to the proper path

mamluk: a slave, more particularly a slave trained to serve as a soldier

mawla (pl. *mawali*): a term of complex meaning, it is used here primarily to indicate a "client," a dependent legal status required of early non-Arab converts

mawlid: birthday, especially that of the Prophet

mihna: a "testing," and more specifically that instituted by the caliph al-Ma²mun ostensibly to enforce the view that the Koran was created

millet: the Turkish form of the Arabic *milla*, meaning "religion" and by extension a religious community; by the eighteenth and nineteenth centuries it was used specifically for the political structure of the non-Muslim communities in the Ottoman Empire

mishna: the collection of Jewish oral laws and tradition, given final form in the early third century CE

mudarris: teacher, especially a teacher of law or one of its ancillary subjects in a *madrasa*

mufti: a jurist qualified to issue a legal opinion (*fatwa*)

muhaddith: a transmitter of hadith

muhtasib: an officer implementing the *hisba*, especially in the urban markets, hence a "market inspector"

mujahid: one who wages *jihad*

mukhtasar: an abridged legal handbook

mulid: see *mawlid*

mulk: royal power or authority, used sometimes to refer to a pre- or un-Islamic notion of political power distinct from that of a proper *khalifa*

nass: designation, specifically, the action by which one (Shi²i) designated his successor

pir: a Persian term corresponding to the Arabic *shaykh*, meaning literally "old man," and used especially by Sufis to indicate a recognized spiritual guide

qadi: a judge of an Islamic law court

qa²im: "one who rises," that is, against an illegitimate regime, a popular term among Shi²is to refer to the messianic restorer of God's justice

qibla: the direction a Muslim faces when praying

rabb: literally, "lord," a common Koranic term for God

rabbaniyun: see *ahbar*

rafidi: "one who rejects," used to refer to those who rejected the authority of the first three caliphs: hence a Shi²i, a partisan of ²Ali

raj²a: literally, "return," as in the return (to life) of a hero or other figure who has disappeared (or died)

ribat: a term used to refer both to a frontier fortress, and later to one type of Sufi hospice

ridda: literally, "return," and by extension, "apostasy," referring especially to the efforts of Arab converts to Islam who sought to renounce their allegiance after Muhammad's death

*sama*ᶜ: literally "hearing," and by extension the hearing of music, or spiritual concert of the Sufis

*shafa*ᶜ*a*: intercession, especially with God

shahid: a martyr

sharaf: nobility, the quality of a *sharif*

sharif (pl. *ashraf*): a "noble" person; in the Islamic context, those who claimed membership or descent in the family of Muhammad

shaykh: literally, "old man," a term used to refer to a Sufi master, a teacher, or any other figure of religious authority

*shi*ᶜ*a*: the "party" of 'Ali, that is, the Shiᶜis who believed that leadership of the community should have passed from Muhammad to ᶜAli and thence to his descendants

silsila: a Sufi *shaykh's* chain of spiritual authority, or spiritual genealogy

sira: a biographical account of the Prophet's life

softa: lower-ranking students in the *madrasas* of Ottoman Istanbul

suhba: "companionship" or "discipleship," a term used to describe the relationship between a teacher and his closest pupils

sultan: one who wields (political) authority, and a common term for a Muslim ruler in the Middle Period

sunna: the normative practice of the Prophet and his companions, as known through hadith

sunni: a Muslim who accepts the legitimacy and authority of the historical caliphate

sura: a chapter of the Koran

taqlid: "imitation," and more specifically in the legal sphere, being bound by a previous juristic consensus on a particular point of law

tariqa (pl. *turuq*): a recognized Sufi "way" or "path" of spiritual discipline, and by extension the various orders of mystics

tassawwuf: Sufism

ᶜ*ulama*ʾ: those who know, i.e., the scholars of the Islamic religious sciences

umma: the community of Muslims

ᶜ*urf*: custom

usul: the "principles" or "foundations," especially of Islamic jurisprudence

wali (pl. *awliya*ʾ): one who is "close" to God, i.e., a saint or "friend" of God

waqf (pl. *awqaf*): a charitable endowment established according to Islamic law, for the benefit of a family, or a religious institution, or for some other pious purpose

wilaya: a complex term which can indicate sovereign power or authority (as in that which Shiᶜis believe is invested in the Imam), and also (more properly as *walaya*) the status of sainthood, especially in Sufi discourse

zandaqa: heretical unbelief generally, and also more particularly Manichaeism

zawiya: a usually small religious institution established by or for the benefit of a Sufi *shaykh*

zuhd: renunciation, i.e., of worldly temptations

zindiq: a freethinker or non-believer, or more specifically a Manichaean

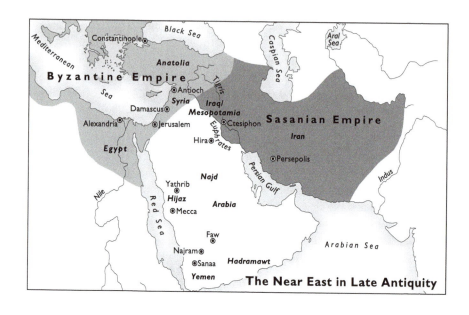

The Near East in Late Antiquity

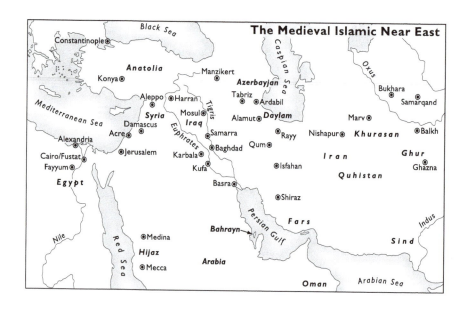

The Medieval Islamic Near East

PART I

The Near East before Islam

CHAPTER 1

Introduction

The millenium or so before the rise of Islam in the early seventh century CE was a period of enormously rich social and cultural development in the lands that form the subject of this book. So much is probably true of any thousand-year interval of human history, but this particular epoch was of special importance in that it saw the crystallization of the religious traditions which have survived into the modern era, and which formed the backdrop to the emergence of the new religion which traces its origins to the preaching of Muhammad in western Arabia.

Marshall Hodgson, in his monumental history of *The Venture of Islam*, identified the period between 800 and 200 BCE, which the German philosopher Karl Jaspers had referred to as the "Axial Age," as decisive in creating the world out of which Islam eventually emerged.[1] Throughout the Eurasian landmass, the Axial Age saw the coalescence of a number of distinct cultures, regionally-based but linked by both trading networks and a common core of principles: the Graeco-Roman or Mediterranean, the Indian, the Chinese. This was an era of leading religious figures and of the production of foundational religious texts in all of these regions: the teaching of Lao-Tzu, Buddha, the Greek philosophers, the Hebrew prophets, and the compilation of the Upanishads in India. From the standpoint of the religious traditions which are studied in this book, the year 200 BCE may be somewhat arbitrary, since the subsequent centuries were, at least in the Near East, equally decisive regarding the articulation of identifiable religious traditions. Indeed, it was the period between 200 BCE and 600 CE – the later portion of what is usually called the "Hellenistic period" and the centuries which comprise the era known as "late antiquity" – which saw the spread of those cultural and religious patterns which are loosely identified as Hellenism; their impact on virtually all social strata throughout the Near East; the fuller articulation of rabbinic Judaism in the academies of Mesopotamia; and of course the career of Jesus and the subsequent emergence of a distinctive Christian faith.

If the millenium or so prior to the rise of Islam had an "axial" character, so too, in a geographic sense, did the region of the Near East. General histories of the Near

---

[1] Marshall Hodgson, *The Venture of Islam: Conscience and History in a World Civilization*, in 3 volumes (Chicago: University of Chicago Press, 1974), 1.111f.

East or of the world commonly speak of the Fertile Crescent, that arc of territory stretching from the Nile River in Egypt to the Tigris and Euphrates in Iraq, as a "crossroads," as the meeting point of three continents, but the characterization is no less true for its overuse. The cultures produced in this region, and in those territories around its periphery (including Anatolia, the peninsula of Arabia, and Iran as far as the Oxus River) which played such critical roles in its historical development, mingled productively if not always entirely freely. Despite their latent hostility to the "barbarians," many Greeks believed that much of their civilization had been borrowed from the East, and even if Athena was not exactly "black" (in the somewhat polemical phrase of a controversial study), it is true that Greek culture owed a considerable debt to the peoples of the east Mediterranean littoral – for example, to the Phoenicians for their alphabet.[2] The conquests of Alexander the Great, and the subsequent penetration of Hellenism into Egypt, Syria, Mesopotamia, and even lands further to the east, "pulled Hellenism's center of gravity sharply eastward."[3]

The crossroads was not without its obstacles. In the centuries before the rise of Islam, the Near East was dominated by two rival states. The Byzantine Empire, with its capital in Constantinople, *was* the old Roman Empire, or what was left of it. Across its eastern border, in the eastern half of the Fertile Crescent and in the lands beyond, lay the empire of the Sasanians, an Iranian dynasty which had come to power in the third century. The two states were bitter rivals, and for much of late antiquity were at war. Their political rivalry, however, did not completely preclude meaningful cultural contact. The Sasanians, even at the height of their conflict with Rome in the sixth century, relentlessly borrowed from Byzantine culture everything from bath-houses to systems of taxation, and the shah Khusrau I Anushirvan (r. 531–579) gleefully welcomed the pagan Greek philosophers whom the Roman emperor Justinian had expelled from their Academy in Athens.[4] Looking back from the vantage point of the Muslim conquests, rather than from the imperial capitals of the two empires, it is equally important to stress not just the Fertile Crescent's character as a crossroads, but also its political vulnerability to powers on its periphery, its historical role as a "vortex that pulls inward and fuses what lies around it."[5] In the millenium or so before the rise of Islam, the region was usually dominated by states based just beyond its physical boundaries, including the Roman and Sasanian empires. The conquests of the Muslim Arabs, who in the seventh century burst into the Fertile Crescent from the remote and inhospitable desert peninsula to the south, represent simply one more example of far older historical patterns.

---

[2] Martin Bernal, *Black Athena: The Afroasiatic Roots of Classical Civilization*, volume 1: *The Fabrication of Ancient Greece 1785–1985* (New Brunswick, NJ: Rutgers U.P., 1987).

[3] Garth Fowden, *Empire to Commonwealth: Consequences of Monotheism in Late Antiquity* (Princeton: Princeton University Press, 1993), 61–2.

[4] Patricia Crone, "Kavād's Heresy and Mazdak's Revolt," *Iran: Journal of the British Institute for Persian Studies* 29 (1991), 30; Averil Cameron, *Agathias* (Oxford: Clarendon Press, 1970), 101; Richard Frye, *The Heritage of Persia* (Cleveland: World Publishing Company, 1963), 218.

[5] A point made brilliantly by Fowden, *Empire to Commonwealth*, 17–18.

Central to the character of Near Eastern society in these centuries was the rise of an urban, mercantile economy. Of course, no pre-modern society reached anything close to the levels of urbanization in our industrial and post-industrial world, and it is worth remembering at the outset that many of the religious developments described in this book reached the ninety percent or more of the population which was rural in attenuated and problematic form. Nonetheless, cities there were, cities which were frequently dominated by merchants and others involved in a commercial economy, and often it was in them, or in response to their needs and uncertainties, that the religious developments which survived and which seemed important to later generations took shape. It was in this period, for example, that the use of currency became a widespread phenomenon, and it is surely not coincidental that two of the more memorable episodes from the accounts of Jesus' life – his encounter with the moneychangers in the Jerusalem temple, and his remark about rendering unto Caesar that which was Caesar's – involved coins.

The urban commercial economy had a decisive impact on religious developments of the era. In the first place, the existence of regional and trans-regional trading networks discouraged cultural and religious parochialism. They helped to make possible, for example, the emergence of traditions which claimed adherents beyond any one city or locality: the household god, or the tutelary god of a city, gradually was eclipsed by (or identified with) deities with a more catholic appeal. Similarly, they encouraged the spread of religious ideas from one place to another. It comes as no surprise that the missionary activities of several of the religions of late antiquity – Manichaeism, for example, and later Islam – were closely associated with merchants. Secondly, and more importantly, urban commercial economies tended to make social inequities more conspicuous and brought social injustices into sharper relief. It was to such problems, made worse by the permanently shifting character of urban life, that many of the new religions addressed themselves.

Although he seems to have glossed over some of the more nuanced questions regarding economic structures and social class, Hodgson drew in a general way upon the sociological analysis of Max Weber; and – if we allow ourselves at the outset to paint with a rather broad brush – it will serve us as well, in part because it informs some of the most basic questions about the origins and character of Islam.[6] Despite the significant differences between the religions of Buddha, the rabbis, and others, they shared many characteristics. Arising against the background of injustice, inequality, and social dislocation, they pointedly spoke to

---

[6] Max Weber, *The Sociology of Religion*, trans. Ephraim Fischoff (Boston: Beacon Press, 1963), esp. Chaps. 6 and 7. Note that Weber drew a distinction between the religious orientation of "commercial" and "capitalist" classes, defining capitalism as "capital continuously and rationally employed in a productive enterprise for the acquisition of profit" (92–3); it was the latter which were especially troubled by social injustice and inequity, and so were attuned to religions of a profoundly ethical (and frequently prophetic) character. His analysis (and that of Hodgson), however, included many merchants under the "capitalist" heading.

the individual conscience, and so had a "confessional" character. Produced by increasingly literate societies, they were frequently affirmed by scriptures, both those for which a divine origin was claimed (the Torah, say, or the Koran) and those of a more exegetical character (the Talmud), as well as those of a more indeterminate nature (the Zoroastrian *Avestan* texts and the surviving commentaries in which they are embedded). A corollary is that, however spontaneous their origins (and frequently they originated as reactions against established traditions), they tended to adopt increasingly systematic form, whether the formal hieratic institutions of the Christian church, or the rabbis' more decentralized and "democratic" structures of authority.[7] Despite radically different solutions to the problems raised by an unjust world, they increasingly looked to a life after death, or to some eschatological future, as the locus of justice and salvation. This was true even of a religion such as Judaism, which, succumbing to the powerful gravitational pull of late antique Hellenism, moved beyond the this-worldly focus of its core Biblical texts.

Two general trends among the religions of the end of the classical and the late antique worlds deserve special mention. First, they tended to be closely associated with states and empires.[8] The most obvious example is Christianity, whose identification with the Roman Empire began under the emperor Constantine (d. 337) and was complete before the reign of his sixth-century successor Justinian. The attachment of Rome's great historical rival, the Sasanian Empire of Iran, to Zoroastrianism developed at an uneven pace, but by the sixth and seventh centuries was substantially complete, and the almost complete collapse of the Zoroastrian community in the centuries following the Islamic conquests was due in part to the destruction of the state structure which had supported it. Islam itself from the beginning represented a close if problematic fusion of political and religious authority, in which condition it once again constituted less a rupture with the Christian Roman past than a continuation of one of the major themes of late antiquity, an opportunity, as it were, to do Constantine one better.[9] Here again, for all its peculiarity, Judaism was not altogether different. Isolated Jewish kingdoms or principalities emerged in various times and places – in Armenia, Chalcis, Cappadocia, Iturea, and Abilene in the first century CE; among the Himyarites, in southern Arabia, during the sixth century; or among the Khazars of Central Asia in the eighth – and the Jewish revolts in Palestine in 66 and 132 CE represented a striking amalgamation of political and religious authority.[10] If the other great religion to emerge from the late antique Near East, Manichaeism, failed to

---

[7] Cf. Peter Brown, "The Religious Crisis of the Third Century A.D.," in *Religion and Society in the Age of Saint Augustine* (New York: Harper and Row, 1972), 83.

[8] On this, see now Garth Fowden's magisterial study, *Empire to Commonwealth*.

[9] Fowden, *Empire to Commonwealth*, 152f, drawing closely on Patricia Crone and Martin Hinds, *God's Caliph: Religious Authority in the First Centuries of Islam* (Cambridge: Cambridge University Press, 1986).

[10] Jacob Neusner, "The Conversion of Adiabene to Judaism: A New Perspective," *Journal of Biblical Literature* 83 (1964), 61. On the Jewish kingdom in southern Arabia, see Gordon Darnell Newby, *A History of the Jews of Arabia from Ancient Times to Their Eclipse under Islam* (Columbia, South

establish a lasting relationship with one of the states of the region, it was not for lack of trying.

A second point concerns the universalist character and claims of the religions of late antiquity. The adherents of the religions of late antiquity – or at least those adherents who took their religion seriously – increasingly associated their faith with a truth which applied to all the world, and not just to a particular people or place. Surely one of the features of Christianity which appealed to Constantine and his successors was its universalism, for it allowed the emperor to present himself as the representative or instrument of a God who stood over all of humankind, a God who could reveal to Constantine his sign and commend it to him as the banner under which to carry out his military campaigns.[11] This union of Roman state and Christian religion, which reached fruition in the early Byzantine state, in fact built upon a connection between religious truth and political power which was implicit in the cult of the emperor as it developed during the centuries immediately preceding Constantine's conversion.[12] The ideal of an association of universalist faith and triumphal state percolated widely through late Roman society. In a famous passage from his Christian cosmography, an early sixth-century Alexandrian merchant named Cosmas glossed a verse from the Book of Daniel which he took to refer to the rough coincidence of the establishment of the Roman Empire and the birth of Christ.

> For while Christ was yet in the womb, the Roman empire received its power from God as the servant of the dispensation which Christ introduced, since at that very time the accession was proclaimed of the unending line of the Augusti by whose command a census was made which embraced the whole world. ... The empire of the Romans thus participates in the dignity of the Kingdom of the Lord Christ, seeing that it transcends, as far as can be in this state of existence, every other power, and will remain unconquered until the final consummation.[13]

And once again, the rise and success of Islam followed rather than digressed from older patterns. It is doubtful that Islam began as anything more than the monotheistic religion of the Arabs. Of course it did eventually become universalist; the existence and permanence of a territorially enormous and explicitly Muslim state probably made that transformation inevitable.

The social dimension was equally significant, as merchants crossing international borders cultivated a truly ecumenical outlook. But more importantly, monotheism itself must have contributed to the phenomenon of universalism, since

Carolina: University of South Carolina Press, 1988), 38f; on the Khazars, see *EI²*, art. "Khazar" (by W. Barthold and P. B. Golden); on the Palestinian revolts, see Fergus Millar, "Empire, Community and Culture in the Roman Near East: Greeks, Syrians, Jews and Arabs," *Journal of Jewish Studies* 38 (1987), 143–64, esp. 147–8.

[11] The universalist claims of Christianity underlie a very interesting letter of Constantine's to the Persian emperor Shapur, expressing horror at Zoroastrian ritual and commending Iranian Christians to the shah's care. See Robin Lane Fox, *Pagans and Christians* (New York: Knopf, 1987), 636–7.

[12] Fowden, *Empire to Commonwealth*, esp. 38, 81–2, 87–8.

[13] Cosmas Indicopleustes, *The Christian Topography*, trans. J. W. McCrindle (London: Hakluyt Society, 1897), 70–1.

the belief in a single god by definition constitutes a narrowing of the scope of what constitutes truth.[14] Polytheistic religious systems by their very nature acknowledge a multiplicity of paths to truth, or salvation, or whatever is the goal of the religious enterprise. The belief in a single god, by contrast, can easily become an assertion that that deity can be understood and approached in only one way. And monotheism, or at least a tendency toward belief in a single god, permeated the late antique world, by no means exclusively in its Jewish or Christian form. The various local and national religions, even the colorful and exuberant polytheism of Egypt, were not immune to the force of the monotheistic ideal.

> O God most glorious, called by many a name,
> Nature's great King, through endless years the same;
> Omnipotence, who by thy just decree
> Controllest all, hail, Zeus, for unto thee
> Behooves thy creatures in all lands to call,

begins the famous "Hymn to Zeus" of the Stoic philosopher Cleanthes (d. 232 BCE).[15] In the Graeco-Roman world, it was the philosophers whose monotheism was most noticeable, but even explicitly polytheistic texts, such as the poems of Homer, and the cultic polytheism of which they formed the basis, do not preclude a more inclusive understanding of divinity in which localized and anthropomorphic gods were merely particular and imperfect manifestations of a single divine power.[16] The situation in Arabia in this period was extremely complex, but even there, on the remote periphery of the Mediterranean world, various monotheisms were known in the years before the beginning of Muhammad's ministry.

From monotheism, it is but a short step to an explicit, and potentially militant, universalism. The example of Judaism in this regard is somewhat problematic, since Jewish monotheism was coupled with the association of Judaism with a particular ethnic group. Even so, there was a strong universalizing streak in the Judaism of late antiquity. One should not overstress the simplistic contrast between the tolerant polytheism of the classical Mediterranean world and the more repressive orthodoxies of the monotheistic faiths. On the other hand, the confessional religions of late antiquity were by nature increasingly exclusive: adherence to one automatically excluded identification with another, even if, as we shall see, it was not always possible or easy to draw fine lines between one

---

[14] Cf. the remarks of Gedaliahu G. Stroumsa, "Religious Contacts in Byzantine Palestine," *Numen* 36 (1989), 16–42, esp. 23, and Fowden, *Empire to Commonwealth*, 106–7.

[15] *Essential Works of Stoicism*, ed. Moses Hadas (New York: Bantam, 1965), 51.

[16] Fowden, *Empire to Commonwealth*, 38–41; Peter Brown, *The World of Late Antiquity, AD 150–750* (New York: Harcourt Brace Jovanovich, 1976), 52; H. Idris Bell, *Cults and Creeds in Graeco-Roman Egypt* (Liverpool: Liverpool University Press, 1953), 1–24, esp. 7–16; E. R. Dodds, *Pagan and Christian in an Age of Anxiety: Some Aspects of Religious Experience from Marcus Aurelius to Constantine* (Cambridge: Cambridge University Press, 1965), 116–18; John Peter Kenney, "Monotheistic and Polytheistic Elements in Classical Mediterranean Spirituality," in *Classical Mediterranean Spirituality*, ed. A. H. Armstrong (New York: Crossroads, 1986), 269–92, esp. 273.

tradition and the next. (This leaves open, furthermore, the analytically separate issue of religious syncretism.)

Confessions which exclude others are a necessary ingredient of a world of distinct religious identities and of competing faiths. And the world we are investigating was, as much as anything else, a world of missionaries, proselytization, and religious competition. Conversion and initiation – more generally, the making of *individual choices* on matters of religion – were common themes in the religious literature of the age, from Apuleius's fictional account of the experiences of an initiate into the cult of the Egyptian goddess Isis, to St. Augustine's autobiographical narrative of his own conversion to catholic Christianity and a life of religious discipline. The dominant factor in the religious turmoil of late antiquity was the rise of Christianity, and the competition between Christianity and paganism was largely of Christian manufacture.[17] But the period was more generally an "age of anxiety."[18] In a work such as Augustine's *Confessions* we can trace the psychological dimensions of the religious stress characteristic of the age. In what follows we will try to elucidate briefly the identities and parameters of the traditions involved in the religious competition of late antiquity.

---

[17] Glen Bowersock, *Hellenism in Late Antiquity* (Ann Arbor: University of Michigan Press, 1990), 5–6.

[18] E. R. Dodds used the phrase to describe the third century, but it is just as descriptive of the ensuing centuries. And cf. Brown, *Religion and Society*, 80: "The 'Age of Anxiety' became, increasingly, the age of converts."

CHAPTER 2

The religions of late antiquity

Judaism

The religion of the people of Israel played a critical role in the religious matrix of late antiquity. Jews constituted a significant minority of the population in many Mediterranean towns, and Judaism had an impact on the religious lives of many non-Jews as well. It was out of Judaism that Christianity first arose, and at least partly through a bitter dispute with its mother faith that the new religion defined itself. As we shall see, the relationship between Judaism and Islam was just as close. Nor were the older pagan traditions immune from the influence of the first of the major monotheistic faiths. Nonetheless, reconstructing the history of Judaism in the Near East in the centuries before and after the rise of Islam is difficult, given the nature of the surviving historical record; much of the story has to be pieced together from sources hostile to the Jews and their faith.

The God of Israel was known throughout the Near Eastern and Mediterranean worlds, thanks to the widespread dispersal of his worshipers. In part their dispersion resulted from the successive deportations of Jews from Palestine, under the Assyrians and Babylonians and, in the wake of the Bar Kochba rebellion in the second century CE, the Romans. By the rise of Islam, for example, the Jewish community of Babylonia was well over one thousand years old. But there was also considerable voluntary migration, especially to flourishing cities such as Alexandria in Egypt and Antioch in northern Syria. In the early first century BCE, the Sibylline oracle had commented that Jews could be found throughout the known world, an observation repeated in a somewhat boastful letter of King Herod Agrippa to the Roman emperor Caligula. Jerusalem, he declared, is

> the mother city, not of one country Judaea but of most of the others in virtue of the colonies sent out at divers times to the neighbouring lands of Egypt, Phoenicia, Syria, the part of Syria called the Hollow and the rest as well and the lands lying far apart, Pamphylia, Cilicia, most of Asia up to Bithynia and the corners of Pontus, similarly also into Europe, Thessaly, Boeotia, Macedonia, Aetolia, Attica, Argos, Corinth, and most of the best parts of Peloponnese. And not only are the mainlands full of Jewish colonies but also the most highly esteemed of the islands Euboea, Cyprus and Crete. I say nothing of the countries beyond the Euphrates, for except for a small part they all, Babylon

and of the other satrapies those where the land within their confines is highly fertile, have Jewish inhabitants.[1]

Several of these far-flung Jewish communities deserve a closer look. Jews had settled, of course in Palestine, but also throughout the Graeco-Roman world, as the apostle Paul well knew. One of the most important Jewish communities in the Mediterranean region was found in Egypt. A permanent Jewish presence in Egypt dated back to at least the sixth century BCE, with the establishment of a mercenary garrison on the Elephantine island near modern Aswan. The Jewish community in Egypt was extremely diverse. Many of the Jews of Egypt were, or had as their forebears, soldiers, as the settlement of Jewish military colonies continued throughout the Ptolemaic period. By the early first century CE, the Alexandrian Jewish philosopher Philo estimated the total Jewish population of Egypt at one million; Jews were found in all the major towns, in the Delta, the Thebaid, and the Fayyum. Communities of Samaritans, too, could be found scattered through the country, from the mid-third century BCE through at least the end of the Islamic Middle Period. Above all, Jews were found in Alexandria, the capital of Ptolemaic and Roman Egypt, in which they formed a distinct and self-regulating community.[2]

Herod Agrippa's apparent pride in his people reflected an extroverted enthusiasm which the Jews of the Mediterranean world shared with the adherents of other religions in the Hellenistic period. In light of what came later, it is worth recalling that many Jews participated freely in the religious dialogue and experimentation which characterized the centuries just before and at the start of the Common Era. Hellenism was a powerful cultural current, one which pulled many Jews into its wake. Many Jews had become speakers of Greek – hence the need for the Septuagint, the Greek translation of the Hebrew Scriptures, produced in that most Hellenistic of cities, Alexandria, in the third century BCE. Moreover, the intellectuals among them (such as the Alexandrian Jewish philosopher Philo) engaged in sustained exchange with their pagan colleagues, an exchange through which the Jews sought to explain and justify their traditions and their faith. No less a figure than the patriarch of the Palestinian Jewish community maintained a friendly correspondence with the pagan rhetor Libanius in Antioch in the fourth century. Their exchange concerned, in part, the patriarch's son, who had been a student of one of Libanius' pupils, but had failed to complete his studies. No

---

[1] Philo, *The Embassy to Gaius*, trans. F. H. Colson (Cambridge, Massachusetts: Harvard University Press, 1962) (Loeb Classical Library, Philo, vol. 10), 143; cited in Emil Schürer, *The History of the Jewish People in the Age of Jesus Christ (175 B.C. – A.D. 135)*, new edition by Geza Vermes, Fergus Millar, and Martin Goodman (Edinburgh: T. & T. Clark, 1986), 3:4–5. On the dispersal of the Jews generally, see Schürer, 3:1–86.

[2] On the Jewish community of Egypt, see Schürer, *The History of the Jewish People*, 3:38–60; H. Idris Bell, *Cults and Creeds of Graeco-Roman Egypt* (Liverpool, 1953), 25–49; J. M. Modrzejewski, *The Jews of Egypt: From Ramses II to Emperor Hadrian* (Philadelphia: The Jewish Publication Society, 1995), 161–225.

matter, the pagan counseled his Jewish friend: "perhaps it will be profitable for him to see many cities – as it was for Odysseus."[3]

There was already a pronounced element of "judeophobia" in the attitudes of many pagans to their Jewish neighbors and their exclusive, monotheistic faith. The tensions were in part theological. Many pagans could not fathom or appreciate the resolutely aniconic character of the Jewish understanding of God, which made it difficult to fit him into the flexible and expandable pantheon of recognized deities. (Some tried nonetheless: Plutarch, for example, identified Yahweh with the Greek god Dionysos.) But the tensions also had a social dimension. Some non-Jews, for example, were perplexed by particular Jewish practices, such as circumcision and their refusal to work on the Sabbath, by which the Jews self-consciously set themselves apart from their neighbors. These tensions and mis-understandings led to accusations that the Jews harbored a deeply-rooted indifference, or even hostility, to non-Jews, and at times to outbursts of anti-Jewish violence.[4]

Despite an underlying level of hostility among both pagans and, increasingly, Christians, Judaism had its appeal for Gentiles, and not only in its Christian form. The Jewish historian Josephus reports that the empress Poppaea, second wife of Nero, felt the attraction of Judaism, and interceded with her husband on its behalf.[5] Jewish monotheism was compelling, the Jewish moral law commanded respect and admiration, and Jewish theology and ritual stressed the expiation for sin which spoke directly to the religious psyche of late antiquity (and which also contributed to the popularity of the various "mystery" cults). Given the sheer size of the Jewish population and its presence throughout the Mediterranean world, Judaism had distinct political advantages, too, another point worth remembering in light of later conditions. This was particularly true in southwest Asia, given the presence there of Palestine and of the significant Jewish population in Babylonia: the conversion of the ruling family of Adiabene in northern Mesopotamia in the first century can be understood at least in part as an attempt to capitalize on the political advantages of being Jewish.[6]

This last point raises the vexing problem of conversion to Judaism, Jewish proselytization, and the broader issue of Jewish universalism. It is probably best to begin by stepping behind the more sharply-delineated religious boundaries of later centuries, and remembering that Judaism as we know it was, like the other

[3] Wayne A. Meeks and Robert L. Wilken, *Jews and Christians in Antioch in the First Four Centuries of the Common Era* (Missoula, Montana: Scholars Press, 1978) (Society of Biblical Literature: Sources for Biblical Study, no. 13), 11–12.

[4] See Peter Schäfer, *Judeophobia: Attitudes Towards Jews in the Ancient World* (Cambridge, Massachusetts: Harvard University Press, 1997).

[5] Schürer, *The History of the Jewish People*, 3:78; Josephus, *Jewish Antiquities* 20.196, trans. Louis H. Feldman (Cambridge, Massachusetts: Harvard University Press, 1965) (Loeb Classical Library), 9:493; idem, *Vita* 16, trans. H. St. J. Thackeray (Cambridge, Massachusetts: Harvard University Press, 1926) (Loeb Classical Library), 1:9.

[6] Jacob Neusner, "The Conversion of Adiabene to Judaism: A New Perspective," *Journal of Biblical Literature* 83 (1964), 60–66.

religious traditions which emerged from late antiquity, still in the process of formation. Beyond the particularism of the notion of a people specially chosen by God, there was a strong universalizing streak in Jewish literature and thought, represented most obviously in biblical passages such as those of the "Second" Isaiah about the Jewish people constituting a "light to the nations." Not all Jews responded favorably to this theme, but among more Hellenized Jews, such as Philo, it was strong, and contributed to the dialogue in which he and others engaged with their pagan neighbors. It is doubtful that Judaism in the Hellenistic and late antique periods produced as active a missionary movement as did, say, Christianity, but proselytization was known and approved, even by some of the rabbis whose opinions are expressed in the Talmud, at least through the fourth century CE.[7] The degree of conversion varied considerably. Full conversion, including (for males) circumcision, was possible and not unusual, although some of the rabbis accorded converts a kind of second class status, and late Roman legislation, such as that outlawing the circumcision of Gentiles, sporadically limited proselytes' opportunities, at least when enforced.[8] But other Gentiles attached themselves to Judaism and to Jewish communities in less categorical fashion, for example, by substituting a purifactory bath for the more off-putting act of circumcision. There has been considerable debate about the meaning of the term "God-fearers," which ancient sources and inscriptions use to refer to groups of Gentiles who attached themselves to synagogues, and who followed some Jewish customs but not all of the law; but whether or not the term was a technical one and the God-fearers formed a distinct grade of Judaizing Gentiles, it indicates both the appeal of Judaism to non-Jews and a significant level of inter-communal exchange of beliefs, values, and practices.[9]

Josephus described Syria as that region of the ancient world in which Jews constituted the largest proportion of the population. But by the fourth century, the cultural and probably the demographic center of Judaism lay to the east, in Mesopotamia. The Jewish community there was old, dating back to the Achaemenid empire, but it grew substantially in late antiquity, in part because the Sasanian emperors encouraged Jewish immigration from the rival (and considerably more hostile) Roman Empire, and in part through a process of conversion among the native Aramaean population with whom the Jews shared a common vernacular. Estimates for the size of the Jewish population in Iraq have

---

[7] On late Jewish proselytization, see Marcel Simon, *Verus Israel* (Oxford: Oxford University Press, 1986), 270–305, and Louis H. Feldman, *Jew and Gentile in the Ancient World: Attitudes and Interactions from Alexander to Justinian* (Princeton: Princeton University Press, 1993), 383–415.

[8] On conversion, see Shaye J. D. Cohen, "Crossing the Boundary and Becoming a Jew," *Harvard Theological Review* 82 (1989), 13–33; idem, "The Rabbinic Conversion Ceremony," *Journal of Jewish Studies* 41 (1990), 177–203; Martin Goodman, "Proselytizing in Rabbinic Judaism," *Journal of Jewish Studies* 40 (1989), 175–85. On fourth- and fifth-century Roman legislation aimed at preventing conversion to Judaism, see Simon, *Verus Israel*, 291–3.

[9] On this subject, see Schürer, *The History of the Jewish People*, 3.150–76 (by Fergus Millar); Garth Fowden, *Empire to Commonwealth: Consequences of Monotheism in Late Antiquity* (Princeton: Princeton University Press, 1993), 65–72; Feldman, *Jew and Gentile in the Ancient World*, 288–415.

ranged from 500,000 in the third century to as much as two million in the year 500, although the number of Jews probably declined somewhat in ensuing decades as the pace of conversion to Christianity grew.[10] The population of a city such as Mahoza was so thoroughly Jewish that the rabbis debated whether the very gates of the city did not require a mezuzah (a small case containing parchment on which was written short Biblical quotations, which Jews traditionally fixed to the doorposts of houses). The size and prestige of the Babylonian community grew at the direct expense of the Jewish community of Palestine. That latter community suffered of course in the wake of the Bar Kochba rebellion, when Jews were forbidden to live within the city of Jerusalem, a prohibition periodically renewed by the Roman emperors, and also from the sharp rise of antisemitic feeling in the later Roman Empire. Rabbi Judah bar Ezekiel confirmed the eminence and authority of the Babylonian community in declaring, "Whosoever emigrates from Babylonia to Palestine breaks a positive biblical commandment, because it is written 'they shall be carried to Babylon, and there shall they be until the day that I remember them, saith the Lord' [Jer. 27.22]."[11]

Viewed with the advantage of historical hindsight, Rabbi Judah's confidence was not misplaced. The experience of Mesopotamian Jews in the centuries before Islam was in fact critical, both for the articulation of Judaism as it has been known since (as it was largely in the rabbinical academies of Iraq that Jewish law took shape), and also in defining the social and political structures which characterized the Near Eastern Jewish experience into the modern period. Under the Sasanian rulers, Jews were afforded a high degree of communal autonomy, an arrangement which in many ways foreshadowed the regime of self-contained communities, rooted in religious identity, which helped to shape the social structure of medieval Islamic cities. At the rise of the Sasanian empire, the community was led by the exilarch, a member of a family claiming Davidic descent. Operating as a sort of "Jewish vassal prince," the exilarch represented the community before the Sasanian emperor, who allowed him to levy taxes, police the community, administer justice, and even, on occasion, raise troops to serve in the imperial army. His authority was shared, however, with the rabbis, who first came to Mesopotamia from Palestine in the wake of the Bar Kochba revolt. Their authority was based, not on descent, but on the claim that they possessed and transmitted an oral law, parallel to the written law, which they traced back to Moses. By the fourth and fifth centuries, the rabbis had created an institutional structure for instruction and learning through which their interpretation of Jewish law came to be dominant, not just in Iraq, but among Jews throughout the diaspora. And by at least the end of the sixth century, the leaders of those schools, the geonim, had

---

[10] On the size of the Jewish population in Iraq, see Jacob Neusner, *Talmudic Judaism in Sasanian Babylonia* (Leiden: E. J. Brill, 1976), 95; Michael G. Morony, *Iraq after the Muslim Conquest* (Princeton: Princeton University Press, 1984), 306–8.

[11] Cited in Salo W. Baron, *A Social and Religious History of the Jews*, 2nd edition (New York: Columbia University Press, 1952–) 2:204–5, 208.

emerged as authoritative spokesmen on questions regarding law, the questions which marked the Jews off as a people and gave them a separate identity.

There is a curious tension in the nature of authority within the Sasanian Jewish community, an authority which was both secular and religious but which could never thoroughly dominate either the sacred or profane sphere of peoples' lives – a tension which in fact was characteristic of medieval Near Eastern institutions of power. The exilarch, for example, functioned at times almost as a courtier of the Sasanian emperor, yet his authority rested in the final analysis on the claim of Davidic descent. Similarly, the rabbis' role as authoritative interpreters of the law had a political dimension which eventually brought them into conflict with the exilarch. The dimensions of that conflict are not entirely clear, but it resulted in the eclipse of the office of the exilarch by the end of the Sasanian period, the rabbis, led by the geonim, emerging as both authoritative interpreters of the law and representatives of the Jewish community.[12] (The denouement of this drama was played out, as we shall see, under the caliph al-Mansur in the late eighth century.)

And the rabbis' victory was decisive, both for the internal character of the Jewish community and for its relations with the broader society of which it formed a part. The Jewish community of Iraq was socially diverse, consisting of townsmen and scholars but overwhelmingly of laborers, peasants, and slaves, and as such knew considerable interaction with the non-Jewish communities of the country. Interaction bred cultural influence – Iranian influence, for example, can be traced in Jewish mysticism and in the magic which came increasingly to be associated with Jews – and social interpenetration, such as intermarriage and conversion. Only in such an open world can the considerable growth in the size of the Jewish community in late antiquity be understood. But the rabbis brought a more refined definition of what it meant to be Jewish, one that required the setting of sharper communal boundaries. It was they, with their concerns about the law and ritual purity, who discouraged contact between Jews and non-Jews, who grew skeptical of conversion to Judaism, and who frowned upon intermarriage.[13] Their victory and their concerns were signs of the times. Their anxieties about the social mixing of adherents of different religious communities were shared by the Zoroastrian priests who grew increasingly identified with the Sasanian state, and reflected the more general process by which religious identities in late antiquity crystallized around a few major traditions.[14]

---

[12] On the exilarch, the rabbinate, and on the structure of the Jewish community in Mesopotamia in general, see Jacob Neusner, "Jews in Iran," in *The Cambridge History of Iran*, vol. 3: *The Seleucid, Parthian and Sasanian Periods*, ed. Ehsan Yarshater (Cambridge: Cambridge University Press, 1983), 909–23; Morony, *Iraq after the Muslim Conquest*, 306–31; Baron, *A Social and Religious History of the Jews*, 2.196–8.

[13] Morony, *Iraq after the Muslim Conquest*, 312–14. The Talmud, however, does not speak with a unified voice. Some rabbis remained warmly disposed to proselytization. See Simon, *Verus Israel*, 274–8.

[14] A process which Baron referred to as "closing the ranks." See *A Social and Religious History of the Jews*, 2.129–71.

The most important aspect of that process is that it was a process, a process which occupied the whole of the late antique period, and one which was certainly incomplete, for Judaism as well as for other religions, in the early seventh century. Above all, the process grew out of a dialectic involving the various faith traditions, as each attempted to define itself more sharply against the others. The process was probably sharpest in the territories of the newly Christianized Roman Empire. Under the Ptolemaic and Seleucid emperors and their pagan Roman successors, Jews had been afforded a fair degree of freedom in the practice of their religion. There were exceptions, of course, such as the efforts of the Seleucid Antiochus Epiphanes to suppress Judaism (which efforts sparked the Maccabaean revolt in the second century BCE), or the reprisals carried out by the Romans in response to the rebellions in Palestine in 66–70 and 132–135 CE, which resulted in the destruction of the Temple in Jerusalem and the banishing of Jews from that city. Spontaneous outbursts of violence against the Jews, conducted not by state authorities but by urban mobs, betray an underlying strain of hostility to Judaism, probably reflecting an impatience with Jewish exceptionalism (as in practices like circumcision, or in the Jewish refusal to participate in the civic cults), which hostility must be set against the philo-semitic feelings of others attracted to Jewish monotheism and doctrines of redemption. But on an official level at least, the Jews formed a relatively favored community. They were, for example, by and large not required to participate in the imperial cult. One mark of their status resides in occasional instances in which Christians suffering from one of the outbreaks of Roman persecution converted to Judaism in order to protect themselves.[15] Even in Palestine, which was quite naturally the center of much opposition to the Roman political order, Judaism remained licit and active, at least outside of Jerusalem.[16]

Under such conditions, religious exchange could take place at a variety of levels. Some Jews, for example, continued actively to proselytize as late as the fourth century, despite the growing strength of Christianity and also the sharpened hostility of the rabbis, one of whom declared that "a gentile who studies the Torah deserves capital punishment."[17] Christians and Jews (as well as pagans) shared what has been called a "religious *koiné*," that is to say, similar patterns of religious belief and behavior, especially but not exclusively on the level of "popular religion": magic, and the belief in spiritual beings, angels, and demons.[18] Christians continued to visit synagogues, or gather for prayer and scripture readings on the Jewish sabbath, or be buried in Jewish cemeteries, despite the efforts of the early church councils to draw sharper lines between Christians and Jews. Communities of Jewish-Christians survived for decades, even centuries,

[15] Schürer, *The History of the Jewish People*, 3.125.
[16] Stroumsa, "Religious Contacts in Byzantine Palestine," 24; Saul Lieberman, "Palestine in the Third and Fourth Centuries," *Jewish Quarterly Review*, n.s. 36 (1945–6), 329–70. On the relatively privileged position of Jews more generally, see Schürer, *The History of the Jewish People*, 3.114–25.
[17] Cited in Baron, *A Social and Religious History of the Jews*, 2.148.
[18] Gedaliahu G. Stroumsa, "Religious Contacts in Byzantine Palestine," *Numen* 36 (1989), 16–42, esp. 21.

after a distinctive Christian church and faith had emerged. They puzzled many, including the patriarch Cyril of Jerusalem. In a sermon in 348, he remarked that these individuals worshiped Jesus Christ, yet refused the name "Christian" and insisted upon calling themselves "Jews."[19]

But despite the exchange, boundaries between the communities were beginning to harden. Even their apparent sharing of a common scripture served to drive Christians and Jews apart, since the theology underlying the Christian identification of the "old" and "new" testaments was irrelevant, even antithetical, to the rabbinical understanding of a dual scripture, written and oral, both revealed at Sinai and possessed in their entirety only by the rabbis.[20] To some degree, the rabbis welcomed and contributed to this process of separation and distinction, for it meshed with their efforts to refine the law and solidify their control over the Jewish community. But even more important was the attitude of the Roman state. Constantine's conversion to Christianity in the early fourth century did not transform the empire overnight into an instrument of Christianization, but it did set in motion the gradual merger of the interests of the Roman state and the Christian faith (or at least certain elements and traditions within the Christian church). By 380, the emperor Theodosius declared Christianity the official religion of the empire. The organized pagan cults were the first to feel the impact of this identification of church and state, but increasingly the Jews, too, felt its onerous weight. In 409 and 438, Jews who attempted to convert Christians were declared subject to capital punishment. The state began to interfere in the practice of Jewish law, subjecting Jews to Roman law in matters such as marriage and inheritance, thereby undermining the juridical foundations of Jewish identity and the autonomy which the Jews had enjoyed under pagan Rome. The assault on Judaism aimed at its bedrock: under Justinian, the state even tried to regulate ritual in the Jewish synagogue, by stipulating which versions of scripture could be read, and over the sixth century instances of forced baptism increased. These developments were the social manifestations of a changing theological climate, in which religions claimed for themselves authority to define the parameters of truth, parameters which applied to and circumscribed the lives of all. Judaism, given its proximity to the origins and basis of Christianity, was especially problematic for Christian theologians and rulers, whose efforts to separate and control the Jews perhaps reflected what Sigmund Freud called the "narcissism of minor difference." Hence Justinian's efforts to force Jews to postpone their observance of the Passover, so that Judaizing Christians might be prevented from celebrating Easter on the Jewish holiday. And hence the term "Jew" became in Christian polemic one of abuse, applied by Christians to all – pagans and Christian sectarians as well as Jews – who deviated from the norm.[21]

---

[19] Stroumsa, "Religious Contacts in Byzantine Palestine," 28.

[20] Jacob Neusner, *Judaism and Christianity in the Age of Constantine* (Chicago: University of Chicago Press, 1987), 128–45.

[21] On the sharpening of communal boundaries and the worsening position of the Jews, see Baron, *A Social and Religious History of the Jews*, 2.129–214, and 3.3–18; Peter Brown, *The World of Late*

Most accounts of the Jews under Sasanian rule have assumed that they fared considerably better than their co-religionists to the west. Peter Brown, for example, has piquantly observed that "[a]t a time when the emperor Justinian was laying down which version of the Scriptures the Jews should be allowed to read in the synagogues of his empire, the rabbis of Ctesiphon were free to conduct a vigorous polemic against the Christian doctrines of the Trinity and the Virgin Birth."[22] Several of the Sasanian monarchs acquired reputations as friends of the Jews, reputations which have left traces in the Talmud. The Jews of Mesopotamia, for example, endeared themselves to Shapur II (309–79) by their refusal to cooperate with the Roman emperor Julian during his invasion of the Sasanian Empire. Yazdigird I (399–420) is reputed to have been on familiar terms with the Jews and even with their scriptures, although the story that he had a Jewish wife may be apocryphal.[23] As Judaism was increasingly defined as hostile to Christianity and to the Roman state, Jews could even identify their interests with those of Rome's great historical rival, the Sasanian Empire, as we shall see.

But the Jews of Mesopotamia also experienced the sharpening of communal boundaries in the centuries before the rise of Islam. In both tenor and substance, Judaism differed profoundly from the Zoroastrianism which grew more closely identified with the Sasanian state. On certain matters of ritual touching intimate areas of human life and expectations, divergence in practice could create real feelings of uneasiness or even revulsion: marriage, for example (in particular the Zoroastrian acceptance of consanguinous unions), or death rites (Jewish in-humation, which seemed to Zoroastrians to defile the earth, versus the Zoroastrian practice of exposing the dead to the elements, which could be construed as threatening the prospects for bodily resurrection).[24] Tensions of this sort may have lain behind outbreaks of violence such as one that occurred in Isfahan in the second half of the fifth century, in which, following a slanderous accusation that the Jews had attacked two Zoroastrian priests, half the Jewish population of the city was massacred and its children turned over as slaves to serve the fire-temples. But the more important nexus for the worsening of the position of Jews in the Sasanian Empire was a political one. Here again, it is important to stress that Jews did not always act as a politically passive minority. They were caught up in some way in the confused events associated with the Mazdakite movement in the Sasanian empire in the late fifth and early sixth centuries (on which, see below); their involvement issued at one point in a rebellion led by the exilarch Mar Zutra II, who established for seven years an independent Jewish state in Mahoza, until it was overrun by the Iranians and Mar Zutra captured and beheaded. During another

Antiquity, AD 150–750 (New York: Harcourt Brace Jovanovich, 1976), 172–187; Stroumsa, "Religious Contacts in Byzantine Palestine," passim; J. F. Haldon, *Byzantium in the Seventh Century: The Transformation of a Culture* (Cambridge: Cambridge University Press, 1990), 345–8; Andrew Sharf, *Byzantine Jewry from Justinian to the Fourth Crusade* (New York: Schocken Books, 1971), 19–41.

22 Brown, *The World of Late Antiquity*, 165.
23 Neusner, "Jews in Iran," 915.
24 Morony, *Iraq after the Muslim Conquest*, 296.

rebellion later in the sixth century, some communities of Jews backed the losing claimant to the Sasanian throne, which again led to pogroms. At any rate, by the end of the Sasanian period, the Jews of Mesopotamia had known massacres and meddling in their internal affairs by the imperial authorities; the office of the exilarch had been periodically suppressed, and the academies which were so central to Jewish religious life had been temporarily closed.[25]

Christianity

The development which contributed most to the process by which the religions of late antiquity defined themselves more sharply was the rise of Christianity. As a historical matter, it would be meaningless to say that Christianity *caused* the process; but that process involved a dialogue, and most of the participants in that dialogue were Christian. The dialogue was not always a friendly one – quite the contrary. One of the characteristic features of the religious literature of late antiquity is its highly polemical nature. Polemics helped the traditions to define themselves, but also betrayed the underlying uncertainties and competition which fueled them in the first place.[26]

Judaism, as we have seen, was increasingly a target of Christian polemic, as the young religion sought to differentiate itself from its parent. No doubt Jews participated in the exchange, but it is significant that surviving examples of Jewish-Christian polemic come exclusively from the Christian side. Christians continued to feel a need to stake out an independent identity well into the common era. Ignatius, bishop of Antioch around the turn of the first century, composed letters condemning, not Jewish Christians, but Gentile Christians who adopted Jewish practices. His concerns match those of John Chrysostom, prelate of Antioch some three centuries later. Chrysostom's sermons suggest that many Christians in Antioch harbored an infatuation with Judaism, reflected in Christian participation in Jewish festivals, and attendance at synagogues. The preacher claimed even to know at least one Antiochan Christian who identified himself as such, but who had submitted to circumcision.[27] It is easy to condemn the rhetorical violence of Chrysostom's sermons for their use of what we would now identify as antisemitic images – he labels Jews, for instance, as "Christ-killers" – but they should also be read as reflecting the profound anxieties generated by a drawn-out process through which the separate identities of the different faiths were confirmed.

---

[25] On the worsening condition of the Jews in Mesopotamia and other Iranian territories, see Geo Widengren, "The Status of the Jews in the Sasanian Empire," *Iranica Antiqua* 1 (1961), 117–62.

[26] Averil Cameron, "The Eastern Provinces in the Seventh Century A.D.: Hellenism and the Emergence of Islam," *Hellenismos: Quelques Jalons pour une Histoire de l'Identité Grecque*, ed. S. Said (Leiden: Brill, 1991), 287–313, esp. 307.

[27] Meeks and Wilken, *Jews and Christians in Antioch*, 20, 30–4; and cf. Robert Wilken, *John Chrysostom and the Jews: Rhetoric and Reality in the Late Fourth Century* (Berkeley: University of California Press, 1983).

Paganism too felt the sting of Christian attack. Pagans had not always treated Christians kindly, as the many martyrs might attest. And pagans too participated in the war of words between the faiths. To cite just one instance, one which may have been known to the emperor Constantine: Hierocles, one of the emperor Diocletian's chief lieutenants during the persecutions of the early fourth century, authored a treatise denigrating Christ and denouncing the Christian belief in his divinity, a treatise which prompted an extended reply from the church historian (and later Constantine's adviser) Eusebius.[28] But Christian memory may have over-stressed the extent and significance of pagan persecution.[29] Certainly once the Roman emperors adopted Christianity, as a practical matter pagans were no longer in a position to cause serious disruption to Christian life and worship, the brief campaign of the pagan emperor Julian against Christianity in the mid-fourth century notwithstanding.

On the contrary, after the early fourth century, it was Christians who persecuted pagans. Constantine's conversion did not lead to the sudden eclipse of paganism, but it did ratchet up the rhetoric of Christian hostility. Constantine's own religious policy presents a somewhat contradictory mien, and historians have come to radically different conclusions about the degree of his personal and political commitment to Christianity. A judicious reading of the evidence may suggest that, while Constantine's conversion was sincere, the overriding goal of his religious policy was to promote peace within the empire, a peace to heal the wounds left by the persecution instigated by his pagan predecessor, Diocletian, and a peace built around a tolerant consensus of all those (pagans included) who acknowledged a supreme god under whose auspices Constantine ruled.[30] Constantine closed a number of pagan temples, but he also at one point exiled the staunchly orthodox bishop Athanasius of Alexandria (albeit for reasons having nothing to do with theology). On the other hand, he himself publically referred to paganism as an "error," and to ritual sacrifice as a "foul pollution," and had his agents break up pagan statues and expose the rubbish with which they were filled.[31] Intentionally or not, his words and actions inspired others, especially bishops and monks, to take up the cudgel, verbal and literal, which they did with increasing vigor. After a period of improved fortunes for pagans under Julian (r. 361–3) and in the years immediately following his death, the pace and tenor of Christian assaults on pagan cults and temples picked up. Imperial legislation called for the closure and

---

[28] H. A. Drake, *In Praise of Constantine: A Historical Study and New Translation of Eusebius' Tricennial Orations* (Berkeley: University of California Press, 1976), 68. Eusebius' treatise is included at the end of the Loeb volume of Philostratus' *Life of Apollonius of Tyana*, trans. F. C. Conybeare in two volumes (London: William Heinemann, 1912), 2.484–605.

[29] See, for example, Peter Brown's comments on W. H. C. Frend's study, *Martyrdom and Persecution in the Early Church: A Study of a Conflict from the Maccabees to Donatus* (Oxford: Blackwell, 1965), in "Approaches to the Religious Crisis of the Third Century A.D.," in *Religion and Society in the Age of Saint Augustine* (New York: Harper and Row, 1972), 86–7.

[30] Drake, *In Praise of Constantine*, 61–74. Robin Lane Fox, by contrast, stresses Constantine's commitment to the new faith and his particular concern with *Christian* unity: *Pagans and Christians* (New York: Knopf, 1987), 609–62.

[31] Lane Fox, *Pagans and Christians*, 666, 673.

dismantling of specific shrines and, in 435, for their general destruction; but it was bishops and, especially in rural areas, unruly monks who led the charge, often in advance of the law. The destruction of the famous Serapeum in Alexandria in 391, for example, was instigated by the city's bishop. By the early fifth century, the movement was in full swing. Bishops seized the moment and, capitalizing on the anxieties stirred up by the violence they had provoked, frequently made certain that attacks on temples were followed by the formal mass conversion of the pagans who had worshiped in them. For example Porphyry, bishop of Gaza from 395 to 420, having overseen the destruction of a pagan temple, welcomed the mass conversion of the terrified pagans, over-riding the objections of fellow churchmen that the converts were driven by fear rather than conviction.[32]

This last point is especially significant. The growing level of Christian hostility is surprising, as late antique paganism shared much with the new religion of Christianity, both on an intellectual level (pagan theology having grown increasingly monotheistic) and on that of popular belief and practice. The emphasis on conversion suggests once again the growing importance to the men and women of late antiquity of formal expressions of religious identity. In that may lie Christianity's greatest legacy to the world which, in the seventh century, Islam inherited.

Christians raised more insistently than others the question of religious identity. "I cannot call myself anything else than what I am," said the young North African martyr Perpetua (d. ca. 203), "a Christian."[33] It is deeply ironical, therefore, that the question of Christian identity should have proved so troublesome to the Christians themselves.[34] Of all the major religions to have emerged from late antiquity, Christianity had the misfortune to be the one which placed the greatest emphasis on doctrine and theology. The principal issues, concerning the nature of Christ, ironically began to emerge just at the moment of Christianity's triumph through the conversion of Constantine, in the form of the Arian controversy. They continued to plague the church through the rise of Islam, and probably contributed to the frustrations felt by Muhammad and his followers at the apparent doctrinal disorder of and internecine squabbling within the Christian community. That the apparent triumph of a monotheistic religion should be accompanied by increasingly bitter debates over doctrinal issues may not be coincidental. As one historian has recently observed, "where polytheism diffuses divinity and defuses

---

[32] Mark the Deacon, *Vie de Porphyre, Évêque de Gaza*, trans. Henri Grégoire and M.-A. Kugener (Paris: Société d'Éditions "Les Belles Lettres", 1930), 72–4; Garth Fowden, "Bishops and Temples in the Eastern Roman Empire A.D. 320–435," *Journal of Theological Studies* n.s. 29 (1978), 53–78.

[33] *Passio Sanctarum Perpetuae et Felicitatis*, ed. James W. Halporn (Bryn Mawr, Pennsylvania: Thomas Library, 1984), 3.2; Elizabeth Alvilda Petroff, *Medieval Women's Visionary Literature* (New York: Oxford University Press, 1986), 70.

[34] Judith Herrin points out that most histories of early Christianity adopt, intentionally or otherwise, the viewpoint of the "orthodox" church which ultimately triumphed, at least in the West. Doing so can obscure "the tentative and hesitant, divisive and competitive aspects of early Christian communities, their idiosyncracies in practice and belief, in short, the relative lack of uniformity." *The Formation of Christendom* (Princeton: Princeton University Press, 1987), 54–5f.

the consequences, if not always the intensity, of debate about its nature by providing a range of options, monotheism tends to focus divinity and ignite debates by forcing all the faithful, with their potentially infinite varieties of religious thought and behavior, into the same mold, which sooner or later must break."[35] This is not the place for anything more than a limited assault on the dizzying edifice of the Christological controversies of the fourth and fifth centuries. The social and historical significance of those controversies, however, is another matter.[36]

To consider the impact of the Christological controversies on Christian identity and the nexus of political and religious authority in the centuries before Islam, let us look in closer detail at the situation in Egypt.[37] By the end of the second century, Christianity was gaining ground throughout the country. A number of factors contributed to its appeal to the population, including several doctrinal parallels with the late pagan cults patronized both by native Egyptians and by Greeks and Romans resident in the country, such as their emphasis on redemption and sacramental mysteries, and perhaps especially the traditional Egyptian preoccupation with immortality (as in, for example, the popular cult of Osiris, god of the Nile and king of the dead). By the fourth century, the church was well-established, with a network of churches down to the village level, and a growing body of Christian literature written in or translated into Coptic, the language of the native population. At the time of the conversion of Constantine, perhaps half the inhabitants of Egypt professed Christianity; by the early fifth century, the figure probably reached eighty percent.[38] Egyptian Christianity had a tremendous impact on the faith beyond the Nile valley, most obviously in monasticism, whose roots lie in the Christian ascetics (such as the hermit Antony) who fled to the Egyptian desert and in the coenobitic movement associated with figures such as Pachomius.[39] But Egyptian influence was more subtle, as well. The ecumenical council of Ephesus in 431 declared Mary the *Theotokos*, the "God-Bearer," and in doing so, it "ratified the fervor of the Copts, who had worshiped her as such."[40] Egyptians were by no means alone in their feelings for Mary, of course. On the other hand, it may be worthy of note that one of the earliest Church fathers to enunciate a doctrine of Mary as Theotokos was Athanasius, and that the major proponent of

---

[35] Fowden, *Empire to Commonwealth*, 106–7.

[36] The Christological controversies are treated in any number of doctrinal histories of the early church. Among the best are Henry Chadwick, *The Early Church* (Harmondsworth: Penguin, 1967), and W. H. C. Frend, *The Rise of Christianity* (Philadelphia, 1984). A non-Chalcedonian point of view is given in Aziz S. Atiya's *History of Eastern Christianity* (Notre Dame: University of Notre Dame Press, 1968), although this work is somewhat sentimental and uncritical.

[37] On early Christianity in Egypt, see C. Wilfred Griggs, *Early Egyptian Christianity: From Its Origins to 451 CE* (Leiden: E. J. Brill, 1991), and the still serviceable work of H. Idris Bell, *Cults and Creeds in Graeco-Roman Egypt* (New York: Philosophical Library, 1953), 78–105.

[38] Roger S. Bagnall, *Egypt in Late Antiquity* (Princeton: Princeton University Press, 1993), 278–81.

[39] The best study of early monasticism is still Derwas J. Chitty, *The Desert a City: An Introduction to the Study of Egyptian and Palestinian Monasticism Under the Christian Empire* (Oxford: Blackwell, 1966).

[40] Brown, *The World of Late Antiquity*, 143.

the doctrine at Ephesus was Cyril; both Athanasius and Cyril were patriarchs of Alexandria. Moreover, what became the principal medieval image of Mary – suckling the infant Jesus – can be traced back iconographically to Egyptian depictions of the goddess Isis nursing her infant son Horus.[41]

Ultimately, of course, the controversy over Mary as Theotokos was a Christo-logical issue, and foreshadowed a larger crisis which plagued the Church as a result of the Council of Chalcedon in 451. The Council's declaration that Christ was both perfect God and perfect man, made known to us in two natures, angered those who came to be known as Monophysites, who insisted on the full mystical union of God and man in a single nature in the person of Christ. Many Egyptians passionately embraced the Monophysite position, as did the churches of Armenia and Ethiopia, and most of the Christians of Syria. Consequently, the aftermath of the conciliar decision was a permanent doctrinal rupture between most Christians of those regions and those adhering to the orthodox or "Melkite" (imperial) church. But there was a more explicit political dimension as well, since the Coun-cil also made it clear that Constantinople was to be regarded as the premier Christian city of the eastern Empire, to the detriment of the authority of the patriarchal sees of Antioch and, especially, Alexandria.

What did this all mean? There has been much debate concerning this issue, particularly over whether the doctrinal rupture between Chalcedonians and Monophysites in any way undermined the unity and strength of the Christian empire, and so paved the way for the Muslims' success in the seventh century. Assertions that the emergence of a distinctively Monophysite Coptic church "must be regarded as the outward expression of the growing nationalist trends" in Egypt seem, at best, anachronistic.[42] Doctrinal tensions between Chalcedonians and Monophysites did not imply an intractable hostility between Greek-speaking, imperial Chalcedonian Christians on the one hand, and Coptic-speaking, Mono-physite Egyptian Christians on the other. Several historians have persuasively argued that the cultural overtones and political implications of the theological division should be minimized: that by the end of late antiquity, there was in fact a close symbiosis of (and not an atavistic struggle between) Greek and Coptic cultures in Egypt, and that Monophysite anger at the Chalcedonian creed did not imply that Egyptian Christians were hostile to the empire itself.[43]

---

[41] Ibid. On the controversy surrounding the conciliar declaration of Mary as Theotokos, see Hilda Graef, *Mary: A History of Doctrine and Devotion* (London: Sheed and Ward, 1963), 101–11; Jaroslav Pelikan, *Mary Through the Centuries: Her Place in the History of Culture* (New Haven: Yale University Press, 1996), 55–65.

[42] Atiya, *History of Eastern Christianity*, 69. Atiya's florid rhetoric sometimes rises to comical heights, as in his assertion (77) that Cyrus, Patriarch of Alexandria at the time of the Muslim conquests, was a "Melkite colonialist" whose "national origin was doubtful" and who was "one of the most hateful tyrants in Egyptian history. He used the Cross as an iron mace to club native resistance."

[43] Fowden, *Empire to Commonwealth*, 100–37, esp. 127; Glen Bowersock, *Hellenism in Late Antiquity* (Ann Arbor: University of Michigan Press, 1990), 67.

On the other hand, it is surely significant that by the end of the fifth century, the majority of Christians in Egypt, Syria, and (for different reasons) Iraq adhered to doctrines which put them at odds with those espoused by the church associated with imperial authority. Their frustration and anger with the imperial church had a profound impact on the Christian identity of those who professed a Monophysite creed. The Melkite patriarch of Alexandria in the wake of Chalcedon, who adhered to the Council's Christological declarations, discovered as much when he was torn apart by a mob of Egyptians in 457. More importantly, the schism resulted in the emergence in both Egypt and Syria of rival networks of bishops, priests and churches, one loyal to the Chalcedonian formulations generally supported (although in varying degrees, and not without efforts to heal the breach) by the emperors, another to the Monophysite creed. And Monophysite frustrations did not dissipate quickly. It would be misleading to suggest that local Syrian and Egyptian Christians systematically betrayed the Christian Roman state to the Arab invaders. On the other hand, the hostility which sometimes characterized their relations with Melkite authorities probably helped to sap the vigor of Roman efforts to resist the Arabs in Syria and Egypt. That, at least, was the suggestion of John, a Coptic bishop in Upper Egypt in the late seventh century, who identified the anger of the Coptic inhabitants of some Egyptian towns towards the Roman emperor Heraclius, "because of the persecution wherewith he had visited all the land of Egypt in regard to the orthodox faith," as having contributed to the Arabs' victory.[44]

The situation faced by Christians in Iraq and the other provinces of the Sasanian empire was completely different.[45] Christianity first penetrated the area to the east of Syria through the sizeable Jewish communities of Mesopotamia. By the third century it was well established and organized, and began to attract the attention of the Zoroastrian priesthood which was growing closer to the Sasanian state. Christianity continued to grow down to and even into the Islamic period, at the expense of Jews, pagans, and Zoroastrians; by the late sixth century, it constituted probably the single largest confessional community in Iraq. There are parallels between its organization and relation to the state and those of the Mesopotamian Jews, parallels which assume a special importance when viewed from the vantage point of the later Islamic period. The experience of both Jews and Christians in the Sasanian empire demonstrates that, in this world of diverse faiths, an individual's social and even political identity derived primarily from his or her religious

---

[44] John of Nikiu, *The Chronicle of John, Bishop of Nikiu*, trans. R. H. Charles (London: Williams and Norgate, 1916), 184; cf. Walter Kaegi, "Egypt on the Eve of the Muslim Conquest," in *The Cambridge History of Egypt*, vol. 1: *Islamic Egypt, 640–1517*, ed. Carl Petry (Cambridge: Cambridge University Press, 1998), 34–61, esp. 45–6; and idem, *Byzantium and the Early Islamic Conquests* (Cambridge: Cambridge University Press, 1992), 265–9.

[45] On Christianity in Iraq and in the Sasanian Empire, see J. P. Asmussen, "Christians in Iran," in *The Cambridge History of Iran*, vol. 3, *The Seleucid, Parthian and Sasanian Periods*, ed. Ehsan Yarshater (Cambridge: Cambridge University Press, 1983), 924–48; Sebastian Brock, "Christians in the Sasanian Empire: A Case of Divided Loyalties," in *Religion and National Identity*, ed. Stuart Mews (Oxford: Basil Blackwell, 1982) (Studies in Church History, 18), 1–19; Morony, *Iraq after the Muslim Conquest*, 332–83; and, more carefully, Atiya, *History of Eastern Christianity*, 237–66.

community, foreshadowing the situation in the Islamic Middle Ages.[46] As with the Jewish leadership, the church "became an agent of the state to secure the loyalty of its Christian subjects": the church led Christians in prayer for the king, and might even excommunicate Christians who rebelled against the state, in exchange for which the ecclesiastical hierarchy expected the state's assistance in enforcing its will on members of its own community. The Sasanian emperors were not, of course, Christian. Like their Christian Roman counterparts, however, they might intervene in church affairs, to convene a council of Christian bishops, for example, or to secure the election of some particular candidate as *catholicos*.[47]

The social and political condition of Christians in the Sasanian empire was even more complex than that of their co-religionists to the west. Christians shared with Jews an underlying aversion to a number of Zoroastrian beliefs or practices – the worship of fire, for example, or consanguinous marriages – and the Zoroastrian priesthood (itself shocked by Christian ideals such as virginity) periodically unleashed waves of persecution of Christians. One of the worst outbreaks occurred during the reign of Shapur II, which produced the horrors recorded in the Syriac "Lives of the Martyrs." On the other hand, Christianity was never formally proscribed by the emperors. Christians served the Sasanians in the army and in the bureaucracy, sometimes in quite senior positions. Thus Christians found themselves owing allegiance to both Christ and the shah, and "under normal conditions there was not any clash of loyalties since membership of the 'People of God' and of the Persian state belonged to separate modes of existence."[48] After the fourth century, troubles arose primarily during periods of conflict and tension with the Christian Roman Empire. So, for example, a treaty with the Roman empire in 561 provided that Christians were to be left alone, allowed to worship freely and construct churches. Under Khusrau Parviz, who regained his throne as a result of Byzantine intervention and who was married to two Christian women, the condition of Christians improved further, but then deteriorated sharply during the cataclysmic war which engulfed the two states in the early seventh century.

The Christological controversies which plagued Roman Christianity also had an impact in the Sasanian world. The majority of Sasanian Christians followed what came to be identified as the Nestorian position, one distinct from the Chalcedonian and hostile to the Monophysite. According to Nestorius, the patriarch of Constantinople who gave his name to the sect, Christ was the locus of two entirely independent natures, the divine and the human: so, for example, while Mary might be considered the mother of Christ, she could in no way be labeled Theotokos, "God-Bearer." But Monophysites, linked to the Jacobite church of Syria, also had a strong and distinct presence in Mesopotamia. The situation was further confused by the presence of significant communities of Melkite Christians, many of them the product of deportations carried out by the Sasanians from

---

[46] A point made by both Brock, "Christians in the Sasanian Empire," and Morony, *Iraq after the Muslim Conquest*.

[47] Brock, "Christians in the Sasanian Empire," 4–5; Morony, *Iraq after the Muslim Conquest*, 334–41 (the quotation is taken from p. 334).

[48] Brock, "Christians in the Sasanian Empire," 14.

territories conquered from Rome or from border areas during the course of their periodic wars, although since the state itself was not Christian, no sect could effectively enforce a claim to representing "orthodoxy."[49] As in Syria and Egypt, the most important consequence of the theological disputes was the emergence of separate and distinct ecclesiastical networks and structures, churches, monasteries, and schools. This fueled sectarian competition, especially between Nestorians and Monophysites. Significantly, the competition grew sharper in the early years of the seventh century, just before the Arab invasions, as churches and monasteries purged their ranks of nonconforming members. Some Iraqi Christians later concluded that the sectarian strife contributed to the ease with which the Muslims took the country, or, in more theological language, that God permitted the Arabs to triumph as a punishment for Christian disunity.[50] On the other hand, the competition also provided a catalyst for vigorous proselytization. Nestorian Christianity in particular proved to be a dynamic force in the religious history of the early medieval period, its missionaries active throughout Central Asia and as far as China at least until the Mongol conquests in the thirteenth century.[51] But the Nestorians failed to establish a permanent relationship with a major political entity, and so in the long run succumbed to the dynamic mix of political and religious authority represented by Islam.[52]

Zoroastrianism and Manichaeism

Inhabitants of the Sasanian empire, even more than those of the Roman, lived in a world of astonishing religious variety in the centuries before the rise of Islam. Judaism and Christianity, as we have already seen, staked out a significant presence in the Sasanian realm, largely but not exclusively in its Mesopotamian provinces. Pagans of various stripes could be found virtually everywhere. Iran's geographic location was a critical factor in giving shape to the religious mix. Lying just beyond the easternmost Roman provinces, it provided a natural refuge for Jews fleeing Roman persecution; and Jews, in their wake, brought Christianity. Further east, Iran borders on the culturally and religiously diverse world of India, and even apart from any prehistoric connections between the Indo-European settlers of the two regions, commercial and strategic imperatives drew them together, particularly under the Sasanians, who cultivated mercantile links to the sub-continent.[53] As a result, Buddhism made its presence felt in late antique Iran, particularly in its easternmost provinces, and through Iran was known to

---

[49] On the Melkite church in the Sasanian empire, see J. Nasrallah, "L'Église melchite en Iraq, en Perse et dans l'Asie centrale," *Proche-Orient Chrétien* 25 (1975), 135–73 and 29 (1976), 16–33.
[50] A. Mingana, *Sources Syriaques*, 2 vols. (Mosul: Imprimerie des Pères Dominicaines, 1907), 2:172–4; Morony, *Iraq after the Muslim Conquest*, 375–80; Asmussen, "Christians in Iran," 946–7.
[51] Brown, *The World of Late Antiquity*, 162; Atiya, *History of Eastern Christianity*, 257–66.
[52] Fowden, *Empire to Commonwealth*, 122–3.
[53] André Wink, *Al-Hind: The Making of the Indo-Islamic World* (Leiden: Brill, 1990), 1.45–64, esp. 48–53.

Manichaeans and others in the Fertile Crescent.[54] When he sought to leave a record in stone of the religious rivals he had fought and vanquished, the zealous third-century Zoroastrian priest Karter listed Jews, shamans, Christians, Manichaeans, and Brahmans.[55]

But the principal religion within the Sasanian realm, because of its roots in Iranian culture and history and because of its intimate connection to the Sasanian state, was Zoroastrianism. Late antique Zoroastrianism, even more than Judaism and Christianity, is difficult to define in any precise and categorical fashion. A distinctive Zoroastrian faith was beginning to emerge in late antiquity, but the process was not complete, even by the time of the Arab invasions. Part of the problem is textual: it is not easy to assign precise dates to the principal Zoroastrian texts, and in any case they tend to incorporate much older material. A more fundamental problem is that Zoroastrian doctrine took shape only slowly, sometimes in response to the theological assertions of other religious traditions. Separate polytheistic, monotheistic, and especially dualist strands can be identified within the broader Zoroastrian tradition. The polytheism of ancient Iranian religion probably continued as the norm for many of the common people, although the priests tended to redefine the multitudinous deities as angelic beings subordinate to the great god Ahura Mazda (Ohrmazd). By contrast, another strand within the Zoroastrian tradition in the Sasanian period subordinated both Ahura Mazda and the personification of the evil principle, Ahriman, to an impersonal god of infinite time and space, Zurvan.[56] Dualism, however, the understanding of the cosmic order as the product of a struggle between good and evil deities, was the dominant theological tendency. Zoroastrian dualism was distinguished from that of Manichaeism by its insistence upon the genesis of the world, or at least most of it (minus things like reptiles, snakes, and the seven planets), at the hands of the good, rather than the evil, deity.

In Iran no less than in the Roman empire, the characteristic process of religious definition in late antiquity was a product of intense competition and not-always-friendly dialogue. Monotheistic passages in Zoroastrian texts may have served as an apologetic response to Jewish and Christian polemic.[57] But in Iran, Manichaeism provided perhaps the most serious threat. Karter's persecution of non-Zoroastrians was very likely inspired in part by the favor shown to the new religion by the king Shapur I (r. ca. 241–273). Shapur was generally tolerant, at one point issuing an edict that "Magi [i.e., Zoroastrians], Zandiks (Manichaeans),

---

[54] Fowden, *Empire to Commonwealth*, 82–4; M. Tardieu, "La diffusion du Bouddhisme dans l'empire Kouchan, l'Iran et la Chine, d'après un kephalaoin manichéen inédit," *Studia Iranica* 17 (1988), 153–82.

[55] Compare Brock, "Christians in the Sasanian Empire," 6, with Martin Sprengling, *Third Century Iran: Sapor and Kartir* (Chicago: Oriental Institute, 1953), 41–2, 51, 58.

[56] See Morony, *Iraq after the Muslim Conquest*, 286–9; J. Duchesne-Guillemin, "Zoroastrian Religion," in *The Cambridge History of Iran*, vol. 3, *The Seleucid, Parthian and Sasanian Periods*, ed. Ehsan Yarshataer (Cambridge: Cambridge University Press, 1983), 866–908; R. C. Zaehner, *The Dawn and Twilight of Zoroastrianism* (New York: G. P. Putnam's, 1961), 175–264.

[57] Morony, *Iraq after the Muslim Conquest*, 287.

Jews, Christians and all men of whatever religion should be left undisturbed and at peace in their belief."[58] The number of Christians especially increased dramatically during his reign.[59] But Manichaeism was tempting to the shah, who met the prophet Mani, gave him license to preach within his realm, and, according to some, may have considered adopting Manichaeism as the official religion of the state. The precise date of the compilation and redaction of the Zoroastrian texts known collectively as the *Avesta* has been much discussed, but they may have taken shape as a direct response of the Zoroastrian priesthood to the challenge posed by Mani and his revelations.[60]

The situation in the Sasanian empire differed somewhat from that in the Roman because Zoroastrianism retained certain traits of a national, i.e., a peculiarly Iranian, religion. There were some non-Iranian converts to Zoroastrianism, even among the tribes of the Arab peninsula. In an ethnically mixed area such as Iraq, however, Zoroastrianism was primarily the religion of the ruling elite, Iranians belonging to the upper classes and serving the Sasanian state.[61] There is little sign among Zoroastrians of active and general proselytization, as practiced by Christians, Jews, and Manichaeans, at least among the non-Iranians of the empire.[62] On the other hand, even the Iranian population included a growing number of converts to Christianity, especially toward the end of the Sasanian period, a phenomenon which may at times have strained relations between the state and the Christian churches.

This is not to say that there was no universalist dimension to Zoroastrian religious life; but what universalism there was derived directly, and to a greater degree than in the case of Rome and Christianity, from the explicit connection between religion and the state.[63] As we have seen, the commitment of the Sasanian emperors to Zoroastrianism was not an uncontested given. As late as the mid-fifth century, Yazdigird II (r. 438–457) made a close study of all the faiths of his subjects, although in the end he remained faithful to Zoroastrianism. But over time, the tendency was toward a union of the outlook and interests of the state and the Zoroastrian hierarchy. The tenth-century Muslim historian Mas'udi quotes Ardashir, the founder of the Sasanian dynasty, as saying that "religion and kingship are two brothers, and neither can dispense with the other. Religion is the

---

[58] Cited in Duchesne-Guillemin, "Zoroastrian Religion," 879.

[59] M.-L. Chaumont, "Les sassanides et la christianisation de l'Empire iranien au 3ᵉ siècle," *Revue de l'histoire des religions* 165 (1964), 165–202.

[60] H. S. Nyberg, "Sassanid Mazdaism According to Moslem Sources," *Journal of the K. R. Cama Oriental Institute* 39 (1958), 1–63, esp. 17–32; cf. Fowden, *Empire to Commonwealth*, 81. Others have credited competition with Islam for encouraging the compilation of definitive Zoroastrian texts. François Nau, "Étude historique sur la transmission de l'Avesta et sur l'époque probable de sa dernière redaction," *Revue de l'histoire des religions* 95 (1927), 149–99.

[61] Morony, *Iraq after the Muslim Conquest*, 296–7; on converts to Zoroastrianism, see the sources cited on p. 280.

[62] Nyberg, "Sassanid Mazdaism," 11. One exception was an effort to convert the population of Armenia, although this probably had principally to do with strategic considerations, Christian Armenia lying on the border between the Sasanian and Roman empires. Zaehner, *Dawn and Twilight*, 187–8.

[63] A point made by Fowden, *Empire to Commonwealth*, 24–36.

foundation of kingship and kingship protects religion."[64] Khusrau Anushirvan was remembered by the Zoroastrian priests as having "put into practice the teachings of the word of the religion and the worship and rites of the gods," and as having challenged the enemies of the orthodox faith.[65] The close connection between religious and political authority in late antique Zoroastrianism is important for its foreshadowing of later developments in Islam. The Sasanian monarch, according to Zoroastrian precepts developed and articulated during this period, was held to be supreme in all affairs, both religious and secular. He "served as the divinely ordained link between man the microcosm and god the macrocosm. Only through the king did the people have access to religion, god, and salvation." Apparently the Zoroastrian priests had to deal with kings whose commitment to the faith was less than perfect, and so they developed a doctrine by which it became a religious duty to contradict a heretical ruler and to overthrow those who threatened the "good religion" with their transgressions. But such errancies aside, Zoroastrian doctrine affirmed the union of kingship and religion, and so enjoined universal obedience to the sacralized monarch.[66]

The importance of the monarch in Zoroastrian thought derived in large part from his role as the lynchpin of an elaborate and (at least in theory) rigid social hierarchy, which itself was believed to reflect the structure of the cosmos. The fundamental distinction within Iranian society was that between nobles, who were exempted from certain taxes and forbidden to marry outside their caste, and commoners. The Zoroastrian literature, however, articulated a much more complicated and baroque social vision, in which humanity was divided among four social strata, variously defined but commonly consisting of priests, the military, cultivators, and artisans. This quadripartite model, the creation of which was ascribed in Zoroastrian legend to the primal and archetypal ruler Jamshid, and which almost certainly had an ancient connection to similar models prominent in Indian thought, formed the ideological foundation of the Sasanian state. The monarch had the responsibility to defend the system and to preserve the integrity of each caste so that, through a "circle of equity" in which each stratum supported the work of the others, both cosmos and society could survive and function. On a practical level, the system obviously served those at the top, in particular the religious hierarchy, who supervised a complex ecclesiastical structure and vast endowments; one leading and sympathetic modern student of Zoroastrianism has referred to late Sasanian society as "priest-ridden."[67]

Zoroastrian thought did not, however, lack a profound egalitarian undercurrent,

---

[64] Duchesne-Guillemin, "Zoroastrian Religion," 877; R. C. Zaehner, *The Teachings of the Magi* (London: George Allen and Unwin, 1956), 85.

[65] From the *Denkart*, as cited by R. C. Zaehner, *Zurvan: A Zoroastrian Dilemma* (Oxford: Clarendon Press, 1955), 53.

[66] Jamsheed Choksy, "Sacral Kingship in Sasanian Iran," *Bulletin of the Asia Institute* 2 (1988), 35–52; the quotation is taken from p. 37.

[67] Mary Boyce, *Zoroastrians: Their Religious Beliefs and Practices* (London: Routledge and Kegan Paul, 1979), 140–44. See also the excellent summary of socio-religious thought and practice in the Sasanian period in Louise Marlow, *Hierarchy and Egalitarianism in Islamic Thought* (Cambridge: Cambridge University Press, 1997), 66–90.

one which perhaps emerged in reaction to the dominant ideology of social division. This undercurrent, which can be traced back at least to a third-century Zoroastrian religious teacher named Zaradusht, surfaced periodically in the late Sasanian period, most notably under the shah Kavad (r. 488–496 and 498–531) and through a revolt led by a certain Mazdak around the time of the succession of Khusrau Anushirvan to the throne in 531. The exact connection between "Kavad's heresy and Mazdak's revolt," and between them and Zaradusht's teaching, has been the subject of much discussion.[68] Zaradusht had apparently identified the private possession of property and women as the root of social injustice and disharmony, and so preached a doctrine of communal access to them. Kavad sought to undermine the purity of lineage, and thus the status and power of the nobility, by insisting upon universal access to women; while Mazdak led a peasant revolt which demanded universal access too, or at least the radical redistribution of, both women and wealth. The efforts of both men failed. Kavad was deposed by his nobles, and Mazdak's rebellion was suppressed by Khusrau around the time of his accession to the throne, for which service to the "good religion" he was given the title Anushirvan, "Immortal Soul." It is difficult to be certain about the details and inter-relationship of the doctrines espoused by Zaradusht, Kavad, and Mazdak, since information about them is drawn almost entirely from sources hostile to them. But individually and collectively they represented a challenge to the dominant Iranian social order and its religious foundation, a challenge which emerged from within Zoroastrianism itself. More importantly, from our perspective, the challenge had a lasting legacy on religious developments in the medieval Near East, since much of the doctrine of Mazdak reappeared among certain sectarian groups in Iran during the first several centuries of the Muslim era.[69]

Mazdak and his creed remind us of the tense but exciting religious atmosphere which existed under the Sasanian emperors, and the same is true of Manichaeism. The prophet Mani himself was born into a family attracted to the Jewish-Christian baptist sects which proliferated in the Fertile Crescent in the first centuries of the Common Era. After receiving a series of revelations from a celestial being as a young man, Mani began to preach a new religion – his "hope," as he called it. His doctrine bore a superficial resemblance to Christianity – Jesus, for example, plays a prominent role in the Manichaean myth – but Mani also drew upon certain Indian ideas (such as metempsychosis) and especially Iranian dualism. The elaborate mythology developed by Mani in his writings posited a universe produced by the conflict between two primal forces, light and darkness, truth and falsehood, expressed sometimes in Christian language as God the Father and the devil, and sometimes in Zoroastrian terms as Zurvan and Ahriman. Physical existence in this

[68] Most recently in a stimulating article by Patricia Crone, "Kavād's Heresy and Mazdak's Revolt," *Iran: Journal of the British Institute of Persian Studies* 29 (1991), 21–42.

[69] On Mazdakism generally, see Crone, "Kavād's Heresy," and Ehsan Yarshater, "Mazdakism," in *The Cambridge History of Iran*, vol. 3, *The Seleucid, Parthian and Sasanian Periods*, ed. Ehsan Yarshataer (Cambridge: Cambridge University Press, 1983), 991–1024.

mythology is conceived as a state of suffering, as the divine sparks present in the progeny of Adam await their separation from dark matter. So Manichaeism developed a gnostic doctrine through which knowledge of the true human condition, and a consequent avoidance of procreation, paved the path to final redemption.[70]

Beyond the baroque and compelling richness of Manichaean doctrine and mythology, several aspects of Mani's preaching and its outcome demand our attention. In the first place, Mani's religious activities took place in a specifically Iranian context. He preached before the emperor Shapur on a number of occasions, dedicated a book to him, and, according to legend, converted the shah's brother. At the Sasanian court, he encountered and came into conflict with the Zoroastrian priest Karter. The two shared the ambition of harnessing the power of the state to their respective religions. In time, however, it was Karter who prevailed: in 276, under the emperor Bahram, Mani was arrested at Karter's urging, and eventually died in prison.

On the other hand, Mani and his followers aimed from the beginning at an even larger target. Of all the religions of late antiquity, Manichaeism was the most explicitly universalist, Islam not excepted. Its universalism is already apparent in the prophet's self-conscious syncretism. "Wisdom and deeds have always from time to time been brought to mankind by the messengers of God," proclaimed Mani. "So in one age they have been brought by the messenger called Buddha to India, in another by Zaradust [Zoroaster] to Persia, in another by Jesus to the West. Thereupon this revelation has come down and this prophecy has appeared in the form of myself, Mani, the envoy of the true God in the Land of Babylon." Mani proclaimed his message as the culmination of all previous revelations from God. "As a river joins another river to form a strong current, so the old books are added together in my Scriptures; and they have formed a great Wisdom, such as has not existed in previous generations." Manichaean missionaries propagated their doctrines well beyond the borders of the Iranian empire. Its appeal may be measured by the varied languages in which translations of Manichaean texts have survived, including Coptic, Turkish, and Chinese. In the Roman Empire, as is well known, Manichaeism was a potent force, which at one point held a powerful attraction for St Augustine. The bishop of Hippo later waged a polemical battle against the faith, as did the third-century pagan philosopher Alexander of

---

[70] For general studies of Mani and Manichaeism, see Geo Widengren, "Manichaeism and Its Iranian Background," in *The Cambridge History of Iran*, vol. 3, *The Seleucid, Parthian and Sasanian Periods*, ed. Ehsan Yarshater (Cambridge: Cambridge University Press, 1983), 965–90; idem, *Mani and Manichaeism* (New York: Holt, Rinehart, and Winston, 1965); Samuel N. C. Lieu, *Manichaeism in Mesopotamia and the Roman East* (Leiden: E. J. Brill, 1994); idem, *Manichaeism in the Later Roman Empire and Medieval China*, 2nd edition (Tubingen: J. C. P. Mohr, 1992). For useful summaries of Manichaean doctrine, see Widengren, "Manichaeism and Its Iranian Background," 972–84; Hans Jonas, *The Gnostic Religion*, second edition (Boston: Beacon Press, 1958), 206–37; Mircea Eliade, *A History of Religious Ideas*, in 3 volumes (Chicago: University of Chicago Press, 1982), 2.384–95.

Lycopolis.[71] Its missionaries were active in Central Asia well into the Middle Ages, and for a time in the late eighth and early ninth centuries Mani's faith was adopted as the official religion of the Uighur Turks.

In the end, however, despite its universalism and its appeal, Manichaeism failed. In part it did so because it never permanently attached itself to any of the principal empires which dominated the Near East from late antiquity into the modern period.[72] The stringent demands which Manichaeism imposed on its followers may also have limited its appeal. Manichaean communities were divided into two groups, the "elect" and the "hearers." The former lived extremely circumscribed lives, sheltered from harmful and soul-entrapping activities such as the eating of meat and, especially, sex and procreation. The "hearers" were not subject to the rigorous asceticism of the "elect." On the other hand, they could not look forward to as perfect or swift a salvation: whereas the elect, according to the Muslim author Ibn al-Nadim, would be returned at death to the "Gardens of Light" from whence they originally came, the "hearers" could expect to remain "in the world like a man who sees horrible things in his dream, plunging into mud and clay," until "his light and spirit are rescued, so that he becomes attached, adhering to the Elect, donning their garments after the long period of his [transitional] uncertainty."[73] In some ways this put the social aspect of Manichaeism at odds with the other universalizing religions of late antiquity, especially Islam, in which the Koranic emphasis on divine mercy provided a path to salvation which even the most humble could follow. On this level, Manichaeism could not compete, and unlike Judaism, Christianity, and Zoroastrianism, eventually became entirely extinct. On the other hand, its failure was not immediately apparent, even to the Islamic conquerors of the Near East in the seventh and eighth centuries. Manichaeism had an appeal even for some early Muslims, as we shall see. And when early Muslim polemicists defended their radical monotheism in the face of Iranian dualism, it was the compelling mythology and syncretistic doctrine of Mani, rather than the Zoroastrianism associated with the Sasanian state, which occupied most of their attention.[74]

Paganism

Of the religious traditions of late antiquity, paganism was the oldest. The use of the term paganism tends to make the historian uncomfortable, for a number of reasons. In the first place, it is employed to indicate religious beliefs and

---

[71] Peter Brown, *Augustine of Hippo* (Berkeley: University of California Press, 1967), 46–60; P. W. van der Horst, *An Alexandrian Platonist Against Dualism: Alexander of Lycopolis' Treatise 'Critique of the Doctrines of Manichaeus'* (Leiden: Brill, 1974). On Manichaean universalism, see Brown, *World of Late Antiquity*, 164; Lieu, *Manichaeism in the Later Roman Empire*, 86–120; Fowden, *Empire to Commonwealth*, 72–6. The first quotation is found in Lieu, *Manichaeism in the Later Roman Empire*, 86, and the second in Eliade, *History of Religious Ideas*, 2:387.

[72] This point is made most forcefully by Fowden, *Empire to Commonwealth*, 75.

[73] Ibn al-Nadim, *Fihrist*, trans. Bayard Dodge (New York: Columbia University Press, 1970), 796.

[74] Crone, "Kavād's Heresy and Mazdak's Revolt," 27.

practices of almost unlimited variety, many of them unconnected in any meaningful sense to others also defined as manifestations of paganism. From one
perspective, there was no such thing as paganism, but there were lots of
paganisms, most of them deeply rooted in local and ethnic communities.
Consequently, as one historian has recently and sensibly put it, "to buy into such
a category is to render oneself immediately imprecise."[75] Secondly, the term's
polemical overtones can also mislead us. The word "pagan" itself (originally
indicating a rustic villager, or boor) was a term of abuse which Christians used to
denote those who followed religions other than their own, in particular the ancient
cults which lingered on in rural areas after the cities of the Mediterranean region
had become predominantly Christian. The term "paganism" tends to conjure
images of Greeks performing sacrifices to Athena and Apollo, or Egyptians
worshiping multiple deities in various animal forms; and no doubt polytheism, and
the belief in and the worship of various localized deities, remained one aspect of
the pagan experience throughout the period, especially perhaps among the common people and in rural settings. But paganism – or more accurately, some of the
paganisms of late antiquity – had moved a good distance from the religion of
Homer and Ramses, and in many respects shared a good deal with the Christian
and Islamic traditions which replaced it.

Despite the imprecision of the term, historians fall back on it, inevitably if
reluctantly, to identify the mass of inter-connected religious traditions and cults
which emerged from the ancient world and which found themselves in competition
with the newly self-conscious communities of Christians, Jews, Zoroastrians and,
later, Muslims. In response to the more precise religious identity of, for example,
Christianity, fourth-century pagans such as Libanius and the Roman emperor
Julian understood themselves to represent an alternative – an *older* alternative – to
the new religions. The commitment of late antique and early medieval defenders
of paganism reflected not only a nostalgic longing for a vanishing faith, but a
genuine appreciation for a tradition which, in its breadth, sophistication, and
universalist outlook, laid the groundwork for and in many ways anticipated the
achievements and vision of the new monotheisms. "Who was it that settled the
inhabited world and propagated cities, if not the outstanding men and kings of
paganism?" asked the Sabian Thabit ibn Qurra (d. 901). "Who revealed the arcane
sciences? Who was vouchsafed the epiphany of that godhead who gives oracles
and makes known future events, if not the most famous of the pagans? ... They
filled the world with upright conduct and with wisdom, which is the chief part of
virtue. Without the gifts of paganism, the earth would have been empty and
impoverished, enveloped in a great shroud of destitution."[76]

In global terms, it is impossible to deny, first, that paganism was locked in
a struggle with the emerging monotheistic traditions, and second, that paganism
was, in late antiquity, in a secular decline. The signs of competition are rampant:

---

[75] David Frankfurter, *Religion in Greco-Roman Egypt: Assimilation and Resistance* (Princeton:
Princeton University Press, 1999), 33.
[76] Cited by Fowden, *Empire to Commonwealth*, 64–5.

in the laws by which Christian Roman emperors sought to marginalize or suppress pagan cults, or in the popular stories of the Christian saints which portray them contesting with "magicians" and "demons" (behind which one can often detect pagan holy men or localized pagan deities). And the decline is measurable, and not merely in the obvious fact that, at some point between the third and seventh centuries, the vast majority of the inhabitants of the Near East formally converted to one of the new faiths. Egypt provides a case in point. An important marker of the decline of paganism there lies in the decay of the active life of the temples and other cultic sites and occasions. Organized paganism in Egypt was in trouble well before the rapid spread of Christianity in the fourth century, and probably contributed to the latter phenomenon, rather than being a product of it. The last attested celebration of the Ameysia, an important festival associated with the goddess Isis, occurred in 257 CE, well before the majority of Egyptians even nominally professed Christianity. Even before this, Egyptian temples had begun to suffer from a decline in the level of financial support from imperial authorities, support which had for centuries been critical to their construction, upkeep, and embellishment. In Egypt, the situation was made worse by the fact that the priests apparently lost their ability to read and write the Egyptian language in its ancient scripts, and so found themselves partially cut off from their pagan religious traditions: other than at the remote temple at Philae in Upper Egypt, there are virtually no hieroglyphic or demotic inscriptions after the mid-third century.[77]

But the story of the struggle and decline of paganism is incomplete, and can obscure a much more nuanced story of religious identity and development. If paganism at some point "died," in the sense that all the inhabitants of Egypt or Syria or wherever came to identify themselves at least formally as Jews, or Christians, or (later) Muslims, the actual death of paganism was a protracted affair – and again, one which was by no means complete at the rise of Islam. Signs of the survival of pagan traditions abound throughout the Near East. At Edessa in Syria, one of the earliest and most important centers of eastern Christianity, a city which the pagan emperor Julian had shunned for its commitment to the Christian faith, pagan rituals and sacrifices were still practiced in the late sixth century.[78] In Iraq, organized pagan cults suffered from the hostility of and active persecution by both Christian bishops and monks and zealous Zoroastrian priests; but the pagans' enemies were still at it when the Muslim Arabs appeared on the scene in the fourth and fifth decades of the seventh century. A Nestorian *catholicos*, shortly after the Muslim conquest (but well before significant numbers of local residents had converted to Islam), complained that there were more pagans than Christians in the

---

[77] Roger S. Bagnall, "Combat ou vide: christianisme et paganisme dans l'Égypte romaine tardive," *Ktema* 13 (1988 [1992]), 285–96; idem, *Egypt in Late Antiquity* (Princeton: Princeton University Press, 1993), 251, 261–73.

[78] Bowersock, *Hellenism in Late Antiquity*, 36; J. B. Segal, *Edessa 'The Blessed City'* (Oxford: Clarendon Press, 1970), 108; Han J. W. Drijvers, "The Persistence of Pagan Cults and Practices in Christian Syria," in *East of Byzantium: Syria and Armenia in the Formative Period*, ed. Nina Garsoian, Thomas Mathews, and Robert Thompson (Washington, DC: Dumbarton Oaks, 1982), 35–43.

district of Beth Aramaye (lower Iraq). Reports of human sacrifices in Iraq should perhaps be approached with some caution, but it is striking that they continue well into the eighth century.[79] In Egypt, too, paganism survived the decline of its temples. There was active resistance to Christianity both among the philosophers in Alexandria, and in the countryside. One historian has described a veritable religious war which traumatized large portions of Upper Egypt in the fifth century, where entire villages remained untouched by Christianity. As late as the early seventh century, bishops could find pagan temples to destroy, and idolaters to baptize.[80] Even in the heartlands of the Byzantine Empire, in northwestern Asia Minor not far from the capital at Constantinople, a Christian missionary in the mid-sixth century claimed to have converted thousands of pagans, and to have destroyed or rededicated their temples. Here as elsewhere, those formally converted to Christianity may have, more or less secretly, preserved their ancient temples and altars, which they might then frequent at night, and there under the cover of darkness replay their pre-Christian rites. According to the Byzantine chronicler Theophanes, when Arab armies besieged the town of Pergamon in 717, its inhabitants in desperation resorted to a magician and his rather startling formula for salvation. At his urging, they "produced a pregnant woman who was about to give birth and cut her up. And after removing her infant and cooking it in a pot, all those who were intending to fight dipped the sleeves of their right arm in this detestable sacrifice." To no avail, recorded the disgusted chronicler; "they were delivered to the enemy." The story may or may not be true, but it is significant that the chronicler could relate it as if it were.[81]

It was not simply a question of paganism surviving in isolated manifestations, as a kind of relic. In the first place, the question of paganism is a reminder that religion and religious identities can be experienced on a variety of levels. The religious identity of a pagan in, say, an Egyptian village may have been related to, and informed by, the dominant myths which have survived in ancient Egyptian literature and the cults of the temples whose finances were increasingly in disarray. But it was also a product of very practical and immediate needs (such as healing, or ensuring a decent crop), and so was served not simply by relatively remote temple priests but by local holy men, local deities, local shrines, local stories, and religious practices defined or administered by local figures – loci of religious

---

[79] Morony, *Iraq after the Muslim Conquest*, 384–400.

[80] Roger Rémondon, "L'Égypte et la suprème résistance au christianisme (Ve–VIIe siècles)," *Bulletin de l'Institut Français d'Archéologie Orientale* 51 (1952), 63–78; see also László Kákosy, "Survival of Ancient Egyptian Gods in Coptic and Islamic Egypt," *Coptic Studies: Acts of the Third International Congress of Coptic Studies, Warsaw, 20–25 August, 1984*, ed. Wlodzmierz Godlewski (Warsaw: Éditions Scientifiques de Pologne, 1990), 175–7; and idem, "Das Ende des Heidentums in Ägypten," *Graeco-Coptica: Griechen und Kopten im byzantinischen Ägypten*, ed. Peter Nagel (Halle: Martin-Luther Universität Halle-Wittenberg Wissenschaftliche Beiträge, 1984), 61–76.

[81] *The Chronicle of Theophanes Confessor: Byzantine and Near Eastern History, AD 284–813*, trans. Cyril Mango and Roger Scott (Oxford: Clarendon Press, 1997), 541; on the situation in western Anatolia more generally, see Frank R. Trombley, "Paganism in the Greek World at the End of Antiquity: The Case of Rural Anatolia and Greece", *Harvard Theological Review* 78 (1985), 327–52.

authority which could survive the unraveling of the more formal networks associated with temples.[82]

Secondly, pagan practices, values, and expectations insinuated themselves in a variety of ways into the spiritual life and frame of reference of the new religious era. In Egypt, for example, thaumaturgy and oracular functions had always played an important role in local manifestations of paganism. Those traditions and the expectations they encouraged may have shaped the particular form of Coptic Christianity: in Coptic literature, the saints often play the role of healer, seer, or wielder of supernatural powers. A story from the early fifth-century *Lausiac History* by Palladius about a holy man named Makarios is suggestive, in part because it is so typical of accounts in late antique sources. An Egyptian approached a (presumably pagan) sorcerer to enlist his aid in attracting the attention of a woman with whom he was infatuated, or barring that, prevailing upon her husband to throw her out. Through his magical charms, the sorcerer caused the woman to assume the shape of a horse. Her husband, naturally distraught, sought the assistance of the Christian saint. Makarios first expressed a certain impatience with the situation, complaining to the husband that "you are the horses, for you have the eyes of horses. Now she is a woman, not at all changed, except in the eyes of self-deceived men." At the same time, however, Makarios took very practical counter-steps: he "blessed water, poured it on her bare skin from the head downward, and made her appear as a woman," and, by way of prophylaxis, enjoined the woman to attend communion regularly.[83]

As Palladius' story suggests, in the popular mind the competition between Christianity and paganism was largely one of power. But at the deep foundational level of mental structures which manifest themselves as folk belief, change naturally worked more slowly. At this level, pagans shared with Christians, Jews, and others certain assumptions, beliefs about the unseen world, and practices related to those beliefs, which we would recognize as (more or less) "religious": a belief in demons, for example, or in the ability of certain spiritually gifted individuals to confront and control them. In Mesopotamia in the early seventh century, the sister-in-law of a Christian deacon sought the assistance of pagan sorcerers to attract his attention. At their direction, she covered herself with oil, causing "the fire of love for her [to] spread in him like the fire of a blazing furnace," which passion was extinguished only through the deacon's anointing with a countervailing oil at the hands of a holy man.[84] The "sphere of magic" did not appear, to the men and women of late antiquity, to be clearly distinct from the

---

[82] This is the compelling argument of Frankfurter, *Religion in Greco-Roman Egypt*.

[83] Palladius, *The Lausiac History*, trans. Robert T. Meyer (New York: Newman Press, 1964), 56–7; cf. Bagnall, *Egypt in Late Antiquity*, 273–5; Frankfurter, *Religion in Greco-Roman Egypt*, passim, esp. 184–95; Françoise Dunand, "Miracles et guérisons en Égypte tardive," in *Mélanges Étienne Bernand*, ed. Nicole Fick and Jean-Claude Carrière (Besançon: Université de Besançon, 1991), 235–50, on the functional similarity of medical cures produced by pagan gods and Christian holy men, despite certain differences in the structures through which the faithful begged a cure.

[84] Morony, *Iraq after the Muslim Conquest*, 389; E. A. Wallis Budge, *The Histories of Rabban Hôrmîzd the Persian and Rabban Bar-ʿIdtâ*, 2 vols. (London: Luzac and Co., 1902), 2:266–7.

"sphere of religion," even if Jewish rabbis and Christian priests did sometimes view magicians and their trade with distrust and horror.[85] And religious authorities were right, in a sense, to be concerned: the magic common among Christians, Jews and others owed much to the pagan religions of the ancient world, for their gods and goddesses often survived as the demons or spirits whose activities the magicians sought to counter or control. For example, a number of Jewish incantation bowls from Mesopotamia have survived which sought to counter-act the evil influence of demons identified as, among others, Ishtar – the name of the prominent ancient goddess of the region.[86] And the astrological preoccupation of ancient Mesopotamian religion of course had an extended afterlife among medieval Muslims, Christians, and Jews.

Despite the rise in the level of rhetorical hostility and its accompanying violence, and despite a corresponding emphasis on formal professions of faith – developments which left a profound mark on the world Islam inherited – a dialogue between the religious traditions persisted through the end of late antiquity. Paganism participated fully in that dialogue, and through it contributed in substantial and subtle ways to the religious life of those who came later. The flexibility and syncretistic potential of Mediterranean paganism are well known, and need no comment here. But other religions, such as Christianity, were also more porous than bishops and others might insist. In some instances, paganism found its channel to the future in the form of Hellenism. Much recent scholarship has tended to minimize the gap in the late antique Near East separating Hellenized cities from the non-Greek (Syriac, for instance, or Coptic) countryside, and has stressed the extent to which Hellenism penetrated all layers of society and provided a common cultural vernacular.[87] The connection between paganism and Hellenism is reflected in the fact that *hellenismos* can mean, in late antique texts, "paganism" itself – a point of which the pagan emperor Julian delighted in reminding Greek-speaking Christians.[88] And so the religious differences between, say, paganism and Christianity were muted by certain astonishing resemblances. Christians had a trinity, but so too did some pagans, such as those in the Hawran in Syria who worshiped a trio of gods, one of which was known by a name which meant "God-man."[89] Holiness, a numinous quality distinguishing certain individuals from the ordinary run of humankind, was a characteristic of Christian

---

[85] For an excellent discussion of the intersection of Judaism and magic in late antiquity, see Judah Goldin, "The Magic of Magic and Superstition," in *Aspects of Religious Propaganda in Judaism and Early Christianity*, ed. Elizabeth Schüssler-Fiorenza (Notre Dame: University of Notre Dame Press, 1976), 115–47.

[86] Neusner, *History of the Jews in Babylonia*, 5:215–43, esp. 231; Morony, *Iraq after the Muslim Conquest*, 384, 387.

[87] On this point, see especially Bowersock, *Hellenism in Late Antiquity*, and Cameron, "The Eastern Provinces in the Seventh Century A.D." Bowersock, for example, says that Hellenism was "a means for a more articulate and a more universally comprehensible expression of local traditions" (9).

[88] Bowersock, *Hellenism in Late Antiquity*, 9–11.

[89] G. W. Bowersock, "An Arabian Trinity," *Harvard Theological Review* 79 (1986), 17–21; idem, *Hellenism in Late Antiquity*, 17–19. "The significance of a god-man deity in an indigenous cult of Semitic paganism," observes Bowersock, "scarcely needs underscoring."

saints, but also of some late antique philosophers, at least as they were remembered by their disciples.[90] Influence flowed in both directions. An epic fifth-century Egyptian poem about Dionysos recounts that "Bacchus our lord shed tears, so that he might bring an end to the tears of mortals," a line which "could never have been written in a Greek pagan poem before the Christian era."[91] On the other hand, Christian tomb frescoes with scenes drawn from Greek mythology, or an encomium to the very Christian emperor Theodosius II comparing him to Achilles, Agamemnon, and Odysseus, bespeak Christian artists, authors, and audiences thoroughly comfortable with the cultural legacy of the pagan past.[92] The precise direction of the influence is not necessarily important; what is important is that the extended religious conversation of late antiquity engaged a variety of religious traditions, and that for all that it came under siege, paganism had not yet spoken its final word.

---

[90] Bowersock, *Hellenism in Late Antiquity*, 15–17; Garth Fowden, "The Pagan Holy Man in Late Antique Society," *The Journal of Hellenic Studies* 102 (1982), 33–59.

[91] Bowersock, *Hellenism in Late Antiquity*, 44. The poem is the *Dionysiaca* of Nonnos of Panopolis, trans. W. H. D. Pouse, in 3 vols. (Cambridge, Massachusetts: Harvard University Press, 1940) (Loeb Classical Library), 12.171.

[92] Bowersock, *Hellenism in Late Antiquity*, 64–5.

CHAPTER 3

Arabia before Islam

To the south of the Fertile Crescent stretches the peninsula which takes its name from the Arabs who inhabit it. Arabia was the setting for the career of the Prophet Muhammad as recounted in the Muslim sources, and so makes a special claim upon the attention of those interested in the subsequent unfolding of Near Eastern history. From the beginning, however, we should bear two caveats in mind. First, the connection between Arabia and its people and their culture, on the one hand, and Islam on the other, is problematic. The religious tradition which we now identify as "Islam" may have begun in an Arabian context, and certainly that context remained central to the later development of the religion for any number of reasons – for example, the fact that the Koran is in Arabic, the language of the inhabitants of the peninsula, or the importance which Muslims later accorded to the behavior of the Prophet and his companions in determining what constitutes a "proper" Islamic life. But is it useful to think of Islam as principally a *product* of Arabia, as the Islamic tradition does? Certainly the demographic and cultural center of gravity in the Islamic world quickly moved beyond the Arabian peninsula. Even if the Arabian crucible is important, what exactly does that mean? To what extent, for example, was Arabia in the sixth and seventh centuries integrated into the larger cultural and religious patterns of the rest of the Near East? Arabia may be where Islam began, but the cultures and traditions of other areas, most notably the more populated regions of the Near East from Egypt to Iran, arguably played a more critical role in the subsequent delimitation of Islamic identity.

Second, the sources available for the reconstruction of pre-Islamic Arabian society are not such as to inspire much confidence. Muslims refer to the pre-Islamic period as the *jahiliyya*, the "time of ignorance" before the coming of the Koranic revelation. From a historical rather than a theological viewpoint, the term is an apt one, although for entirely different reasons. Almost all of the Muslim sources on the pre-Islamic period and the years spanning Muhammad's career are relatively late, having been written a century and a half or more after the events they purport to describe. (They were of course based at least in part on material which circulated *orally* much earlier.) In recent years, several scholars have cast serious doubt upon the accuracy of the traditional picture of pre- and early-Islamic

Arabian society, much of it relying on those late Muslim sources. The problem with those sources, in a nutshell, is that they were put together and used by Muslims to settle later controversies and to justify retrospectively an Islamic *Heilsgeschichte*, and so reflect more what later Muslims wanted to remember than what was necessarily historically accurate.[1] We will discuss the source problems more fully in a later chapter, but for now the reader should at least understand that the usual accounts of the origins of Islam are based on sources of dubious historical value.

With these warnings in mind, what can we say about religious conditions and their social and political underpinnings in Arabia in the decades before the coming of Islam, or at least about how the sources portray those conditions? In some ways it was a very different world than that of Egypt, the Fertile Crescent, and Iran, in which Judaism, Christianity, Zoroastrianism, Manichaeism, and a residual paganism contested for followers and for authority. The inescapable fact that much of the peninsula consists of desert produced a radically different social and political dynamic, particularly in those regions dominated by bedouin. These regions lay beyond the uncontested reach of centralized, territorial states such as the Roman or Sasanian empires, and, except in certain limited regions, also lacked indigenous traditions of permanent political institutions. In this world, social identity rested upon perceived patterns (either real or fictive) of kinship. In the same way, what political authority there was focused on kin groups, on members of particular lineages who through military accomplishment or through control of cultic sites acquired a certain "nobility" (*sharaf*), and on temporary alliances and federations between tribes and clans, rather than on individuals and institutions. Particularly respected men might be accorded a limited and temporary authority, especially as a *hakam*, a mediator selected through a process of consensus to provide limited guidance to and to negotiate differences between individual or tribal rivals. A more effective social "glue" was the blood-feud, which placed realistic constraints on the anarchy of nomadic life and limits on the endemic violence.[2]

To be sure, not all of Arabia was desert, and not all Arabs were bedouin. The Arabian environment was in fact quite diverse, and produced societies as various

---

[1] For an especially clear example of this revisionist scholarship, see Patricia Crone, *Meccan Trade and the Rise of Islam* (Oxford: Blackwell, 1987), 203–30; and see below, pp. 57–60.

[2] There are a number of useful surveys of social and political conditions in pre-Islamic Arabia; many of them, however, serve as introductions to biographical studies of Muhammad or interpretive accounts of the rise of Islam. Among them: Ignaz Goldziher, *Muslim Studies*, trans. C. R. Barber and S. M. Stern, 2 vols. (London: George Allen and Unwin, 1966–71), 1:11–97; Marshall Hodgson, *The Venture of Islam: Conscience and History in a World Civilization*, in 3 volumes (Chicago: University of Chicago Press, 1974), 1:147–57; Ira Lapidus, "The Arab Conquests and the Formation of Islamic Society," in *Studies on the First Century of Islamic Society*, ed. G. H. A. Juynboll (Carbondale and Edwardsville: Southern Illinois University Press, 1982), 49–72; Maxime Rodinson, *Mohammed* (New York: Pantheon, 1971), 1–37; Irfan Shahid, "Pre-Islamic Arabia," in *The Cambridge History of Islam*, ed. P. M. Holt et al. (Cambridge: Cambridge University Press, 1970), vol. 1, *The Central Islamic Lands from Pre-Islamic Times to the First World War*, 3–29. Especially to be recommended is Fred M. Donner, *The Early Islamic Conquests* (Princeton: Princeton University Press, 1981), 11–49.

in character as those of the northern regions of the Near East. At least one corner of Arabia supported an agricultural and citied civilization on a par with those of the Fertile Crescent. The southwestern corner of the peninsula, focused on the modern country of Yemen, was *Arabia Felix*, "fruitful" or "happy Arabia," a land (unlike the rest of the peninsula) of significant rainfall and lush vegetation. In the centuries before the rise of Islam, its environmental conditions and agricultural and trading economy (situated as it was at a strategic point on the sea route from the Mediterranean to both India and East Africa) supported a material culture and political traditions much more like those of the rest of the Near East than those of central Arabia, and the religious situation there was markedly different than that elsewhere in the peninsula. In Arabia as a whole, the true nomads represented only a fraction of the total population. Even outside of Yemen, more or less permanent settlements could be found. Some of these were quite large, such as the agricultural oasis of Yathrib in which the Islamic community first took shape, or more limited urban centers such as Mecca, site of Muhammad's birth and early life. But even here, the bedouin and the inhabitants of settled regions were tied together by bonds of both economy and culture, and in particular by their distinctive patterns of kinship ties.[3] The story from the *sira* (biography) of the Prophet in which the infant Muhammad was entrusted to a Bedouin woman for suckling, whether or not it is literally true, suggests a symbiotic relationship binding together the various social groups of the Arabian peninsula.[4]

If that describes social and political conditions in much of pre-Islamic Arabia, obviously "religion" was likely to mean something very different there than it did in the settled and increasingly urban societies of the north. Gods there were aplenty, and as we shall see, even monotheism had made its mark in Arabia well before the coming of Islam. The Arabs, at least as much as inhabitants of other regions of the Near East, lived in a world saturated with the supernatural, which took for them the form of multitudinous and ubiquitous spirits (*jinn*) as well as gods. But the *moral* order of their society depended less on reference to a framework of supernatural origin than it did to the exigencies of social life in the demanding world of their difficult environment. The late antique obsession with formal expressions of religious identity must have seemed to the Bedouin, if it intruded onto their consciousness at all, as incomprehensible. Religion was something immediate and real – could some deity help you find a lost camel? – rather than a matter of abstract doctrine and principle. (Such "practical" concerns were not, of course, irrelevant to the religious experiences of most people in the more "sophisticated" regions of the Near East.) Moreover, in the absence of a state, the kind of identification between religious and political authority which was becoming increasingly characteristic of societies in the Fertile Crescent and

---

[3] A point made forcefully by Hodgson, *Venture of Islam*, 1:147–8, and Donner, *Early Islamic Conquests*, 26–8.

[4] The story can be found in Ibn Ishaq, *The Life of Muhammad*, trans. Alfred Guillaume (Oxford: Oxford University Press, 1955), 70–3.

the other settled and urbanized regions to the north of Arabia was, obviously, out of the question.

The dominant religious traditions of pre-Islamic Arabia remained polytheistic, but little can in fact be known with certainty about them. There has been much debate among historians of religion about the origin and character of Arabian religion – for example, whether it represented a "primitive" form of Semitic religion, or instead a degenerate form of the more sophisticated traditions of the Fertile Crescent (paralleling the traditional Muslim account according to which Muhammad's role was to restore a primitive monotheism associated with Abraham). There are signs of litholatry among the Arabs, although by the time of Muhammad most of the various deities had acquired faces and personalities. Several hundred Arabian deities are known from the Muslim sources, the most prominent of which were those identified by the Arabs as the three "daughters of Allah" – Manat, Allat, and al-ʿUzza – a trinity which was, according to the later Muslim tradition, accorded a special place among Muhammad's tribe of Quraysh and their allies around the advent of Islam, and to which prominent (although ambiguous) mention is made in the Koran.[5] Behind the specific deities, the Arabs were also probably aware of Allah. For some he may have represented a remote creator god, possibly related to the Semitic El; some Western scholars have suggested (again, paralleling in a way the traditional Muslim account) that he represents a *deus otiosus* who had over the centuries been eclipsed by more particularized and localized deities.[6] Allah apparently played little role in religious cult, although the Muslim tradition associates him with the Kaʿba in Mecca. Cultic life focused on a number of practices which survived, in revalorized form, in Islam, including sacrifice and pilgrimage to shrines. It is often assumed that the most important of those shrines was that centered on the Kaʿba at Mecca, and that it was the object of a widely-shared pilgrimage cult among the pre-Islamic Arabs. This cult, so the traditional story goes, was tended to by the Quraysh, the tribe to which Muhammad belonged, and who acquired thereby a special and privileged status among the pre-Islamic Arabs. However, even this story, which forms such an important part of many traditional Muslim narratives of Islam's origins, has recently been shown to rest on dubious historical foundations.[7]

It is in fact difficult to say much with confidence regarding pre-Islamic Arabian religion. The situation may not, however, be completely bleak. If we are to understand the rise of Islam, it may be that we can say *something* by looking

---

[5] What exactly the three goddesses were, and what light they shed on pre-Islamic Arabian religion, is however difficult to say. See now G. R. Hawting, *The Idea of Idolatry and the Emergence of Islam: From Polemic to History* (Cambridge: Cambridge University Press, 1999), 130–49. Compare, on the pre-Islamic deities more generally, Toufic Fahd, *Le panthéon de l'Arabie centrale à la veille de l'hégire* (Beirut: Institut Français d'Archéologie de Beyrouth, 1968), 41–4 (on Allah), 111–20 (on Allat), 123–6 (on Manat), and 163–78 (on al-ʿUzza).

[6] See, for example, Joseph Henninger, "Pre-Islamic Bedouin Religion," in *Studies on Islam*, ed. Merlin Swartz (New York: Oxford University Press, 1981), 6–7, and Tor Andrae, *Mohammed: The Man and His Faith* (Freeport, N.Y.: Books for Libraries Press, 1971), 31–4.

[7] Crone, *Meccan Trade*, 168–199.

beyond the particular condition of the Arabs to their place in the wider world of the Near East and of the cultural and religious patterns of late antiquity.

There were in fact a wide array of links which bound the Arabs of the peninsula to the states and religions of the Near East. One dominant theme in Western scholarship has suggested that among the most important links were commercial ones. According to this account, the Arabs, and in particular Muhammad's own tribe of the Quraysh, played important roles in an international transit trade between the Roman world and the East, the religious significance of which is, first, that it brought about social changes and gave rise to tensions within Mecca which formed the backdrop to the Koranic revelations, and second, that commercial contacts made possible more extensive cultural and religious exchange.[8] Like much else in the traditional narratives, this account is now difficult to accept.[9] Nonetheless, the religious history of Arabia in the years leading up to Islam is tied to the larger story of Near Eastern religion in late antiquity, and the Muslim conquests of the seventh century can be seen as part of a much longer process by which Arabia and the rest of the region grew closer culturally, religiously, and politically.[10]

Contacts were especially strong and intimate with the Hellenistic and Roman Near East.[11] The Hellenism which saturated the Fertile Crescent before and during late antiquity penetrated at least as far as Faw, in the interior of the Arabian peninsula, 700 kilometers southwest of the modern city of Riyadh, and 180 kilometers northeast of the important town of Najran, astride an ancient trading route leading from Yemen to Mesopotamia and other points in the northern Near East. Here, in this "thoroughly Arab society," archeological evidence nonetheless reveals signs of strong Hellenistic influence, including wall paintings with a pronounced Hellenistic flavor, as well as statues of the Graeco-Egyptian god Harpocrates and possibly Minerva.[12] Further north, along the edge of the Fertile Crescent, the exchange of people and ideas between Arabs of the interior and predominantly Aramaic-speaking inhabitants of Syria was, and had been for centuries, a routine element of life. That exchange touched on religious matters, perhaps more self-consciously so after the widespread Christianization of the

---

[8] A dominant theme of W. Montgomery Watt, *Muhammad at Mecca* (Oxford: Clarendon Press, 1953), esp. 72–9. Watt observes that "[t]he Qurʾān appeared not in the atmosphere of the desert, but in that of high finance" (3).

[9] Again, Crone, *Meccan Trade*, passim, where she argues not that there was no trade, but rather that historians have exaggerated the importance of the international transit trade through Arabia, and that Qurashi control of that trade on the eve of Islam cannot be confirmed by the sources.

[10] Lapidus, "The Arabs Conquests and the Formation of Islamic Society," passim.

[11] On this subject, see the magisterial works of Irfan Shahid: *Rome and the Arabs: A Prolegomenon to the Study of Byzantium and the Arabs* (Washington, D.C.: Dumbarton Oaks, 1984); *Byzantium and the Arabs in the Fourth Century* (Washington, D. C.: Dumbarton Oaks, 1984); *Byzantium and the Arabs in the Fifth Century* (Washington, D.C.: Dumbarton Oaks, 1989); *Byzantium and the Arabs in the Sixth Century* (Washington, D. C.: Dumbarton Oaks, 1995).

[12] A. R. al-Ansary, *Qaryat al-Fau: A Portrait of Pre-Islamic Civilisation in Saudi Arabia* (New York: St Martin's Press, 1982), 15, 24–5, 104–5, 113. The characterization of Faw as "thoroughly Arab" is that of Glen Bowersock, *Hellenism in Late Antiquity* (Ann Arbor: University of Michigan Press, 1990), 74–5.

Roman Empire. Bishop Theodoret of Cyrrhus (d. ca. 458), in his account of the life of the Syrian saint Simeon Stylites, records that Arabs used to visit him "in bands of two or three hundred at a time, sometimes even of a thousand," and, moved by the saint's piety, renounced their "ancestral error," smashed their idols, and abandoned the "orgies of Aphrodite" – by which he may have meant the Arab goddess Allat or al-ʿUzza – whom they had been accustomed to worship.[13] The continual movement of people back and forth from the settled regions to the desert was of course potentially destabilizing, and the Romans attempted by various means to control the large Arab population just beyond their frontiers. Several Roman military expeditions, from the time of Augustus to that of Justinian, reached as far as southern Arabia, although the empire was never able to establish a permanent military and political presence in the region. The line of Roman forts which extends southward from Syria to the Gulf of Aqaba testifies to their concerns about the potential military threat posed by the Arabs, and their worry – prophetic, as it turned out – that the Arabs might one day wish to take from Syria something more than new religious ideas and models.[14] Another tactic employed by the Romans – employing some Arab tribes as "federates" and allies of the imperial army – in fact increased the level of cultural exchange, and contributed to the spread of Christianity among the Arabs.[15] Chief among them was the tribe of Ghassan, who in the sixth century ruled a buffer kingdom between Byzantine Syria, on the one hand, and on the other, both tribal Arabia and a similar Arab kingdom (the Lakhmids) allied with Iran.

The example of the Ghassanid kingdom is worth a closer look, for its experience reflects the complex historical conditions under which Arabia was being drawn into the Near Eastern orbit and its intricate nexus of politics and religion. Both geographically and culturally, Ghassan straddled the Roman and Arabian worlds. Its rulers were Arabs, who shared with the Bedouin the cult of poetry which loomed so prominently in pre-Islamic Arabian culture – the famous Arab poet and panegyrist Hassan ibn Thabit was among those who visited and composed verses for the Ghassanid kings. But by the first half of the sixth century at the latest, they were also Christian. The Ghassanids contributed to the Christianization of Arabia by actively supporting missions there, particularly to the south of the peninsula, to cities such as Najran which became during the sixth century the major center of Arabian Christianity.[16] On the other hand, their Christianity was Monophysite, and so the bonds binding them to the Chalcedonian empire partook of an ambivalence similar to that felt by Egyptians and Syrians.

[13] Robert Doran, *The Lives of Simeon Stylites* (Kalamazoo, Michigan: Cistercian Publications, 1992), 76–7.

[14] Fergus Millar, "Empire, Community and Culture in the Roman Near East: Greeks, Syrians, Jews and Arabs," *Journal of Jewish Studies* 38 (1987), 164.

[15] On the Arab *foederati*, see Shahid, *Byzantium and the Arabs in the Fourth Century*, 476–90, 498–510, 542–9; *Byzantium and the Arabs in the Fifth Century*, 459–520; and *Byzantium and the Arabs in the Sixth Century*, passim.

[16] On Najrān, see *EI*², art. "Naḏjrān" (by Irfan Shahid); Irfan Shahid, *The Martyrs of Najran: New Documents* (Brussels: Société des Bollandistes, 1971).

The Ghassanids were federated allies of Rome, and served Roman interests in Arabia and on the Sasanian frontier; but Byzantine wariness of Monophysitism contributed to the decision to arrest two Ghassanid kings during the second half of the sixth century, and so to a severe straining of ties between the empire and its subordinate Arab allies on the eve of the devastating Sasanian invasion of the early seventh.[17] The tensions grew worse, and by the eve of the Muslim conquests, according to Theophanes, a Roman official in Palestine rudely dismissed Arab soldiers claiming their pay, driving them away and insulting them as "dogs."[18]

More generally, the condition of Christianity in pre-Islamic Arabia was fraught with tension. The Christian Roman emperors made a conscious effort to draw the Arabs into their fold. Constantius, for example, in the middle of the fourth century sent a bishop, Theophilus Indus, to convert the South Arabians. His mission was not a great success, but it already suggests an understanding of the complex intersection of religious, strategic, and commercial interests in Arabia: the region was known to Romans in part through the activities of Roman merchants there, and Theophilus's embassy was spurred in part through Constantius's appraisal of the strategic threat posed by Sasanian interest in the region.[19] Roman interest in Arabia continued through the end of late antiquity. One interesting indication of this interest is found in a story recorded by the Muslim historian al-Tabari, according to which Byzantine artisans, stone masons and mosaic artists, helped to construct a church in the city of Sanaa in Yemen out of marble and with mosaics sent from Constantinople.[20] Such examples indicate that Arabia was, at the end of late antiquity, very much a center of religious competition, and that the game was one which the Romans played to the best of their ability. By and large, however, the Arabs seem to have consciously avoided the specifically imperial (i.e., Chalcedonian) version of the Christian faith. In eastern Arabia, Christianity was a presence, for example in the oasis of al-Yamama from which Muhammad's prophetic rival Musaylima emerged and among tribes such as the Banu Hanifa. Christianity came to this region largely through al-Hira, the important Arab settlement on the borders of Sasanian Iraq, and so was Nestorian in orientation.[21] By contrast, among the Ghassanids and in Najran, as we have seen, Monophysite Christianity predominated. Other groups of Arabs may have been Christianized, but only partially or imperfectly so. Some reflection of this may be present in the Koran itself, which seems to suggest that some Arabs understood the Christian

---

[17] Shahid, *Byzantium and the Arabs in the Sixth Century*, 455–79, 529–622.

[18] *The Chronicle of Theophanes Confessor: Byzantine and Near Eastern History, AD 284–813*, trans. Cyril Mango and Roger Scott (Oxford: Clarendon Press, 1997), 466.

[19] Shahid, *Byzantium and the Arabs in the Fourth Century*, 86–106.

[20] Muhammad ibn Jarīr al-Ṭabarī, Tārīkh al-rusul waʾl-mulūk, ed. M. J. De Goeje and others (Leiden: E. J. Brill, 1879–1901), 934–6, = *The History of al-Ṭabarī*, vol. 5, trans. C. E. Bosworth (Albany, New York: SUNY Press, 1999), 217–21; R. B. Serjeant and Ronald Lewcock, "The Church (al-Qalis) of Ṣanʿāʾ and Ghumdān Castle," in *Ṣanʿāʾ: An Arabian Islamic City*, ed. R. B. Serjeant and Ronald Lewcock (London: World of Islam Festival Trust, 1983), 44–8, esp. 47.

[21] Dale F. Eickelman, "Musaylima: An Approach to the Social Anthropology of Seventh Century Arabia," *Journal of the Economic and Social History of the Orient* 10 (1967), 17–52, esp. 31–2.

trinity to consist of God, Jesus, and Mary: "And when God said: 'Oh Jesus, son of Mary, did you say to men, "Take me and my mother as gods next to Allah"?'" (5.116). Whether or not Muhammad himself understood the Christian idea of the trinity in this sense, the Koranic verse suggests that some Arabs had at best a very attenuated notion of what constituted Christian doctrine.[22]

To further complicate the situation, Christianity was not the only major Near Eastern religion with a stake in Arabia. There were significant Jewish communities, too, possibly larger and certainly better organized. Not surprisingly, the origins of these communities are somewhat obscure. Foundation legends ascribe the origin of the Jewish tribes at Yathrib variously to a priestly tribe dispatched by Moses to destroy the Amalekites who, the legends claim, had settled in the Hijaz, or to Jews fleeing the Roman destruction of the second temple, and that of the community in Yemen to the union of Solomon with the Queen of Sheba. As a historical matter, it is likely that some Jews sought refuge in Arabia after the suppression of the rebellions in Palestine in the first and second centuries, and that their numbers were augmented by proselytization and conversion, both of individuals and, more commonly in the Arabian context, of entire kin groups.[23] By the middle of the fourth century, Constantius's emissary Theophilus noted the presence in South Arabia of a large Jewish community. Whatever their origins, by the rise of Islam these Jews were thoroughly Arabized and integrated into the Arab society in which they lived: they spoke Arabic (although sometimes in a particular Judaeo-Arabic dialect), and had Arabic names; they functioned in a variety of occupations, as merchants, scholars, bedouin, craftsmen; they produced poets composing odes thoroughly in the traditional style of the bedouin.[24]

Through its Jewish as well as Christian communities, Arabia was drawn into the Near Eastern theater of religious developments. The Jews of Arabia were Arabized, but they were not unknown to or cut off from their religious brethren elsewhere in the Near East. The Koran uses terms such as *rabbaniyun* and *ahbar*, which seem to suggest the presence of some kind of rabbinical organization in western Arabia and so perhaps a connection to late antique Judaism as it took shape in Palestine and Iraq. Moreover, the Mishna (the collection of Jewish legal traditions compiled around the year 200 CE) itself reveals an awareness on the part of Near Eastern rabbis with the condition and problems of the Jews of Arabia.[25] For some Arabian Jews, the political connection was an Iranian one. In the second half of the sixth century, for example, the Sasanian official in charge of relations

[22] See *EI*[2], art. "Maryam" (by A. J. Wensinck and Penelope Johnstone).

[23] On the foundation legends and the origins of the Jewish communities of Arabia, see Gordon Darnell Newby, *A History of the Jews of Arabia from Ancient Times to Their Eclipse under Islam* (Columbia, South Carolina: University of South Carolina Press, 1988), 14–21, 31–2, 52–4.

[24] Newby, *History of the Jews of Arabia*, 21, 49, 55–7; Ilse Lichtenstadter, "Some References to Jews in Pre-Islamic Arabic Literature," *Proceedings of the American Academy for Jewish Research* 10 (1940), 185–94.

[25] Koran 5.47. Cf. Newby, *History of the Jews of Arabia*, 54–8. Others, however, have argued that the primary Jewish influences on Muhammad were sectarian and anti-rabbinic in character; see Chaim Rabin, *Qumran Studies* (Oxford: Oxford University Press, 1957), 112–30.

with the desert Arabs may have appointed a member of one of the principal Jewish tribes at Yathrib as his representative in the oasis, charged with the collection of certain taxes or tribute.[26]

Jewish and Christian activity in Arabia needs to be viewed against the background of competition between the Roman and Sasanian empires, and between the various religious traditions of the Near East in late antiquity. A particularly rich and suggestive example is that of Dhu Nuwas, a king of Himyar in South Arabia who converted to Judaism in the early sixth century and then led an attack on and persecution of Christians, particularly at Najran, reportedly in retaliation for the burning of a synagogue there. His Judaism is interesting, in the first place because it indicates the possibility of Jewish proselytization in the region, and in the second because it too suggests an Iranian connection. According to a Syriac source, Dhu Nuwas's mother may herself have been Jewish, from Nisibis in Mesopotamia, within the Sasanian empire. His persecution of Christians at Najran and elsewhere may have been provoked more broadly by concern about the political implications of the Christian presence there, since the Christians, although Monophysite, maintained links to the Byzantine empire. At any rate, the persecution led the emperor Justinian to urge the ruler of the Ethiopian kingdom of Axum, himself a Christian (although, again, Monophysite) to intervene in South Arabia. An Ethiopian expeditionary force defeated and slew Dhu Nuwas, and the occupation which resulted lasted for half a century – until, significantly, it was forcibly brought to an end by the Sasanians in the second half of the sixth century.[27]

Iranian religions also staked a claim in Arabia. Zoroastrianism was known to the Arabs, through the Sasanian military presence along the Persian Gulf and in South Arabia, in a pair of temples constructed by Iranian colonists at a mining site in Najd, and through commercial and political links between Iraq and the Hijaz. Apparently some Arabs even converted to the Iranian national faith, at least among the tribe of Tamim in the northeast of the peninsula.[28] References in several early sources to the presence of individuals among the Quraysh who espoused *zandaqa* seem to suggest that at least a few Meccans had adopted some form of Iranian dualism. The term *zandaqa* entered Arabic from Middle Persian, in which it indicated "Manichaeism," and so there is a strong likelihood that Manichaeans were present in Mecca, although another interpretation would render the term in this context as "Mazdakism."[29] More generally, there is evidence for the

[26] M. J. Kister, "Al-Ḥīra. Some Notes on Its Relations with Arabia," *Arabica* 15 (1968), 143–69, esp. 145–9.

[27] On Dhu Nuwas and the confusing events in South Arabia during the sixth century, see Newby, *History of the Jews of Arabia*, 39–47; C. E. Bosworth, "Iran and the Arabs Before Islam," in the *Cambridge History of Iran*, vol. 3: *The Seleucid, Parthian and Sasanian Periods*, ed. Ehsan Yarshater (Cambridge: Cambridge University Press, 1983), 602–8; Sidney Smith, "Events in Arabia in the 6th Century A.D.," *Bulletin of the School of Oriental and African Studies* 16 (1954), 424–68, esp. 456–63.

[28] Ibn Qutayba, *Kitāb al-maᶜārif*, sixth edition, (Cairo: al-Hayʾa al-ᶜAmma al-Miṣriyya, 1992), 621; Morony, *Iraq after the Muslim Conquest*, 280; Francois de Blois, "The 'Sabians' (Sābiʾūn) in Pre-Islamic Arabia," *Acta Orientalia* (1995), 39–61, esp. 48–9; Crone, *Meccan Trade*, 46.

[29] Ibn Qutayba, *Kitāb al-maᶜārif*, 621. Compare de Blois, "The 'Sabians'," 48–50, and Kister, "Al-Ḥīra," 144–5.

circulation of Iranian religious ideas in Arabia in the form of Persian loan words in the Koran, most notably *firdaws*, "paradise." And so the extensive influence of Iranian civilization on Islam after the seventh-century conquests would seem in fact to continue much older trends among the Arabs.[30]

Thus through various channels were the Arabs drawn into the cauldron of religious and political competition which characterized the Near East at the end of late antiquity. Penetration of Arabia by the Roman and Sasanian empires, and by Christianity, Judaism, and Zoroastrianism, was always tentative, its implications and consequences always ambiguous. What, for example, did it mean to be an Arabian Jew? For Dhu Nuwas, it clearly involved struggle with both Christianity and Rome, and probably implied some alignment of interest with the Sasanian empire, itself of course the home of the largest and most vibrant Jewish community of late antiquity. For Arab Christians, the situation was equally confusing: their religious identity might result in alliance with external Christian powers; on the other hand, the dominance of Monophysitism and Nestorianism among those Arabs who were Christian must have limited their identification with the interests of the dominant Christian power in the region, Rome.[31]

It is against this ambiguous background that the question of the *hanifiyya* should be considered. The early Arabic sources, including the Koran, make reference to individuals identified as *hunafa'* (sing. *hanif*; the religion they practiced: *hanifiyya*), and suggest that they professed a monotheistic faith which was neither Jewish nor Christian, but was linked in a general way with the figure of Abraham. The Muslim tradition presents Muhammad himself as seeing his mission as that of restoring a primitive monotheistic cult which, among the Arabs, had over time been corrupted and forgotten. There has been much debate about the precise significance of the *hunafa'*. For present purposes, however, two possible points stand out. In the first place, if there were those who professed some sort of vague (i.e., not specifically Jewish or Christian) monotheism, their presence, along with that of other Arabian contemporaries of Muhammad claiming prophethood, may reflect the degree of religious ferment and confusion in Arabian society. The religious message preached by Muhammad, in other words, whatever its ultimate source, was a response to religious developments already underway. A second point would interpret the phenomenon somewhat differently. While the precise contours of the doctrines and practice of the *hunafa'* are more than a little obscure, they probably included adherence to what its practitioners identified as the "religion of Abraham" (*din ibrahim*), respect for the sanctity of the Ka'ba (which in turn was identified with Abraham), and "Abrahamic" practices such as circumcision. Some have suggested that the *hunafa'* reflect a yearning on the

---

[30] Bosworth, "Iran and the Arabs Before Islam," 609–11.

[31] Garth Fowden, *Empire to Commonwealth: Consequences of Monotheism in Late Antiquity* (Princeton: Princeton University Press, 1993), esp. 100–137, has stressed this ambiguity. In particular, while acknowledging a certain cultural and political tension resulting from the doctrinal differences which plagued Christianity, he argued that the Monophysitism of the Arabs did not mean that they (or, for that matter, Syrians or Egyptians) were necessarily hostile to the empire.

part of some Arabs for a monotheistic creed which was independent of Judaism, Christianity, and their ethnic or political baggage.[32] That interpretation is not impossible, but it may be a bit teleological, assuming that the end product – Islam as a specifically Arabian monotheism, distinct from the earlier religions – was present or at least foreshadowed from the beginning. In the context of time and place, the connection to Abraham may instead have provided the Arabs with a link to other religious traditions of the Near East, since the notion that the Arabs were descendants of the Hebrew patriarch through his son Ishmael circulated widely in the Near East, among the Arabs as well as other peoples, and confirming that link would lend credibility to the new religious message preached by Muhammad.[33] In this light, the phenomenon of the *hanifiyya* might indicate, once again, that Islam's origins, even in the Arabian environment, were very much a part of wider religious patterns embracing the whole of the Near East.

---

[32] G. E. von Grunebaum, *Classical Islam: A History 600 A.D.–1258 A.D.* (Chicago: Aldine Publishing Company, 1970), 25–6; W. Montgomery Watt, *Muhammad at Medina* (Oxford: Clarendon Press, 1956), 143.

[33] Cf. now Hawting, *The Idea of Idolatry*, 36–7, and 42–4.

CHAPTER 4

The early seventh century

Virtually all accounts of the rise of an Islamic state and then empire in the seventh century stress its extraordinary character, the suddenness of the appearance on the scene of the Muslim Arabs and the wholly unexpected nature of their success – what Marshall Hodgson referred to as "a breach in cultural continuity unparalleled among the great civilizations."[1] Explanatory models for the Muslim success – at least those which do not focus upon the Arabs themselves, on the demographic, economic, or religious factors propelling them forward – tend to look for causes in the chaotic developments in the Near East in the late sixth and early seventh centuries. In this, of course, there lies the danger of an easy retrospective teleology, of the assumption that the Near Eastern civilizations experienced on the eve of the Muslim conquests a crisis which weakened them fatally, and so rendered those conquests (or something like them) virtually inevitable. The cautious historian should eschew such a dramatic viewpoint, tempting as it may be. On the other hand, conditions in the Near East in the early seventh century were indeed highly charged and unstable. From a broader perspective, they demonstrate, not the inevitability of the Muslim conquests, but the degree to which those events marked a stage in a longer-term process by which the Arabs were drawn into the cultural orbit of the Fertile Crescent and surrounding territories and, in their Muslim guise, contributed to its evolution.

The most spectacular development in the decades before the Muslim conquests was the brutal conflict between the Roman and Sasanian empires. Khusrau II apparently harbored dreams of restoring the hegemony over the whole of the Near East which Iran had wielded under Cyrus and Xerxes, and came close to success: by 620, Sasanian armies had occupied Syria, Egypt, and Asia Minor as far as the Bosphorus. In the end, the Byzantine empire was saved by a remarkable come-from-behind victory led by the emperor Heraclius, who restored the Asian provinces and Egypt to Roman rule, invaded Iran itself and plundered the royal palace at Dastagird. Such events were traumatic enough to the non-combatants

---

[1] Marshall Hodgson, *The Venture of Islam: Conscience and History in a World Civilization*, in 3 volumes (Chicago: University of Chicago Press, 1974), 1:103. Hodgson did, however, go on to point out a high degree of cultural continuity between Islam and the civilizations of late antiquity as well.

whose lives were disrupted by them, but reflect only the most obvious dislocations of the era. Military uncertainty was accompanied by political instability in both the Roman and Sasanian empires: Heraclius came to power on the wings of a coup against the ineffective military tyrant Phocas, while the disastrous sacking of Dastagird led to the murder of Khusrau in 628.[2] At a deeper level, the foundations of Near Eastern society, particularly in the Roman provinces, were suffering from a process of erosion independent of the course of political and military events. Both historical and, especially, archaeological evidence suggests that, from some point in the early- or mid-sixth century, cities such as Antioch, Aleppo and Latakia experienced economic decline, depopulation, and a contraction of that civic space and life which had supported a flourishing urban life in late antiquity. The decline affected as well Roman defenses on the southern desert frontier, where forts were abandoned (to be occupied, in some cases, by solitary monks) and security turned over to nomadic or semi-nomadic tribes (like the Ghassanids) in tentative alliances with the Roman authorities – from an Arabian viewpoint, of course, an especially pregnant development.[3]

Against that background the developments which had characterized the religious sphere in late antiquity took on a sharper relief. Religious polemic between Jews and Christians, for example, became more heated, especially in the context of war between Rome and Iran. Chafing at the rising level of Christian Roman hostility, and with an eye to the generally more favorable conditions under which their Iranian brethren lived, many Jews in Syria and elsewhere reacted warmly to the Sasanian invasion: a Jewish riot in Antioch, for instance, contributed to its fall to the shah's army. Upon occupying Jerusalem, the Iranians turned over administration of the city to the Jews, although a few years later they suddenly suppressed the Jewish regime there. When Heraclius restored Syria to Roman rule, the Jews found themselves politically exposed to a vengeful regime. The Roman emperor's unsuccessful attempt to force their wholesale conversion in 632 is just as telling, if less dramatic, a sign of the culmination of the process of resolving religious identities which had characterized late antiquity as the Arab conquests which followed rapidly upon the death of Muhammad in that same year. It highlights the degree to which Roman society and its polity had become identified with a distinct religious tradition, and one which claimed universal authority.

In a sense, the religious sphere had expanded so as to absorb everything, and in particular an individual's identity – social, political, cultural. Vestiges of pre-Christian classical culture survived in the East, of course, far more than they did in the West, but they did so increasingly in a Christian guise, like the figure of

[2] Peter Brown, *The World of Late Antiquity, AD 150–750* (New York: Harcourt Brace Jovanovich, 1976), 169–70; Judith Herrin, *The Formation of Christendom* (Princeton: Princeton University Press, 1987), 187–203.

[3] Hugh Kennedy, "The Last Century of Byzantine Syria: A Reassessment," *Byzantinische Forschungen* 10 (1985), 141–83.

Aphrodite (= the Arabic goddess al-ʿUzza) found in a church in southern Syria dedicated to the Virgin Mary.[4] What civic life remained in Roman cities in the late sixth and seventh centuries was overseen by the bishop or patriarch, and so it was with them that the Muslim Arabs would negotiate the terms of the cities' surrender. In this world, an individual identified himself first and foremost as a Jew or a Christian (or later a Muslim), rather than as a Roman, let alone a Syrian or an Egyptian. The Near East inherited by the Muslim Arabs was more than anything else a mosaic of religious identities, the pieces of which were colored by distinct traditions. As such, it resembled the situation which had existed for some time in Sasanian Mesopotamia; the Muslim conquests confirmed the process by which the Mesopotamian model extended over the whole of the Near East, and locked it into a specifically Muslim form.[5]

So most of the inhabitants of the Near East in the seventh century took their religion seriously. For such, the situation facing them appeared especially grave because of a heightened sensitivity to apocalyptic fears and expectations. Millenialism and messianism were rife in most of the religious traditions which emerged from late antiquity, no doubt heightened by the political and military chaos of the period.[6] They are to be expected as a matter of course in Christianity, but they infected Zoroastrianism as well.[7] Above all, Jews in the Near East looked forward to divine intervention and messianic salvation, and for them, significantly, messianism thoroughly folded a political dimension into the religious. In late antique Judaism, the Messiah was an explicitly political figure, and the relatively recent memory of the Maccabean and Bar Kochba revolts must have kept alive hopes of imminent delivery. The Sasanian invasions of the early seventh century certainly stoked the flames of messianism among the Jews of Palestine and Syria, and inspired among them a colorful apocalyptic literature. Judaism as known in the Arabian peninsula around the time of the rise of Islam, too, was infused with messianism and, more generally, a potent brew of religious ferment: Muhammad himself may have encountered in Yathrib Jews claiming prophetic status or a messianic role.[8] Indeed, various groups and individuals in the Near East in the seventh and eighth centuries – some Jewish and some not

---

[4] Glen Bowersock, *Hellenism in Late Antiquity* (Ann Arbor: University of Michigan Press, 1990), 72; Fawzi Zayadine, "Peintures murales et mosaïques à sujets mythologiques en Jordanie," in *Iconographie classique et identités régionales*, ed. Lilly Kahil, Christian Augé, and Pascale Linnant de Bellefonds (Athens: École Française d'Athènes, 1986), 407–28, esp. 421–4.

[5] The best general discussion of the process of the merging of religious with social, cultural, and political identities around the time of the Muslim conquests is to be found in Brown, *World of Late Antiquity*, 172–87.

[6] On this subject generally, see A. Vasiliev, "Medieval Ideas of the End of the World: West and East," *Byzantion* 16 (1940), 462–502.

[7] Michael G. Morony, *Iraq after the Muslim Conquest* (Princeton: Princeton University Press, 1984), 302–5.

[8] David Halperin, "The Ibn Ṣayyād Traditions and the Legends of al-Dajjāl," *Journal of the American Oriental Society* 96 (1976), 213–225; Newby, *A History of the Jews of Arabia*, 49, 59–63. On Jewish messianism in the seventh century more generally, see Salo W. Baron, *A Social and Religious History of the Jews*, 2nd edition (New York: Columbia University Press, 1952–) 3:18–19, 21.

– understood the appearance of the Muslim Arabs in the context of Jewish messianism.[9] Whatever the precise contours of the relationship between Judaism and emergent Islam, it is certain that the new faith can only be understood against the background of Jewish messianism and, more broadly, of the religious turmoil which characterized the Near East at the end of late antiquity.

[9] Patricia Crone and Michael Cook, *Hagarism: The Making of the Islamic World* (Cambridge: Cambridge University Press, 1977), 4–9; Chaim Rabin, *Qumran Studies* (Oxford: Oxford University Press, 1957), 112–30, esp. 123f; Bernard Lewis, "An Apocalyptic Vision of Islamic History," *Bulletin of the School of Oriental and African Studies* 13 (1950), 308–38.

PART II

The Emergence of Islam, 600–750

CHAPTER 5

Approaches and problems

The term "Islam," like any other historical abstraction of comparable scope, indicates a phenomenon of great complexity and constantly evolving dimensions. This should go without saying; unfortunately, given how easily and naturally we fall back on the simple term to describe the complex organism, it bears repeating. Islam was not fully formed at the death of the Prophet Muhammad in 632, nor a few years later when it burst out of its Arabian homeland, nor even many decades later when it was clear that the rule of those who called themselves "Muslims" was permanent. The story of the emergence during the seventh and eighth centuries of particularly Islamic identities and patterns of religious authority can be read as a continuation of that of the focusing of religious identities which characterized the late antique Near East. The questions posed by the unexpected appearance on the scene of enthusiastic monotheists from the Arabian desert forced adherents of the older faiths to articulate more precisely those contours which defined them against their rivals. But it is also true that Islam itself only took shape through a process of dialogue with the other faith traditions. Indeed, it is misleading to speak of the "appearance" or "rise" of Islam, if those words convey a sense of unproblematic apparition as sudden as that of the Arab warriors before the bewildered Byzantine or Sasanian armies. It would be safer to say that Islam "emerged," gradually and uncertainly, over the decades – an "ill-defined period of gestation"[1] – which followed the death of the Prophet Muhammad in 632.

The reader should bear two caveats in mind. First, the period between Muhammad and the ʿAbbasid revolution in the mid-eighth century was extraordinarily rich in events which, from a later Islamic perspective, were pregnant with meaning. Narratives of classical and medieval Islamic history therefore conventionally devote considerable space to the century and a half which witnessed the career of the Prophet, the rule of his four "rightly-guided" successors, and the establishment of the first dynasty of Muslim rulers, the Umayyads – and that despite the paucity of contemporary sources for the period. By the time that members of the ʿAbbasid family seized power, a recognizable Muslim tradition, society, and polity had emerged. Second, while much of this chapter will be

[1] Marshall G. S. Hodgson, *The Venture of Islam*, vol. 1: *The Classical Age of Islam* (Chicago: University of Chicago Press, 1974), 104.

concerned with events and actors labeled, at least by posterity, as Muslim, we should maintain a sense of scale and proportion. In the middle of the eighth century, despite a quickening pace of conversion of non-Arabs to Islam, the Muslims remained a small minority of the total population of the Near East, at least outside of Arabia.

The reconstruction of the earliest decades of Islamic history is a particularly delicate matter. For Muslims, of course, the events of those years are foundational, and the narratives that reconstruct them undergird the institutions and ideas that have come to constitute Islam. Sunnis and Shiᶜis, for instance, distinguish themselves largely through their reconstructions and interpretations of certain pivotal events of these formative years, but this is only the most obvious example of a larger pattern. For most if not all Muslims, the personalities and events in question provide the symbolic vocabulary of continuing and contemporary debate. For the historian, however, the problem lies in the reliability of the sources available for a reconstruction of those events. The ninth-century belle-lettrist Ibn Qutayba quoted the Prophet's companion Hudhayfa ibn al-Yaman as blithely acknowledging that: "We are Arab people; when we report, we predate and postdate, we add and we subtract at will, but we do not mean to lie."[2] The difficulties however go considerably beyond this charming acknowledgment of unintentional tendentiousness. The oldest surviving Arabic sources for the earliest years of Islam, although based on earlier orally-transmitted material, date from a period more than a century after the events they describe. And so as one recent study has succinctly put it, it is difficult to know what "Islam" was a century or so after the start of the Muslim era, since "none of the Islamic texts available to us yet existed."[3] By the time those texts were actually written down in the form in which we now have them, the normative traditions were already almost complete, and diverse and competing parties had developed within Muslim society. As a result, these sources inevitably reflect later attitudes and interests as much as, if not more than, those of the earliest Muslims, and project those attitudes and interests back upon the people and events they describe. Source critical problems similar to those involved in the study of the Christian gospels absolutely permeate the earliest Islamic historical record.

This problem has in fact been recognized for some time. Of late, however, the degree to which the traditional Arabic literary sources can be relied upon at all to provide a narrative of events has been a matter of vigorous debate. Several published surveys can now guide the interested reader to a fuller examination of the historical and historiographical questions.[4] But the issue bears directly on

---

[2] Quoted by Moshe Sharon, "The Umayyads as *Ahl al-Bayt*," *Jerusalem Studies in Arabic and Islam* 14 (1991), 115.

[3] G. R. Hawting, *The Idea of Idolatry and the Emergence of Islam: From Polemic to History* (Cambridge: Cambridge University Press, 1999), 13.

[4] A very convenient starting point is R. Stephen Humphreys, *Islamic History: A Framework for History*, revised edition (Princeton: Princeton University Press, 1991), 69–91. See also Albrecht Noth with Lawrence I. Conrad, *The Early Arabic Historical Tradition: A Source-critical Study*, trans. Michael Bonner (Princeton: Darwin Press, 1994), and Fred Donner, *Narratives of Islamic Origins: The Beginnings of Islamic Historical Writing* (Princeton: Darwin Press, 1998).

certain questions of the emergence of an Islamic identity and of patterns of Islamic authority, and so some brief introduction to it is necessary.

In *Hagarism: The Making of the Islamic World*, a book published in 1977 which its authors provocatively described as "written for infidels by infidels," Patricia Crone and Michael Cook speculated that the Islamic literary tradition from which the usual narrative of Muslim origins has been reconstructed might be "without determinate historical content."[5] In part their speculation was based on the well-known fact that the earliest surviving Muslim sources are comparatively late, and so reflect less what happened than what later Muslims wanted to remember as having happened. This is a point which has been a staple of at least Western scholarship since Ignaz Goldziher's pioneering study of *hadith* (i.e., the "traditions" which purport to record the deeds and words of Muhammad and his companions), in which he demonstrated that many hadith were later fabrications, although the degree of the material's unreliability has always been a matter of some debate. The point may be illustrated by a later and more precise, although more limited, discussion of one particular aspect of the narrative of Islamic origins, in which Crone pointed out how much of that narrative was a product of traditions which served to explain Koranic verses which, to later Muslim audiences, seemed opaque. In other words, the Koran and the exegetical problems it poses in some sense generated the stories that were used to explain them.[6]

The problem is compounded by lingering uncertainties involving the Koranic text itself. The Muslim tradition gives a variety of accounts of how the Koran, consisting of verses revealed to Muhammad over the twenty or so years of his prophetic career, came to be collected. The best known, at least to Sunnis, ascribes the beginnings of the collection process to ʿUmar (r. 634–644), the second caliph to lead the Muslim community after Muhammad's death, and gives the third caliph, ʿUthman (r. 644–656), credit for establishing the received recension of the Koranic text. But other, incompatible accounts survive in the sources, attributing the collection of the Koran to other, later figures, such as the Umayyad caliph ʿAbd al-Malik (r. 685–705) or his lieutenant, al-Hajjaj ibn Yusuf (d. 714). The earliest surviving Koranic texts, such as the verses inscribed in the Dome of the Rock in Jerusalem, are not entirely reassuring to the traditional account, since they display minor variations from the received text and, in any case, their presence there "does not of course give any indication of the literary form in which these materials normally appeared at that time."[7]

---

[5] Patricia Crone and Michael Cook, *Hagarism: The Making of the Islamic World* (Cambridge: Cambridge University Press, 1977), 3.

[6] Patricia Crone, *Meccan Trade and the Rise of Islam* (Oxford: Blackwell, 1987), 203f. Crone gave a concise statement of the historiographical problem in *Slaves on Horses: The Evolution of the Islamic Polity* (Cambridge: Cambridge University Press, 1980), 1–17.

[7] Crone and Cook, *Hagarism*, 18. The most radical challenge to the historicity of the received Koranic text appears in the studies of John Wansbrough, *Quranic Studies: Source and Methods of Scriptural Interpretation* (Oxford: Oxford University Press, 1977), and *The Sectarian Milieu: Content and Composition of Islamic Salvation History* (Oxford: Oxford University Press, 1978); a convenient summary of Wansbrough's ideas can be found in Andrew Rippin, "Literary Analysis of Qurʾān,

Others have adopted a considerably less skeptical approach to the Muslim sources, accepting earlier rather than later dates for the writing down of the various sources and arguing that the new religion brought with it a conviction of the Muslim community's obligations to posterity, which contributed to the development of a more refined historical sense and to an early commitment to preserving a written record of events.[8] A systematic and sensitive, although not credulous recent study has identified in several factors – most notably, the "marked agreement" of the sources on at least the broad outlines of the "traditional origins story," despite the existence from the beginning of competing, even hostile points of view within the Muslim community; and also the fact that what little *documentary* evidence survives more or less complements, rather than undermines, the narrative derived from literary sources – grounds for accepting that narrative as at least a framework for inquiry.[9] On the other hand, even if the more extreme claims of the skeptics are put aside – for example, that the Koran did not take its final shape until two hundred years or more after the Prophet's death – their arguments point to several valuable lessons for the present study. The first is that the whole process of the formation of an Islamic identity was a protracted and uneven one. Anything we can now recognize as a distinctively *Islamic* tradition did not coalesce until relatively late – the end of the seventh or beginning of the eighth century. The second, related point is that Islam, for all its roots in western Arabia, is even more a product of the encounter between the Arab followers of Muhammad and the existing religions and cultures of Syria and Iraq. Islam, in other words, was less a disruption than a continuation of some of the important cultural and religious developments of late antiquity.[10]

Tafsīr, and *Sīra*: The Methodologies of John Wansbrough," in *Approaches to Islam in Religious Studies*, ed. Richard C. Martin (Tucson: University of Arizona Press, 1985), 151–163. See also John Burton, *The Collection of the Qurʾān* (Cambridge: Cambridge University Press, 1977).

[8] Fuat Sezgin, *Geschichte der arabischen Schrifttums* (Leiden: E. J. Brill, 1967–); A. A. Duri, *The Rise of Historical Writing among the Arabs*, trans. Lawrence I. Conrad (Princeton: Princeton University Press, 1983).

[9] Donner, *Narratives of Islamic Origins*; see also idem, "The Formation of the Islamic State," *Journal of the American Oriental Society* 106 (1986), 283–96.

[10] Compare Oleg Grabar's thoughtful review of *Hagarism* in *Speculum* 53 (1978), 795–9.

CHAPTER 6

The origins of the Muslim community

The religious and cultural tradition of Islam came to be identified as the legacy of Muhammad the son of ʿAbdallah. Muhammad, as depicted in the Muslim narrative of Islamic origins, was an inhabitant of the western Arabian town of Mecca. According to those sources, in the early decades of the seventh century Muhammad embarked upon a prophetic career, preaching faith in the single God and articulating to his followers God's revelations to him. Having provoked the wrath of the leaders of the pagan society in which he lived, Muhammad and his small band of followers fled to the oasis of Yathrib some 200 miles north of Mecca in the year 622, an event known to the Muslim tradition as the *hijra* and which marks the beginning of the Muslim calendar. In Yathrib, also known as Medina (from *madinat al-nabi*, "the city of the prophet"), Muhammad first established a Muslim *umma* or "community." Over the final decade of his life, Muhammad continued to receive revelations which after his death in 632 were collected into the Koran as we now know it, and gradually brought the inhabitants of virtually the whole of the Arabian peninsula to embrace Islam and to acknowledge the political supremacy of his *umma*.

The Muslim tradition thus clearly situates the origins of the faith in an Arabian context. The attribution, however, masks a much larger question about the origins of Islam: whether it owes more to the Arabian society in which it first appeared, or to the larger Near Eastern context to which its attention was shifted within a few years of Muhammad's death. The question, of course, is not a "zero-sum" one – Arabian roots do not preclude a Near Eastern identity, and the latter should not obscure the fact that, without the former, there would be no Islam. Islam is doubly continuous: with its particular past, the western Arabian context into which Muhammad was born, and the attenuated presence there of Near Eastern monotheism; and also with its ecumenical future, its full absorption into the larger religious and political traditions of the empires, Byzantine and Sasanian, which it replaced. The story of Islam's first one hundred and fifty years is the story of how one continuity was gradually replaced by the other.

Muslims, quite naturally, stress the uniqueness of the "Islamic event," but historians must view the emergence of Islam against the background of developments in both Arabia and the Near Eastern provinces which fell to the newly converted

Arabs in the middle years of the seventh century. In doing so, in fact, they find themselves in good company. The Muslim historian Masᶜudi, writing in the tenth century, understood Islamic civilization to have inherited much from the older cultures of the peoples the Arabs conquered or with whom they came into contact – statecraft from the Persians, science and philosophy from the Greeks and Indians, and so on.[1] But the contributions of pre-Islamic peoples and cultures run much deeper than those familiar examples. The Dome of the Rock in Jerusalem, for example, which as we shall see marks an important stage in the crystallization of a distinctly Islamic identity, incorporates much in the way of Byzantine architectural motifs, and was in fact built with the help of Byzantine craftsmen. Some of the distinctive features of medieval Islamic societies, such as the organization of semi-autonomous communities built around sectarian identities and responsible for ordering and administering some aspects of community life, grew out of institutions and attitudes already present in the pre-Islamic Near East.

The pattern of cultural interchange between nascent Islam and the older Near Eastern religious traditions was a complex affair. It would be naive to think of it as a one-way street of Muslim borrowing, as an earlier generation of Western scholarship suggested by posing in stark form questions such as, "What has Muhammad taken from the Jews?"[2] We will see points at which Islam contributed to developments within Judaism, Christianity, and Zoroastrianism, too. Moreover, when Muslims adopted ideas, practices, or institutions from the older religious traditions, they did so in a creative spirit. So, for example, while Muslims leaned heavily on the vocabulary of pre-Islamic art and architecture, they used them to fashion a distinctively Islamic visual language, one which in the religious sphere produced a simple but unambiguously Islamic artifact – the mosque.[3]

The important point, however, is that Islam emerged in a Near East which was saturated with the ideas, institutions, and values of other religious traditions. An historian approaching the subject from the disciplinary standpoint of comparative religion will inevitably stress the parallels between the new faith, its practices, texts and vocabulary, and those of other traditions of the late antique Near East. It is of course particularly with Judaism and Christianity that the new religion engaged in protracted dialogue, but other traditions also left their mark. The story of Muhammad ascending to heaven and meeting God, for example, is one that has parallels in both Zoroastrian and Manichaean texts – it forms a *topos*, that is,

---

[1] Tarif Khalidi, *Islamic Historiography: The Histories of Masᶜūdī* (Albany, NY: SUNY Press, 1975), esp. 81–116.

[2] The question is taken from the title of Abraham Geiger's book, *Was hat Mohammed aus dem Judenthume aufgenommen?*, originally published in 1833. On the tendency of Western scholars to posit questions about Islam in a Jewish or Christian framework, see Maxime Rodinson, "A Critical Survey of Modern Studies on Muhammad," in *Studies on Islam*, ed. Merlin Swartz (New York: Oxford University Press, 1981), 23–85.

[3] Oleg Grabar, *The Formation of Islamic Art* (New Haven: Yale University Press, 1973), 104–38.

which links Islam to the other faith traditions of the Near East, whether or not the Muslim story was actually borrowed from them.[4]

As we saw in the previous chapter, Judaism and Christianity both had staked out significant presences in Arabia by the end of the sixth century. The precise nature of what a Meccan Arab such as Muhammad around the year 600 would have known of the older monotheistic faiths is problematic, but the biographical traditions about the Prophet and the Koran itself both indicate some level of awareness. Muhammad's knowledge was certainly not perfect. As we have seen, the Koran at one point seems to suggest an understanding that the Christian doctrine of the Trinity involved the deification of Mary as well as Jesus. But Muhammad, and even more importantly his audience, clearly had gleaned something, either from Jews or Christians resident in Mecca, or from others they encountered during the course of commercial expeditions outside of the Hijaz. Hence the "referential" character of the Koran, its tendency to allude to stories about the Biblical prophets in a fashion which presumes a certain level of familiarity with the underlying and unexpressed narratives.[5] The scripture's character therefore invites a comparative approach.

Certain ritual and conceptual parallels are especially strong between Islam and Christianity as understood and experienced by the native Christians of Syria, Iraq and Egypt, whose versions of the faith, as we saw in the previous chapter, were those most familiar to the Arabs of the peninsula.[6] For example, the special respect in which the Koran holds Mary (Jesus is often referred to as Ibn Maryam, the "Son of Mary") recalls the mariology of some eastern Christians. On the other hand, it is also possible that the Koranic verse cited mocking the notion that Mary constituted one element of a divine trinity may have reflected polemics waged by some Nestorian Christians against the Orthodox doctrine that Mary was the "Mother of God."[7] Koranic apocalyptic, and even more so that associated with non-scriptural Islamic tales, is also reminiscent of Christian literature: the familiar image, common in the Koran, that a trumpet blast will announce the Day of Resurrection, or the warnings that the hour of judgment, while close, cannot be known, and even the very lush and physical Koranic descriptions of paradise, all would hardly have been unfamiliar to Near Eastern Christians.[8]

[4] See, for example, Geo Widengren, *Muhammad, the Apostle of God, and His Ascension* (*King and Savior*, vol. 5) (Uppsala: A.-B. Lundequistska Bokhandeln, and Wiesbaden: Otto Harrassowitz, 1955). Cf. the famous story about the mysterious light which emanated from the belly of Muhammad's mother during the pregnancy in which she carried the future prophet, which may also have Zoroastrian antecedents; see Jamsheed K. Choksy, *Conflict and Cooperation: Zoroastrian Subalterns and Muslim Elites in Medieval Iranian Society* (New York: Columbia University Press, 1997), 60f.

[5] John Wansbrough, *Quranic Studies: Source and Methods of Scriptural Interpretation* (Oxford: Oxford University Press, 1977), 1, 38–43, 51–2, 57–8; Andrew Rippin, "Literary Analysis of *Qurʾān*, *Tafsīr*, and *Sīra*: The Methodologies of John Wansbrough", in *Approaches to Islam in Religious Studies*, ed. Richard C. Martin (Tucson: University of Arizona Press, 1985), 159–60.

[6] For a survey of the literature, see Neal Robinson, *Christ in Islam and Christianity* (Albany: State University of New York Press, 1991), 15–22.

[7] Ibid., 20.

[8] Joseph Henninger, "L'Influence du Christianisme Oriental sur l'Islam naissant," *L'Oriente Cristiano nella Storie della Civiltà* (Rome: Accademia Nazionale dei Lincei, 1964), 379–411.

Indeed, the very Koranic term for resurrection – *qiyama* – was probably borrowed from Syriac Christianity.[9]

But it is the connections between Islam and Judaism that are most powerful and intriguing. The presence of significant numbers of Jews in Yathrib/Medina, and their complicated and ultimately unhappy relationship with the Prophet, constitutes a major component of most narratives of Islamic origins. In those accounts, framed by the expulsion of first one, and then a second Jewish tribe from the oasis, and the massacre of the male members of a third (the Banu Qurayza), the Jews usually serve as a sort of foil to Muhammad, and their deteriorating relations as a catalyst for the articulation of a more explicitly Islamic identity. So, for example, the growing suspicion and hostility of the Medinese Jews to Muhammad's religious and political claims is said to have provided the context for a change in the direction of the *qibla*, the direction faced by Muslims during their formal prayers. At an earlier stage, Muhammad had led his followers in facing Jerusalem; then, in verses which in the ultimate recension of the Koran were the 142nd to144th of *sura* 2, God instructed the believers instead to turn their faces to the Ka'ba in Mecca. And so the Koran could now demand of the believers a far more antagonistic stance towards the adherents of older monotheistic faiths, Judaism as well as Christianity: "Fight against those among the people who have been given the scriptures who do not believe in God or the Last Day, and who do not forbid that which God and his Messenger have forbidden, and who do not follow the true faith, until they pay tribute out of hand and are humbled" (9.29).

In fact, however, the story of the relationship between Judaism and nascent Islam is far more complex. The position of the Jews as described in the "Constitution of Medina," a record of several agreements outlining the political form of the evolving Muslim *umma* (community) and the terms of Muhammad's leadership, was famously ambiguous – they were said to form "one community with the believers," but on the other hand they "have their religion and the Muslims have theirs" – and it seems likely that that ambiguity survived even the massacre of the Banu Qurayza.[10] That act of violence perhaps broke the back of organized Jewish political opposition to Muhammad, but it did not end the Jewish presence in Medina, let alone other localities in which Muslims lived, or were soon to live. The story that the caliph 'Umar, responding to an injunction of the dying Prophet, expelled the Jews of the Hijaz almost certainly reduces to one dramatic moment a process – the reduction in the power and presence of the Jews throughout Western Arabia – which began before the Prophet's career and extended well beyond the seventh century.[11] And so the expulsion and massacre of some of the Jewish tribes

[9] Joseph Horovitz, "Jewish Proper Names and Derivatives in the Koran," *Hebrew Union College Annual* 2 (1925), 186.

[10] The ambiguous position of the Jews is discussed in R. B. Serjeant, "The *Sunnah Jāmi'ah*, Pacts with the Yathrib Jews, and the *Taḥrīm* of Yathrib: Analysis and Translation of the Documents Comprised in the So-called 'Constitution of Medina,'" *Bulletin of the School of Oriental and African Studies* 41 (1978), 1–42, and Frederick M. Denny, "*Ummah* in the Constitution of Medina," *Journal of Near Eastern Studies* 36 (1977), 39–47.

[11] Gordon Darnell Newby, *A History of the Jews of Arabia from Ancient Times to Their Eclipse under Islam* (Columbia, South Carolina: University of South Carolina Press, 1988), 49–108.

of Medina, even if true, did not mark the end of the complicated story of creative interaction between Judaism and Islam.

That story involved more than the borrowing by a new faith of the religious artifacts of an older one. Ideas and stories that we would now identify as "Jewish" probably circulated more widely in late antique Arabia than is commonly suspected, and so the boundaries there between Judaism, Christianity, early Islam, even the "pagan" traditions of pre-Islamic Arabia, are not always easy to discern. Even the spatial reorientation by which Muhammad and his companions focused on Mecca and the Kaʿba to the exclusion of Jerusalem may not reflect the clear distancing from Judaism that, on the surface, it would seem to indicate, since certain elements of the structure and their understanding in Muslim tradition turn out to be closely connected to Jewish tradition and practice.[12] The environment in which Muhammad conceived and the forms in which he articulated his religious mission were saturated with the prophetic and messianic expectations which also shaped the experiences of Arabian Jews. At the very moment that Muhammad laid the groundwork for the new religion of Islam, he was confronted not only by other Arabs asserting their prophethood (such as Musaylima of the tribe Banu Hanifa), but by a Jewish boy in Medina who wrapped himself in a cloak (as did Muhammad), uttered incantations in a trance-like state (as did Muhammad), and claimed to be an apostle of God – a claim which Muhammad was apparently unable or unwilling directly to refute.[13]

Islam, in short, emerged from a religious matrix pregnant with ideas, stories, and attitudes that also informed the religious expectations of contemporary Jews. Even according to the traditional Muslim accounts, the close interaction of Judaism with what came to be identified as Islam continued well after the Prophet's death, as the Arabs conquered and began to culturally absorb the lands to the north of Arabia. It is therefore hardly surprising that Patriarch Sophronius, preaching a sermon in Jerusalem on Christmas Day, 634, referred to the Arab soldiers, encamped only a few miles away, as "Hagarenes" and "Ishmaelites," after Abraham's concubine (Hagar) and son (Ishmael), thereby fitting them, via a genealogy accepted by most of the Arabs themselves, into the framework of salvation history familiar to Christians from their reading of the Hebrew Scriptures, or that Syrian Christians continued for decades to use these terms to refer to their new rulers.[14] The origins of Islam, in other words, cannot be understood without taking into account a pattern of creative interaction with the other Near Eastern monotheistic faiths, and especially Judaism. Moreover, channels of mean-

---

[12] G. R. Hawting, "The Origins of the Muslim Sanctuary at Mecca," in *Studies on the First Century of Islamic Society*, ed. G. H. A. Juynboll (Carbondale and Edwardsville: Southern Illinois University Press, 1982), 23–47.

[13] Later Islamic traditions identified the boy, Ibn Sayyad, as the *Dajjal*, the Anti-Christ, but that element appears to have been alien to the original material concerning his encounters with Muhammad. See David Halperin, "The Ibn Ṣayyād Traditions and the Legends of al-Dajjāl," *Journal of the American Oriental Society* 96 (1976), 213–225.

[14] S. P. Brock, "Syriac Views of Emergent Islam," in *Studies on the First Century of Islamic Society*, ed. G. H. A. Juynboll (Carbondale and Edwardsville: Southern Illinois University Press, 1982), 9.

ingful communication between the traditions identified as Judaism and Islam remained intact for decades, as we will see shortly when we discuss the discipline of Koranic exegesis and the early use of traditions known as *isra'iliyyat*.

All of this, however, is not to deny any importance to the specifically Arabian setting in which Muhammad was born and in which his career unfolded. Earlier generations of Orientalists stressed this Arabian setting, and even more the influence of bedouin culture and values. For them, Islam was principally an expression of the "nomadic semitic spirit."[15] By the mid-twentieth century, the perspective of Western historians had shifted; increasingly they came to emphasize the urban origins of Islam, stressing the mercantile nature of Meccan society and understanding the Koran's message and Muhammad's career as a response to the peculiar needs and concerns of a newly assertive, internationally-oriented Arab bourgeoisie.[16] Both of these formulations are too sharp, and rely upon either superseded assumptions about ethnic identities and categories (e.g., about the "Semites" and semitic culture) or simplistic models of socio-economic development. But the Arabian context was nonetheless important. Matters such as Arabian tribal identity continued to shape the political and social history of the early Muslims. And even if Mecca was not the thriving metropolis and Muhammad's contemporaries the bourgeois individualists that some have made them out to be, the development of the new faith and all that it entailed (including, of course, the Arab conquest of the Near East) should be seen as part of a larger and longer-term process whereby the inhabitants of the peninsula were drawn into the social and religious patterns which dominated the more urbanized societies to the north.

The Arabian setting made itself felt in numerous ways. Most obviously, there is the Koran, which was revealed in Arabic, and which the Muslim tradition has understood as a response to the particular historical environment of early seventh-century Arabia. This is not to deny the linguistic and exegetical difficulties posed by the Koranic text, nor to ignore the elements of language and ideas which link the Koran itself to other Near Eastern scriptures and religious traditions.[17] Neither is it to accept uncritically the Muslim exegetical tradition which, as we have seen, may have generated the stories circulated to explain obscure passages of the holy book. Indeed, insisting on an Arabian framework for investigating the Koranic text can lead to conclusions at odds with dominant Muslim views, as for example with the Koran's description of Muhammad as an *ummi* prophet, which the tradition has interpreted as meaning that he was illiterate (and which, it claims, proves the

---

[15] The phrase is from Henninger, "L'influence du Christianisme oriental," 380, describing the attitude of leading early Orientalists such as Ernest Renan (1823–1892).

[16] A good example can be found in the chapter on "The Geographical Setting" in the *Cambridge History of Islam*, ed. P. M. Holt, Ann K. S. Lambton, and Bernard Lewis (Cambridge: Cambridge University Press, 1970), 2:443–68, in which the author, Xavier de Planhol, while drawing attention to the impact of the deserts of Arabia and acknowledging the dynamic force which the bedouin contributed to Islam, nonetheless concluded that, from the very beginning, "in Islam it is the town-dwellers who were set above the nomads."

[17] See now G. R. Hawting, *The Idea of Idolatry and the Emergence of Islam: From Polemic to History* (Cambridge: Cambridge University Press, 1999).

miraculous nature of the book), but which some Western commentators have understood to mean that Muhammad was a prophet to an un-scriptured people, to the Arabs who had not before received a revelation of their own.[18] But it is to say that the Koran provided one anchor that secured the new tradition to the Arabian context. Whatever the origins of the Koran itself, Muslim commentaries on it have assumed that it was revealed in western Arabia in the early seventh century, and so the tradition has looked to Arabia for answers as to how the Koran is to be understood.

The Arabian context was characterized by assumptions and attitudes that Islam would eventually seek, explicitly or implicitly, to overcome. Take, for example, the question of tribal identity. In pre-Islamic Arabia, an individual's social position depended first and foremost on those ties of kinship which bound him to an overlapping network of families, clans, and tribes. There are of course Koranic verses which demand a rejection of blood ties in favor of those of faith, and eventually the primacy of the bonds of personal commitment to the faith group would (more or less) prevail. But the earliest Muslims were Arabs and members of particular Arab tribes, and their descendants retained for several generations their ethnic and kin-group loyalties alongside and in competition with the newer claims of faith. A hadith captured both the tension and the persistence of tribal and kin-group loyalties and hierarchies perfectly: Muhammad is said to have commented that "the best of the people in Islam are the best of them in the *jahiliyya* [that is, the pre-Islamic period], if they are instructed in religion."[19] One need only remember the famous advice of the caliph ʿUmar to the Arabs, to remember their genealogies and not become like the settled and tribe-less Nabataeans – whether the story is apocryphyal or not hardly matters. While many factors gave rise to the Arab conquests, among them were the pressures generated by the nature of the state founded by Muhammad, a state which on one level amounted less to a rejection of tribalism than to a supra-tribal confederation of a sort not completely unfamiliar to the Arabs, and as one historian has observed, "tribal states *must* conquer to survive."[20] In this context, the Muslim tradition's identification of Abraham as a proto-typical worshiper of Allah is doubly important, because it provided a point of reference for the Arabs which was at once theological (there is one God) and genealogical (since most Arabs, like others in the Near East, accepted that Abraham was, through Ishmael, their common ancestor).

The political structure of Muhammad's *umma* as reflected in the "Constitution of Medina" and in other sources owed a good deal to traditional Arabian practice and values. This should not be surprising. The opportunity to remove himself from Mecca, where his fellow townsmen were growing increasingly annoyed by and hostile to the religious message he was preaching, presented itself as a result of a

[18] Kenneth Cragg, *The Event of the Qur'an: Islam in its Scripture* (London: Allen & Unwin, 1971), 56f.
[19] Al-Bukhārī, *al-Ṣaḥīḥ*, "Kitāb al-Anbiyā'" nos. 8, 14, 19; cf. Louise Marlow, *Hierarchy and Egalitarianism in Islamic Thought* (Cambridge: Cambridge University Press, 1997), 26–7.
[20] Patricia Crone, *Meccan Trade and the Rise of Islam* (Oxford: Blackwell, 1987), 243.

persistent feud between tribes in Yathrib, to settle which Muhammad was called in as an arbitrator (*hakam*), a position which traditionally conferred on its holder a very limited authority. In this capacity, Muhammad functioned in a manner which was familiar to the Arabs of his day and which grew out of the needs of a society with almost nothing in the way of permanent traditions and institutions of political power, a society in which politics was largely a matter of kin-group relations. It is significant that this supra-tribal confederacy chose to deal with certain critical issues such as murder and the blood feuds to which it gave rise – a matter which was indeed critical in the tribal society in which its members lived – in a "customary" (*ma'ruf*) way.[21]

On the other hand, of course, eventually Islam moved decisively away from the Arabian and tribal context. In doing so, it either suppressed or minimized many pre-Islamic values, assumptions, and institutions (such as tribal loyalty and a severely restricted notion of political leadership), or revalorized them (such as the pilgrimage to and worship at the Ka'ba in Mecca). Some of these changes came about through Islam's encounter with the older religious traditions after the Arabs' conquest of places such as Egypt, Syria, and Iraq, but that encounter drew on elements and ideas that were at least implicit in Muhammad's own message and career. It may be overstating the case to claim that the appearance of Islam responded to a social crisis in Mecca, a crisis caused by rampant materialism and a deracinated individualism which were themselves the product of a sophisticated international trade which undermined the traditional tribal order.[22] Such a viewpoint presumes a conception of religion in which conversion results from deliberate personal choice as a response to some perceived inadequacy of traditional doctrines and explanations, a conception of religion which was perhaps increasingly common of the societies of the northern Near East, but which was unlikely to be characteristic of a tribal context. The Muslim tradition understandably emphasizes the conversion of individuals such as the Prophet's friend and collaborator 'Umar, who were apparently convinced of the truth of his claims, but most Arabs must have converted to the new religion through the agency of a tribal decision. But Muhammad laid the groundwork for a radically different approach. The Koran, for example, enunciates a moral vision bounded by abstract notions of justice, judgment, and mercy which, whether or not they were borrowed from Judaism and Christianity, gave Muslims a vocabulary with which to communicate with the other inhabitants of the Near East. And if at first Muhammad functioned as a traditional arbitrator, he also claimed the status of an apostle of God, and acceptance of that claim formed the basis of identity in the new

---

[21] R. B. Serjeant, "The Constitution of Medina," *The Islamic Quarterly* 8 (1964), 3–16; idem, "The Sunnah Jāmi'ah, Pacts with the Yathrib Jews, and the Taḥrīm of Yathrib: Analysis and Translation of the Documents Comprised in the So-called 'Constitution of Medina,'" *Bulletin of the School of Oriental and African Studies* 41 (1978), 1–42.

[22] See W. Montgomery Watt, *Muhammad at Mecca* (Oxford: Clarendon Press, 1953); compare Crone, *Meccan Trade*, and R. B. Serjeant, "Meccan Trade and the Rise of Islam: Misconceptions and Flawed Polemics," *Journal of the American Oriental Society* 110 (1990), 472–73.

community, and of the Prophet's personal authority. To participate in the new umma required from the beginning a commitment to an identity grounded in Muhammad's religious message, rather than in traditional tribal relations. By the end of his life, Muhammad (as described by the earliest Muslim sources) presided over a polity that was broader in its geographical reach, uniting almost the whole of the peninsula, and characterized by a greater centralization of power than anything most Arabs had previously known. In short, although Muhammad was in many ways a traditional Arabian figure and his career can only be understood in that traditional context, his message set the stage for the consuming dialectic which characterized Islam's encounter with Judaism, Christianity, and the other religions of the Near East, a dialectic through which Islam became the heir of late antique civilization.

CHAPTER 7

Early Islam in the Near East

Muhammad's unexpected death in 632 threw his community into confusion, and the difficulty it had in simply surviving speaks volumes about the absence at this stage of a fully formed religious identity, or at least of the failure of that identity to claim the unremitting allegiance of many of those who had joined it. A number of points of tension surfaced, but probably no set of issues proved so contentious to Muslim posterity, or so critical in subsequent definitions of what it meant to be a Muslim, than that surrounding the question of leadership after the Prophet's death. Consequently this terrain is particularly dangerous for the historian. According to the standard Sunni account, Muhammad's friend and father-in-law Abu Bakr prevented the Medinese Muslims setting themselves up as a separate community from Muhammad's close circle of Meccan companions, and then was named through acclamation as the first caliph, or successor, of the Prophet. Shi°is, however, have a different recollection, and stress a story according to which Muhammad, sometime prior to his death, identified his cousin °Ali as his presumptive heir. Of course both the Sunni and Shi°i recollections in fact reflect the fully formed expectations of the later sectarian groups and political parties.[1]

It is virtually certain that Muhammad had not made arrangements for the organization and leadership of his community before his death. There are dozens of separate traditions which suggest that the Prophet intended one person or another to succeed him, but as others have pointed out, their very number, let alone their inconsistency, demonstrate that in fact he had not made (or at least had not publicly revealed) any decision concerning this critical question.[2] Sunni tradition projects backwards upon the first decades after Muhammad's death a memory of the period as a golden age, when what are identified as the "rightly-guided" caliphs ruled in the Prophet's spirit, if not with his authority. According to

---

[1] Wilferd Madelung has, nonetheless, systematically reviewed the sources in his reconstruction of the political development of the early post-Muhammad Muslim community. See *The Succession to Muhammad: A Study of the Early Caliphate* (Cambridge: Cambridge University Press, 1997). His conclusions are far too diverse to summarize here, but in some ways he arrives, through largely Sunni sources, at a viewpoint sympathetic to the claims of °Ali to priority, and thus to the expectations of the later Shi°i community.

[2] Moshe Sharon, "The Development of the Debate Around the Legitimacy of Authority in Early Islam," *Jerusalem Studies in Arabic and Islam* 5 (1984), 125.

that account, Muhammad was succeeded first by his close friend and confidant Abu Bakr as caliph. Abu Bakr in turn was succeeded by other companions of the Prophet each one selected through the consensus of the leaders of the community: first ᶜUmar, then ᶜUthman, and finally ᶜAli, Muhammad's cousin and son-in-law. But that viewpoint did not take final shape until much later: for example, ᶜAli's status as one of the "rightly-guided" caliphs was not a firm fixture of Sunni thought until the ninth or tenth century. Moreover, the actual circumstances of their accessions and reigns, even as described by the Sunni sources reflect a polity in turmoil, at best. Abu Bakr came to power only through a last-minute sleight-of-hand, while ᶜUmar and ᶜUthman were both assassinated. ᶜAli was raised to power by the rebels responsible for ᶜUthman's death, fought a long civil war against ᶜUthman's cousin Muᶜawiya ibn Abi Sufyan, and was himself at last murdered, a chain of events which the tradition remembers as the community's first *fitna*, "trial" or "temptation," i.e., "civil war."

Quite naturally, much of the secondary literature about early Islam has focused on this issue of leadership. We cannot hope to summarize the discussion here, but can only identify some of the major themes touching upon the question of religious identity and authority. In the first place, the tribal factor continued to play an important and destabilizing role in the development of what would come to be identified as the Islamic polity. In the wake of the Prophet's death, the community was shaken by the so-called Wars of *Ridda*, of "return" or, more grandly, "apostasy," when the *umma* under the leadership of Abu Bakr fought against those tribes which considered the tribal confederation suspended and their allegiance to it terminated, now that Muhammad was gone. The Sunni tradition casts this as a defining moment for the Muslim state. The Muslims' victory is credited with both preserving a unitary state, and cementing the identification of Islam with the Arabs. But at least as important was ᶜUmar's subsequent decision (reversing the exclusionary policy of Abu Bakr) to allow those tribes which had rebelled during the course of the *Ridda* wars and been subdued to participate in the expanding incursions into and attacks on the Fertile Crescent. On one level, ᶜUmar's decision reincorporated the defeated Arabs into the polity as Muslims; at the same time, however, it also acknowledged at least implicitly the continuing claims of the tribes to the self-identities of their members, as well as the *umma*'s need for their participation.[3] Under the caliphate of ᶜUthman, the "tribal factor" continued to destabilize the *umma*, and now from its very core. That caliph pursued a well-known policy of favoring members of his own clan of Umayya from within the larger tribe of Quraysh. The Banu Umayya had held a sort of aristocratic status in pre-Islamic Meccan society. Since, however, most of them had been among the most implacable enemies of the Prophet until shortly before his death, this policy appeared to some Muslims to represent the return to prominence of the pre-Islamic

---

[3] Compare M. A. Shaban, *Islamic History, A.D. 600–750 (A.H. 132): A New Interpretation* (Cambridge: Cambridge University Press, 1971), 28–9, where he sees ᶜUmar's decision as re-establishing the principle of "Islamic Co-Operation."

Meccan nobility, and so it alienated many within the community, and contributed to the tensions which led to ʿUthman's murder.[4]

Those tensions were possible, however, only because Muhammad's preaching had generated a new and competing dynamic. One of the themes of this book has been that of the indeterminacy of the identity of "Islam" at least until the late seventh century, or even later. Nonetheless, the movement led by Muhammad and those who succeeded him, however it is to be identified, was a religious one, or more precisely had important religious components, and those components had considerable force, even if (from the standpoint of those looking for categorical clarity) they lacked a crystalline character. The monotheism preached by Muhammad was of central importance, since it both demanded a radical break from the polytheism of pre-Islamic Arabia (Arabian polytheism had acknowledged Allah's existence, but not his jealous claims), and provided a channel for dialogue with Near Eastern Judaism and Christianity.[5] More importantly, Muhammad's religious message had social and political implications, which were reflected most acutely in ʿUmar's establishment of a *diwan*. The *diwan* was essentially a list of those who were entitled to a share in the booty acquired during the course of military campaigns and distributed by the state; rank within it depended not on tribal identity, but on *sabiqa*, "precedence" according to one's contributions to the new polity.

The new religious imperatives were not *necessarily* contradictory to those of the tribal order. Indeed, they could even work hand in hand. Historians have given various explanations for the Arab conquests in the Near East in the fourth and fifth decades of the seventh century: some have stressed various social and environmental factors peculiar to tribal Arabia, others the newly-found religious fervor of the Arabs.[6] But again, a nuanced answer to the question need not be a zero-sum one. The tribal factor played an unmistakable role in the initial stages of Muslim history, and continued to do so for some time. In Arabia, tribal politics involved *ghazw*, the practice of collecting booty by conducting raids on commercial caravans, rival tribes, or settled (and relatively defenseless) communities. And as is well known, the Arab conquests began as an extension and redirection of the older practice of *ghazw*: having united the Arabs of the peninsula for the first time in a single state, the leaders of the community sought an outlet for this tribal imperative, and conveniently found one in the rich but weakened societies of Syria and Iraq. But the monotheism preached by Muhammad contributed its own imperatives. The Koran is not a squeamish document, and exhorts the believers

---

[4] Martin Hinds, "The Murder of the Caliph ʿUthmān," *International Journal of Middle East Studies* 3 (1972), 450–69; cf. Madelung, *Succession*, 80f.

[5] Z. D. H. Baneth, "What Did Muḥammad Mean When He Called His Religion 'Islām'? The Original Meaning of Aslama and its Derivatives," *Israel Oriental Studies* 1 (1971), 183–90. See G. R. Hawting, *The Idea of Idolatry and the Emergence of Islam: From Polemic to History* (Cambridge: Cambridge University Press, 1999), for a sustained challenge to the idea that the Koran was in fact a response to Arabian polytheism.

[6] Fred M. Donner, *The Early Islamic Conquests* (Princeton: Princeton University Press, 1981), 3–9, gives a useful summary of the various interpretations.

to *jihad*. Verses such as "Do not follow the unbelievers, but struggle against them mightily" (25.52) and "Fight [those who have been given a revelation] who do not believe in God and the last day" (9.29) may originally have been directed against Muhammad's local enemies, the pagans of Mecca or the Jews of Medina, but could be redirected once a new set of enemies appeared. To the contemporary eye, piety and the desire for loot were not incompatible, and so we are told that Koran readers were instructed to recite to the Arab soldiers *Surat al-Anfal*, a chapter of the Koran dealing largely with the spoils of war, as a means of encouraging them and strengthening their hearts before battle, a practice for which the tradition claimed Prophetic precedent. The complex nature of the Muslim Arab conquests is captured nicely in the historian al-Tabari's account of Arab general Saʿd ibn Abi Waqqas's exhortation to his soldiers as they prepared for a pivotal battle against the Persians in 635:

> This land is your inheritance and the promise of your Lord. God permitted you to take possession of it three years ago. You have been tasting it and eating from it, and you have been killing its people, collecting taxes from them, and taking them into captivity. ... You are Arab chiefs and notables, the elect of every tribe, and the pride of those who are behind you. If you renounce this world and aspire for the hereafter, God will give you both this world and the hereafter.[7]

Whatever inspired them, the Arab conquests must have come as a shock to the inhabitants of Iraq, Syria, and Egypt. They knew *of* the Arabs, of course, as nomads from the desert had for centuries been moving in and out of the settled areas of the Fertile Crescent. Moreover, as we saw earlier, the Byzantine and Sasanian Empires had, in the century or so before the conquests, maintained a master–client relationship with the Arab states of the Ghassanids and the Lakhmids which served as buffers between the imperial provinces and the ungovernable tribes and wastes of the peninsula. But nothing prepared the citizens of Damascus or Ctesiphon for the tremendous victories of the Arabs over Byzantine and Sasanian forces at the battles of Yarmuk in Jordan (636) and Qadisiyya in Iraq (636 or 7), nor for the possibility that these provinces would be permanently occupied and administered by a new Arab state.

The bewilderment of the inhabitants of the Near East was long-lasting, and testifies to the drawn out gestation of a distinctive Muslim identity. Contemporary non-Muslim sources indicate a protracted effort on the part of the non-Arab inhabitants of the Near East to comprehend these unexpected rulers in terms which

---

[7] Muhammad ibn Jarīr al-Ṭabarī, *Tārīkh al-rusul wa'l-mulūk*, ed. M. J. De Goeje and others (Leiden: E. J. Brill, 1879–1901), 1.2289 = *The History of al-Ṭabarī*, vol. 12, trans. Yohanan Friedmann (Albany, NY: SUNY Press, 1992), 84–5; cf. al-Ṭabarī, *Tārīkh*, 2294–5 = *History* 12.89-90; al-Ṭabarī, *Tārīkh*, 2095 = *History*, vol. 11, trans. Khalid Yahya Blankenship (Albany, New York: SUNY Press, 1993), 94. See also Martin Hinds, "Kūfan Political Alignments and Their Background in the Mid-Seventh Century A.D.," *International Journal of Middle East Studies* 2 (1971), 346–67, esp. 358; G. H. A. Juynboll, "The Qur'ān Reciter on the Battlefield and Concomitant Issues," *Zeitschrift der Deutschen Morgenländischen Gesellschaft* 125 (1975), 11–13; Patricia Crone, *Meccan Trade and the Rise of Islam* (Oxford: Blackwell, 1987), 244–5.

made sense to them.[8] So, for example, the Christians of Syria knew the Arab conquerors as "Saracens," "Hagarenes," "Ishmaelites," or even "Amalek." A century after the Prophet's death the last of the Church Fathers, John of Damascus, still used these terms to describe the Muslims, and furthermore suggested that Muhammad's religious ideas were in part the outcome of his encounter with a monk subscribing to the Christian Arian heresy.[9] Seventh-century Byzantine sources devote much more polemical attention to Judaism than to the Arabs' new faith. On the one hand, that may simply reflect the inertia of the Byzantine polemical tradition, and a lingering perception that the hated Jews posed a more serious religious threat. On the other, it may also reflect the predominance of the Jewish contribution to the religious matrix from which Islam emerged. Christians writing in Syriac, who were often better informed about the Arabs and their faith than were their more remote Byzantine colleagues, also at first seem to have understood the Muslim phenomenon in a Jewish framework, describing, for example, the construction of the Dome of the Rock as a rebuilding of the ancient Temple, and asserting that Muhammad and his followers accepted the Jewish law. A monk writing in a monastery in northern Iraq in the 680s referred to Muhammad as a "guide" who instructed the Arabs in the "ancient law," by which he meant the Torah.[10]

To the inhabitants of the Near East, what the Arabs were was – Arabs. In the wake of the *Ridda* wars, and of the Arabs' sudden conquest of most of the Near East, the new religion became identified more sharply as a monotheism for the Arab people. As is well known, the Arabs made no attempt to impose their faith on their new subjects, and at first in fact discouraged conversions on the part of non-Arabs. A caliph such as ʿUmar seems to have regarded himself, first and foremost, as the leader of the Arabs, and their monotheistic creed as the religious component of their new political identity. So, for example, while he recognized the right of some Christian Arab tribes to retain their own faith, he did not impose on them the humiliating head-tax (*jizya*) to which other non-Muslims were now subject. And so, too, when the Christian Arabs of the tribe of Iyad sought refuge in the Byzantine Empire, ʿUmar wrote to the emperor demanding their return, and threatening to drive non-Arab Christians out of lands under Arab control if he did not comply.[11] Similarly, Syriac sources from the mid- to late-seventh century

---

[8] The best survey of these sources is now Robert G. Hoyland, *Seeing Islam as Others Saw It: A Survey and Evaluation of Christian, Jewish and Zoroastrian Writings on Early Islam* (Princeton: Darwin Press, 1997).

[9] Daniel J. Sahas, "The Seventh Century in Byzantine-Muslim Relations: Characteristics and Forces," *Islam and Christian–Muslim Relations* 2 (1991), 11, and idem, *John of Damascus on Islam: The "Heresy of the Ishmaelites"* (Leiden: E. J. Brill, 1972).

[10] Averil Cameron, "The Eastern Provinces in the Seventh Century A.D.: Hellenism and the Emergence of Islam," *Hellenismos: Quelques Jalons pour une Histoire de l'Identité Grecque*, ed. S. Said (Leiden: Brill, 1991), 287–313, esp. 294–5; G. J. Reinink, "The Beginnings of Syriac Apologetic Literature in Response to Islam," *Oriens Christianus* 77 (1993), 165–87, esp. 166–7; S. P. Brock, "Syriac Views of Emergent Islam," in *Studies on the First Century of Islamic Society*, ed. G. H. A. Juynboll (Carbondale and Edwardsville: Southern Illinois University Press, 1982), 11–12.

[11] Madelung, *The Succession to Muhammad*, 74.

referred to Muhammad in political rather than religious terms, as king of the Arabs, rather than as prophet.[12]

In hindsight, of course, both Muhammad and his religion amounted to much more. The sharpening of the Muslims' religious identity took place during a period – the second half of the seventh and the beginning of the eighth centuries – which is sometimes referred to as that when the Muslim state was in essence an "Arab kingdom." The formation of this distinct religious identity and the consolidation of the empire dominated by Arabs, were really the culmination of the longer-term process by which the Arabs of the peninsula were incorporated into the dominant social and cultural patterns of the Near East.

[12] Brock, "Syriac Views," 14.

CHAPTER 8

The Umayyad period

The murder of ʿAli in 661 and the establishment of the caliphate of his rival Muʿawiya, cousin of ʿUthman and Arab governor of Syria, is generally taken to mark the advent of the Umayyad dynasty, the first Islamic state built explicitly on the claims of one family (the Banu Umayya) to the right to rule. Muʿawiya was succeeded in 680 by his son, Yazid, and then by members of collateral branches of the Umayyad family. In fact, however, the political situation was more complex, and its complexity reflects and is central to the process through which Islam emerged. The third caliph ʿUthman had appointed many members of his own clan to important administrative posts, provoking considerable opposition among Muslims who resented the favors granted to the family, particularly as many members of the Banu Umayya had been late and reluctant converts to Islam. ʿUthman's policy may have extended to efforts to ensure that he was succeeded as caliph by one of his sons.[1] If that is the case, then the dynastic policies of the Umayyads could be regarded as having commenced earlier than the reign of Muʿawiya, with the regime of ʿAli constituting a mere interregnum. On the other hand, no Umayyad "state" was firmly established and widely recognized for some time. The intense opposition among the Arabs to Muʿawiya's nomination of Yazid as his successor, and the abortive rebellions on behalf of one member or another of ʿAli's family, such as that led by his son al-Husayn which ended in disaster at Karbala in 680, or more importantly that carried out in the name of ʿAli's son Muhammad ibn al-Hanafiyya in Iraq between 685 and 687, were in some ways the least of the problems facing the Umayyads. Far more significant at the time was the rebellion led by ʿAbdallah ibn al-Zubayr, the son of one of the most prominent early Muslims. Between 681 and 692, he refused to recognize the authority of Yazid or his successors, and established his own caliphate based in the Hijaz. This rebellion was no flash in the pan: at times, Ibn al-Zubayr's authority extended beyond Arabia to include Egypt, Iraq and probably Iran as well. Support for the Umayyads was not uniform even in Syria, which province served as the base of their power, since some of the tribal Arabs settled there acknowledged the

---

[1] Wilferd Madelung, *The Succession to Muḥammad: A Study of the Early Caliphate* (Cambridge: Cambridge University Press, 1997), 88f.

caliphate of Ibn al-Zubayr. All this political chaos reminds us of several of the themes we have been developing. First, the institutions of Islam at this point were still grounded in Arabian identities: on one level, the political competition between the Umayyad family, Ibn al-Zubayr, and the various descendants of ʿAli involved simply the bedrock question of which clan of the tribe of Quraysh would have the right to lead the new polity. And second, it may yet be too early to speak with confidence of *any* unified Muslim polity: with different claimants to the title of "commander of the believers" spread throughout Syria, Iraq, and Arabia, and with the nature of caliphal authority itself vague and untested, the ruling institutions of the Muslim *umma* had yet to be clearly defined.[2]

The Arab character of the *umma* under the Umayyads is unmistakable. It can be measured in any number of ways – graphically, for example, in the well-known fact that at this stage a non-Arab generally could convert to the new religion only by simultaneously becoming a "client" (*mawla*, pl. *mawali*) of the Muslim Arab at whose hands he had converted. This requirement stemmed from the need to incorporate non-tribesmen into what was still a largely tribal society, for example, by insuring that the convert had a relationship with someone who would make the customary payment of compensation in the event the convert inflicted bodily harm upon a Muslim Arab.[3] The social discrimination which these non-Arab Muslims experienced also testifies to the Arab character of the Umayyad polity, as does the replacement of Greek by Arabic as the language of Umayyad administration in Syria at the end of the seventh century.

But the polity's Arab identity was not static; on the contrary, it experienced a marked evolution in response to the changed dynamic of a state which grew increasingly centralized, even imperial. In the first place, there was a small but growing number of non-Arab converts, and these *mawali* fairly quickly came to play an important role in the army, government, and administration, and even in religious scholarship. Secondly, the foundations of Muslim society gradually changed, too, as larger numbers of Arabs settled down to routine life in the provinces their militant fathers had conquered. Politics and the structure of the Umayyad army had a distinctly Arab feel. Governors, for example, ruled the tribesmen settled in their provinces through an aristocracy (the *ashraf*) drawn largely from the ranks of the pre-Islamic Arab nobility, meeting them in audiences which resembled the informal councils of clan elders of the pre-Islamic period.[4] But tribal identities were themselves in flux, and increasingly took the form of constructs manipulated for social or political ends. Lineages (and therefore alliances) could be manufactured or changed as political circumstance dictated,

[2] For an extreme formulation of this argument, see Moshe Sharon, "The Umayyads as *Ahl al-Bayt*," *Jerusalem Studies in Arabic and Islam* 14 (1991), 115–52, esp. 122–30.

[3] The complex question of the "clientship" of non-Muslim Arabs is discussed in Patricia Crone, *Roman, Provincial and Islamic Law: The Origins of the Islamic Patronate* (Cambridge: Cambridge University Press, 1987), and *EI²*, art. "Mawlā" (by P. Crone).

[4] The system is clearly described by Patricia Crone, *Slaves on Horses: The Evolution of the Islamic Polity* (Cambridge: Cambridge University Press, 1980), 30–2.

and the broad tribal groupings of "Qays" and "Yaman," the violent struggle between which sapped the late Umayyad state of both strength and legitimacy, became in fact coalitions competing for the resources of the imperial state–military factionalism expressed in the language of Arabian tribalism.[5]

A perfect example of both the underlying Arabness of the Umayyad state, and also of its transitional character, can be found in the palaces constructed by caliphs or other leading figures of the Umayyad court on the margins of the settled area of Syria. On the one hand, their placement in the countryside, beyond the circle of citied life, reflects the political reality of the Umayyad state: that it was here, away from the still overwhelmingly Christian urban settlements, that the Muslim Arab commanders could meet more easily with the nomadic and semi-nomadic tribes, with their chiefs and their mass of followers, which still constituted the backbone of the Muslim army. Certain architectural features, too, such as the apparent absence of elaborate bedrooms or indoor kitchens may reflect the persistence of tastes and lifestyles associated more with a desert lifestyle than that of an urban aristocracy. On the other, the buildings also draw on a variety of pre-Islamic Near Eastern patterns and conventions – the presence of complex baths, for example, which had been a characteristic feature of urban Roman life. The iconography of the art – wall paintings, floor mosaics, sculpture – which decorates these palaces, too, draws freely on Roman and Iranian (and distinctly non-Arabian) images: geometric and vegetal designs; scenes of dancing, music-making, acrobatics; figures dressed in Byzantine or Sasanian princely costumes.[6]

Those images of Roman and Iranian princes reflect a larger development: the imperialization of the Muslim polity. Under the Umayyads, that polity remained Arab, but its Arab leaders had to learn to speak in the idiom of the Near Eastern empires which they either challenged (the Roman) or replaced (the Sasanian). Their success can be measured in Umayyad art – in, for example, the jewels, crowns, and other symbols of imperial authority and wealth which decorate the interior of the Dome of the Rock – or in certain ceremonial practices of the caliphs' court.[7] When in the early eighth century the caliph al-Walid I sent to the Byzantine emperor the princely gift of twenty thousand pounds of pepper, he demonstrated an easy fluency in the Near Eastern imperial language. For their success, however, the Umayyads paid a price. The Shi'i tradition of course is hostile to them, for having replaced the caliphate of 'Ali, but so is the Sunni. The Umayyads have been presented, both in Islamic literature and, as a result, in modern secondary studies, as irreligious and (somewhat contradictorily) as usurping a religious function which did not inhere either in their persons or their

---

[5] Crone, *Slaves on Horses*, passim, and G. R. Hawting, *The First Dynasty of Islam: The Umayyad Caliphate AD 661–750* (Carbondale and Edwardsville: Southern Illinois University Press, 1987), 36–7 and 53f.

[6] Oleg Grabar, *The Formation of Islamic Art* (New Haven: Yale University Press, 1973), 141–64.

[7] See, for example, Oleg Grabar, "Notes sur les cérémonies umayyades," in *Studies in Memory of Gaston Wiet*, ed. Myriam Rosen-Ayalon (Jerusalem: Institute of Asian and African Studies, 1977), 51–61.

office. They stand accused – with the exception of the pious caliph ᶜUmar ibn ᶜAbd al-ᶜAziz (r. 717–20) – of corrupting the polity and the new religion, abandoning the path laid down by the Prophet and followed by the first four "rightly-guided" caliphs, and transforming the caliphate into *mulk*, "secular kingship."[8]

The latter charge is not merely political, but central to a Sunni argument concerning the nature of religious authority in Islam. So, it is said, the inherent nature of the caliph's authority was limited, since the paramount religious authority of Muhammad, seal of the Prophets, could not survive his death. Abu Bakr, the first caliph, humbly chose for himself the limited title of *khalifat rasul allah*, the "deputy of the prophet of God"; it was the corrupt Umayyads who transformed the office into an imperial one with their impious assumption of the grandiose title of *khalifat allah*, "deputy of God." In doing so, they attempted to arrogate to themselves a religious authority which by rights was invested only in God and his community, as expressed through the consensus of the men of religion.

The problem with such a narrative is that it projects backwards upon the Umayyads a view of religious authority and the correct religio-political order which only emerged later. The Umayyads did apparently conceive of the caliph's office as the locus of authority over religious as well as political affairs. In the absence at the time of a precise definition of what "Islam" meant, however, it is difficult to characterize their claims and actions as departing from an accepted model rather than adapting to the changed circumstances of a state which, by the early eighth century, stretched from the Atlantic Ocean to Central Asia. There is plenty of evidence to suggest that the Umayyad caliphs did in fact function as arbiters of "religious" issues, acting for example as judges (*qadis*) and as articulators of God's law, and also that many Muslims regarded them and their office as central to their understanding of what it meant to be a Muslim. Their controversial governor of Iraq, for example, al-Hajjaj ibn Yusuf (admittedly not the most impartial authority), is recorded as having professed in the most striking language that

> there is no god but God, who has no partner, that Muhammad is His servant and messenger, and that he [al-Hajjaj] knew of no obedience except to [the Umayyad caliph] al-Walid ibn ᶜAbd al-Malik; on this he would live, on this he would die, and on this he would be resurrected.[9]

And so the Umayyad caliphs, or at least some of them, made enormous contributions, as the "deputies of God," to the articulation of a distinctive Islamic tradition. It is significant, for example, that it is only in the final two decades of the seventh century that we find in the documentary record – coins, papyri,

---

[8] For a useful survey of the hostility to the Umayyads in the Islamic tradition, both Sunni and Shiᶜi, see Hawting, *The First Dynasty of Islam*, 11–18.

[9] Patricia Crone and Martin Hinds, *God's Caliph: Religious Authority in the First Centuries of Islam* (Cambridge: Cambridge University Press, 1986); the description of al-Hajjaj's profession of faith is found on p. 41.

inscriptions, etc. – clear and consistent references to Muhammad the prophet of God as a marker of Muslim identity. Earlier evidence suggests a preoccupation with God, the coming judgment, and other religious themes, but little concerning the person or historical role of the Prophet. Under the Umayyads, however, the Muslims began to set themselves apart more distinctly from the other monotheisms, and for this Muhammad now began to play an important role – as the model for Muslim behavior, and ultimately as the "seal" of the line of prophetic revelation.[10] The critical moment was not, as one might expect from later histories, the reign of the proverbially pious ᶜUmar ibn ᶜAbd al-ᶜAziz, but rather that of his uncle ᶜAbd al-Malik. The challenges ᶜAbd al-Malik faced threatened to divide and conquer the Muslim Arabs, and his policies and achievements should be read as the assertion of a newly-unified and self-conscious Islamic polity. ᶜAbd al-Malik had to deal with direct assaults on the unity of the *umma*, in the form of Shiᶜi rebellions in Iraq and that of Ibn al-Zubayr in the Hijaz, and it is significant that the year in which the latter's revolt was finally crushed (692, or 73 in the Muslim calendar) was known to the later Arab chroniclers as the "year of unity."[11] Conceptually, too, ᶜAbd al-Malik's policies defined more precisely the parameters of Muslim life. A paramount example lies in his reform of the coinage, in particular the minting of coins devoid of any iconic or representational illustrations, and bearing simply bald expressions of the new faith, in the form of the assertion that "there is no god but God" and other Koranic statements. ᶜAbd al-Malik's issue apparently was designed to replace the Byzantine *denarii* which were then circulating in the Islamic empire, coins which posed an explicit religio-political challenge to the Arabs with their triumphalist depiction of both Christ and emperor. The traditional explanation for these new coins, that they reflect an inherent Islamic opposition to any sort of figural representation, again probably puts the cart before the horse, as that very attitude was only in the process of formulation. But they did mark a step toward the assertion of a distinctive Islamic attitude towards representation, and thus toward an assertion of Islamic identity.[12]

The supreme example of ᶜAbd al-Malik's contributions to the articulation of a distinctively Islamic tradition in the context of inter-sectarian rivalry sits atop the Temple Mount, what Muslims refer to as the Noble Sanctuary, in Jerusalem. Jerusalem of course was a natural battleground between the different faith traditions, and the Temple area a flashpoint. Its significance for Judaism is obvious, as both the site of the ancient Temple and also, at least in legend, that of Abraham's near sacrifice of Isaac. And indeed, in the fleeting period shortly before the Arab conquests when the Sasanians, who had defeated the Roman armies and occupied the Syrian provinces, temporarily restored the city to Jewish rule, Jewish attention

[10] Crone and Hinds, *God's Caliph*, 25–33; Fred Donner, *Narratives of Islamic Origins: The Beginnings of Islamic Historical Writing* (Princeton: Darwin Press, 1998), 85–94, esp. 88, and 147–9.

[11] Sharon, "The Umayyads as *Ahl al-Bayt*," 133–4. The term "year of unity" was also applied to that in which Muᶜawiya had become caliph.

[12] Grabar, *Formation of Islamic Art*, 93–95; G. R. D. King, "Islam, Iconoclasm, and the Declaration of Doctrine," *Bulletin of the School of Oriental and African Studies* 48 (1985), 267–77, esp. 275.

and expectations were focused again on the Temple area, as the Jewish leader who took the name Nehemiah briefly restored the sacrificial worship associated with the ancient sanctuary.[13] Christians of course concerned themselves primarily with other sites, especially the Church of the Holy Sepulcher, which they considered the location of Christ's burial and resurrection, but they did not ignore the Temple area: archaeological evidence suggests that the Romans paid considerable attention to the Temple Mount in the years just before the Arab conquest.[14] Quite naturally, then, the Arab monotheists – who had, according to the Muslim tradition, at an early point prayed with their faces turned in the city's direction, before the Koran instructed them to face the Ka‘ba – quickly came to appreciate the enormous symbolic power of Jerusalem and in particular of the vicinity of the ancient Temple. Stories about the Arab conquest of the city describe the signing of the treaty of capitulation and the caliph ‘Umar's subsequent triumphal tour, accompanied by the patriarch Sophronius, and while they are encrusted with legend, they suggest the caliph's particular interest in the Temple Mount. Those stories may be apocryphal, but there was certainly a simple wooden mosque on the Mount at least by Mu‘awiya's time – it is mentioned by the French pilgrim Arculf around the year 670. But it was ‘Abd al-Malik who decisively appropriated the Temple area for the new faith.

The monument known as the Dome of the Rock dominates the topography of the city, occupying a spot of supreme importance to Jewish tradition, and looking down on the site of the Church of the Holy Sepulcher. There has been considerable discussion of when exactly the structure was built, but the most thorough study of the question has put the date of construction in 692 and the years following – in other words, at precisely the moment that ‘Abd al-Malik was accomplishing the uniting of the Islamic state and beginning the project of identifying a distinctively Islamic type of coinage.[15] Even more controversial has been the question of the structure's purpose. Later Muslim writers perceived in the decision to build the Dome an attempt to create an alternative locus of pilgrimage at a time when Mecca was still under the control of Ibn al-Zubayr, although again this probably reflects more the hostility of the fully-developed tradition to the Umayyads than any deliberate impiety on the part of ‘Abd al-Malik or anyone else.[16] Far from representing an attempt to turn the community from its already-established practice, the Dome reflects the process by which Islam gradually came together in a distinctive shape by the end of the seventh century. The entire building amounts to a graphic statement of the identity and superiority of the Arabs' faith in the

---

[13] M. Avi-Yonah, *The Jews of Palestine: A Political History from the Bar Kochba War to the Arab Conquest* (New York: Schocken Books, 1976), 266.

[14] Cyril Mango, "The Temple Mount AD 614–638," in *Bayt al-Maqdis: ‘Abd al-Malik's Jerusalem*, ed. Julian Raby and Jeremy Johns (Oxford: Oxford University Press, 1992), 1–16.

[15] Sheila Blair, "What is the Date of the Dome of the Rock?" in *Bayt al-Maqdis*, 59–87.

[16] See S. D. Goitein, *Studies in Islamic History and Institutions* (Leiden: E. J. Brill, 1966), 135–8, rejecting the earlier conclusions of Goldziher. For a defense of Goldziher's argument, at least in modified form, see Amikam Elad, "Why Did ‘Abd al-Malik Build the Dome of the Rock? A Re-Examination of the Muslim Sources," in *Bayt al-Maqdis*, 33–58.

context of Near Eastern monotheism. From a Jewish perspective, not only did the monument occupy the site of the ancient Temple, but it appropriated for the Arabs a spot associated with Abraham, and so amounted to an architectural expression of the Koran's reconceptualization of the patriarch's identity as the first Muslim. The building's challenge to Christianity was no less deliberate or acute, not merely through its commanding physical presence in the city, but also in its shape (it took the form, not of an open mosque, but of a Byzantine reliquary, a common form of Christian martyria and churches, in Jerusalem and elsewhere) and in the Koranic inscriptions – possibly the earliest surviving Koranic texts – which grace its walls: "Say: God is one, God the eternal, he has not begotten, nor is he begotten, and there is no one comparable to him" (*sura* 112) and, more pointedly

> O people of the Book, do not go beyond the bounds in your religion, and do not say anything of God except the truth. Truly, the Messiah Jesus son of Mary was an apostle of God and his Word, which he conveyed to Mary, and a spirit from Him. So believe in God and his apostles, and do not say [that God is] three. Stop – it is better for you. Surely God is one God. He is exalted beyond having a son (4.171).[17]

Given the significance of Jerusalem to both Jews and Christians, it is perhaps not surprising that it provided the backdrop for a development which, while it may not mark the beginning of Islam, nonetheless represents an important watermark, one still visible some thirteen centuries later, in the articulation of the new religion's identity. As the setting suggests, that identity was not entirely separate from the other Near Eastern monotheistic traditions, as their subsequent interaction will demonstrate. But it was now distinct from those of Judaism and Christianity. Having defined itself more clearly, however, Islam now also began to feel the pressure of internal schism.

[17] For a full discussion of the building and its significance, see Oleg Grabar, "The Umayyad Dome of the Rock in Jerusalem," *Ars Orientalis* 3 (1959), 33–62, and idem, *Formation of Islamic Art*, 48–67.

CHAPTER 9

The beginnings of sectarianism

There is an old and well-developed heresiographical tradition in Islam. In response to reported dicta of the Prophet to the effect that his community would ultimately fracture into seventy-three (or seventy-two – the precise number varies with the reports) sects, theologians composed extensive treatises identifying the different religious groups and their relation to what the authors identified as legitimate Islam. Of course, as Islam has generally lacked an institutional authority constituted to make definitive pronouncements about matters of religious interest, what exactly the parameters of Islamic legitimacy embrace has tended to shift with the perspective of the viewer. The very terms "heresy" and "orthodoxy" (since the former cannot exist without the latter) as they are used in the Western Christian tradition are in some ways misleading in an Islamic context. On the other hand, the flexibility of the Islamic tradition has not prevented Muslims from fervent denunciations of those who (in their view) falsely claim the mantle of Islam.[1] Indeed, the very lack of an authoritative institutional structure has probably helped to make conflicts over issues of religious identity sharper and more intense. Those conflicts were central to the history of Islam in the first century and a half of the new religion when, as we have seen, it only gradually carved out for itself an identity distinct from those of the earlier Near Eastern monotheisms. The Umayyads were not heretics, nor were they as a group especially bad Muslims, but as an Islamic identity began to coalesce during the period of their rule, so too did the tensions and fissures which ultimately would distinguish one Islamic sect from another. And once again, the critical issue, that around which the sectarian groups tended to form, was that of leadership. Now that the new faith distinguished itself through its understanding of the distinctive historical role of the Prophet Muhammad, the issue of leadership subsumed other points of difference. The question, put simply, was: who would be recognized as the "heir[s] of the Prophet," and how would the community understand the nature of their authority?

---

[1] Bernard Lewis, "The Significance of Heresy in Islam," *Studia Islamica* 1 (1953), 43–63; Alexander Knysh, "'Orthodoxy' and 'Heresy' in Medieval Islam: An Essay in Reassessment," *Muslim World* 83 (1993), 48–67.

Opposition to the Umayyad caliphs was, by the first half of the eighth century, both intense and widespread. Much of that opposition was unfocused, as the experience of the rebel ᶜAbdallah ibn Muᶜawiya suggests. Ibn Muᶜawiya (no relation of the Umayyad caliph, rather a descendant of ᶜAli ibn Abi Talib's brother Jaᶜfar) led a rebellion in Kufa and, later, Iran beginning in 744, and although the revolt failed, he drew momentarily at least on support from diverse groups and interests, including some who would later be identified as Shiᶜis as well as Kharijis (on whom, see below), disaffected Umayyads as well as supporters of the ᶜAbbasid family, disgruntled Arabs as well as non-Arab converts (*mawali*), in addition to a core group of extremists whom the later heresiographers labeled the Janahiyya. (The Janahiyya are linked with the idea that Ibn Muᶜawiya was actually an incarnation of God, and that, after his apparent murder, he had not in fact died, but instead had gone into hiding somewhere around Isfahan, and would one day return in triumph.)[2]

Not all of the opposition was explicitly religious in nature. The Islamic state was still principally an Arab state – indeed, with policies such as that of making Arabic the official language of government administration, the Umayyads had in some ways made the state's Arabness more acute. Consequently, it is hardly surprising that internal fissures were expressed in the language of tribal solidarity and competition (*ᶜasabiyya*) – as, for example, in the struggles between "Qays" and "Yemen" which plagued the Umayyads' final years. There has been some debate as to what exactly those ostensibly tribal confederations actually reflected; but whether they represented real tribal alignments or merely served the political and military interests of certain groups, it is difficult to perceive in them and in their fratricidal conflict consistent ideological positions or religious issues.[3]

Nonetheless, there was ideological opposition aplenty, and most of it can be associated with the outlook and concerns of a faction of growing size and significance within Muslim society for whom religious issues and concerns were of paramount importance. Western historians have called this large and amorphous group different things: the "Piety-Minded," and the "General Religious Movement."[4] The social and intellectual origins of this group were as diverse as the conclusions which they began to draw about the problems facing the Islamic *umma* and the correct solutions to them. The group included those who had been sympathetic to the rebels who had murdered ᶜUthman for his alleged transgressions, as well as those who looked with special reverence on the family of Muhammad, especially his descendants through his cousin and son-in-law ᶜAli; it

[2] William F. Tucker, "ᶜAbd Allāh ibn Muᶜāwiya and the Janāḥiyya: Rebels and Ideologues of the Late Umayyad Period," *Studia Islamica* 51 (1980), 39–57.

[3] See now Patricia Crone, "Were the Qays and Yemen of the Umayyad Period Political Parties?" *Der Islam* 71 (1994), 1–57, which rebuts the earlier contention of M. A. Shaban that the labels served as markers for groups advocating particular ideological positions. Compare *Islamic History, A.D. 600–750 (A.H. 132): A New Interpretation* (Cambridge: Cambridge University Press, 1971), 120–37.

[4] Marshall G. S. Hodgson, *The Venture of Islam*, vol. 1: *The Classical Age of Islam* (Chicago: University of Chicago Press, 1974) 241–79; W. Montgomery Watt, *The Formative Period of Islamic Thought* (Edinburgh: Edinburgh University Press, 1973), esp. 63–81.

included the conservative Arab elements who had supported the counter-caliphate of Ibn al-Zubayr, as well as those sympathetic to the claims of the non-Arab converts for full social inclusion within the fraternity of Muslims. If anything united them, it was simply the opportunity to express a political or social ideal in Islamic terms, an opportunity which would not have been fully realized without the crystallization of an Islamic identity in the late seventh and early eighth centuries, for which the Umayyads themselves were at least partly responsible. In this respect, the Umayyads didn't resist Islam – they made it possible. But since they constituted the ruling clan, they became the target of the principled wrath of the pious.

Given their diverse outlooks, no single member of this group can be taken as typical, but in the career of Hasan al-Basri (d. 728) we can at least trace some of the ideas which circulated among and the tensions which plagued them. The historical Hasan is somewhat enigmatic, although his figure looms large in much later Muslim tradition. A pious preacher and scholar who briefly served as *qadi* in the Iraqi town of Basra under the caliph ᶜUmar ibn ᶜAbd al-ᶜAziz, Hasan spoke for those for whom being a Muslim meant an uncompromising adherence to the principles enunciated in the Koran. Hasan himself came from a mixed background – he was born in Medina to a Persian freedman – and his outlook reflects a society in which Islam had crystallized as a distinct faith tradition, and in which, for all its continued Arabness, that tradition now aspired to the mantle of Judaic and Christian universalism. It may be too much to see in Hasan, as did the French scholar Louis Massignon, the "first historical manifestation of Sunnism," since a distinctively Sunni Islam was a response to the sectarianism which was only just beginning. It is however entirely appropriate to perceive in his ideas the ideological manifestation of the developments reflected architecturally in the Dome of the Rock. Hasan also demonstrates the pressures which a self-conscious Islam could bring to bear against the Umayyads themselves. His asceticism may have mirrored and in some sense been inspired by the contempt for worldly goods and pleasures which was so characteristic of late antique Christianity, but its immediate stimulus was the wealth and ostentation of some of the later Umayyad caliphs which distressed many of the pious who now began to look back to the example of the Prophet for guidance. He explicitly rejected the option of open rebellion to which many pious Muslims felt themselves pushed, dismissing the proposition that grave sin vitiated a ruler's right to demand obedience, and so foreshadowed the quietist streak which ran through much later Islamic political thought: it was ascetic penance that would bring about the divine redress of social injustices. At the same time, however, he insisted on his right, even duty, to criticize the Umayyads and their governors for what he considered reprehensible behavior, discharging that responsibility in his sermonizing, and in this way contributed to the growing tide of religiously-inspired dissatisfaction with the established Muslim regime.[5]

---

[5] On Hasan, see Louis Massignon, *Essai sur les origines du lexique technique de la mystique musulmane* (Paris: J. Vran, 1954), 174-201; *EI*[2], art. "Ḥasan al-Baṣrī" (by H. Ritter).

The example of the Kharijis (Ar. *khawarij*, literally "those who go out"), identified by the heresiographers as the first clearly-defined sectarian group to emerge from the pious opposition, reinforces several of the themes concerning the identity and nature of early Islam which we have stressed. In actual fact their origins are somewhat obscure. The first Muslims identified as Kharijis are those who abandoned ᶜAli's army during his dispute with the Umayyad leader Muᶜawiya following the murder of ᶜUthman. According to the sources, these Kharijis objected to ᶜAli's acceptance of a proposal to settle the dispute through arbitration; their opposition stemmed from their conviction that ᶜUthman had in fact been guilty of serious misdeeds, and so Muᶜawiya's demand for vengeance for his kinsman's death was void. Whatever the precise connections between these malcontents and those associated with the various Khariji sects as they crystallized at the end of the seventh and beginning of the eighth centuries, the emergence of the Kharijis reminds us again of the centrality of the question of political leadership in the shaping of Islamic religious identity, since the starting point for their opposition was their disapproval of the behavior of ᶜUthman and, indeed, of subsequent caliphs. More importantly, their opposition to Umayyad rule, as expressed in a number of bloody rebellions, reflected the crystallization of Islam itself. The Khariji impulse was rooted in the elevation of religious principle to a pre-eminent rung: in the conviction, for example, that grave sin excluded an individual from the Muslim community and from the promise of salvation, or that the caliph should be required to rule on the basis of Koranic directives and doctrine, or that tribal distinctions did not matter and so the caliph could be any-one willing to follow the will of God. As such, the Kharijis both reflect and gave impetus to the emergence of a self-conscious Islamic identity: they were, in the somewhat dramatic words of a nineteenth-century Orientalist, "true sons of Islam." It comes therefore as no surprise to find that, in a Muslim society still dominated by Arabs, Kharijism soon attracted as partisans a number of non-Arab Muslims, particularly in Iran.[6]

Khariji rebellions in the first century and a half of the Islamic period were numerous but mostly ineffective. The rebels who seceded from his army were wiped out by ᶜAli at Nahrawan in Iraq in July 658, although the victory eventually cost the caliph his life, as his assassin was urged on by his wife, who had lost her father and brother in the battle. A more significant challenge was posed by a Khariji leader named Najda ibn Amir, who for a time in the late seventh century controlled large territories in eastern Arabia, Yemen, and the Hadramawt, and threatened the rule of both the Umayyad ᶜAbd al-Malik and the Hijaz-based Ibn al-Zubayr. Kharijis identified by the later heresiographers as the Azariqa, after

---

[6] On the early Kharijis, see Julius Wellhausen, *Die religiös-politischen Oppositionsparteien im alten Islam* (Berlin, 1901), trans. R. C. Ostle and S. M. Walzer, *The Religio-Political Factions in Early Islam* (Amsterdam: North-Holland Publishing Company, 1975), 1–91; Watt, *The Formative Period of Islamic Thought*, 9–37; idem, "Kharijite Thought in the Umayyad Period," *Der Islam* 36 (1961), 215–31; and Wilferd Madelung, *Religious Trends in Early Islamic Iran* (Albany: Bibliotheca Persica, 1988), 54–76.

their leader Ibn al-Azraq (d. 685), terrorized southern Iraq and Iran in the late seventh century in the name of their purified view of the new religion. Ibn al-Azraq held that those who claimed to be Muslims but who did not "go out" with them could legitimately be robbed or killed, since in his view they had ceased to be Muslims when they compromised with a corrupt regime and so showed themselves insufficiently committed to following the will of God. Most Khariji groups eschewed such extremism, but the language in which the Azariqa expressed their doctrine is notable for drawing on what now can be identified as expressly Muslim terminology. So, for example, they described the action of a Muslim in "going out" from and leaving behind a corrupt community as a *hijra*, using the word which also referred to the flight of Muhammad and his companions from Mecca to Yathrib, which marked the start of the Islamic era. The *hijra*, in other words, was for the Kharijis not simply a historical event, but a model for proper Muslim behavior. On the one hand, the Khariji phenomenon marks another stage in the process by which the Muslim identity became fully self-conscious. On the other, the bewildering variety of Khariji sects identified by the Muslims heresiographers testifies to the degree to which that identity was, in its first century and a half, still in significant flux.

Although it eventually proved a much more serious sectarian challenge, Shiᶜism took somewhat longer to mature. From the beginning, it seems, there was a "party" (Ar. *Shiᶜa*) of those who supported the claims of ᶜAli, Muhammad's cousin and son-in-law, to the leadership of the community after the Prophet's death. Their preference was later recorded in an account of an event during the last year of the Prophet's life, when at a place called Ghadir Khumm Muhammad identified ᶜAli as his chosen successor. The numbers of this party, however, were apparently limited. ᶜAli was passed over several times as successor to the Prophet before his eventual and almost accidental elevation, suggesting that there was opposition to any claims he might have put forward. His son al-Husayn led the famous rebellion against the Umayyads that ended in disaster at Karbala in Iraq, when al-Husayn and the other members of his party were wiped out by an Umayyad army. Its ignominious conclusion was due in part to the fact that he had been able to muster the active support of only seventy or so men. The essential element of Shiᶜism, as it came to be formulated in the eighth and ninth centuries, lies in the conviction that leadership of the community should have passed to ᶜAli and his descendants after Muhammad's death – that the community should be ruled not merely by a "successor" (caliph) of the Prophet chosen through consensus, but by a divinely-selected leader, or *Imam*, from among the Prophet's descendants. It is possible to read the record to suggest that Muhammad expected and the Koran reflected the assumption that authority would remain in the Prophet's own family.[7] It is difficult, however, to conclude that most Muslims at the time accepted the proposition.

---

[7] This is one of the central themes of Wilferd Madelung, *The Succession to Muḥammad: A Study of the Early Caliphate* (Cambridge: Cambridge University Press, 1997).

Part of the difficulty lay in the uncertainty of who exactly the "family of the Prophet" included. By the end of the seventh century, the idea had taken root among some Muslims that leadership was the prerogative of some member of the "people of the house" (Ar. *ahl al-bayt*). The term is a Koranic one, but it appears there in contexts that are ambiguous. In pre-Islamic usage, the phrase signified the leading family of a tribe; in the Islamic context, of course, it referred to the family of Muhammad. The question, however, was how that family was to be defined, a question made more acute by the fact that the Prophet left no surviving male descendants. The uncertainty of the term's meaning allowed many to stake a claim, including the Umayyads, who were collaterally related to the Prophet and who represented a family widely recognized among the pre-Islamic Quraysh as the most noble.[8] Gradually, however, a more refined meaning emerged, one which focused on Muhammad's nearer relations (the clan of Hashim) and more specifically his descendants through his cousin and son-in-law ꜤAli. The tortured process through which this occurred in the late seventh and eighth centuries constitutes the background to the emergence of ShiꜤism and the convulsive events which brought the Umayyad period to a close.

A turning point was the disaster of Karbala and the martyrdom there of ꜤAli's son al-Husayn in 680. In itself the affair was a minor one, but its consequences were tremendous. The events at Karbala spurred a movement of pious penitence among Muslims who felt shame at having failed to come to al-Husayn's support. Within a few years, anger at the tragic events at Karbala had taken on a political cast by providing a rallying cry for opponents of the Ummayads – revenge for the murdered family of the Prophet. It is interesting, therefore, that one of the most important rebellions inspired by these sentiments was carried out on behalf of Muhammad ibn al-Hanafiyya, a son of ꜤAli not by Fatima, Muhammad's daughter, but by another of his wives, and so not a descendant of the Prophet. The apparent disjuncture may be explained by the fact that it was descent on the father's side which counted in Arab society, and by the fact that by 685, when this rebellion began, Ibn al-Hanafiyya was the senior surviving son of the Prophet's cousin.[9] But it also demonstrates clearly that, while a distinctive "party" of ꜤAli may have been crystallizing, the doctrinal form of what came to be known as ShiꜤism – for example, tracing a line of Imams (leaders) in direct and exclusive descent from the Prophet through ꜤAli and then through his son al-Husayn – belonged still to the distant future.

Muhammad ibn al-Hanafiyya did not participate in the revolt carried out on his behalf, and may not even have authorized it; its leader, rather, was a figure named al-Mukhtar ibn Abi ꜤUbayd. The rebellion, centered in Kufa, survived for two years, until the town was retaken and al-Mukhtar killed – significantly, not by an Umayyad army, but by forces loyal to Ibn al-Zubayr. The timing, however, was

---

[8] Moshe Sharon, "The Umayyads as *Ahl al-Bayt*," *Jerusalem Studies in Arabic and Islam* 14 (1991), 115–52.
[9] Moshe Sharon, *Black Banners from the East* (Jerusalem: Magnes Press, 1983), 108.

critical, and al-Mukhtar's rebellion another in the series of developments and crises through which a distinctive although not yet stable Islamic identity emerged around the end of the seventh century. al-Mukhtar appealed to and drew support from *mawali*, but the significance of this is not entirely clear. It used to be argued that the prominence of *mawali* in al-Mukhtar's army indicated that the rebellion and the Shiʿism of which it represents an early manifestation had from the first a peculiarly non-Arab or Persian cast. This conclusion, however, is not well founded – al-Mukhtar was an Arab, as of course was Ibn al-Hanafiyya, as well as the leading figures in the movement. Nor is there any indication that the rebellion was fought for the general principle of ethnic equality in Islam. But the movement did have distinct apocalyptic overtones. For example, al-Mukhtar explicitly named Ibn al-Hanafiyya as the "Mahdi," possibly the first time this pregnant term was used in an Islamic context to indicate a messianic figure. This is significant for many reasons, not least because millenarian expectations circulated ever more widely among Islamic movements over the next half century, culminating in the campaign which resulted in the establishment of the ʿAbbasid caliphate. But it also marks the degree to which the new religion began to adopt as its own the motifs and obsessions of the other religious traditions of the late antique Near East. It is interesting in this regard, for example, that Muslims were not the only ones to view al-Mukhtar's rebellion in messianic terms. The contemporary Christian Syriac chronicle of John bar Penkaye, too, viewed events in Iraq in the 680s through an apocalyptic glass, and saw the rebellion, and in particular the prominence within it of non-Arab soldiers, as heralding "the destruction of the Ishmaelites."[10]

The particular sectarian group associated with al-Mukhtar is usually identified as the Kaysaniyya by the heresiographers, who in turn include it among the various parties labeled Ghulat, or "extremists." The Ghulat, including the Kaysaniyya, are portrayed by later writers, both Sunni and Twelver Shiʿi, as the radicals among the partisans of the family of ʿAli because of their apparent espousal of doctrines which later offended widely-accepted Muslim theological postitions. Such rigid categorization, however, once again should be read as the projection backwards of sectarian identities as they hardened at a much later period. We necessarily tread on thin ice, since information on the Ghulat comes almost exclusively from sources hostile to them, but the doctrines ascribed to al-Mukhtar and other figures are odd only when viewed from the standpoint of Sunnism or Twelver Shiʿism as they later took shape. Al-Mukhtar and the Kaysaniyya, and the Ghulat more generally, represent in fact the doctrinal ferment at the heart of Islam at the very moment the new religion became conscious of its distinct historical identity, and also the degree to which the new Muslims found a bewildering variety of religious ideas, many of them drawn from older Near Eastern traditions, appealing. The Kaysaniyya, for example, included both Arabs with living memories of their pre-Islamic beliefs and practices and converts with disparate religious heritages, and

---

[10] Sebastian Brock, "North Mesopotamia in the Late Seventh Century: Book XV of John Bar Penkāyē's *Rīš Mellē*," *Jerusalem Studies in Arabic and Islam* 9 (1987), 51–75, esp. 53, 63–73.

their doctrines drew on the traditions of both. For instance, the doctrine of *raj°a*, which asserts that some heroic figure may return to life, may have precedents in pre-Islamic Arabian belief, but certainly looks forward to the Shi°i doctrine of the "return" of the Hidden Imam. Already in the late seventh and early eighth centuries one finds departed °Alid leaders whose return is anticipated, among them Ibn al-Hanafiyya, who was reputed, after his apparent death in 700 (or 703, or 705 – there is some uncertainty), to be still living on a hill near Medina, guarded by a pair of lions, and fed by two springs, one of honey and one of water.[11] The heresiographers allege that, to inspire his soldiers, al-Mukhtar had a chair carried into battle which he identified as having belonged to °Ali, and that he explicitly drew a comparison between °Ali's chair and the Israelites' Ark of the Covenant. Most significantly of all, there are reports that al-Mukhtar claimed to receive visits and revelations from Gabriel. This reminds us that the critical doctrine that Muhammad was the "seal" of prophets, in the sense of having categorically closed the door of prophecy, was only now taking shape, and that before it was widely accepted it was possible for Muslims to expect continuing prophetic contact between God and mankind.[12]

---

[11] Sharon, *Black Banners*, 117.

[12] The literature on the emergence of Shi°ism is vast, and is addressed in most works on this early period of Islamic history. One place to begin, beyond the various entries in the *Encyclopaedia of Islam*, is with Marshall Hodgson's still serviceable "How Did the Early Shi°a Become Sectarian?" *Journal of the American Oriental Society* 75 (1955), 1–13. On the critical issue of the finality of prophethood, see Yohanan Friedmann, *Prophecy Continuous: Aspects of Aḥmadī Religious Thought and Its Medieval Background* (Berkeley: University of California Press, 1989), 49–82.

CHAPTER 10

The non-Muslims of early Islam

Of course non-Muslims constituted the vast majority of the inhabitants of those lands ruled or fought over by the early caliphs. Popular stereotypes about Islam spreading by the sword, and older scholarly assumptions that most of the inhabitants of the Near East converted fairly quickly to the new faith in order to escape the onerous personal and agricultural taxes levied on non-Muslims, both radically misrepresent the complex situation faced by Jews, Christians, Zoroastrians and others in the century or two following the initial Arab conquests. In fact, what came to be known as the *dhimmi* communities, those monotheists who lived under a pact of protection (*dhimma*) with the Muslim state, survived and in many cases thrived for many generations. Eventually, of course, most regions did emerge with Muslim majorities, but the process of conversion took some time, and was uneven, the actual pace varying according to local circumstance and the specific character of relations between the particular faiths and the Muslim polity.

At the beginning, relations between the Arab conquerors and the inhabitants of the lands they occupied were, if not entirely amiable, likely free of the pervasive tension which sometimes characterized them in later centuries. In a famous passage, the ninth-century historian al-Baladhuri records the people of the Syrian city of Hims, both Christians and Jews, proclaiming their preference for Muslim rather than Byzantine rule, begging the Arab soldiers to stay when the emperor Heraclius threatened to retake the city, and, upon the defeat of the Roman army, welcoming the Muslims back from battle with music and dance.[1] The Syrians' enthusiasm for their conquerors may reflect wishful thinking on the part of a Muslim historian living more than two centuries after the event, but given the tensions which had plagued relations between the native Christians of Egypt and Syria and the Melkite authorities in the decades before the Arab conquests, let alone the poisonous relations which had developed between the Jews and the Christian Roman state, a certain feeling of relief would hardly be surprising. Moreover, there is plenty of evidence to suggest that at least some non-Muslim

---

[1] Aḥmad ibn Yaḥyā al-Balādhurī, *Kitāb futūḥ al-buldān*, ed. Ṣalāḥ al-Dīn al-Munajjid (Cairo: Maktabat al-Nahḍa al-Miṣriyya, 1956), 162; trans. Philip Hitti, *The Origins of the Islamic State*, vol. 1 (New York: Columbia University, 1916 [reprinted Beirut: Khayats, 1966]), 211.

communities continued on trajectories of growth and development which had begun in the pre-Islamic period. In Iraq, for example, the religious and legal institutions, which both Christian and Jewish communities had developed through their interaction with the Sasanian state and which presumed a degree of communal autonomy, survived the conquest; after some initial hesitation, the Muslims accepted them as the basis for their own relationship with the non-Muslim communities.[2] There, the Nestorian community at first benefitted from the Arabs' destruction of the Sasanian state, constructing new monasteries and augmenting its numbers through the conversion of both pagans and Zoroastrians.

The trend of most recent research has been to understand the emergence of Islam in the larger context of Near Eastern religious history, and thus to stress continuity between the pre- and post-conquest periods, while at the same time acknowledging the complexity of that continuity: non-Muslim groups both were shaped by and themselves had an impact upon the emerging religion of Islam. This should be seen as a corrective to a perspective which, intentionally or not, facilely presumed from the first a sharp distinction between Muslim and non-Muslim. A number of factors conspired to produce that mistaken, or at least incomplete perspective. As a historiographical matter, it may have been a function of the disciplinary boundaries in Western academia, which have tended to isolate students of Arabic and Islam from those of the languages and religions of the pre-Muslim Near East. It also of course reflects the undoubted suddenness of the Arab conquests, and the massive political dislocation which they involved and which was surely obvious to all contemporary observers. Moreover, the character of the surviving source material encourages a kind of intellectual ghettoization of that which is Muslim and that which is not. In the first place, there is the general tendency of the Muslim tradition to project later developments backward onto earlier authorities: so, for example, one the best known documents outlining the terms by which non-Muslims would relate to the Muslim polity is cast in the form of a negotiated settlement between the second caliph and the Christians of Syria, and is persistently known as the "Pact of ᶜUmar," although in fact it cannot, in the form in which we now have it, date to the early decades of the Muslim period. More generally, the Arabic sources for the early period are relatively uninterested in non-Muslims and the complex and nuanced lives they must have led, and in them the rich social and religious scene of the late antique Near East, full of colorful figures like the Syrian ascetics who perched for years atop pillars, largely disappears.[3]

The story of what became of the non-Muslim inhabitants of the Near East in the decades following the Arab conquest constitutes another chapter in the larger

---

[2] Michael G. Morony, *Iraq after the Muslim Conquest* (Princeton: Princeton University Press, 1984), passim. On this as on all matters regarding Iraq in the late antique and early Islamic periods, Morony's work is essential, and provides an important model for understanding the origins and development of early Islamic society throughout the Near East.

[3] See the cogent remarks of Patricia Crone, *Slaves on Horses: The Evolution of the Islamic Polity* (Cambridge: Cambridge University Press, 1980), 11–12.

tale of the resolution of religious identities which, as we have seen was a defining motif of late antique Near Eastern history, and which itself involved the slow emergence of Islam. Here is where the true continuity between late antiquity and early Islam is to be found. The condition and experience of non-Muslims in the late seventh and early eighth centuries cannot be properly understood without first grasping the very gradual articulation of a separate Muslim identity, which we have traced in the earlier chapters of this book. John of Damascus insisted upon portraying Islam as, in part, an outgrowth of a Christian heresy, Arianism. By the time he wrote, however, in the middle of the eighth century, there was good reason to think of Islam as an independent tradition. By that time, the Dome of the Rock dominated the topography of Jerusalem, and Hasan al-Basri was criticizing the ruling authorities in distinctly if not uniquely Islamic terms.

The first century and a half after the Arab conquests may have been as critical to the formation of medieval Judaism as they were for Islam. Broadly speaking, the period was a propitious one for the Jews who lived under Muslim rule. Jewish communities in Palestine in particular recovered from the tumultuous and difficult final decades of Byzantine rule, Jews for example returning to Jerusalem in large numbers under the early Muslim caliphs.[4] Even in new cities such as Basra and Kufa in lower Iraq, founded specifically as garrisons for the conquering Arab armies, Jews fairly quickly established a presence (some of them perhaps as refugees from the Hijaz) and deep roots: when the rabbi Benjamin of Tudela arrived in Kufa in the mid-twelfth century, he was shown an elaborate tomb which the local Jewish population venerated as that of a Jewish king who died at the court of Nebuchadnezzar.[5]

Despite its head start, some have still perceived in Judaism in the early Islamic period an "underdefined entity."[6] Many of the characteristic features of medieval Judaism were coming into focus, but neither the internal orientation of the Jewish community nor its relationship to the non-Jewish Near Eastern population were yet set in stone. In Iraq, the period spanning the last decades of Sasanian and the first of Muslim Arab rule saw the crystallization of the authority of the rabbis and of the *geonim*, the heads of the major rabbinical academies there. The office of the exilarch, which had lapsed from about the year 590, was revived by the Arab conquerors, but over the first few centuries of Muslim rule became increasingly ceremonial. Real authority over the community passed to the *geonim* and to the rabbis under a process, rooted in the rabbis' claim to authoritative interpretation of the written scripture and sole possession of the oral one, which had already begun under the later Sasanians. This development was decisive for both the Jewish

---

[4] Moshe Gil, *A History of Palestine, 634–1099* (Cambridge: Cambridge University Press, 1992), 68–74.
[5] Benjamin of Tudela, *The Itinerary of Benjamin of Tudela* (Malibu, California: Pangloss Press, 1983), 105.
[6] The phrase is from Steven M. Wasserstrom, *Between Muslim and Jew: The Problem of Symbiosis under Early Islam* (Princeton: Princeton University Press, 1995), 45.

communities of the Near East and also for the shape of relations between the government of the Muslim Arabs and the other religious communities over whom they ruled. Internally, it set the stage for sectarian developments within Judaism itself. More significantly, the model of ruling a subject non-Muslim population through religious leaders and institutions who exercised considerable autonomy and authority over internal communal matters was ultimately extended beyond the former territories of the Sasanian Empire. Indeed, perhaps the greatest impact of the Arab conquests on the Jews of the Near East lay in the uniting of disparate communities under the rule of a single political and cultural entity. The experience of Jews living under Roman and Sasanian rule had been radically divergent. Now, for a time at least, the Jews of the Near East – who made up as much as ninety percent of world Jewry – came to know and to operate under a single ruling institution.

From the perspective of the rabbis, therefore, the early Islamic moment was a propitious one for the creation of a large community with a stable identity, bounded and defended by the moral and religious authority of the rabbinate, operating within but also with a limited independence from a political framework controlled by the Muslim Arab conquerors. But several persistent dangers threatened this vision and rabbinic authority. The first arose from within Judaism itself, namely, the messianism latent in the Jewish historical vision. Jewish messianism, in the context of early Islam, was not a mere historical oddity. Indeed, it is important to remember that Jews of this period would not have despaired of a political future. A strong Jewish state was not unheard of (consider, for example, Dhu Nuwas's kingdom in South Arabia), and would shortly again become a reality, when the Khazar tribe (or at least its king and ruling class), which battled the Arabs for control of the Caucasus from the mid-seventh century, converted to Judaism at some point in the late eighth century. For some Near Eastern Jews, the political possibilities were not a distant hope: both the pre- and early-Islamic periods were punctuated by Jewish revolts, in Palestine, Iraq, Iran, and elsewhere. More generally, messianic expectations were rampant, encouraged by the prolonged and cataclysmic war between the Roman and Sasanian empires, and then by the appearance of a Judaizing prophetic cult from Arabia. A Jew announcing the arrival of the Messiah led an uprising in southern Iraq just a few years after the Arab conquest, a rebellion which was suppressed by Arab troops from Kufa.[7] Indeed, it was in Iraq and Iran that Jewish messianism made its greatest impact. As the eighth century wore on, that messianism dovetailed with similar apocalyptic expectations among those Muslims, especially the partisans of ʿAli, who opposed the Umayyad regime with increasing vigor. Its most colorful manifestation may lie in the rebellion, probably in the last decades of Umayyad rule, led by Abu ʿIsa al-Isfahani, a figure who claimed, among other things, to have risen to heaven where he encountered God, who "stroked" (the Arabic word is etymologically linked to the term "messiah") his head. Abu ʿIsa's complex and somewhat obscure

---

[7] Morony, *Iraq after the Muslim Conquest*, 327.

doctrines seem to have drawn on, or been formulated in order to mobilize, the messianic expectations of Christians (Abu ᶜIsa means the "father of Jesus") and followers of Muhammad as well as Jews, and though his rebellion failed, his movement lived on for several centuries, both as a Jewish sect known as the ᶜIsawiyya, and through its impact on groups of Shiᶜi extremists.[8]

Naturally the later Muslim tradition, as well as the rabbis, looked with alarm on movements such as that of Abu ᶜIsa. That Jewish messianism, and in particular its eruptions in the Muslim east, was perceived to be a threat is demonstrated by the unforgettable hadith which warns that "the anti-Christ will be followed by seventy thousand Jews of Isfahan wearing Persian shawls." But the example of Abu ᶜIsa points to a second possibility, a more diffuse although perhaps greater threat, which alarmed both the rabbis and, later, their Muslim counterparts: namely, the very real possibility, at this tumultuous moment of Near Eastern religious history, of creative interaction between the Muslim and Jewish traditions. There are hints (if the sources can be credited) in Abu ᶜIsa's program of an effort on the part of this Jewish leader to propitiate the new Muslims: for example, he is said to have preached that Muhammad was a genuine prophet (that is, at least to his own people, the Arabs), and some sources even identify Abu ᶜIsa's personal name as that of the founder of Islam. On the Muslim side, there is the problematic issue of the relationship between Judaism (and Jewish messianism in particular) and the incipient Shiᶜi movement. At some point, of course, labeling someone or some idea "Jewish" became a way of discrediting it, so it is possible that when the sources make such connections, they are reflecting later polemic rather than original linkages. But the evidence is persistent and tempting: for example, those accounts which trace certain doctrines associated with the Shiᶜi Ghulat (such as the assertion that ᶜAli stood to Muhammad as Aaron [or Joshua] did to Moses, or that ᶜAli had not died but would reappear to establish the realm of truth and justice) through the followers of al-Mukhtar to an individual, ᶜAbdallah ibn Sabaᵓ, identified as a Yemeni Jewish convert to Islam. More generally, there are the close connections, of language, image, and structure, between Jewish messianism and the millenial expectations which, while not unknown among those who came to be called Sunnis, were characteristic of Shiᶜism from the start.[9]

The really important point, however, is that the channels of interaction and cross-fertilization were not limited to radicals or those with accentuated millenarian expectations. On the contrary, the evidence suggests a considerable exchange of texts and ideas between Judaism and Islam in the first Islamic century. The Jewish convert Kaᶜb al-Ahbar is routinely cited as one individual responsible for the introduction of legends and pious lore about the Hebrew prophets which the Muslim tradition came to know as the israᵓiliyyat. In fact, however, quite a few of the first Muslims, including several of those most responsible for shaping the early

[8] Wasserstrom, *Between Muslim and Jew*, 68–89; idem, "The ᶜĪsāwiyya Revisited," *Studia Islamica* 75 (1992), 57–80.

[9] On the connections between Jewish messianism and proto-Shiᶜism, see Wasserstrom, *Between Muslim and Jew*, 47–71, and the sources cited there.

religious life of the community, had fertile contact with Jews and Jewish traditions. Several of Muhammad's chief companions and those whose names most frequently appear in the "chains of authority" (*isnads*) through which his words and stories of his deeds were transmitted to posterity are credited with extensive knowledge of the "Torah" (by which is probably meant the Jewish tradition and scripture generally); they include Abu Hurayra, the Persian convert Salman al-Farsi, and the Prophet's cousin ʿAli himself. Ibn ʿAbbas, perhaps the most important transmitter of Prophetic hadith, is sometimes identified as the *hibr al-umma*, the "rabbi of the [Muslim] community." According to one report, Muhammad himself once asked his adopted son Zayd ibn Thabit to learn *al-yahudiyya*, probably meaning an Arabic dialect in common usage among Arabian Jews, in order to learn from them and their scriptures. The exchange of texts continued after the new religion had worked its way out of Arabia; the so-called *israʾiliyyat* (which include tales about the Hebrew prophets, Jesus and other biblical figures) left profound traces in the Muslim historical imagination and also in Koranic commentaries. It is true that, eventually, the developed Muslim tradition came to look askance on the *israʾiliyyat*, and with suspicion on those, such as Kaʿb al-Ahbar, most closely connected with them. That attitude, however, is the product of a later time, of a point in Muslim history when the faith defined itself more explicitly in opposition to others. The early years were characterized by a freer exchange of ideas. Nor should we assume that that dialogue was one-sided, since the actual mechanisms of exchange can rarely be traced. It was not simply that Muslims borrowed texts and ideas from Jews (or Christians); rather, individuals adhering to each of the three faiths drew creatively on a common pool of stories and traditions to shape their understanding of the scriptures they believed that God had given them.[10]

For Christians, more than for Jews, the Arab conquests were likely to have meant a traumatic rupture with the communal and political patterns which had developed over the previous centuries. The importance of those provinces which became the heartland of the Islamic empire – Egypt, Syria, and Iraq – to the development of late antique Christianity can hardly be overstated. It was largely in Egypt and Syria, after all, that the traditions of asceticism and monasticism had first taken shape. The Nestorian church in Iraq represented one of the most dynamic Christian communities at the time of the Arab invasions; by the early seventh century, it was probably the largest religious community there, its numbers augmented by the conversion of pagans, Zoroastrians, and Jews. Now, however, those provinces were ruled by Arabs who came to call themselves Muslims, a condition which was to prove more or less permanent.

In fact, however, Near Eastern Christians' experience of the reality of Arab rule, and their reaction to it, was a complex affair. Links between them and the church and government of the Roman Mediterranean were not immediately and

---

[10] Jacob Lassner, *Demonizing the Queen of Sheba: Boundaries of Gender and Culture in Postbiblical Judaism and Medieval Islam* (Chicago: University of Chicago Press, 1993), esp. 120–4.

completely severed. During the period of Umayyad rule, for example, as many as five Syrians were elevated to the papacy in Rome. From a Roman perspective, the Arab conquests could not be understood outside of the consuming and persistent problem of Christological differences. During the seventh century, emperors and church councils sought a theological compromise that would bridge the gap between the Chalcedonian and Monophysite christologies, efforts that represented at least in part an attempt to secure the Roman connection to the Christians of the provinces now (temporarily, it was hoped) occupied by the Arabs.

Near Eastern Christians could hardly have been unaware of their new Arab rulers, but they may well have been confused as to what the new regime meant for them. Several Christian communities continued on trajectories of growth established in late antiquity. In Iraq, for example, the conquests brought inevitable disruptions, including the sacking of ecclesiastical establishments and the killing of a number of monks; but it was not long before the Christian communities recovered. The Nestorian church in particular proved vital: new monasteries were constructed in the wake of the conquests, and the momentum behind the process of conversion to Christianity among Jews and Zoroastrians continued. Indeed, in the centuries which followed, the Nestorian church undertook an extensive (although ultimately unsuccessful) missionary program to the east, in Iran, Afghanistan, and Central Asia, one of the least appreciated aspects of early medieval Christian history. It comes as no surprise, therefore, to find a number of Nestorian sources from the period following the Arab conquest commenting favorably upon the new rulers, recognizing them as worshipers of the one true God and describing them as respectful of churches, monasteries, the clergy and their prerogatives within the Christian community. In Palestine, too, despite the complaints of churchmen such as the patriarch Sophronius that the "Saracens" destroyed churches and pillaged monasteries, there is archaeological evidence for the continued construction of new churches in the period of and just after the Arab conquests, and the change in regime did not prevent a flourishing of monastic culture in the late seventh and early eighth centuries.[11]

What seems to us clear and unambiguous – for example, the permanent disappearance of Roman political authority from the Near East – may have seemed less so at the time. The temporary withdrawal of the Roman army in the face of the Sasanian advance just a few decades before the Arab invasions may have already suggested to the Christians of Egypt and Syria that Roman authority was subject to limits, and that their religious identities were not inseparably tied to that of the imperial state. On the other hand, just as the legions had returned in the wake of the Persian retreat, so they might again. Christians participated along with Jews

[11] Robert Schick, *The Christian Communities of Palestine from Byzantine to Islamic Rule* (Princeton: Darwin Press, 1995), passim, esp. 77–80, 96–7. See also Morony, *Iraq After the Muslim Conquest*, 332–83; Garth Fowden, *Empire to Commonwealth: Consequences of Monotheism in Late Antiquity* (Princeton: Princeton University Press, 1993), 122–3; S. P. Brock, "Syriac Views of Emergent Islam," in *Studies on the First Century of Islamic Society*, ed. G. H. A. Juynboll (Carbondale and Edwardsville: Southern Illinois University Press, 1982), 15–17.

and the new Muslims in the heady millenarianism of the time. Not surprisingly, a number of Christians, Monophysites especially, quickly came to view the Arab conquests as the catalyst for ushering in the apocalyptic age: according to this view, God unleashed the "Ishmaelites" on the unsuspecting Christians to punish them for their own sins, that is, for Roman ecclesiastical policy and efforts to impose unwanted christological doctrines. But by the end of the seventh century, an apocalyptic vision emerged in which, the Christian community having been properly chastised, the Byzantine emperor comes to play the role of God's avenger, driving the Arabs from the "land of promise" and attacking them in the "desert of Yathrib" itself. The source of this vision is unclear, and the text which expresses it may have been composed by a Chalcedonian Christian, that is, one loyal to the christological position and ecclesiastical authority of the Melkite church; but the text circulated in Syriac, and so presumably was popular with Syrian and Iraqi Christians as well. If the text was composed around the year 690–1, as has been proposed, we may see in it a Christian response to the more sharply delineated Muslim identity associated with ʿAbd al-Malik's reforms and the building of the Dome of the Rock; and if that is the case, the ascription of a redemptive role to the Byzantine emperor is especially suggestive.[12]

Of course, the apocalypse did not come, and the Romans did not return. Ultimately, therefore, Near Eastern Christians had to make their peace with the Muslim Arabs. After the conquests, the local Christian communities were thrown entirely back on their own resources, as much of the Greek-speaking elite in Syria and Egypt, for example, fled to what was left of their Empire. Long centuries of interaction between the Arabic-speaking bedouin and the Syriac-speaking peasants of Syria and Iraq, in addition to their linguistic affinities, may have encouraged their passive acceptance of Arab rule, but the decimation and disappearance of the Greek-speaking elite contributed as well. Christian communities remained, but it is striking how rapidly the native languages, Coptic and Syriac, died out as instruments of everyday communication, especially given how small, demographically speaking, the Arab presence in the conquered territories was. Even what survived in the Near East of the Melkite church had to adjust. By the end of the eighth century, Near Eastern Christian writers loyal to the Chalcedonian church had developed an Arabic literature, one in which the linguistic and theological impact of the Koran is expressly visible, and one which was directed more to shoring up the religious identity of its Christian audience than to a direct polemic with Arabic-speaking Muslims.[13]

---

[12] There is considerable recent literature on the apocalypse of Pseudo-Methodius; the interested reader could start with Brock, "Syriac Views of Emergent Islam," 17–19; Hoyland, *Seeing Islam as Others Saw It*, 263–7; G. J. Reinink, "Pseudo-Methodius: A Concept of History in Response to the Rise of Islam," in *The Byzantine and Early Islamic Near East*, ed. Averil Cameron and Lawrence Conrad (Princeton: Darwin Press, 1992), 149–88; Andrew Palmer, Sebastian Brock, and Robert Hoyland, *The Seventh Century in the West-Syrian Chronicles* (Liverpool: Liverpool University Press, 1993), 222–42.

[13] See, for example, Sidney H. Griffith, "The First Christian *Summa Theologiae* in Arabic: Christian *Kalām* in Ninth-Century Palestine," in *Conversion and Continuity: Indigenous Christian*

The experience of the adherents of other faith traditions with their new Arab rulers was equally complex, although perhaps, for us, somewhat more obscure. Pagan traditions were already in a secular decline before the coming of the Arabs in most of those lands they conquered. Nonetheless, their remnants did not disappear overnight. Ultimately Islamic law came to distinguish sharply between monotheists possessing a revealed scripture and others, tolerating the former but offering the latter the choice of conversion or death; but such clear-cut discrimination did not necessarily characterize the experience of pagans in the first Islamic centuries.

In the first place, intact communities of pagans survived the Islamic conquests, in some cases for several centuries. The most famous example is that of the so-called "Sabians" of Harran, a town in northern Mesopotamia which the Church Fathers already knew as Hellenopolis, "the pagan city," because of the tenacity of its religious traditions. The town was peacefully occupied by the Arabs in 640, and for a brief period at the end of the Umayyad period served as the capital of the empire under Marwan II. The Harranians' religious traditions centered on an astral cult – among other reports about them is that they kept the body of a man believed to resemble the deity Mercury in a mixture of oil and borax, and removed his head every year when the planet was at its height, at which time its soul spoke, "relating what was happening and replying to questions." But the town also sheltered an academy devoted to philosophy, the members of which eschewed the sacrificial cult and ceremonies of the temple and its worshipers. According to the well-known story reported by the tenth-century bookseller and cataloguer Ibn al-Nadim, the Harranian pagans in the early ninth century came under the scrutiny of the ʿAbbasid caliph al-Maʾmun, who offered them the choice of conversion or death. Some succumbed, and converted to Christianity or Islam, but others successfully escaped the dilemma by claiming that they were "Sabians," in reference to an otherwise obscure term used in the Koran to refer to a group who believed "in God and the last day" (e.g., 2.62). In any case, both academy and temple long survived the coming of Islam: the historian Masʿudi visited the school in the middle of the tenth century, while the last temple was not closed until the eleventh.[14]

Manichaeism presented Islam with a deeper challenge, because of the appeal of its sophisticated theological thought. Despite its explicit dualism, the religion survived, although relatively little is known about the history of the sect in the first Islamic century. One point of confusion is that the term generally used to describe Manichaeism, *zandaqa* (an adherent was a *zindiq*), came to be used more generally as an epithet for freethinking or unbelief. On the evidence of Ibn al-Nadim,

[14] On the Sabians of Harran, see Ibn al-Nadīm, *Fihrist* 2:746–73; Michel Tardieu, "Ṣābiens Coraniques et 'Ṣābiens' de Ḥarrān," *Journal asiatique* 274 (1986), 1–44; and *EI*², art. "Ḥarrān" (by G. Fehervari) and "Ṣābiʾa" (by T. Fahd).

however, the Manichaean community had sufficient structure to have a "head" and sufficient internal dynamism to have experienced sectarian splits over various points of doctrine. The tradition also apparently had significant appeal, at least for some among the elite in early Islamic society. The famous government secretary and belle-lettrist Ibn al-Muqaffaᶜ, for example, was credited with having written an apologia for Manichaeism, one which both defended the phantasmagorical Manichaean cosmogony and also attacked the fideism of Islam and the other monotheistic traditions. Whether or not he actually penned the treatise, the ascription, along with ubiquitous reports of the Manichaean sympathies of courtiers, writers, and even theologians, suggests the persistent attraction of this elitist faith, and also the danger it posed to Islam: that one could formally identify oneself as a Muslim, yet hold beliefs inimical to prophetically-grounded monotheism. (Even the Umayyad caliph al-Walid was, according to some accounts, a follower of Mani.) In the early ᶜAbbasid period, Manichaeism came under sharper attack and persecution, although the tradition had an exciting if ultimately doomed future in Central Asia and China, and may have survived in attenuated form in some later Muslim, especially Shiᶜi, philosophical and mystical speculation.[15]

Zoroastrianism presented a peculiar challenge to the new Muslims. It did not share a prophetic past with Islam, as did Judaism and Christianity, but could it be considered a monotheistic faith, despite the apparent dualism at its core, and one which possessed a revealed scripture? There is one Koranic reference to adherents of the Iranian national religion (22.17), but it is fleeting, and does not make clear whether the Muslim holy book views Zoroastrianism as comparable in character and status to Judaism and Christianity, or to the rejected and despised polytheisms. Ultimately, Zoroastrians were explicitly accepted as *dhimmis*, although Islamic law as later formulated betrays a peculiar and sharpened suspicion of Zoroastrianism. As a result, Zoroastrians were not granted the same rights and status as Jews and Christians. So, for example, Zoroastrians were forbidden entrance to mosques, a prohibition which, at least in the early Islamic period, did not extend to Jews and Christians; also they were denied access to Muslim bathhouses, on the grounds that their bodies were polluting.[16]

Zoroastrians benefited from the initial absence of a clearly-articulated Muslim policy toward non-Muslim traditions. Here as elsewhere, the Arab conquerors entered into treaties of capitulation with their new non-Muslim subjects. There was no single pattern, and the terms by which the natives submitted and the Arabs agreed to their protection varied considerably from place to place. In Iraq, the political center of the Sasanian state, Zoroastrian institutions were viewed as appendages of the royal government and family, and suffered much destruction and confiscation. In other regions, the disruption, at least at first, was considerably

---

[15] On al-Walid as a Manichee, see Abūʾl-Faraj al-Isfahānī, *Kitāb al-aghānī*, 24 vols. (Cairo: Dār al-Kutub, 1935), 7.83. On Manichaeism under early Islam, see Ibn al-Nadīm, *Fihrist*, 2:773–805; G. Vajda, "Les zindīqs en pays d'Islam au début de la période abbaside," *Rivista degli Studi Orientali* 17 (1937), 173–229; *EI*², art. "Ibn al-Muḳaffaᶜ" (by F. Gabrieli).

[16] Jamsheed K. Choksy, *Conflict and Cooperation: Zoroastrian Subalterns and Muslim Elites in Medieval Iranian Society* (New York: Columbia University Press, 1997), 124–9.

more limited. In Sistan, at the far east of the Persianate cultural area, the local Muslims in 671 actually interceded to prevent the Arab governor from executing the leading Zoroastrian priests and extinguishing their sacred fires, on the grounds that doing so would violate the treaty of capitulation and protection.[17]

It used to be argued that Zoroastrianism, because it was so closely tied to the Sasanian state, quickly collapsed in the wake of the Arab conquests. In fact, the process by which Zoroastrianism became a minority faith in its own native land was drawn-out and complex. In the first place, it should be noted that already, before the Arab conquests, conversion from the state religion (especially to Christianity) had presented a serious problem for the Zoroastrian authorities, and that conversions to Christianity continued after the Arab conquest. Once again, from a broader perspective the early Islamic centuries appear continuous with those of late antiquity. Secondly, Zoroastrianism was displaced not simply through a process of conversion, but also through settlement of Iran by Muslim Arabs. This in itself was a protracted affair, and the movement of Arab tribes into Iran continued well into the ʿAbbasid period. Still, in the long run, the ancient Iranian religious tradition all but disappeared from its homeland, in which Zoroastrians today make up only a tiny minority, and in this respect the Zoroastrian encounter with Islam differs significantly from that of Near Eastern Judaism and Christianity. There were a number of high-profile cases in which Iranians accepted the faith of the conquerors during the course of and just after the early conquests, such as that of the Hamraʾ, a division of the Sasanian army the members of which submitted to the Arabs and embraced their cause (some of them even before the pivotal battle of Qadisiyya), becoming clients (*mawali*) of the tribe of Tamim. But in general the pace of conversion in the territories of the former Sasanian empire was at first slow. It was probably fastest in the urban settlements in which Arab troops were garrisoned. Moreover, rural Iranian converts may well have migrated to Muslim-dominated cities since, from the standpoint of the Zoroastrian community, abandoning the Zoroastrian faith implied a sort of social death. And so Zoroastrianism came increasingly to be associated with rural regions, which in the long run put it at a sharp disadvantage to Islam. Still, by the end of the Umayyad period, Zoroastrianism was hardly moribund, and even in the cities, the Muslim community may have represented only a small minority of the population.[18]

---

[17] On the incident in Sistan, see Choksy, *Conflict and Cooperation*, 33–4, and C. E. Bosworth, *Sīstān Under the Arabs, From the Islamic Conquest to the Rise of the Ṣaffārids (30–250/651–864)* (Rome: IsMEO, 1968), 24.

[18] On the conversion of Iran, see Richard Bulliet, *Conversion to Islam in the Medieval Period* (Cambridge, Massachusetts: Harvard University Press, 1979), esp. 16–63, and the response of Michael Morony, "The Age of Conversions: A Reassessment," in *Conversion and Continuity: Indigenous Christian Communities in Islamic Lands, Eighth to Eighteenth Centuries*, ed. Michael Gervers and Ramzi Jibran Bikhazi (Toronto: Pontifical Institute of Mediaeval Studies, 1990) (Papers in Mediaeval Studies 9), 135–50. Efforts to quantify as obscure a historical process as conversion will inevitably invite criticism. Nonetheless, Bulliet's general conclusion that the conversion of Iranians to Islam was still relatively limited in the mid-eighth century is confirmed by Choksy's excellent study, *Conflict and Cooperation*.

CHAPTER 11

The ʿAbbasid revolution

As we have stressed, the Umayyad caliphs have been treated somewhat unfairly by later Muslim tradition. They were dismissed by some Muslims as impious usurpers, and by the middle of the eighth century, there is evidence of deep-seated dissatisfaction with their rule. The fault lines were many and overlapping. Non-Arab converts, still limited in number but constituting an increasingly large component of Muslim society and the army, resented the social inferiority which they experienced. Some of the dissatisfaction was now effectively local or regional, as Iraqi Arabs, or those settled in more remote provinces, chafed at domination by the Syrian soldiers who had formed the core of Umayyad support. Competition among the Arab elite reached critical proportions, too, as factions identified as one tribal grouping or another contended for power and access to the wealth of the state. In particular, violence between the broad tribal alliances of Qays and Yemen reached endemic proportions, and finally consumed the Umayyad state itself, precipitating the murder of the caliph al-Walid II by a group of Yemenis, and a movement of bloody vengeance on behalf of Qays led by the last Umayyad caliph, Marwan II.[1]

Above all, the middle of the eighth century was a period of turmoil in the realm of ideas, values, and expectations, as the inhabitants of the Near East witnessed and participated in a process, inflamed by millenarian dreams, of disruptive struggle over the ordering of their political and religious worlds. The Khariji impulse, for all its persistent failure, was never uprooted, and continued to provoke violent insurrections, particularly at the end of the Umayyad period, when a series of Khariji rebellions in Iraq helped to pave the way for the advance of the ʿAbbasids from Iran. More generally, the Kharijis, by articulating a set of principles and expectations which made the religious message of the Koran the centerpiece of social and political thought, helped to set the standards for the Muslim community as a whole. The Kharijis' insistence on the necessary righteousness of the caliph, for example, focused the attention of the community

---

[1] On factional conflict in the late Umayyad period, see Patricia Crone, *Slaves on Horses: The Evolution of the Islamic Polity* (Cambridge: Cambridge University Press, 1980), 37–48, and Paul Cobb, *White Banners: Contention in ʿAbbasid Syria, 750–880* (Albany, NY: SUNY Press, 2001), 68–75.

102

on the person and office of the ruler from the very beginning, while the bizarre policy of the Azraqis in "questioning" (istiᶜrad) individuals to discover whether they were true Muslims (by Azraqi standards), and then murdering those who failed to pass muster, at least raised in no uncertain terms the question of what it meant to be a Muslim. Shiᶜi hopes, too, grew more focused as the Umayyad period rushed to its close and, as we shall see, played an important role in the advent of ᶜAbbasid power. Apocalyptic anticipation among Jews and Christians as well as Muslims in the middle of the eighth century heightened the sense that the coming years would bring radical change; moreover, the expectations of the adherents of one faith fueled those of the devotees of another. So, for example, while the ᶜAbbasids themselves encouraged and capitalized upon the millenial dreams of Muslims, a contemporary Jewish text on the signs of the coming of the Messiah names the ᶜAbbasid caliph al-Mansur as the ruler of Ishmael at the approach of the last days.[2]

Who exactly were the ᶜAbbasids, and what was the nature of their "revolution"? A preliminary word of caution is in order. Reconstructing the narrative and the meaning of the ᶜAbbasid movement is difficult, because of the nature of the sources. For the most part those sources are fairly late, and reflect the viewpoints of later generations. More precisely, they reflect the ideology of ᶜAbbasid apologists some years after the events which brought them to power. That is significant, because apparently the nature of the ᶜAbbasids' ideological claims shifted radically over time. The ᶜAbbasid movement was a direct response – one among many – to the religious turmoil of the mid-eighth century, but its very success altered the political and religious terrain, and subsequent ᶜAbbasid caliphs and their supporters adjusted to the changed circumstances by constructing new justifications for their rule. Reconstructing the narrative and the evolution of the ᶜAbbasids' claims amounts therefore to what some have called an exercise in historical archeology, an attempt to sift through the "stratigraphy" of the literary remains to chart the changing character of the ᶜAbbasid state. The project is, however, central to an understanding of the evolution of Islamic religious identity and authority.[3]

The ᶜAbbasid family took its name from al-ᶜAbbas, a paternal uncle of Muhammad, but their claim to leadership through their descent from the oldest surviving male relative of the Prophet at the time of his death post-dated their

---

[2] Bernard Lewis, "An Apocalyptic Vision of Islamic History," *Bulletin of the School of Oriental and African Studies* 13 (1950), 331.

[3] Jacob Lassner, *Islamic Revolution and Historical Memory: An Inquiry into the Art of ᶜAbbāsid Apologetics* (New Haven: American Oriental Society, 1986), esp. xi–xv and 4–36. Accounts of the ᶜAbbasid revolution itself can be found in Moshe Sharon, *Black Banners from the East* (Jerusalem: Magnes Press, 1983), and M. A. Shaban, *The ᶜAbbāsid Revolution* (Cambridge: Cambridge University Press, 1970); there is also a short, convenient narrative summary in G. R. Hawting, *The First Dynasty of Islam: The Umayyad Caliphate AD 661–750* (Carbondale and Edwardsville: Southern Illinois University Press, 1987), 109–15. For a good survey of the historiographical issues surrounding the ᶜAbbasid revolution, see R. Stephen Humphreys, *Islamic History: A Framework for History*, revised edition (Princeton: Princeton University Press, 1991), 104–27.

accession to the caliphate by several decades. In the decades which preceded the insurrection which brought them to power, the nature of their claim was quite different, and says a good deal about the tumultuous state of Muslim religious identity at mid-century. The clandestine ᶜAbbasid movement probably begins with ᶜAli, the son of ᶜAbdallah ibn al-ᶜAbbas, one of the most prominent of early hadith transmitters and a cousin of the Prophet. He and his son Muhammad took up residence at Humayma, in Jordan, and during frequent visits to the Umayyad court in Damascus, Muhammad became intimately associated with Abu Hashim, a son of that Muhammad ibn al-Hanafiyya on whose behalf al-Mukhtar had led a revolt several decades previously. (In fact the connection between the ᶜAbbasid family and that of Ibn al-Hanafiyya may have begun even earlier, when both resided in the Hijaz.) A portion of the surviving supporters of al-Mukhtar had recognized Abu Hashim as leader or Imam after his father's death, and Abu Hashim now introduced Muhammad ibn ᶜAli to them. According to later texts explaining and justifying the ᶜAbbasids' claims, Abu Hashim, who had no sons, recognized and "appointed" – the term was a pregnant one in Shiᶜi usage – Muhammad ibn ᶜAli as his heir. In this way the ᶜAbbasid family came to lead an underground movement of opposition to the Umayyads (usually identified as the Hashimiyya), one which emerged from the bedrock of pious support for the claims of the Prophet's family, and particularly his ᶜAlid descendants, to rule.

At first glance, of course, this seems odd, since the ᶜAbbasids were only collaterally related to the Prophet: how could supporters of ᶜAli's family support their claims? Several things should be kept in mind, however. The first is that the movement over which the ᶜAbbasids exerted leadership was, at first, quite small. Its center was in Kufa, where its adherents numbered only thirty or so; it was only through painstaking missionary work, particularly in Khurasan, that it attracted a wider following. More importantly, while Shiᶜisim as a movement, with its distinctive acknowledgment of the leadership of the Prophet's direct descendants, was now coming into shape, the understanding of the concept of the "people of the house" – that is, of those relations of the Prophet whose genealogical standing gave them special status – was not yet so firm and exclusive as it would later become. Indeed, to some extent it was the phenomenon of the ᶜAbbasid movement itself which spurred the Shiᶜis to identify themselves and their claims more precisely. Perhaps most decisively, the ᶜAbbasid movement was deliberately clandestine, and its proponents and the "missionaries" they sent out made a point of not naming the exact individual for whose sake they toiled, and of trying to cultivate support simply for "the chosen one from the family of Muhammad" – a vague phrase which by design carried a more ecumenical appeal, and in particular one which would resonate with the growing number of Muslims whose hopes centered on a descendant of Muhammad through ᶜAli and Fatima.

The narrative of the clandestine organizing and finally the open insurrection, begun in Khurasan under the leadership of the ᶜAbbasid client Abu Muslim, which brought the ᶜAbbasid family to power lies beyond the scope of this book; the interested reader will find several full accounts in the bibliography. But a number of points can be made, especially concerning the themes of religious identity and authority. The first and most important is that the upheaval which resulted in the ᶜAbbasid seizure of power was a product of the religious turmoil of the mid-eighth century. It reflected broad and systemic developments in the structure and direction of Islamic society and of the religious universe in which Muslims moved: it was not, that is, simply a coup d'état, through which one ruling family replaced another. By the middle of the eighth century, "Islam" was an unmistakable entity, and the ᶜAbbasids had to justify their claims in a specifically Islamic idiom. Their efforts to do so betray some uncertainty and experimentation. Hence, for example, while their movement may have had its roots in the unfocused Shiᶜi expectations of its day, the ᶜAbbasids eventually dispensed with a Shiᶜi claim in favor of other religious justifications of their rule. But the point is that their claim had to be articulated in religious form. So, for example, their supporters used the term *dawla* to describe their accession to rule. The term meant literally a "turning" as in a passing of time or a change of fortune, and so by extension suggested both a radical break with the corrupt Umayyad past and also a "*re*-turning," that is, the restoration of an ideal Muslim order associated now with the Prophet and the primitive Islamic community.[4] This is not to say that Islam was now fully formed – on the contrary, one of the arguments of subsequent chapters of this book is that much of what we take to be typically "Islamic" was in fact the product of a later period. Nor is it to deny that the *vision* of Muhammad and his community which inspired the ᶜAbbasids and their supporters reflected more the conditions and values of their own historical experience rather than that of Muhammad – that is, that that vision was thoroughly idealized, rather than historical. But it is to say that the ᶜAbbasid revolution, like the construction of the Dome of the Rock two generations earlier, marked a high point in the development of a self-conscious Islamic tradition.

A second point concerns the character of the "revolution" itself. An older line of Western scholarship, traceable back to some of the leading Orientalists of the late nineteenth and early twentieth centuries, saw in the ᶜAbbasid revolt, which began in the eastern province of Khurasan and which resulted in the shift of the center of political gravity to the former Sasanian province of Iraq, an Iranian national rebellion against Arab domination. This view has been largely discredited by more recent scholars, who have perceived in it both the influence of the ethnic nationalism which saturated Western assumptions a century ago, and also an overly teleological explanation of events of the mid-eighth century by consequences which could not in fact have been foreseen at the time.[5] Ideologically, the movement was oriented toward the restoration of an ideal society associated with the Arab prophet Muhammad, rather than any resurgence of Iranian culture and

---

[4] A point made by Jacob Lassner, in "The ᶜAbbasid *Dawla*: An Essay on the Concept of Revolution in Early Islam," in F. M. Clover and and R. S. Humphreys, eds., *Tradition and Innovation in Late Antiquity* (Madison: University of Wisconsin Press, 1989), 247–70, and idem, *Islamic Revolution and Historical Memory*, xi–xv.

[5] See, for example, Lassner, "The ᶜAbbasid *Dawla*," 250f, and the sources cited there.

identity. It is true that the ᶜAbbasids drew on the support of some *mawali*, many of them Iranian in origin, but their expressed goal was the organization of society around Islam, rather than any ethnic identity, and so those Iranian clients who joined the rebellion did so in order to assimilate more fully into Muslim society, rather than to re-orient it in an Iranian direction. Sociologically, too, the movement had a deeply Arab coloring. Most of its leaders, including of course members of the ᶜAbbasid family themselves, were Arabs, and the rivalry between Qays and Yemen played an important role in determining which Arabs settled in Khurasan joined the rebellion, and which opposed it (the ᶜAbbasids themselves, as well as most of their Arab followers, belonging to the Yemeni confederation).[6]

Still, if one looks at the event from a longer view, it is possible to see in the ᶜAbbasid revolution a step, one among many, toward the gradual re-orientation of Islamic civilization, toward a deepening of the ecumenical spirit of Islam and in particular of its more enthusiastic embrace of elements of the Iranian tradition. This general trend was already at work before the ᶜAbbasid revolt. Sasanian-Iranian influence can already be detected in the architecture, art and ceremonial of the Umayyad court, for example.[7] In Iran itself, the Muslim Arab authorities had for years relied on the local aristocracy and native bureaucracy, only some of them converts to Islam, to mediate the central government's authority and in particular to collect its taxes. In other words, the power and influence of Iranian servants of the ᶜAbbasid caliphs, such as Ibn al-Muqaffaᶜ and the Barmakids, had strong roots in pre-ᶜAbbasid practice. The province which first rose in rebellion to the ᶜAbbasid call was an Iranian one, Khurasan, and there was a strong Iranian element alongside those Muslim Arabs who rallied to the ᶜAbbasids' banner, including *mawali* who served in the ᶜAbbasid armies. On an ideological level, something in the ᶜAbbasid program may have appealed to certain groups which grew out of specifically Iranian religious traditions. If the Muslim historians and heresiographers can be trusted, Iranians who followed the teachings of Mazdak (see above, pp. 29–30) and who were known in the early Islamic centuries as the Khurramiyya identified themselves with various Shiᶜi sectarian groups, and through them participated in (although they also ultimately grew disenchanted with and alienated from) the movement which swept the ᶜAbbasids to power.[8] Observers at the time noted the extent of Iranian penetration of the ranks of ᶜAbbasid supporters, and in some cases viewed (with or without alarm, depending on their point of view) the ᶜAbbasid triumph as that of client Iranian Muslims.[9]

---

[6] On the last point, see Khalid Y. Blankenship, "The Tribal Factor in the ᶜAbbāsid Revolution: The Betrayal of the Imam Ibrāhīm b. Muḥammad," *Journal of the American Oriental Society* 108 (1988), 589–603.

[7] Oleg Grabar, *The Formation of Islamic Art* (New Haven: Yale University Press, 1973), 156–63.

[8] Wilferd Madelung, *Religious Trends in Early Islamic Iran* (Albany: Bibliotheca Persica, 1988), 7–9; *EI*², art. "Khurramiyya" and "Kaysāniyya" (both by W. Madelung).

[9] For examples, see Crone, *Slaves on Horses*, 61; idem, "The 'Abbāsid Abnāʾ and Sāsānid Cavalrymen," *Journal of the Royal Asiatic Society* (Series 3) 8 (1998), 1–19, esp. 11–13; and Michael Bonner, *Aristocratic Violence and Holy War: Studies in the Jihad and the Arab–Byzantine Frontier* (New Haven: American Oriental Society, 1996) (American Oriental Series, vol. 81), 52.

The example of the Khurramiyya brings us back to the central question of the relationship of the ᶜAbbasid movement to Shiᶜism. The matter is extraordinarily complex, and has formed the subject of extensive debate among contemporary historians, but can only be dealt with here in a summary fashion.[10] Things are complicated further by the fact, already noted, that most of what we know comes from later, partisan sources, and so its tendentiousness is difficult to measure. But in a nutshell, the story is this:

By acquiring the leadership of at least a portion of the Hashimiyya, the ᶜAbbasids effectively threw in their lot with the welter of proto-Shiᶜi groups which lent such color to the late-Umayyad religious scene. It is important to remember that Shiᶜi sectarian identities were still at this stage imprecise, as demonstrated clearly by two critical matters, the first of which was the question of leadership. While the hope of those Muslims who sought leadership from among the "people of the house" increasingly focused on the descendants of Muhammad through ᶜAli, the precision of the view later associated with the Twelver sect – that Muhammad was succeeded as the locus of religious authority by a series of Imams, beginning with ᶜAli, followed by his sons by Fatima, and then al-Husayn's own sons, grandsons, and later descendants – had not yet crystallized. The second matter concerns the doctrines espoused by the different proto-Shiᶜis which, as we have already noted, varied tremendously. Some of these – for example, the idea that the imamate could be assigned or appointed, from one Imam to his chosen successor, or the idea that an apparently deceased Imam could be expected to return, either from death or from a hidden location to which he had secretly been spirited, both of which circulated among the Hashimiyya – had a prominent future with Twelver Shiᶜism. Others – for example, the idea that the divine presence could itself be incarnated in some human individuals, which also circulated among some Shiᶜi groups attached to the ᶜAbbasid movement – would eventually be rejected by mainstream Shiᶜism, and the Muslims who espoused them identified as "exaggerators," or Ghulat.

It was this complex and still-evolving welter of religious ideas and expectations that the ᶜAbbasids tapped in their efforts to establish themselves as leaders of the Muslim community. Once they had come to power, however, their resolution of the tensions between their dynastic aspirations to lead the *umma* and the programs of their diverse supporters contributed significantly to the crystallization of Shiᶜi identity. In the revolutionary phase, the question of leadership, and the possibility that some supporters of the *ahl al-bayt* might be disappointed by ᶜAbbasid leadership, were obscured, since the identity of the ᶜAbbasid candidate – who was, of course, not an ᶜAlid, or even a descendant of the Prophet, but only a collateral relation – was, for practical reasons, kept secret. Even when the rebellion of the Hashimiyya had broken into the open in 747, its organizer, the ᶜAbbasid client Abu

---

[10] In addition to the works by Lassner, Sharon and Madelung cited above, see Marshall G. S. Hodgson, "How Did the Early Shiᶜa Become Sectarian?" and Claude Cahen, "Points de vue sur la 'révolution ᶜabbāside'," *Revue historique* 230 (1963), 295–338.

Muslim, publicly identified the still clandestine leader of the revolt only as "the chosen one from the family of Muhammad." It was not until the rebellion had spread out of Khurasan, and the city of Kufa had been captured, in late 749, that a member of the ᶜAbbasid family, Abuʾl-ᶜAbbas, was publicly proclaimed the Imam. The delay resulted from the reluctance of some supporters, now that the critical moment was at hand, to recognize anyone other than a descendant of ᶜAli as Imam. Even more telling was a series of rebellions that plagued the ᶜAbbasids during their early years in power and reflected the disillusionment of those who expected deliverance from an ᶜAlid. The most threatening of these was that led by Muhammad "the Pure Soul" and his brother Ibrahim, great-grandsons of al-Hasan, the elder son of the Prophet's cousin ᶜAli and brother of al-Husayn, in 762–3. Its failure marked the end of active Shiᶜi political opposition for half a century, but not the end of Shiᶜism itself: it was at this very moment that Jaᶜfar al-Sadiq, a respected scholar and great-grandson of al-Husayn ibn ᶜAli, quietly laid the foundations for what was to become Shiᶜism as it is now known. Within a few decades, the tension between their own position and the expectations of their ᶜAlid supporters forced the ᶜAbbasids to articulate a new claim to rule: not as having received the appointment of Abu Hashim (who after all, while a grandson of ᶜAli, was not himself a descendant of Muhammad) as Imam, but rather through their descent from al-ᶜAbbas, the Prophet's uncle and, arguably, his legal heir as the oldest surviving male relative at the time of his death. That change, which shifted the focus of expectations for leadership from the Prophet's descendants to the broader clan (the Banu Hashim) to which he had belonged, proved critical to the formation of a specifically Sunni identity. Sunni Islam, in this respect at least, was really a response to Shiᶜi priorities and preferences.

On the matter of doctrine, the ᶜAbbasids had to deal not so much with the disappointment of erstwhile supporters as with their own embarrassment, once they had become rulers of the *umma*, at the positions taken by some of their followers. To illustrate the point, consider the famous case of the Rawandiyya, a proto-Shiᶜi group of Khurasani origin who formed a part of the ᶜAbbasid movement. Accounts by later historians and heresiographers suggest that the Rawandiyya held a number of doctrines, including a belief in metempsychosis and divine incarnation, at odds with Muslim teaching as it came to be known. Apparently the ᶜAbbasids were happy to draw on their support during the clandestine and revolutionary phases of their movement; once in power, however, the odd doctrines of the Rawandiyya proved embarrassing, and the new caliphs sought to distance themselves from the group. So, shortly after his accession, the ᶜAbbasid caliph al-Mansur (r. 754–75) confronted an unruly crowd of the Rawandiyya who proclaimed that he was their God or "lord" (*rabb*) and who began to circumambulate his palace (as Muslim pilgrims do at the Kaᶜba); the caliph's efforts to suppress their public display resulted in the violent dispatch of the crowd.[11]

---

[11] See Lassner, "The ᶜAbbasid *Dawla*," 252–3, and *EI²*, art. "Rāwandiyya" (E. Kohlberg).

In such ways did the ᶜAbbasids seek to resolve the tension created by the diverse expectations of those who had supported their movement. Of course they were not entirely successful: the radical expectations and millenarian dreams which the convulsive events of the first century of Islam had raised both among Muslims and non-Muslims could not be so easily disposed of, and would continue to shape the religious experiences of the inhabitants of the Near East for some time to come. But from an internal Muslim perspective, the ᶜAbbasids' political success did set the stage for a more precise articulation of Sunni and Shiᶜi Islam.

PART III

The Consolidation of Islam, 750–1000

CHAPTER 12

Issues of Islamic identity

The master narrative of the two and a half centuries which followed the ᶜAbbasid Revolution might be characterized as one that took the institution of the caliphate from revolution to autocracy, and thence to disintegration and the concomitant fragmentation of the *umma* – that, at least, was the political framework within which radical transformations in the society and religious identity of Muslims transpired. What follows is a very brief sketch of some of the political highlights of the period, from the accession of al-Saffah, the first ᶜAbbasid caliph, to the end of the tenth century.[1]

In 762, al-Mansur, the second ᶜAbbasid caliph, established a new capital for the empire in Iraq. The foundation of Baghdad, which al-Mansur actually called the "City of Peace," reflected the growing tensions between the ᶜAbbasids and the supporters of ᶜAli's family, who were especially strong in Kufa, the principal Muslim settlement in Iraq which had served as the ᶜAbbasid caliphs' first capital. In many ways the city can stand as a metaphor for the character of the Islamic empire in this period, and for its greatness. The city, like the state of which it was the capital, was an ambitious enterprise. Much of it was occupied by and organized around explicitly imperial structures – palaces, gardens, vast reception halls – with a domed room housing the caliph's throne at the very center. Everything about the city – its spatial arrangement and decoration, the ceremony of the caliphs and their courtiers within it, its very location not far from the old Sasanian capital of Ctesiphon – signaled the unabashed absorption of pre-Islamic imperial traditions, as well as a sharpening of Iranian influence on the character of the civilization. And the whole was not without effect, if we are to believe the historian al-Tabari's famous account of the visit to Baghdad in 917 of Byzantine ambassadors who, though representing themselves a state with a well-developed imperial tradition and ceremonial, were suitably overwhelmed by the splendor of the ᶜAbbasid court and the majesty of the caliph.[2]

---

[1] The best comprehensive history of the ᶜAbbasid period can be found in Hugh Kennedy, *The Prophet and the Age of the Caliphate* (London: Longman, 1986).

[2] On Baghdad, its palaces, and the ideology behind them, see Oleg Grabar, *The Formation of Islamic Art* (New Haven: Yale University Press, 1973), 67–72, 166–78; Jacob Lassner, *The Topography of Baghdad in the Early Middle Ages* (Detroit: Wayne State University Press, 1970); and C. Wendell, "Baghdad: *Imago Mundi* and Other Foundation Lore," *International Journal of Middle East Studies* 2 (1971), 99–128.

Some Muslims came to think of Baghdad as the *omphalos*, the navel of the world, and so it is no surprise that the civilization and culture associated with the ᶜAbbasid capital has loomed large in later accounts of early Islamic history. The popular view is reflected, for example, in texts such as the *Thousand and One Nights*, in which many of the tales are set "in the days of Harun al-Rashid," the fifth ᶜAbbasid caliph (r. 786–809), even though the collection itself took its present shape many centuries later – as if to recall a golden age of prosperity and peace. Such Islamic viewpoints may also have encouraged some Western historians to think of the early ᶜAbbasid period as a sort of "classical" one, in which Islamic civilization, having outgrown the parochialism of an Arab faith, embraced a truly cosmopolitan world-view, and in which many of the norms and artifacts which defined "Islam" in later centuries took recognizable shape.[3] The grounds for such a viewpoint are obvious. From a political perspective, the ᶜAbbasids were markedly successful, at least until the middle of the ninth century. There was a tremendous concentration of wealth in cities like Baghdad, which provided the material foundations for a vibrant cultural life. Most importantly from our perspective, the late eighth and ninth centuries did see some consolidation of foundational texts and patterns of religious authority within the Muslim community – for example, in the early coalescence of the schools of law (*madhahib*), and the collection and writing down of the first and most important compilations of hadith. But the term "classical" is too strong, and deceptive if it is taken to imply that the state of Islam in this period constitutes a model against which all later incarnations and permutations must be measured. The period was one of growth, struggle, and contention, in which Muslims thought (and fought) very seriously about what it meant to be a Muslim, and in which those struggles took on ever greater significance, as the portion of the population which was Muslim grew relatively larger and as the *dhimmi* communities adapted themselves to a state of permanent inferiority. But much of what was later taken to be characteristic of Islam in fact took clearer shape in the centuries which followed those which form the subject of this chapter – in the period which has been identified as the "Middle Period" of Islamic history.

Moreover, from at least the mid–late ninth century, the political power of the central ᶜAbbasid administration was undermined and fragmented by developments both at the center and on the periphery, and some of these developments had a profound impact on the evolution of religious identities and practice. From at least the reign of al-Muᶜtasim (r. 833–42) on, the military power of the state centered on imported slaves, freedmen, and tribesmen hired as mercenaries, many of them of Turkish origin. These Turks and others, who replaced the Arab (and also Iranian) soldiers who had hitherto constituted the core of the Muslim armies, were extremely effective from a military standpoint. However, their mercenary ties to the state or to its leaders contrasted sharply with the religious and ethnic links

---

[3] As, for example, G. E. von Grunebaum, *Classical Islam: A History 600–1258* (Chicago: Aldine, 1970), esp. 7.

which had previously characterized the ties between the *umma* and its armies.[4] From this point on, therefore, the development of religious institutions and patterns of authority unfolded under circumstances characterized by the exclusion of native Muslim populations from military, and later political, power. This would have an especially great impact on the emergence of the religious scholars, the ulama, as a critical social group.

At roughly the same moment that the character of the military supporting the central state was transformed, that central authority itself began to succumb to centrifugal forces. While the caliphal regime remained a symbol of Islamic unity, effective political power in the provinces outside of Iraq passed into the hands of local regimes. In Egypt, for example, Ahmad ibn Tulun, a Turkish soldier sent out from Baghdad as governor of the province, established an autonomous local government which he was (briefly) able to pass on in dynastic fashion to his son. This pattern – of a nominal acknowledgment of caliphal authority overshadowed by administration of real power by a local regime – turned out to be characteristic of political arrangements in the Near East from the tenth century onward, at least until the Mongol destruction of the caliphate in Baghdad in 1258. Some of the local regimes had profound impact on religious developments. Various autonomous Iranian dynasties, for example that of the Samanids, cultivated a renascence of Persian culture and language, which would prove to be the medium for much medieval religious growth in Islam, especially in the area of Sufi mysticism. The Buyids, originally from the region of Daylam south of the Caspian Sea, actually occupied Baghdad in the mid-tenth century and, while formally acknowledging the position of the caliph, ruled the central provinces of the Islamic empire for over a century. That development was all the more striking as the Buyids were Shi'is, and it was under their patronage that Twelver Shi'ism began to take more explicit doctrinal form. The fragmentation of political power posed its most serious threat to Islamic unity, and to the ultimate authority of the caliphs, in the Fatimid regime. The Fatimids, as Isma'ili Shi'is, rejected completely the authority of the caliphs and established a rival Imamate which claimed for itself supreme religious authority and political sovereignty. The Fatimids established their capital in Cairo, in Egypt, but the Fatimid caliphate was recognized at different times much more widely: in North Africa, western Arabia (including the holy cities of Mecca and Medina), Yemen, parts of Syria, and places as far afield as Sind.

The articulation of a specifically Islamic tradition

As we saw in the previous chapter, there is some controversy as to the point at which we can safely speak of a distinctive Islamic tradition. It is likely that what

[4] On the new military patterns, see Patricia Crone, *Slaves on Horses: The Evolution of the Islamic Polity* (Cambridge: Cambridge University Press, 1980); Daniel Pipes, *Slave Soldiers and Islam: The Genesis of a Military System* (New Haven: Yale University Press, 1981); and Matthew Gordon, *The Breaking of a Thousand Swords: A History of the Turkish Military of Samarra, AH 200–275/815–889 CE* (Albany, NY: SUNY Press, 2001).

later generations would recognize as a distinctively Islamic identity did not exist in anything but a very rudimentary state at the death of the Prophet. On the other hand, by the middle of the eighth century, the ᶜAbbasids were able to lead an insurgency on explicitly Islamic grounds, advancing a process which was already well underway when the Dome of the Rock was built at the end of the seventh century. Even so, the process was by no means complete, and further developments were both enriched and complicated by the nature of the ᶜAbbasids' success.

One can trace the outlines of the fuller articulation of the Islamic tradition in its relations with its sister religions, Judaism and Christianity, in this period. As we saw in the last chapter, there was considerable exchange of ideas and stories between Muslims, Jews and Christians in Islam's early years, for example, in the form of narratives about the pre-Islamic prophets known collectively as the isra'iliyyat. Those exchanges mark not only a relatively open cultural atmosphere, but also the fluidity of religious identities at the time, a fluidity perhaps encouraged by the oral nature of cultural transmission.[5] The preference among Muslims for the oral transmission of texts is well known, and is reflected in the very terms by which the earliest Muslim texts are known – hadith, for example, meaning "narrative," "story," or "news," that is, "something that is talked about." But the ninth century was one in which those orally-transmitted texts took a more definitive written form. It was then, for example, that Muhammad ibn Ismaᶜil al-Bukhari (d. 870) and Muslim ibn al-Hajjaj (d. 875) produced their compilations of hadith, each titled the Sahih, the "sound" or "healthy" (i.e., marking the hadith they included as genuine and authoritative), compilations which over time acquired a definitive, almost iconic status among Sunni Muslims. In part, this represented the growing importance of the sunna, the normative practice of Muhammad, in the delineation of Muslim standards and practice, for that sunna was known principally through the hadith. But it also reflected the inscription of authority, and its corollary was the assertion by the ulama, the scholars of the religious and legal sciences, of their principal responsibility for defining and defending the Islamic tradition – a development which we will discuss more fully below and in the following section. Not surprisingly, therefore, this was also the period when the isra'iliyyat acquired a suspect reputation among most of the ulama, and while they continued to be transmitted as entertainment and in popular preaching circles, the very term isra'ilyyat came to have a negative connotation.[6] In such ways did Muslims begin to assert the independence and exclusivist identity of their religion.

---

[5] A point made by Reuven Firestone, Journeys in Holy Lands: The Evolution of the Abraham–Ishmael Legends in Islamic Exegesis (Albany, NY: SUNY Press, 1990), 15–18.

[6] Gordon Newby, "Tafsir Isra'iliyat: The Development of Qur'an Commentary in Early Islam in its Relationship to Judaeo-Christian Traditions of Scriptural Commentary," Journal of the American Academy of Religion 47, Thematic issue S (1980), 685–97. Newby, however, sees this as a marker that the Muslim "community turned toward the inner values of Islam after the period of seeking external confirmation" (694). That approach strikes me as too essentialist. It makes more sense, I think, to see it as part of a longer-term process by which Islam first asserted its distinct identity, rather than as one in which Muslims returned to the "true" Muslim path.

One of the principal unresolved tensions concerned the cultural orientation of the new faith. We have seen how questions of Arab, even tribal identity continued to shape the political life of the Islamic community right down to the ᶜAbbasid revolution. The central importance of a sacred scripture self-consciously revealed in Arabic made some sort of link between Arab cultural orientation and Islam unbreakable. From certain perspectives, especially the linguistic, it was Arabian Islam that triumphed. The Islamic government had already begun to use Arabic as a language of administration under the Umayyads, and in much of the Near East, the momentum was unstoppable, as Arabic gradually squeezed out other languages such as Syriac and Coptic, either eliminating them or reducing them to local liturgical usage. The issues of Arabization and Islamization are related but not identical, and on the whole the Arabs' language spread further and faster than did their religion, at least in the western regions of the Islamic world. In Palestine by the late eighth and ninth centuries, even Christians from the Melkite Church were writing in Arabic, and – which suggests that Arabic was in common usage among their congregants – translating older liturgical works from Greek into the conquerors' tongue. Similarly in Egypt, while Coptic survived longer as a spoken language in some remote villages, by at least the tenth century it was being largely eclipsed, among Christians as well as native Egyptian Muslims, by Arabic.[7] It is notable that the one Near Eastern language which survived on a large scale (albeit in a form heavily influenced by Arabic) was that of the non-Arab cultural tradition which, in the years following the ᶜAbbasid revolution, shaped Islam more than any other: namely, Persian.

The question of the cultural orientation of Islam is closely linked to that of conversion to the new faith on the part of the native inhabitants of the territories conquered by the Arabs. The empirical evidence available on the subject is intriguing but limited, and the few attempts which have been made to put it to systematic use have been controversial. Still, we may carefully venture a few propositions. In the first place, the process had begun in a limited way already in the decades before the ᶜAbbasid seizure of power. During the conquests, many defeated soldiers, their families, and other captives were enslaved and, later, manumitted after embracing the new faith. The number of converts increased during the later Umayyad period, as the government, especially in Iraq, tightened its methods of tax collection, inadvertently encouraging the flight of (non-Muslim) peasants from the land. Some of these peasants (those who were not caught and sent back to their villages) ended up in the garrison towns established to house and to isolate the Muslim Arab immigrants, and successful integration into those societies effectively required their conversion. The pace of conversion only

---

[7] Sidney H. Griffith, "The View of Islam from the Monasteries of Palestine in the Early ᶜAbbāsid Period: Theodore Abū Qurrah and the *Summa Theologiae Arabica*," *Islam and Christian-Muslim Relations* 7 (1996), 9–28; W. B. Bishai, "The Transition from Coptic to Arabic," *The Muslim World* 53 (1963), 145–50; Ira M. Lapidus, "The Conversion of Egypt to Islam," *Israel Oriental Studies* 2 (1972), 248–62; L S. B. MacCoull, "Three Cultures Under Arab Rule: The Fate of Coptic," *Bulletin de la Société d'Archéologie Copte* 27 (1985), 61–70; and idem, "The Strange Death of Coptic Culture," *Coptic Church Review* 10 (1989), 35–45.

quickened during the first century of 'Abbasid rule, although there must have been tremendous regional variation. Places such as Egypt and Syria, for example, retained considerable non-Muslim minorities down into the modern period. In Iran, after a slow start, conversion probably proceeded more quickly, so that, by the beginning of the tenth century, the new religion was demographically as well as politically dominant. Secondly, converts came from a variety of different social classes. At first, most were probably from lower social orders – prisoners of war, slaves, and those peasants driven from their farms by oppressive taxation. But certainly some of the upper classes of the non-Arab peoples who came under Muslim rule converted – one need think only of Ibn al-Muqaffaᶜ, *mawla*, belle-lettrist, and officer of the state in the first years of ᶜAbbasid rule, who came from a noble Iranian family, or the various Barmakids, officials and ministers to several ᶜAbbasid caliphs, at least one of whose ancestors probably held important religious (Buddhist) positions before their descendants converted to Islam.[8]

Finally, the growing numbers of non-Arab converts enriched the new religion and the culture which grew up around it, contributing significantly to the shape taken by Islam in these and later centuries; we will trace some of those contributions in the remainder of this chapter. Whether Islam became a majority religion in most regions of the Near East in the eighth century or the ninth or even later, at some point the number of Muslims whose ancestry was non-Arab must have come to outnumber the descendants of the original conquerors. Of course the situation was increasingly confused by inter-marriage, and despite the rather strong feelings which miscegenation could stir up – an Umayyad governor of Mecca had once had a non-Arab *mawla* flogged, and had the man's hair and beard removed, for his temerity in marrying an Arab woman, while the essayist and polemicist al-Jahiz in the ᶜAbbasid period could still compare intermarriage between Arabs and non-Arab converts to fornication with donkeys and mules – it must in practice have become the rule rather than the exception. But the triumph in much of the Near East of the Arabic language, and of what would in the modern world be called an Arab ethnic identity, cannot disguise the considerable contributions of non-Arabs to the historical construction of Islam. Such contributions became considerably more pronounced in the years following the ᶜAbbasid seizure of power, as the number of converts grew, as the capital shifted to the east and as the state began to rely more markedly on Persian clients and even the older Iranian imperial traditions.[9]

[8] See Richard Bulliet, *Conversion to Islam in the Medieval Period* (Cambridge, Mass.: Harvard UP, 1979); Michael G. Morony, "The Age of Conversions: A Reassessment," in *Conversion and Continuity: Indigenous Christian Communities in Islamic Lands, Eighth to Eighteenth Centuries*, ed. Michael Gervers and Ramzi Jibran Bikhazi (Toronto: Pontifical Institute of Mediaeval Studies, 1990) (Papers in Mediaeval Studies 9), 135–50; and Crone, *Slaves on Horses*, esp. 50–55.

[9] On the dynamics of "social conversion," see Bulliet, *Conversion to Islam*, 35–40. The same author, in *Islam: The View from the Edge* (New York: Columbia University Press, 1994), stresses the contributions of non-Arab Muslims in the formation of Islam. The citation to al-Jahiz can be found in that work in a note on p. 213, while the incident in Mecca, taken from Abū'l-Faraj al-Isfahānī's *Kitāb al-Aghānī* (Cairo, 1929), 16:107, is cited in Roy Mottahdeh, "The Shuᶜūbīyah Controversy and the Social History of Early Islamic Iran," *International Journal of Middle East Studies* 7 (1976), 174–5.

Islam: an urban phenomenon?

Much scholarship on early Islamic civilization has affirmed its fundamentally urban character. Part of the argument's appeal stems from the fact that it flies in the face of so many Western stereotypes which link Islam to the desert Arabs and to a nomadic lifestyle. So, for example, historians have cited the central importance to Muslim self-definition of communal prayer, the coming together of the male Muslim population for prayers and exhortation on Fridays at noon in a *masjid jami*^c (literally, a "gathering mosque" or "collecting mosque"), to Muslim self-definition. Christian ascetics in Egypt and elsewhere had fled the temptations of the towns and escaped to the desert, in a process known as *anachoresis*; but the Muslim jurists spoke of migration from the countryside to the city as a *hijra*, valorizing the migration by employing the term used to describe the archetypal "flight" of Muhammad to Yathrib to avoid persecution in Mecca. A famous hadith, which may reflect less the attitudes of Muslims in the Prophet's own day than the biases and expectations of the urban jurists as they crystallized during the early ^cAbbasid period, purports to quote Muhammad as saying: "What I fear for my people is milk, where the devil lurks between the froth and the cream. They will love to drink it and will return to the desert, leaving the places where men pray together."[10]

Too much perhaps can be made of an urban bias in the formation of Islamic society and Islamic attitudes. To some extent, the perception may be an optical illusion, a product of the urban origin of the surviving source material, most of which comes from a high literary tradition which was closely associated with life in the cities. Moreover, the spread of Islam from Arabia to the more populous regions of the Near East certainly constitutes one instance of a larger pattern, of the periodic intrusion into settled regions of nomadic peoples living on its periphery. As we have seen, the Arab tribal element remained an important factor in the politics of the nascent Islamic state, at least down to the ^cAbbasid Revolution. Finally, one can point to the continuing importance of certain non-urban or at least non-metropolitan regions to the development of Islamic ideas, values, and practices. In the early ^cAbbasid period, special mention should be made of the frontier areas, particularly that separating the Islamic and Byzantine empires. The frontier was necessarily a preoccupation of a state which found a portion of its ideological justification in waging *jihad* to expand the borders of the "house of Islam," and some of the early ^cAbbasid caliphs took their responsibilities to the frontier and its

---

[10] See, for example, W. Marçais, "Islamisme et la vie urbaine," *Comptes rendus de l'Académie des Inscriptions* (1928), 86–100; Xavier de Planhol, "The Geographical Setting," *Cambridge History of Islam* (Cambridge: Cambridge University Press, 1970), 2.445–7; G. E. von Grunebaum, *Medieval Islam: A Study in Cultural Orientation*, 2nd edition (Chicago: University of Chicago Press, 1953), 173–4; idem, "The Structure of the Muslim Town," in *Islam: Essays on the Nature and Growth of a Cultural Tradition* (London: Routledge, 1964), 141–58; and also now Paul Wheatley, *The Places Where Men Pray Together: Cities in Islamic Lands, Seventh Through the Tenth Centuries* (Chicago: University of Chicago Press, 2001). The hadith can be found in Aḥmad ibn Ḥanbal, *Musnad* (Cairo: Dār al-Maʿārif, 1956), 2:176.

expansion especially seriously. This region, in northern Mesopotamia and Syria and south-eastern Anatolia, was of course not devoid of cities, but it was removed from the more familiar metropolises such as Baghdad and Damascus. And here, in figures such as ʿAbdallah ibn al-Mubarak (d. 797) and the pious warrior Ibrahim ibn Adham (d. 777–8), there crystallized a distinctive Islamic ascetic tradition which, over time, would take on a mystical dimension and so have an impact on the religious movement which came to be known as Sufism.[11]

But that Islam should take shape in a largely urban milieu – or more precisely that the Islam that developed in an urban context should acquire a normative character among those who called themselves Muslim – is hardly surprising, given the long history of urban life and culture of those lands which, after the initial conquests, formed the heart of Islamdom. By the latter half of the eighth century, the garrison camps constructed for the conquering Arab armies, such as Kufa and Basra, had become real cities in which the Arab settlers, despite the fact that many of them had (or claimed) nomadic roots and that they were originally distributed along tribal lines, had become in fact town dwellers. The foundation of Baghdad itself testifies to the urban orientation of the Muslim elite. The process of conversion on the part of non-Arabs may have functioned in such a way as to strengthen the urban character of the crystallizing Islamic tradition. In a world in which religious identity was so closely linked to social status, the very act of conversion may have stimulated a movement to the cities, that is, to the places in which the convert would be more likely to find those social networks in which he could live his new life as a Muslim.[12]

In fact, the late eighth and ninth centuries were, at least in the heartland of the Islamic empire in Iraq and eastern Iran, a period of considerable urban growth. Baghdad, and later Samarra, the new capital founded by the caliph al-Mutawakkil north of Baghdad, were ʿAbbasid creations, and both became (and Baghdad long remained) major urban centers, the population of Baghdad dwarfing by a factor of ten or more the nearby Sasanian capital of Ctesiphon. The vitality of these cities is critical to an understanding of the religious history of this period, as they provided the crucible for the development of Islamic values and institutions.[13]

This is most clearly visible in Islamic law as it took shape in precisely this period. The Islamic tradition is historically continuous with the Arabian context in which it originated, and tribal concerns had a role in giving that tradition its initial impetus. But the tradition was a living one, which means that the law was shaped as much by the contingencies of the moment as by an increasingly remote and idealized past. So, for example, while Islamic law insists upon the collective

[11] On asceticism on the frontier, see Michael Bonner, *Aristocratic Violence and Holy War: Studies in the Jihad and the Arab-Byzantine Frontier* (New Haven: American Oriental Society, 1996), 107–34.

[12] See Bulliet, *Conversion to Islam*, esp. 49–54, and idem, *Islam: The View from the Edge* (New York: Columbia University Press, 1994), 67–79.

[13] On the size of Baghdad and Samarra, see Bulliet, *Islam*, 131; Robert McC. Adams, *The Land Behind Baghdad: A History of Settlement on the Diyala Plains* (Chicago: University of Chicago Press, 1965), 84–102.

responsibility of the social group for, say, the harm inflicted by one individual on another, that law was not simply a relic of ancient tribal practice. It was also a practical response to the pressures evident in the new Muslim cities. There, an individual's social status rested on his membership in larger groups: on the one hand, in religious communities, and on the other, within the Muslim collective, in social units which were still identified by (an increasingly fictive) tribal genealogy but which functioned now primarily as a means of assimilating non-Arab converts and of imparting a sense of social identity in large and growing urban conglomerations.[14] Many of the jurists and scholars who shaped Islamic law were themselves merchants or from commercial families, and so the *shariᶜa* quite naturally reflects the tastes and priorities of the urban middle classes. Islamic law constitutes more a discursive tradition informed by competing principles than a fixed body of rules, and so generalizations are inevitably dangerous; but the values of thrift, a disciplined work ethic, and – within the limits imposed by a society in which a person's status was so contingent on that of a larger social or religious group – individual privacy, responsibility, and initiative are readily apparent in the writings of the early jurists. One of the more colorful examples is found in a treatise, *Kitab al-Kasb* (roughly, "on earning"), attributed to the Hanafi jurist al-Shaybani (d. 804), which reports a story about ᶜUmar ibn al-Khattab. The caliph saw a group of pious and penitent (and inactive) men and, told that they were the *mutawakkilun*, "those who patiently rely upon God," responded: No, they are the *mutaᵓakillun*, "those who eat up [other people's money]."[15]

Much of Islamic law is designed to encourage the commercial spirit. The extensive sections of the law books which deal with sales, partnerships, and other commercial matters afford merchants a considerable freedom to enter into binding contracts, at least in so far as those contracts do not violate basic Islamic principles. So, for example, the Islamic lawyers would generally not allow the law to be used to enforce the sale of a forbidden substance, say, wine; but they also took it upon themselves to develop a series of "tricks" (*hiyal*), that is, legal manoeuvers which enabled them to give tacit acceptance to practices (such as the taking of interest on loans) which, while offensive to certain religious principles (usury is explicitly condemned in the Koran), were nonetheless essential to the smooth functioning of an urban, mercantile economy. More significantly, the lawyers recognized the claims of "custom" (*ᶜurf*) in the resolution of disputes and the setting of commercial standards – the custom, that is, of the urban marketplaces. The role of custom is even more prominent in the jurisdiction and activities of the official known as the *muhtasib*. Usually translated as "market inspector," the *muhtasib*'s authority was rooted partly in the Koranic injunction to "command what is good and forbid what is wrong," a religious obligation incumbent on Muslims generally. More specifically, however, he also had a responsibility to insure that commercial transactions were completed fairly and honestly. The office

[14] Norman Calder, *Studies in Early Muslim Jurisprudence* (Oxford: Clarendon Press, 1993), 198–208.
[15] See S. D. Goitein, "The Rise of the Middle Eastern Bourgeoisie in Early Islamic Times," in *Studies in Islamic History and Institutions* (Leiden: E. J. Brill, 1966), 217–41.

of the *muhtasib* probably did not derive directly from that of the *agoranomos* and other officials who supervised market affairs in the ancient and late antique worlds, as a previous generation of Western scholars assumed, but his prominence in medieval Islamic cities did testify more generally to the continuity of religious experience in the late antique and Islamic Near East and to the importance of cities and the commercial milieu as the crucible in which Islamic law took shape.[16]

All this is not to suggest that early Islamic cities were a sort of Whiggish paradise of a liberal and libertarian character. There were competing actors and values, as well as contradictory principles and impulses which were woven into the fabric of the law and of the social experience of religion. Those contradictions are especially visible in Muslim women's experience of the Islamic reality. The status and position of women in early and medieval Islamic societies is an especially complex topic, due in part to the multiple layers of cultural and religious suspicion through which Western observers have historically contemplated and criticized Islam, and cannot be dealt with adequately here. But it may serve for the moment to observe that women provide a revealing focus into the tensions and contradictions of Islamic jurisprudence and the relationship between legal theory and social practice. On the one hand, Islamic law accorded women a number of rights and privileges commensurate with the law's general respect for human dignity, responsibility and equality, rights and privileges which eclipsed those held by women in many (including Western) pre-modern societies – the right, for example, of a married woman to own and inherit property in her own right, property which was not at the disposal of her husband. On the other, a number of debilitating social customs were able to attach themselves to Muslim values and so achieved recognition and valorization, either through the law itself or through popular interpretation of legal principles. So, for example, while the custom of ritually excising the external genitalia of women was never universally practiced in the Islamic world, those Near Eastern Muslims who did practice it were able to perpetuate and disseminate it by describing it as a means of protecting the sexual honor of Muslim women, and so justifying it in the name of preserving sexual decorum, an important concern of the Islamic jurists.[17]

---

[16] On the *muhtasib* and his jurisdiction, see Benjamin R. Foster, "Agoranomos and Muhtasib," *Journal of the Economic and Social History of the Orient* 13 (1970), 128–44, and R. P. Buckley, "The Muhtasib," *Arabica* 39 (1992), 59–117. Michael Cook has thoroughly studied the consequences of the Koranic injunction to "command what is right and forbid what is wrong" in *Commanding Right and Forbidding Wrong in Islamic Thought* (Cambridge: Cambridge University Press, 2000). For a case study of the influence of the bourgeoisie on Islamic law, see Abraham L. Udovitch, *Partnership and Profit in Medieval Islam* (Princeton: Princeton University Press, 1970).

[17] On female excision, see Jonathan P. Berkey, "Circumcision Circumscribed: Female Excision and Cultural Accommodation in the Medieval Near East," *International Journal of Middle East Studies* 28 (1996), 19–38. There is of course an extensive literature on the question of women and gender in Islamic society and law, of very uneven quality, much of it of more polemical than historical value. Readers interested in broad introductions to the subject might be best advised to await the forthcoming volume in the present Cambridge series, by Leslie Peirce and Everett Rowson. A very brief introduction can be found in Jonathan P. Berkey, "Women in Medieval Islamic Society," in *Women in Medieval Western European Culture*, ed. Linda E. Mitchell (New York: Garland, 1999), 95–111. If approached with caution, Leila Ahmed's *Women and Gender in Islam: Historical Roots of a Modern Debate* (New Haven: Yale University Press, 1992) is a stimulating discussion.

Other elements in early Islamic society competed with the urban bourgeoisie, in particular the imperial and aristocratic orientation of the caliphs, their court, and the government scribes. And it is important to remember that Islamic law took shape at precisely the same moment that alien military elites secured a monopoly over real political power that was to last down to the modern period. In other words, the cultural and social power of which the *shariʿa* is a reflection carried with it no guaranteed access to the actual mechanisms of rule, and so politics in the later centuries would consist of constant negotiation between the Turkish military rulers and the native Muslim elites. But the contribution of the urban middle classes to the parameters of Islamic civilization as they took shape in this period was decisive, if only because of the persistent centrality of the *shariʿa* to Islamic identity. It is true that Sufism, which much later became an important, perhaps even dominant mode of Islamic piety, rejected or at least looked with suspicion on many of the values and principles of the jurists. But asceticism, even while rejecting bourgeois values, inadvertently reaffirms their significance; and in the later medieval Near Eastern urban landscape, the Sufi was as much a fixture as the merchant or judge.

CHAPTER 13

Religion and politics

As we have seen, the issue of leadership was a point of serious contention in early Islamic society, so it comes as no surprise that the ᶜAbbasid state was plagued from the beginning by disputes over the identity and legitimacy of the ruler. There was a bloody tone to these disputes, for which the ᶜAbbasids themselves are partly responsible, since upon coming to power they set an unfortunate precedent with their slaughter of as many members of the Umayyad family as they could find. To some extent the violence was simply a product of inter- and intra-dynastic disputes, without any particular ideological significance: when al-Mansur had the chief ᶜAbbasid propagandist and the prime organizer of the ᶜAbbasid revolt Abu Muslim murdered, on one level he was simply removing a dangerous alternative locus of power. But the violence and the challenges to the persons and authority of the ᶜAbbasid caliphs also had a deeply religious coloring. The bloody treatment of the Umayyads was partly the product of the apocalyptic overtones of the movement which swept the ᶜAbbasids to power. The assassination of Abu Salama, another leading propagandist and servant of that movement, at the instigation of the first caliph al-Saffah, probably reflected lingering tensions over who the ruler should be and disappointment among some in the movement's ranks that the "chosen one from the family of Muhammad" had turned out not to be a descendant of ᶜAli ibn Abi Talib. Nor did at least the *idea* of an Umayyad alternative to ᶜAbbasid rule disappear altogether. There were a number of pro-Umayyad rebellions in Syria during the first years of the new dynasty, which suggests that the ᶜAbbasid "triumph" was less complete at first than might otherwise be thought. More significantly, the struggle for the leadership of the Islamic state continued to have a religious dimension. Widespread apocalyptic expectations of the return of a messianic "Sufyanid" (i.e., a descendant of the Umayyad caliph Muᶜawiya ibn Abi Sufyan) provided the vehicle for expressions of disapproval of the ᶜAbbasids well into the ninth century.[1]

---

[1] On the complicated history of Sufyanid apocalypticism, and on continuing problems posed by Umayyad claimants in the early ᶜAbbasid period, see Wilferd Madelung, "Apocalyptic Prophecies in Ḥimṣ in the Umayyad Age," *Journal of Semitic Studies* 31 (1986), 141–85; idem, "The Sufyānī Between Tradition and History," *Studia Islamica* 63 (1986), 5–48; and Paul Cobb, *White Banners: Contention in ᶜAbbasid Syria, 750–880* (Albany, NY: SUNY Press, 2001), 43–65.

Beyond the issue of who should rule lay that of the nature of the ruler's authority, and on this question the ᶜAbbasids found disagreement even among those who supported their rule. The caliphs benefited from the reluctance of many Muslims to inflict civil strife upon the community by challenging the political authority of the rulers. So, for example, Ahmad ibn Hanbal, despite having suffered at the hands of the caliph's agents during the *mihna* (see below), nonetheless declared that

> whoever rebels against one of the Imams of the Muslims – once the people have agreed upon him, and acknowledged him as caliph, in any manner, whether out of pleasure [with him] or by force – that rebel has broken with the community, and deviated from the traditional practice handed down from the Prophet of God … Fighting against authority [*sultan*, here, the Imam-caliph's authority] is not permitted, nor is anyone permitted to rebel against it. Whoever does so is an unlawful innovator, outside the *sunna* and the way.[2]

But the relationship of political to religious authority was a matter of considerable contention and evolution during the first centuries of ᶜAbbasid rule. These issues were central to the distinction between what came to be called Sunni and Shiᶜi Islam, a distinction which was clarified in precisely this period. It would be anachronistic, therefore, to expect a clear articulation of the differences at the beginning of the ᶜAbbasid era, but with the advantage of hindsight, the issue can be expressed as a contradiction. In Sunni Islam, there is no necessary connection between political and religious authority: prophethood as a legislative project came to an end with Muhammad, and what religious authority remained devolved upon the ulama as expressed through their consensus. (In fact, of course, the matter is rather more complicated than this concise description would suggest, and its ambiguities, and the course of their development, will form the subject of much that follows.) In practice, however, the caliphs (and later rulers with other titles) addressed themselves to and intervened in religious issues both directly and indirectly. In Shiᶜi Islam, by contrast, religious authority is in theory closely connected to political authority, both being vested in the person of the Imam. In practice, however, while there was nothing to prevent Shiᶜis giving substance to their Imams' claims to religious authority, their political authority proved completely chimerical (at least until the rise of the Fatimids in the tenth century).[3]

There were plenty of sources on which the ᶜAbbasids could draw in an effort to articulate and make permanent the authority of the caliph over religious matters. As we have seen, the Umayyad caliphs themselves, for all of their reputation among some Muslims as godless profligates and secular kings, had had considerable influence over the shaping of Islamic practice at an early stage in the

---

[2] Ibn Abī Yaᶜlā, *Ṭabaqāt al-ḥanābila*, 2 vols. (Cairo: Maṭbaᶜat al-Sunna al-Muḥammadiyya, 1952), 1.244.

[3] Said Arjomand defines the contradiction in *The Shadow of God and the Hidden Imam: Religion, Political Order, and Societal Change in Shiᶜite Iran from the Beginning to 1890* (Chicago: University of Chicago Press, 1984), 32–9.

tradition's formation. Under the influence of Persian courtiers and scribes, the ʿAbbasids also drew upon older Sasanian models which positioned the ruler at the apex of a structure of religious authority, dispensing justice on behalf of God. But the effort encountered considerable resistance. A critical opportunity was missed early in the new era, during the reign of the second ʿAbbasid caliph, al-Mansur. Observing the inconsistencies in the emerging Islamic legal system in which the standards applied reflected the living and evolving (and therefore irregular) *sunna* or "practice" of the community, the Persian scribe and belle-lettrist Ibn al-Muqaffaʿ urged the caliph to regularize the system by, in effect, codifying the law. That is, he urged the caliph to invoke his prerogative as ruler to determine what the law would be, rather than leaving it to the decentralized authority of the qadis and early jurists. Had the proposal been adopted and successfully imposed, the result would have been a ruling institution more closely approximating the Sasanian monarchy, with the caliph supervising a subservient religious hierarchy who were in effect, even if not in name, priests.[4]

The Sasanian model did have a considerable impact on the shape and public projection of the caliph and his office under the ʿAbbasids. Under the influence of Persian courtiers and bureaucrats, and also of the enormous wealth which accrued to them, the caliphs grew to be remote and awesome figures. Court ceremonial stressed the incomparable majesty of the caliph, separating him from public view and demanding graphic demonstrations of obedience and subservience from those permitted to approach him. The well-known *Kitab al-Taj* ("Book of the Crown"), describing life and ceremonial at the caliphal court in the ninth century and sometimes attributed to the famous litterateur al-Jahiz, paints a picture of an Islamic ruler reminiscent of the Sasanian shahs, but which Muhammad and his companions would hardly have recognized.

But the failure to adopt Ibn al-Muqaffaʿ's proposals reflected an underlying process of disengaging religious from political authority. The "inquisition" (*mihna*) inaugurated by the caliph al-Maʾmun (r. 813–33) and its ultimate failure represented the denouement of this historical drama. Under the terms of the *mihna*, al-Maʾmun and his immediate successors imposed a test on *qadis* and other religious figures, requiring them to conform publically to the doctrine of the createdness of the Koran, a position associated with the theological school of the Muʿtazila. What is of particular interest about the *mihna* is less the theological dimension than the impact of the struggle on the relationship of caliphal and religious authority. The *mihna* may have been connected to al-Maʾmun's efforts to reconcile the ʿAbbasids to the Shiʿa, and in that context his effort to determine the contours of acceptable religious thought brought the office of the caliph more closely into line with the Shiʿi conception of the Imam – a title which al-Maʾmun explicitly took for himself. But the notion that the caliph, as the "deputy of God" (*khalifat allah*), had a responsibility and authority over religious matters was one

---

[4] Ibn al-Muqaffaʿ's suggestions are discussed in S. D. Goitein, "A Turning Point in the History of the Muslim State," in *Studies in Islamic History and Institutions* (Leiden: E. J. Brill, 1966), 149–67.

that had non-Shi'i roots as well. In the fourth and fifth decades of the ninth century, however, when al-Ma'mun and, after him, the caliphs al-Mu'tasim and al-Wathiq sought to deny a public platform for those who insisted that the Koran was uncreated and eternal, the effort encountered resistance, most famously by the popular traditionist Ahmad ibn Hanbal. Ibn Hanbal was subjected to imprisonment and torture, and whether he heroically resisted, maintaining a principled insistence on the uncreated nature of the Koran and the literal force of its words, or capitulated after the flogging had begun (the reports are contradictory on this point), his opposition to the official creed was shared by other religious scholars, particularly the partisans of the Prophetic traditions (the *ahl al-hadith*) as the locus of authoritative religious knowledge and guidance. The position of the traditionalists and religious scholars grouped around Ibn Hanbal enjoyed considerable support among the population of Baghdad. In the face of continuing opposition, the new caliph al-Mutawakkil abandoned the *mihna* shortly after his accession in 847. The bottom line was clear: the failure of the *mihna* marked the definitive triumph of the ulama, rather than the caliph, as the principal locus of religious authority in Islam.[5]

It is important to understand the *mihna* and its fallout on their own terms, in the context of the development of a specifically Islamic constellation of political and religious power, and not as an attenuated reflection of ideas and institutions of European genealogy. So we should not look at the failure of al-Ma'mun's *mihna* as an indication that Islam developed in its early years anything approximating the modern, Western doctrine of the "separation of church and state." Political and religious authority are deeply connected in most discussions of them which have arisen in a Muslim context, since what we can call "political science" forms "a department or branch of theology."[6] Ideologically the 'Abbasid regime was rooted in a promise to make Islam the centerpiece of social and political organization, and so the caliphs inevitably took an interest in religious matters. The regnal names of the early 'Abbasids had a messianic tone, and suggest a self-conscious identification of their interests and role with that of religion, or even God: al-Mansur,

---

[5] An excellent account of the *mihna* can be found in Martin Hinds' article on the subject in the *Encyclopaedia of Islam*. For other discussions, see W. M. Patton, *Ahmed Ibn Ḥanbal and the Miḥna* (Leiden: E. J. Brill, 1897); Dominique Sourdel, "La politique religieuse du calife 'abbaside al-Ma'mun," *Revue des études islamiques* 30 (1962), 27–48, esp. 42–4; Ira Lapidus, "The Separation of State and Religion in the Development of Early Islamic Society," *International Journal of Middle East Studies* 6 (1975), 363–85; Patricia Crone and Martin Hinds, *God's Caliph: Religious Authority in the First Century of Islam* (Cambridge: Cambridge University Press, 1986), 92–7; John Nawas, "A Reexamination of Three Current Explanations for al-Ma'mun's Introduction of the *Miḥna*," *International Journal of Middle East Studies* 26 (1994), 615–29; Bulliet, *Islam: The View from the Edge*, 118–19; Michael Cooperson, *Classical Arabic Biography: The Heirs of the Prophet in the Age of al-Ma'mūn* (Cambridge: Cambridge University Press, 2000), 33–40, and 107–53. For a different reading of the *mihna*, see Muhammad Qasim Zaman, *Religion and Politics under the Early 'Abbasids: The Emergence of the Proto-Sunni Elite* (Leiden: Brill, 1997).

[6] The phrase is A. K. S. Lambton's, from *State and Government in Medieval Islam: An Introduction to the Study of Islamic Political Theory: The Jurists* (Oxford: Oxford University Press, 1981), 1, a useful survey of juristic discussions of Islamic rulership. A briefer account can be found in *EI²*, art. "Imāma" (by W. Madelung).

"the one granted victory [by God]," or al-Mahdi, "the one who is rightly-guided [by God]."[7] The ʿAbbasids ostentatiously draped themselves in the cloak of religion, literally, in fact, through their careful preservation of the Prophet's "mantle" (*burda*), which they donned in public on solemn occasions. Even after the collapse of the *mihna*, the ʿAbbasid caliphs performed essential functions within the religious sphere, for example through the patronage of scholars and some limited encouragement of the collection and propagation of religious knowledge (*ʿilm*).[8]

But the underlying trajectory of Islamic history, in the wake of the execution of Ibn al-Muqaffaʿ and the failure of the *mihna*, made the ulama, and not the caliph, the arbiters of religious authority. Caliphs might still take an interest in religious affairs: they might, for example, participate actively in the public transmission of hadith, the fundamental activity of those engaged in the cultivation of the religious sciences. Their doing so, however, constituted a tacit acknowledgment that, once the caliphs had abandoned any claims to the divine authority the Shiʿis invested in their Imams, the process of defining the religious tradition was fundamentally under the control of the ulama. The central ideological component of that process was the doctrine of *ijmaʿ*, "consensus," a point to which we will return shortly. From a historical perspective, however, these developments seem most important as a sign that the traditionalist ulama, those committed to the cultivation and propagation of religious knowledge rooted in the Koran and especially the practice of Muhammad (*sunna*) as recorded in hadith, had emerged as an important social group, one that would henceforth have a predominant role in the shaping of the religion.[9] Al-Mutawakkil's action in bringing the mihna to a close can be read as representing a dramatic acknowledgment of the fact. In the year 849, he called together a number of legal scholars and hadith transmitters (*muhaddithun*) and after distributing to them gifts and allotting them stipends, instructed them to go out among the people and recite hadith condemning the doctrines of the Muʿtazila.[10] A few years later, support for the traditionalists was so strong that an individual publicly professing doctrines inimical to their own could risk a fatal attack at the hands of the ulama's supporters among the masses.[11] (In the late twelfth and early thirteenth centuries, there was an effort to revive caliphal religious authority. But the caliph al-Nasir sought to implement his program of reform in a very different religious environment – he relied heavily, for example, on the Sufi orders that were then prominent. And in any case, his reforms, for all their excitement and promise, came to naught.)

---

[7] Bernard Lewis, "The Regnal Titles of the First Abbasid Caliphs," In *Dr Zakir Husain Presentation Volume* (New Delhi, 1968), 13–22.

[8] Zaman, *Religion and Politics*, 12, makes an argument for a defining pattern of "collaboration between the caliphs and the ʿulamā".

[9] Crone and Hinds, *God's Caliph*, esp. 92–97.

[10] Al-Khaṭīb al-Baghdādī, *Tārīkh baghdād*, 14 vols. (Beirut: Dār al-Kitāb al-ʿArabī, 1966), 10.67, cited in Zaman, *Religion and Politics*, 145.

[11] Ibn Qutayba, *Taʾwīl mukhtalif al-ḥadīth* (Cairo: Maṭbaʿat Kurdistān al-ʿIlmiyya, 1326 A.H.), 20, cited in Zaman, *Religion and Politics*, 168.

What is really startling about this caliphal abandonment of any pretensions to special religious authority is that it occurred at the same moment in which circumstances were depriving the caliphs of effective *political* authority as well. It is this which helps to explain why, within a few years of the very anti-traditionalist *mihna*, the most traditionalist of the ulama had become the most ardent supporters of the institution of the caliphate. For the ulama, the ʿAbbasid caliphs, having abandoned the revolutionary Shiʿi fervor which brought them to power and surrendered the religious authority which tempted al-Mansur and which al-Maʾmun had arrogantly claimed, no longer posed a threat. On the contrary, they served an important legitimizing function: namely, affirming historical continuity with the *umma* of the Prophet which was increasingly identified as the source of religious guidance and which could only be known through the activities and opinions of the ulama themselves. The irony was that, in practical terms, the caliphs now held little political power, which had passed to Turkish amirs at the center and to governors and semi-autonomous dynasties on the periphery. In the long run, the ulama were therefore forced to seek accommodation with a very different set of political figures and institutions, the military regimes which dominated the Islamic world in the Middle Period. It is that story which constitutes the central narrative theme of the next several centuries of Islamic history.

CHAPTER 14

Shi°ism

The partisans of °Ali were not terribly successful at persuading the Muslim community to acknowledge the authority of their Imams. After the troubled caliphate of °Ali himself, none of his descendants or close collateral relations, i.e., those whom the various proto-Shi°i groups recognized as the rightful leader of the community and instrument of God's will, secured the broad allegiance of the *umma*. Still, the late eighth and ninth centuries were fruitful ones for Shi°ism, as it was then that it acquired a more precise sectarian identity.

The success of the °Abbasids resulted in the proto-Shi°is defining their expectations more sharply. The subversive movement had its roots in proto-Shi°ism, as it drew on the widespread but unfocused support for "the chosen one from the family of Muhammad." But the chosen one turned out not to be a direct descendant of the Prophet, and eventually the °Abbasids had to deal with the disappointment of those who expected something more, or at least something different. By 762, the °Abbasids had the embarrassment of defending themselves against a revolt in the Hijaz, led by Muhammad ibn °Abdallah, *al-Nafs al-Zakiyya* ("the Pure Soul"), the great-grandson of Muhammad's grandson son al-Hasan, who rejected the °Abbasids explicitly on the grounds that they had usurped a position and power which rightfully belonged to a descendant of the Prophet. As Muhammad ibn °Abdallah put it in a letter of challenge dispatched to the caliph al-Mansur,

> Our paternal ancestor, °Ali, was the *wasi* [i.e., the authorized legatee of Muhammad] and the *imam*, so how could you have inherited his *wilaya* [i.e., his sovereign authority] when his own descendants are still alive. Further you well know that no one has laid claim to this office who has a lineage, nobility, and status like ours. By the nobility of our fathers, we are not the sons of the accursed, the outcasts, and the freedmen! No one from the Banu Hashim [the larger clan to which Muhammad belonged] has the sort of bonds we can draw upon through kinship, precedence, and superiority.[1]

---

[1] Muhammad ibn Jarir al-Tabari, *Tarikh al-rusul wa°l-muluk*, ed. M. J. De Goeje and others (Leiden: E. J. Brill, 1879–1901), 1/3.209–11 = *The History of al-Tabari*, vol. 28, trans. Jane Dammen McAuliffe (Albany, NY: SUNY Press, 1995), 167–9.

But if the weakness of the °Abbasids' pretensions to °Alid support was now laid bare, so too was the power of the reigning dynasty: Muhammad ibn °Abdallah's rebellion was easily crushed, as was another and larger revolt led by his brother Ibrahim in Basra.

The failure of these rebellions did not, however, spell the end of Shi°ism. In the first place, their suppression may have contributed in some ways to the diffusion of °Alid sentiments throughout the territories ruled by the Islamic state. Much of the support for the family of °Ali had traditionally been based in Iraq, particularly in the town of Kufa – southern Iraq remains to this day one of the demographic centers of Shi°i Islam – but in the late eighth and early ninth centuries there are signs that the movement was taking root elsewhere. The close identification of Iran and Shi°ism of course belongs to a much later period, but already in the late eighth century the city of Qum had become associated with °Alid partisans, albeit that most of them were Arabs and not Iranians. Refugees from the rebellions of 762 also ended up in Daylam, a mountainous province to the south and east of the Caspian Sea, and their presence there may be linked to the Shi°i inclinations of Daylami Muslims, from amongst whom emerged in the tenth century the Buyid amirs who played such an important role in the development of a sectarian Shi°ism.[2]

More importantly, it was at precisely this moment that the Shi°is began to distance themselves from the °Abbasid state, and lay the doctrinal foundations for what was to become sectarian Shi°ism. The central figures in this process included Ja°far al-Sadiq (d. 765), a scholar respected by Muslims of all schools and a descendant of Muhammad through his grandson al-Husayn, and Hisham ibn al-Hakam (d. 795–6), a pro-°Alid theologian of the late eighth century. For those of proto-Shi°i inclination, as perhaps for Muslims generally, the most vexing question was that of leadership. The Shi°i doctrine of the Imamate, as articulated by Ja°far, Hisham, and others, is of course immensely complicated, and in its Twelver (Imami) form cannot have been finalized until the tenth century. Even so, by the late eighth century, the contours of a distinctively Shi°i understanding of Muslim leadership could probably be discerned. At its core lies the conviction that God provides each generation of Muslims with an Imam, who as the rightful leader of the community is imbued with sovereignty over the world (*wilaya*), a sovereignty which comprises both religious and, at least in theory, political authority. The Shi°i Imam received his appointment by "designation" (*nass*) from his predecessor, as the Prophet had, in Shi°i recollection, appointed his cousin °Ali as his successor at Ghadir Khumm. Several characteristics of this Imam distinguish him from the ideal caliph as he was described by Sunni theologians. For example, the Imam is said to be *ma°sum*, free of sin. Indeed, while strictly speaking his authority is not prophetic, in that the Imams do not bring with them a new law, as did Muhammad,

---

[2] On Qum, see Wilferd Madelung, *Religious Trends in Early Islamic Iran* (Albany, NY: Bibliotheca Persica, 1988), 79–82; on Daylam, see Hugh Kennedy, *The Early Abbasid Caliphate* (London: Croom Helm, 1981), 206–7.

Moses, and Jesus, they do nonetheless speak authoritatively on matters both religious and political. In the eyes of their followers, the Shiᶜi Imams retained that role as authoritative interpreters of divine law which in Sunni Islam gradually passed into the hands of the community as a whole, expressed through the consensus of the ulama. In later Shiᶜi theological speculation, the institution of the Imamate came to have a mystical character: it was described in different ways as forming a part of the cosmic fabric. Consequently, the Imamate is for Shiᶜis a *necessary* institution: that is, there *must* always be an Imam, an individual who can speak authoritatively on God's behalf.[3]

The Shiᶜi understanding of the Imamate implied a break with the rest of the Muslim community on doctrinal grounds, but also because it rested on the rejection of the actual course of early Muslim history. The problem is that, from a Shiᶜi perspective, the community had gone seriously astray in recognizing the authority first of Abu Bakr, and then of ᶜUmar and ᶜUthman, let alone their Umayyad and ᶜAbbasid successors. The centrality of this issue in the dynamic through which Sunni and Shiᶜi identities emerged is evident in the fact that, in these early stages, the name most commonly given to those we would now recognize as Shiᶜi was *rafidi*, as a group the *rafida* or *rawafid*, terms with a number of competing etymologies but which were commonly understood to reflect that they rejected (Ar. *rafadu*) the leadership of Abu Bakr and ᶜUmar.[4] For these Rafidis, later Shiᶜis, the Imamate was to be held by a member of the *ahl al-bayt*, "the people of [Muhammad's] house." The first Imam, of course, was ᶜAli, and most partisans of the *ahl al-bayt* identified the second and third Imams as his sons al-Hasan and al-Husayn. The trick lay in identifying those who followed. The ambiguity, as we have seen, allowed the ᶜAbbasids, collateral relations of the Prophet, to harness temporarily the passions of the partisans of his family; and indeed, as long as that uncertainty persisted, it is difficult to speak with any precision about a distinctive Shiᶜi group, as opposed to a general tendency to privilege the family of the Prophet on questions of leadership. But gradually over the first few decades of ᶜAbbasid rule, that ambiguity dissipated. The pivotal figure was probably Jaᶜfar al-Sadiq who was recognized by many of the proto-Shiᶜa as the rightful Imam. Jaᶜfar's imamate shaped the future of Shiᶜism in several ways, most immediately by focusing the expectations of the partisans of the House of ᶜAli on the Husaynid line, that is, on ᶜAli's descendants through his son al-Husayn, which in this generation was represented most notably by Jaᶜfar. Moreover, Jaᶜfar explicitly accepted political realities, and – unlike those who came to be known as Zaydi Shiᶜis, who in principle accepted as Imam any member of the Prophet's family who actively resisted the rule of an unjust Muslim – made no effort to rebel against the ᶜAbbasids and assert his right to rule. Jaᶜfar's quietism in effect

---

[3] For summaries of the Shiᶜi doctrine of the Imamate, see Abdulaziz Sachedina, *Islamic Messianism: The Idea of the Mahdi in Twelver Shiᶜism* (Albany, NY: SUNY Press, 1981), and Moojan Momen, *An Introduction to Shiᶜi Islam: The History and Doctrines of Twelver Shiᶜism* (New Haven: Yale University Press, 1985), 147–60.

[4] See *EI*², "al-Rāfiḍa" (by. E. Kohlberg).

provided a model for later Shiᶜis, through which it was possible to reconcile the authority of the Imam with the actual and, from a Shiᶜi perspective, tragic course of historical events within the Muslim community.

The early ᶜAbbasid period proved fruitful for Shiᶜism. The imperial metropolis, Baghdad, along with Kufa and Qum, acquired a significant Shiᶜi population. Eventually, much of that population was concentrated in the Karkh quarter, to the south of the original round city. Partisans of the family of ᶜAli could be found in the highest circles. The Shiᶜi theologian Hisham ibn al-Hakam was an intimate courtier of the vizier Yahya ibn Khalid, of the famous Barmaki family, which itself may have had Shiᶜi inclinations. Other Shiᶜis, including members of the al-Furat family, served the ᶜAbbasids as viziers and in other high administrative offices. The circulation of both Shiᶜis and Shiᶜi ideas at the ᶜAbbasid court itself is a reminder that, at this fertile moment in the development of Islam, terms such as *Shiᶜi* must be used cautiously, or at least as indicating a much broader group than it now does. For a moment in the early ninth century, it appeared that the emerging gap between ᶜAbbasids and Shiᶜis might be bridged, when the caliph al-Maʾmun suddenly appointed ᶜAli al-Rida, the grandson of Jaᶜfar al-Sadiq and the family member recognized by many contemporary Shiᶜis as the living Imam, as his successor. It is not clear exactly what al-Maʾmun intended by this move, not least because ᶜAli was twenty years senior to the caliph, but it surely reflected an effort on the part of the ᶜAbbasids to re-harness, or at least to co-opt, the political allegiance of those Shiᶜa who were uneasy with ᶜAbbasid leadership – which is, if nothing else, testimony to the strength of the Shiᶜi movement within Islamic society at this historical moment.[5]

But Shiᶜism's relationship to the ᶜAbbasid state remained problematic, and this made publicly identifying oneself as a partisan of the House of ᶜAli somewhat precarious – a situation which encouraged Shiᶜis to practice what they called *taqiyya*, according to which it is permitted to dissemble regarding one's Shiᶜi convictions in the face of persecution. Al-Maʾmun's flirtation with a political alliance with the Shiᶜi Imam may have cooled in the face of persistent Shiᶜi rebellions, and in any case, ᶜAli died – poisoned at the caliph's orders, say a number of sources – while accompanying al-Maʾmun on his journey from Marv, in eastern Iran, to Baghdad to re-assert his authority in the capital. The situation of later Imams grew more and more difficult, the tenth and eleventh in succession from the Prophet, ᶜAli al-Hadi and his son Hasan al-ᶜAskari, living under virtual house arrest in Samarra. The ᶜAbbasids appear to have cultivated rivalries within the family of the ᶜAlid Imams, as a way of weakening the potential influence of any one claimant to the Imamate, and even went so far as to assign midwives the task of monitoring the women of the Imams' households so as to detect

---

[5] On the strength of Shiᶜism in the late eighth and ninth centuries, see Andrew J. Newman, *The Formative Period of Twelver Shīᶜism: Ḥadīth as Discourse Between Qum and Baghdad* (London: Curzon, 2000), 1–11; on ᶜAli al-Rida and his abortive appointment as caliphal heir, see Michael Cooperson, *Classical Arabic Biography: The Heirs of the Prophet in the Age of al-Maʾmūn* (Cambridge: Cambridge University Press, 2000), 28–32, and 70–106.

pregnancies, any one of which could, in theory at least, pose a significant challenge to their authority. As a distinctive Shi^ci identity crystallized around a persistent dissatisfaction with the ruling house, public expressions of devotion to the House of ^cAli grew more difficult and dangerous. As a mark of the tension, in 850 the caliph al-Mutawakkil ordered the destruction of the tomb of al-Husayn ibn ^cAli at Karbala, explicitly, it appears, to prevent the pious visitation of the tomb which had become an important ritual for Shi^ci Muslims. According to the report recorded by al-Tabari, the authorities threatened to arrest anyone found visiting the grave after its destruction. In Baghdad itself, Shi^ci worshipers could find their mosques destroyed by agents of the ^cAbbasid authorities, and those who gathered there arrested and imprisoned.[6]

Over the ninth century, the Shi^ci community was forced to begin the process of developing structures of authority, built around the leading Shi^ci ulama, independent of the Imams themselves. Several Imams in this period were minors. Moreover, with the Imams living under varying degrees of enforced isolation, contacts with the Shi^ci faithful were necessarily more erratic. The tenth and eleventh Imams, for example, communicated furtively with their followers and received from them financial support through a network of agents, some of whom passed messages and money hidden in containers of cooking fat. Such difficulties may have encouraged the development of alternative loci of religious and judicial authority within the Shi^ci community, theoretically subservient to but to some extent independent of the Imams, and so enabled them to survive this moment of persecution as well as the longer period of occultation which followed.[7]

The critical moment for Shi^cism came at the end of the ninth century. In late 873, the eleventh Imam, Hasan al-^cAskari, living in confinement in Samarra, became ill and, after a short time, died. He was young – only twenty-nine years of age – and the question arose as to whether or not he had produced an heir. The uncertainty produced a predictable range of answers: that Hasan had not actually died, but merely gone into temporary occultation; that the Imamate had passed to other members of his family; finally, that he had in fact had a son, named Muhammad, whose identity and whereabouts were kept secret to protect him from persecution at the hands of the ^cAbbasids and other enemies. It was the latter conviction that proved to have the most promising future, and over the tenth and early eleventh centuries, particularly under the patronage of the Buyid amirs who came to power under the titular rule of the ^cAbbasid caliphs in the mid-tenth century, gave rise to the Twelver or Imami sect, today numerically the largest Shi^ci grouping. The twelfth Imam was identified as Hasan's son, Muhammad *al-Muntazar*, "the awaited one." His disappearance and occultation took on cosmological significance: it was he who would return at the end of time to usher

---

[6] Al-Ṭabarī, *Tārīkh*, 1/3.1407 = *History*, vol. 34, trans. Joel L. Kraemer (Albany, NY: SUNY Press, 1989), 110–11; Jacob Lassner, *The Topography of Baghdad in the Early Middle Ages* (Detroit: Wayne State University Press, 1970), 97–8.

[7] Etan Kohlberg, "Imam and Community in the Pre-Ghayba Period," in *Authority and Political Culture in Shi^cism*, ed. Said Amir Arjomand (Albany, NY: SUNY Press, 1988), 25–53, esp. 37–40.

in the final days, when God's plans for the Muslim community would at last be fully realized.[8]

Over the ensuing decades, the Twelver Shi'i community took a distinctive sectarian as well as doctrinal shape. It was in this period, for example, that the Shi'i scholar al-Kulayni (d. 941) compiled the collection of traditions (*Kitab al-kafi*) that came to play a foundational role for Shi'i law roughly comparable to that played by al-Bukhari's and Muslim ibn al-Hajjaj's collections of hadith in the formation of Sunni jurisprudence. Shi'i scholars in the late ninth and tenth centuries began to construct a theological system which could account for the disappearance of the infallible Imam and, in part by drawing on the Mu'tazili emphasis on the exercise of human reason, justify the prerogative of the scholars to interpret the Imam's will in his absence.[9] This would prove critical both to the emergence of a distinctive Twelver Shi'i communal identity, and also to later Twelver doctrines that stressed the authority of the leading Shi'i ulama, including the doctrine of the "deputyship of the jurist" which the Ayatollah Khomeini would, in the twentieth century, employ to such effect.

The arrival on the scene of the Buyid amirs in the middle of the tenth century proved especially propitious for Twelver Shi'ism. The Buyids, originally Zaydi Shi'is, did not eliminate the 'Abbasid caliphate, but they did cultivate the support of Twelver Shi'is once they had come to power in Baghdad. Doing so may have been convenient for them – since the last Imam of the Twelver line had disappeared some seven decades before their arrival in Baghdad, recognizing the sovereignty of the "Hidden Imam" would involve no limitation on the Buyids' own authority. In any case, the Buyids supported the articulation of a distinctive Twelver identity, for example by patronizing Twelver scholars. They also strengthened the Shi'i community by honoring its leading figures, such as the brothers al-Sharif al-Radi (d. 1016) and al-Sharif al-Murtada (d. 1044), who served as *naqibs* (representatives or supervisors) of those claiming membership in the Prophet's family, and relying on them for a variety of political and diplomatic functions. The public cursing of the first three caliphs – i.e., those who had, in Shi'i eyes, usurped 'Ali's rightful position – contributed to an atmosphere of religious tension. When the Buyid amir Mu'izz al-Dawla in 962 went so far as to order that curses of the first caliphs be painted on the walls of Baghdad's mosques, it is reported that opponents of the Shi'a furtively blotted out the slogans, a clear sign of heightened religious competition. The Shi'is now distinguished themselves in various ways, in particular through their public commemoration of various key events in the Shi'i reconstruction of early Islamic history – the martyrdom of al-Husayn at Karbala was remembered, for example, with noisy public penance on 'Ashura' (the tenth day of the month of Muharram), while the Prophet's alleged

---

[8] For the development of this doctrine, see Etan Kohlberg, "From Imamiyya to Ithna-'Ashariyya," *Bulletin of the School of Oriental and African Studies* 39 (1976), 521–34, and Sachedina, *Islamic Messianism*, passim.

[9] Andrew J. Newman, *The Formative Period of Twelver Shi'ism: Hadith as Discourse Between Qum and Baghdad* (London: Curzon, 2000), 12–31.

recognition of his cousin ᶜAli as his successor at Ghadir Khumm became an occasion for major Shiᶜi celebration.

But the central issue was one of religious authority, for it went to the heart of how the different religious communities defined themselves. So, for example, as the Muslim scholars came to insist upon the importance of the Prophetic *sunna* in establishing what was genuinely Islamic, and upon the priority of hadith in determining what that *sunna* consisted of (a process critical to the formation of what came to be a "Sunni" identity, and which we will discuss more fully below), and upon the authority of the community through its consensus (*ijmaᶜ*) in determining which hadith were genuine, the Shiᶜis marked themselves off by their distinctive approach to the question. They did so either by tracing the transmission of hadith through individuals closely associated with the ᶜAlid cause, rather than those who came to be recognized by the Sunni tradition as authoritative transmitters, or (more radically) by insisting that all hadith must be traced back either to the Prophet or to those descendants of his identified as their Imams, thereby shifting the locus of authority from the community as a whole to the Imams. The distinctiveness of the Shiᶜi community is reflected in the advice allegedly given by an Imam regarding Shiᶜi Muslims who needed legal guidance but who could not locate an acceptable (i.e., Shiᶜi) scholar: that they should seek the opinion of a Sunni *faqih* (jurist) and then do the opposite.[10]

Not, of course, that the Shiᶜis themselves were united. Shiᶜism began as a rather vague and undefined movement of support for the leadership of someone from the family of the Prophet, and as we have seen there were many who claimed that role. Most of this discussion has focused on the group that hindsight would identify as the Twelver Shiᶜis. In the modern world, the Twelver form of Shiᶜism is dominant, but that was not necessarily true in the early centuries, when the specific Shiᶜi sects did not yet exist in their later, precise formulation. There were many individuals and lineages which competed for the support of those inclined to look to a descendant of ᶜAli's for leadership. Of the non-Twelver Shiᶜi sects which emerged from this doctrinal turbulence, the most important was the Ismaᶜiliyya. In the eyes of many medieval Muslims, the Ismaᶜilis constituted the Islamic heresy *par excellence*. The Islamic heresiographical tradition, both Sunni and Twelver Shiᶜi, engaged in a highly critical, at times vitriolic attack on Ismaᶜilism, and one of the problems in reconstructing the history of the sect is that most of the relevant sources were produced in anti-Ismaᶜili circles. The situation is further complicated by several other factors, including the diversity of the Ismaᶜili tradition, which survived into modern times in a bewildering variety of sects, and also the Ismaᶜili emphasis on transmitting and understanding the inner secrets (*batin*) of things, as opposed to the obvious but incomplete external meaning (*zahir*), secrets which adepts were sworn not to reveal to the uninitiated, on pain

---

[10] Kohlberg, "Imam and Community," 38. The anecdote is attributed to several Imams, although it is preserved in a work of the tenth-century Shiᶜi scholar Ibn Babawayh.

(according to a relatively late Sunni source) of forfeiting their slaves, their property, and their wives.[11]

The issue that separated Isma^{c}ili from Twelver, and then one Isma^{c}ili group from another, was that of the identity and authority of the Imam. The point of departure from the main stem of Imami identity and allegiance was the eldest son of Ja^{c}far al-Sadiq, Isma^{c}il, although a distinctively Isma^{c}ili *sectarian* group probably did not emerge until a century or more after Isma^{c}il's death. Isma^{c}il was a problematic figure in several respects. Hostile Sunni and Twelver sources describe him as a drunkard and a heretic; moreover, he appears to have died before his father. For both reasons, Twelver Shi^{c}is rejected the claim of his followers that he was the rightful Imam. His partisans, naturally, thought otherwise, some arguing that Isma^{c}il had not in fact died, but rather had gone into occultation, others recognizing his son Muhammad as the heir, either of Isma^{c}il or directly of Ja^{c}far himself. What is important to the historian is the confusion itself, as a reminder that the lines of successive Imams recognized by later Shi^{c}is were not so clearly defined at the time.

Isma^{c}ilism posed an active challenge to the identity and authority of the Islamic tradition as it crystallized in the ninth and tenth centuries. The history of Isma^{c}il's followers in the decades following his death (or disappearance) is difficult to trace, as are the precise connections between them and the later, fully-formed Isma^{c}ili groups; but suddenly in the second half of the ninth century organized groups of Isma^{c}ilis appear in the historical record, conducting a highly-disciplined missionary campaign the goal of which was to reorient the *umma* in an Isma^{c}ili direction. It was only natural that the Isma^{c}ili mission (*da^{c}wa*, the "calling" or "summoning") would be active in southern Iraq, given the historical concentration of Shi^{c}is there and the proximity of the imperial metropole. But the diffusion of that mission, with its appearance in Sind, Khurasan and other eastern provinces, Azerbaijan, Iran, Iraq, Yemen, as well as (ultimately, to greater effect) North Africa, reflected the scope and ambition of the movement, which sought a radical reorientation of the Islamic world.[12] Isma^{c}ili Shi^{c}ism demonstrated a pronounced tendency to fracture into competing sects, divided over points of doctrine and especially over who was to be recognized as Imam. But despite their fissiparousness, the Isma'ilis resisted the dominant Islamic order, actively and sometimes violently. Isma^{c}ili uprisings and organized military campaigns were a recurrent feature of life in Syria and especially Iraq during the early tenth century.

[11] See Heinz Halm, "The Isma^{c}ili Oath of Allegiance (*^{c}Ahd*) and the 'Sessions of Wisdom' (*Majalis al-hikma*) in Fatimid Times," in *Mediaeval Isma^{c}ili History and Thought*, ed. Farhad Daftary (Cambridge: Cambridge University Press, 1996), 91–115, esp. 96–7. For general studies of the Isma^{c}ili sect, see Wilferd Madelung, "Fatimiden und Bahrainqarmaten," *Der Islam* 34 (1959), 34–88; idem, "Das Imamat in der frühen ismailitischen Lehre," *Der Islam* 37 (1961), 43–135; Farhad Daftary, *The Isma^{c}ilis: Their History and Doctrines* (Cambridge: Cambridge University Press, 1990), S. M. Stern, *Studies in Early Isma^{c}ilism* (Jerusalem: The Magnes Press, 1983); *EI*^{2}, art. "Ismā^{c}īliyya" (by W. Madelung).

[12] See, for example, S. M. Stern, "Isma^{c}ili Propaganda and Fatimid Rule in Sind," and "The Early Isma^{c}ili Missionaries in North-West Persia and in Khurasan and Transoxania," in *Studies in Early Isma^{c}ilism*, 177–88 and 189–233.

The most serious challenge to emerge from Isma'ili Islam was that posed by the Fatimids. Until the end of the ninth century, Isma'ili expectations focused on the imminent return of Muhammad ibn Isma'il. At this point, however, a leader of the sect named 'Ubayd Allah claimed the imamate for himself. 'Ubayd Allah's genealogy – that is, his relation to the expected Muhammad ibn Isma'il – is a matter of some dispute, but the consequences of his assertion were twofold. In the first place, it provoked a split within the sect (of a sort which was to become common), as some Isma'ilis refused to recognize his claims and remained loyal to the hidden (and awaited) Imam, Muhammad ibn Isma'il. Secondly, 'Ubayd Allah himself moved to North Africa, where the way had been prepared for him by his missionaries, and where he now established a caliphate to rival that of the 'Abbasids and took for himself the *al-Mahdi*, an explicitly messianic term by which the hidden Imam was to be known upon his return. By 969, the Fatimids had conquered Egypt, where they constructed a new capital city, Cairo, and from which they pursued an active campaign to convince Muslims everywhere of the authority of their imamate.

Not all Isma'ilis accepted the claims of 'Ubayd Allah and the Fatimids. Among them were the followers of several Isma'ili missionaries operating in Iraq, Bahrayn, and elsewhere, who came to be known as the Qarmatians. The Qarmatians established a state based in Bahrayn in the Persian Gulf in the early tenth century, which for long posed a significant threat to both the Fatimids and the 'Abbasids. In the 920s, the Qarmatians, driven by expectations of the imminent return of Muhammad ibn Isma'il, pressed a campaign against the 'Abbasids which almost resulted in the capture of Baghdad itself. The Qarmatian challenge threatened the foundations of 'Abbasid legitimacy. Among their favorite targets, for example, were caravans of pilgrims passing through, under 'Abbasid protection, to the holy cities in Arabia. Finally, in 930 the Qarmatians of Bahrayn conquered Mecca during the pilgrimage season, slaughtering thousands of Muslim pilgrims and carrying off the venerated Black Stone, which was only returned in 951 after the 'Abbasid government had paid a considerable ransom.[13]

The Isma'ili challenge to Sunni Islam was immediate and political, but it was also doctrinal. The fully-formed Isma'ili tradition itself is characterized by considerable diversity, but several areas of Isma'ili doctrine claim our attention here. Isma'ili views on the central issue of leadership reveal a creative and syncretistic stratum in early Islamic thinking which can easily be obscured by the sheer mass and momentum of the matured Sunni and Twelver Shi'i traditions. Isma'ilism asserts the fundamentally cyclical character of human history, which has known six "speaking" (*natiq*) prophets, bearers of law in its external guise (*zahir*) – Adam, Noah, Abraham, Moses, Jesus, and Muhammad – each of whom was followed by a "silent" (*samit*) one, who secretly reveals the hidden, inner meaning (*batin*) to the initiated. The work of the *samit* is furthered by seven successive Imams in each cycle. In that beginning with Muhammad's *samit* 'Ali,

---

[13] *EI²*, art. "Ḳarmaṭī" (by W. Madelung).

the seventh Imam is identified as Muhammad ibn Ismaᶜil, who has gone into occultation but who upon his reappearance will be recognized as the seventh and final *natiq*, and as the *qa'im* ("one who rises") and *mahdi* ("rightly-guided one") who brings God's final and most complete revelation and will, in the process, usher in the final days of judgment. In the tenth and eleventh centuries, further Ismaᶜili theological speculation drew explicitly on neo-Platonic concepts to fashion an even more elaborate cosmology. More generally, there was an inclusive, almost latitudinarian outlook in much early Ismaᶜili speculation, which contributed to the hostility with which Sunnis viewed the Ismaᶜilis, whom they accused of succumbing to "the efforts of the faiths superseded by Islam to insinuate themselves into Islam and thus eventually to destroy and replace it."[14] That open-ness to dialogue with other religious traditions, and especially the influence of neo-Platonism, is fully at work in the treatises known as the "Epistles" of the *Ikhwan al-Safa*, or "Brethren of Purity," which probably emerged from Ismaᶜili circles in Basra in the early- or mid-tenth century. And it had practical consequences, too, for example in the generally tolerant religious policies of the Fatimid caliphs, once they had come to power.[15]

Above all, the Ismaᶜili movement aimed not simply at replacing the existing caliph with an Imam recognized by his followers as the rightful leader of the *umma*, but rather at the revolutionary transformation of Islamic society. Messianic movements in general tend to have a revolutionary coloring, as expectations of the imminent arrival (or return) of an individual charged by God with implementing his will and ushering in the end of time can easily stoke and feed upon social and economic grievances. Ninth- and tenth-century Ismaᶜilism was fully messianic in this sense. The Ismaᶜili doctrine of cyclical history implied that, in returning, the *mahdi/qaʾim* would surpass or complete the work of the Prophet. His appearance would mark the abrogation of the law which Muhammad had brought; his followers would from this point be able to live exclusively according to the *batin*, the inner truth. For some Ismaᶜilis, such as the Qarmatians, the imminence of the hidden Imam's return was not just a rhetorical matter: it was the expectation that the messianic age and the abrogation of the law was upon them that drove the Qarmatians to such radical steps as, for example, their attacks on pilgrims and

---

[14] Bernard Lewis, *The Origins of Ismaᶜilism* (Cambridge: Heffer and Sons, 1940), 90.

[15] There has been considerable discussion of the origins and authorship of the Epistles; compare *EI²*, art. "Ikhwān al-Ṣafāʾ" (by. Y. Marquet) with S. M. Stern, "New Information about the Authors of the 'Epistles of the Sincere Brethren," in idem, *Studies*, 155–76, and Ian R. Netton, *Muslim Neoplatonists: An Introduction to the Thought of the Brethren of Purity* (London: George Allen & Unwin, 1982), 95–104. On the theological inclusiveness of Ismaᶜilsm and its connections to Gnosticism and neo-Platonism, see Lewis, *Origins*, 93–6; Henri Corbin, "De la gnose antique à la gnose ismaélienne," in *Oriente e Occidente nel Medioevo* (Rome: Accademia Nazionale dei Lincei, 1957), 105–43; Netton, *Muslim Neoplatonists*, 53–77; Heinz Halm, "The Cosmology of the pre-Fatimid Ismaᶜiliyya," in *Mediaeval Ismaᶜili History*, ed. Daftary, 74–83; Azim A. Nanji, "Portraits of Self and Others: Ismaᶜili Perspectives on the History of Religions," in *ibid.*, 153–60; Paul Walker, *Early Philosophical Shiism: The Ismaili Neoplatonism of Abū Yaᶜqūb al-Sijistānī* (Cambridge: Cambridge University Press, 1993), and idem, *Ḥamīd al-Dīn al-Kirmānī: Ismāᶜīlī Thought in the Age of al-Ḥākim* (London: I. B. Tauris, 1999).

the Muslim holy sites. The Fatimids, who came to rule over a large and diverse state, had to make certain adjustments in Ismaᶜili doctrine. For example, they toned down the antinomianism which was characteristic of more radical Ismaᶜili groups, and supported the work of Ismaᶜili jurists such as the *qadi* al-Nuᶜman (d. 974) in developing a body of Ismaᶜili law, an Ismaᶜili *shariᶜa*. But they could not fully suppress the revolutionary impulse of Ismaᶜili Islam, as we shall see in the following chapter. Ismaᶜilism constitutes a reminder that Islam, by the late ninth and tenth centuries, no longer represented a novel response to the religious challenges of late antiquity or the ideological bond of a narrow and alien elite, but had instead become the ideology undergirding the Near Eastern status quo.

CHAPTER 15

The formation of Sunni traditionalism

With the full development of sectarian movements within the Islamic *umma*, the stage was set for the crystallization of a specifically Sunni Muslim identity, which took shape largely in response to the threat of sectarian fragmentation. Khariji Islam survived in peripheral areas of the Islamic world, but in the central Near East in this period posed little threat. It did play some role in the revolt of African slaves (the "Zanj") in southern Iraq in the late ninth century. This rebellion was driven by the appalling conditions in which slaves worked harvesting natron in the region's extensive and virtually impenetrable marshes, but it also relied heavily on its charismatic instigator, an enigmatic figure named Muhammad ibn ʿAli. The Khariji slogan *la hukma illa lillah*, "judgment is God's alone," appeared on Muhammad's banners and coins which were minted in his name. But Muhammad was an opportunist, drawing on support wherever he could find it – at one point he claimed ʿAlid descent, and unsuccessfully sought an alliance with the Ismaʿili leader Hamdan Qarmat, whose name survived in that of the Qarmatians. As a result, the ideological orientation of the Zanj rebellion is somewhat confused. From hindsight, perhaps the most important aspect of the Zanj revolt was simply its timing, in the late ninth century, at just the moment that an active Ismaʿili movement appeared, the Imams most widely recognized by the Shiʿa were disappearing, and the fragmentation of effective political authority called into question the precise significance of the ʿAbbasid caliphate. Ultimately the rebellion was suppressed, albeit with difficulty, and later manifestations of sectarian Kharijism were largely limited to the fringes of the Islamic world: North Africa, for example, and Oman.[1]

Shiʿism, however, was a more serious concern, and what we now call Sunni Islam is, in a way, simply *non-Shiʿi* Islam. The claims of the ʿAlids had understandably concerned the ʿAbbasids, and of necessity their response tended to downplay their rivals' claims, the caliph al-Mutawakkil, for example, associating only with those who scorned ʿAli and ordering that ʿAli be cursed from the pulpits

---

[1] On the Zanj rebellion, see Alexandre Popovic, *The Revolt of African Slaves in Iraq in the 3rd/9th Century* (Princeton: Markus Wiener, 1999); and on Kharijism more generally, W. Montgomery Watt, *The Formative Period of Islamic Thought* (Edinburgh: Edinburgh University Press, 1973), 9–37.

in mosques. Opposition to the claims of the ʿAlids persisted, sometimes in rather bizarre forms which might make even the ʿAbbasids uncomfortable: in a cult in Damascus which made the Umayyad caliph Muʿawiya's tomb an object of pilgrimage, or in the insistence of some Muslims in Isfahan that the first Umayyad caliph had in fact held the status of a prophet.[2] But the sort of open rivalry represented by al-Mutawakkil's hostility to the descendants of ʿAli soon dissipated, in part perhaps because, after the late ninth century, the ʿAlid Imams themselves had disappeared, in the process transmuting the threat they posed from an imminent one to a latent and finally eschatological one. (The Fatimids, of course, were another matter.) Indeed, veneration of the Prophet's family, including of course ʿAli ibn Abi Talib and his descendants, was common among Sunni Muslims too, even if Sunnis did reject the Shiʿi understanding of ʿAli's cosmological role and the particular celebrations through which that understanding was popularly expressed.

The distinction between Sunni and Shiʿi Islam as the two sectarian identities formed over the eighth, ninth, and tenth centuries rests in the first place upon different memories of what occurred in the earliest years of Islam, and second on radically different views of the nature and locus of religious authority. The Sunni and Shiʿi accounts of the pivotal events of early Islam are incompatible, and in this period those different memories became fixed in competing religious rituals and celebrations. So, for example, if Shiʿis in the tenth century learned to express their sectarian identity in celebrations of Muhammad's alleged recognition of ʿAli as his intended successor at the pool of Khumm during his final pilgrimage, Sunnis in response began to celebrate the Prophet's taking refuge in a cave outside Mecca during the *hijra* in the company of Abu Bakr, as a marker that he had intended his friend, and not his cousin, to be his immediate successor. Those competing historical memories buttressed starkly different conceptions of religious authority. What was central to the Sunni view of history, and so to the emerging Sunni identity, was the idea that the community as a whole had got things right, that at least in broad outlines it was following the will of God. That viewpoint is expressed clearly in the famous statement attributed to the Prophet, that "my community will never agree upon an error." Where Shiʿis insisted that Muhammad, as the bearer of God's guidance, had named ʿAli as the divinely-inspired Imam who was to follow him, Sunnis accepted the consensus of the community through which (according to the stories) Abu Bakr was selected as the caliph, the successor to at least the political authority of the Prophet. Similarly, while Shiʿis look for guidance to their divinely-appointed Imam, Sunnis came to rely upon the consensus of the scholars, the ulama, whom a famous hadith identified as the "heirs of the Prophet."[3] We take the name *Sunni* from the Arabic *sunna*, the normative practice of the Prophet, as in the phrase *ahl al-sunna waʾl-jamaʿa*,

[2] Adam Mez, *The Renaissance of Islam* (London: Luzac, 1937), 64; Charles Pellat, "Le culte de Muʿawiya au iiiᵉ siècle de l'hégire," *Studia Islamica* 6 (1956), 53–66.
[3] Al-Bukhārī, *Ṣaḥīḥ*, "Kitāb al-ʿilm" 10.

"the people of the *sunna* and the community [or collectivity]." But Shi^{c}is have their *sunna*, too. What really sets the Sunnis apart is their emphasis on the community, the *jama^{c}a*, as the locus of religious authority, the will of which is expressed through its consensus, *ijma^c*.

The privileging of the consensus of the community brings us to the central question of the law, and of the formation of a science of jurisprudence. We may take as our starting point the common observation that Islam is a religion of law, that the fully-formed *shari^{c}a* makes of Islam something more than a "religion" in the Western sense, but rather an "all-embracing way of life." Islamic law is the product of a science of jurisprudence (*fiqh*) which is probably the most significant field of religious discourse in the Muslim world. The law is not embodied in a code, but rather in texts in which the jurists expressed their opinions as to what constituted proper Islamic behavior. Put another way, it is not simply a collection of rules, but what we would now call a "discursive system." Since there is no code, the opinions recognized by the ulama could in many cases vary enormously – there was considerable scope, that is, for disagreement and variations. But the development of Islamic law served in other ways as a unifying force within the Islamic community. The scope of the law is vast: the jurists expressed opinions on almost every conceivable arena of social life, from how to pray, to how to structure a business partnership, to how to trim one's beard. Islamic law, in other words, was not simply a matter for courts, judges (*qadis*), and the various institutional mechanisms of legal discipline. Rather, it was something which touched on believers' lives in intimate ways, and so all Muslims needed to have at least some rudimentary understanding of it. They might acquire that understanding through their own study of legal texts, or more likely by consulting members of the ulama with training in jurisprudence and a reputation for learning and piety. Marshall Hodgson, in his survey of Islamic history, saw in the religion's "aspiration ... to form all ordinary life in its own mould" the defining characteristic of Islamic civilization, and the central accomplishment of the first century or two of ^{c}Abbasid rule. So, he said, the particular challenge of this era: that the circumstances of empire – when the original Arab ruling elite was dispersed over a vast area, when the number of Muslims had begun to grow significantly through conversion, when through both conversion of non-Arabs and the simple passage of time one could no longer rely on a universal, Arab cultural homogeneity – demanded the articulation of a legal system which would bind an increasingly disparate Islamic *umma* together.[4]

So Islamic law was central to cementing a specifically Islamic identity, not least because other religious communities in the Near East had well-developed legal systems of their own. This was especially true of the Jews, and it is widely accepted that the Jewish model, as developed in the rabbinical academies in Iraq

---

[4] Marshall G. S. Hodgson, *The Venture of Islam: Conscience and History in a World Civilization* (Chicago: University of Chicago Press, 1974), 1.315–58, esp. 315–26.

in late antiquity and just after the Muslim conquests, influenced the development of Islamic law by the Muslim jurists, many of whom lived in Iraq.[5] For all its importance to Muslim identity and to the social organization of Muslim societies, however, we need to remember that Islamic law took a considerable period to come together, and that the process was not without disruption and controversy. Traditionally, the eighth and ninth centuries are mentioned as the time when the law crystallized, since that was the period in which there lived those scholars who gave their names to the four surviving "schools" (*madhahib*, sing. *madhhab*, lit., "way") of Sunni law – Abu Hanifa (d. 767), Malik ibn Anas (d. 795), al-Shafi‘i (d. 820), and Ahmad ibn Hanbal (d. 855).[6] However, the identification of those schools with their eponymous founders – the Hanafis with Abu Hanifa, for example, or the Hanbalis with Ibn Hanbal – was historically a kind of pious fiction. The crystallization of distinct schools was not so much the work of the eponyms themselves as it was of their students or intellectual descendants of later generations, who collected their juridical opinions, wrote extensive commentaries on them, and ultimately compiled biographical dictionaries of scholars and jurists who, in retrospect, belonged to discrete juristic traditions. This process of forming self-reflective schools of Islamic law, to which individual jurists and students consciously adhered, was probably not substantially complete until the late ninth or tenth century.[7]

In later centuries, it was an accepted principle among Sunnis that the four surviving *madhahib* all had equal standing, at least in the sense that the fundamental legitimacy of any particular school was not subject to debate. But the policy of mutual toleration was a later development.[8] In their early days, in the tenth and eleventh centuries, the schools of law often functioned as the focus of intense religious and social rivalries. In Iranian cities, representatives of various *madhahib* competed and clashed repeatedly, legal identities providing a cover for struggle over diverse social, political, and theological differences – as, for example, in the city of Nishapur, where sometimes violent social disturbances pitting political and theological factions identified as "Shafi‘is" and "Hanafis" continued well into the Middle Period. In Baghdad, it was the Hanbali school that provided the rallying point and the bodies for sometimes violent social

---

[5] Joseph Schacht, *On the Origins of Muhammadan Jurisprudence* (Oxford: Clarendon Press, 1950); Patricia Crone and Michael Cook, *Hagarism: The Making of the Islamic World* (Cambridge: Cambridge University Press, 1977), 29–32.

[6] Joseph Schacht, "The Schools of Law and Later Developments of Jurisprudence," in *Law in the Middle East*, ed., Majid Khaduri and Herbert J. Liebesny (Washington, D.C.: Middle East Institute, 1955), 57–84, esp. 63.

[7] Richard Bulliet, *Islam: The View from the Edge* (New York: Columbia University Press, 1994), 92–4; Christopher Melchert, *The Formation of the Sunni Schools of Law, 9th and 10th Centuries C.E.* (Leiden: E. J. Brill, 1997); Norman Calder, *Studies in Early Muslim Jurisprudence* (Oxford: Clarendon Press, 1993), 245–7; George Makdisi, "The Guilds of Law in Medieval Legal History: An Inquiry into the Origins of the Inns of Court," *Zeitschrift für Geschichte der Arabisch-Islamischen Wissenschaften* 1 (1984), 233–52.

[8] Bulliet, *Islam*, 110.

disturbances, movements directed against various perceived enemies, from Shiᶜis
to rationalist theologians.[9]

The broad outlines of the emergence of a science of Islamic jurisprudence and
a working body of Islamic law are well known, and what follows is a very cursory
survey of that process. What we know as Islamic law began as a disparate and
ad hoc system in which communities of Muslims and the individuals who served
as their judges (*qadis*) developed and applied principles and rulings to meet the
juridical needs of their scattered societies. There was considerable diversity in the
law as applied in the early centuries, both because Muslims in different regions
developed different responses to the particular problems they faced, and also
because the law as applied was derived from a variety of different sources: the laws
formulated by pre-Muslim communities, the practice of earlier Muslims, as well
as basic principles of equity. Gradually, however, a more precisely delineated
system emerged.

Two matters in particular merit mention. First, it grew to be recognized that the
principal source of Islamic law was the normative practice of Muhammad (*sunna*),
as reflected in *hadith*. (The Koran itself of course takes formal precedence, but as
a practical matter it proved of only limited value as a source of law. Some in the
early Muslim community propounded a kind of "fundamentalist" or "scripturalist"
emphasis on the Koran to the exclusion of hadith, but their point of view was
overcome by the sheer number and the practical value of the hadith reports.) The
dating of this development is a controversial matter: al-Shafiᶜi is usually identified
as the figure most responsible for it, although some have suggested a later date,
while a more conservative Muslim viewpoint would claim that the community
recognized much earlier the Prophet's central normative role. Leaving the claims
of piety aside, what is most striking is how long it took for this principle to be
clearly articulated and widely held, and to eclipse other, broader definitions
of what constituted *sunna*. Second, the regional schools of the earlier period
gradually gave rise to a series of juridical traditions identified with particular
scholars. Originally, there were dozens of these traditions, although eventually
their number was whittled down to four. Ultimately the four which survived – the
Shafiᶜi, Hanafi, Maliki, and Hanbali – came to rest on a science of jurisprudence
which discovered the law from a hierarchy of sources or "foundations" (*usul*): the
Koran; the *sunna*; the selective use of analogical reasoning, *qiyas* (although this
source was not accepted by all); and the consensus (*ijmaᶜ*) of the recognized body
of religious experts.[10]

[9] Bulliet, *Islam*, 110–12; idem, *The Patricians of Nishapur: A Study in Medieval Islamic Social
    History* (Cambridge, Mass.: Harvard University Press, 1972), esp. 28–46; Wilferd Madelung,
    Religious Trends in Early Islamic Iran (Albany, NY: Bibliotheca Persica, 1988), 26–38; George
    Makdisi, *Ibn ʿAqīl et la résurgence de l'Islam traditionaliste au xiᵉ siècle (vᵉ siècle de l'Hégire)*
    (Damascus: Institut Français de Damas, 1963), 293–383; Simha Sabari, *Mouvements populaires à
    Bagdad à l'époque 'abbaside, ixᵉ-xiᵉ siècles* (Paris: Librairie d'Amérique et d'Orient, 1981), 101–20.
[10] The pioneer work in this field was done by Joseph Schacht, particularly in his study of the *Origins
    of Muhammadan Jurisprudence* (Oxford: Clarendon Press, 1950). On al-Shafiᶜi as the architect of
    Islamic jurisprudence, see Makdisi, "The Juridical Theology of Shāfiʿī: Origins and Significance

Such, in a very small nutshell, is the story of the origins of Islamic law. What can we say about the process, and in particular about its relationship to the broader assertion of a distinctively Sunni identity?

In the first place, the formation of Islamic law constituted a critical step in the consolidation of a unifying if not entirely uniform Muslim identity, a means for delineating what it meant to be a Muslim while at the same time accommodating the growing diversity of outlook and practice within the Muslim community. Islamic law sought to balance the two competing imperatives – the need for a clearly defined Islamic identity, and the need to deal with the existing diversity of belief and practice – in a variety of ways. This is clear from a consideration of the most important of the two "sources" of the law. One method of balancing centripetal forces (the need for a clear Muslim identity) with centrifugal ones (the diversity of actual Muslim practice) was to focus on the person of the Prophet and invest his behavior with a normative status. Hence the emergence of the *sunna* principle: that which was "Islamic" was to be found in the *sunna* of the Prophet, and that *sunna* could be found in *hadith*. On the surface, this principle would seem to favor a precise, "Muhammadan" identity, and to restrict the range of practices which could be recognized as authentically Islamic. In fact, however, the diversity of actual practice trumped the homogenizing tendency of the *sunna* principle. As Ignaz Goldziher famously demonstrated some time ago, the privileging of *sunna* led to the widespread fabrication of hadith to support one viewpoint or practice or another.[11] Once the hadith were written down in collections that acquired an authoritative status, such as those compiled by al-Bukhari (d. 870) and Muslim ibn al-Hajjaj (d. 875), the centrifugal tendencies may have receded. Even so, the residue of diversity was enormous: Ahmad b. Hanbal's collection of hadith, the *Musnad*, contains many thousands of traditions, embracing a considerable range of (sometimes contradictory) ideas and practices.

Of even greater practical importance as a source of law, and also as a means of balancing the centripetal and centrifugal forces, was the doctrine of consensus, *ijmaᶜ*. Jurists defined *ijmaᶜ* in different ways, but the general outlines of the issue can be discerned fairly clearly. The doctrine of *ijmaᶜ* was essential to the identity and authority of the *madhahib*. In theory, *ijmaᶜ* represented the fourth of the four

---

of Usūl al-fiqh," *Studia Islamica* 59 (1984), 5–47. Schacht's conclusions on al-Shafiᶜi's contribution to Muslim jurisprudence, and more generally on the dating of the whole process by which Islamic law took shape and, in particular, the normative status of prophetic *sunna* was recognized, have been challenged recently, from very different perspectives. Compare Calder, *Studies*, 245–7, and Wael Hallaq, "Was al-Shāfiᶜī the Master Architect of Islamic Jurisprudence?" *International Journal of Middle East Studies* 25 (1993), 587–605, with M. M. al-Azmi, *On Schacht's Origins of Muhammadan Jurisprudence* (Oxford: Oxford Centre for Islamic Studies, 1996). For a balanced survey of the sources, see Devin Stewart, *Islamic Legal Orthodoxy: Twelver Shiite Responses to the Sunni Legal System* (Salt Lake City: University of Utah Press, 1998), 26–37.

[11] Ignaz Goldziher, *Muslim Studies*, trans. C. R. Barber and S. M. Stern (London: George Allen and Unwin, 1966), volume 2, chapters 2, 3, and 4. Bulliet, *Islam*, 81–6, makes a compelling case for the "local" origin of hadith – that is, for their diverse, heterogeneous, even contradictory character. More generally, his book presents an argument for the pervasive heterogeneity of Islamic societies in the early centuries.

usul of Sunni Islamic law. In practice, however, it came to have a critical, defining function, one that was reflected in a hadith, in which the Prophet is alleged to have declared that "my community will never agree upon an error." The doctrine was a powerful one, powerful enough, for example, to enable the community to inscribe in its law principles and practices which seem to violate express Koranic statements. So, for example, the doctrine of *ijma*ᶜ enabled the jurists to respond to the prevailing sexual standards of late antique and early medieval Near Eastern societies and accept a punishment for adultery – death by stoning, at least under certain conditions – in direct violation of an explicit Koranic verse, which called for a more lenient penalty. More broadly, the doctrine of consensus constituted the foundation of the authority that the ulama, and especially the jurists among them, claimed over the Islamic tradition. Where the jurists differed over a given legal question, there was *khilaf*, "disagreement" – that is, the tradition recognized a diversity of opinion and practice. But once the jurists of a given *madhhab* had agreed through consensus on a given point, it was taken as binding on those who followed. In this way the doctrine served to reinforce the growing social and cultural authority of the ulama, the educated religious elite, an issue to which we shall return shortly.[12]

The importance of *ijma*ᶜ to the Islamic tradition can hardly be overstressed. It was central to the process of forming the *madhahib* and defining the law, but also in a more general way to establishing the parameters of what constituted Sunni Islam. It is true that, as Western scholars have frequently remarked, there is no "church" in Islam, no institutional structure of authority, and so that the use of terms such as "orthodoxy" and "heresy" are inherently problematic in an Islamic context. That does not mean, however, that questions about what constitutes proper Muslim thought and behavior had no meaning. The doctrine of consensus was one of the principal tools that the tradition developed for answering those questions, and it formed the theoretical basis for the authority of the ulama, and of the jurists in particular. To go against the consensus was, in a very real sense, to step outside the tradition, to become in fact a heretic.[13]

A second point about the development of Islamic law derives from the fact that it overlapped with a series of issues of a more specifically theological nature. This is not surprising, since the fundamental ground over which both theological and jurisprudential battles were fought was the same: namely, the competing claims of human reason, on the one side, and revelation and scriptural (including Prophetic) authority on the other, to determining the "Islamic" position on everything from how to regulate family life to the attributes of God. So, for example, the crystal-lization of the *madhahib* grew out of a fundamental disagreement between what were originally known as the *ashab al-hadith*, the supporters of the paramountcy

---

[12] A full investigation of the doctrine of consensus remains an important desideratum in the field of Islamic studies. The best general work on the subject to date is that of Stewart, *Islamic Legal Orthodoxy*, 25–59, esp. 37–45. See also Wael Hallaq, "On the Authoritativeness of Sunni Consensus," *International Journal of Middle East Studies* 18 (1986), 427–54.

[13] Stewart, *Islamic Legal Orthodoxy*, 45–53.

of Prophetic tradition, and the *ashab al-ra'y*, those who were willing to acknow-ledge considerable scope for the exercise of relatively unfettered human reason in the articulation of the law. So, too, in the theological sphere, the poles of debate were represented by those such as Ahmad ibn Hanbal, who demanded the un-questioning acceptance of scriptural authority even on matters on which a literal reading seemed to lead to absurd conclusions – for example, that when the Koran said that "God's throne was upon the water," it meant precisely that – and on the other extreme by the Mu°tazila, who argued on rationalistic grounds for the createdness of the Koran.

In general there was no absolute correlation between an individual's adherence to one *madhhab* and his position on theological matters. One might, for example, be a Mu°tazili in theology, and adhere to the Hanafi or Shafi°i school of law. But the trends in both areas of debate were similar. On the surface, the victors were those willing to compromise. In law, that compromise took the form of the *madhahib* themselves. So, for example, the jurists all acknowledged the norma-tive value of the Prophetic *sunna* as reflected in *hadith*, even the Hanafis, who originally had given considerable weight to the exercise of human reason. (It was said sarcastically of the early Hanafi jurist Abu Yusuf that he could, through analogy, make sexual relations with virgins and boys licit.) And so, on the other side, the followers of Ahmad ibn Hanbal, despite their absolute reliance on *hadith* and the explicit reluctance of Ibn Hanbal himself to allow his own rulings to become the basis for a systematic jurisprudence, found it necessary to preserve and propagate their traditions in the institutional form of a *madhhab*.[14] In theology, the compromise between Mu°tazili rationalism and Hanbali literalism took the form of the school of thought associated with Abu°l-Hasan al-Ash°ari (d. 935–6). Al-Ash°ari's opinions were in fact as diverse and sometimes contradictory as those who were identified as his followers, but in general it may be said that Ash°ari theology used the tools of scholastic theology to support the theological positions of a fideistic reading of the Koran: for example, that Koranic statements about God sitting on his throne, while not indicating that God had a body as such, must nonetheless be understood literally and not explained away as metaphors.[15]

Beneath the surface, however, the real winners were the traditionalists. *Ijma°* was the means by which the Muslim community agreed on what was Islamic, but the ideological standard was that of tradition: whether one position or practice or another had the authority of Prophetic example. Intellectually, one marker of the traditionalist triumph is to be found in the jurisprudential system conventionally credited to al-Shafi°i, which ascribed the Prophetic *hadith* a predominant norma-tive function. Its repercussions were much wider, however, and left their mark on the thinking of all later Sunni jurists, of whatever *madhhab*, and on Sunni theology and politics. One consequence of the caliph al-Mutawakkil's decision to suspend

---

[14]   See Melchert, *Formation*, passim. The remark about Abu Yusuf is cited on p. 10.
[15]   On al-Ash°ari and Ash°arism, see George Makdisi, "Ash°arī and the Ash°arites in Islamic Religious History", *Studia Islamica* 17 (1962), 37–80, and 18 (1963), 19–39.

the rationalist *mihna* was a need to find a new basis for political legitimacy. And it was on traditionalism that ᶜAbbasid and therefore Sunni legitimacy now came to rest. The popularity of traditionalism manifested itself repeatedly in Baghdad in the late ninth, tenth and eleventh centuries, as crowds responded violently to what they perceived as provocations, destroying mosques identified with Shiᶜis or shouting down preachers who publicly propounded rationalist theological doctrines. Despite its disruptive potential, however, traditionalism was a fundamentally conservative force. On a theoretical level, traditionalism set itself firmly against *bidᶜa*, "innovation," the opposite of *sunna*, and while the jurists inevitably found it necessary to distinguish different kinds of innovations, ranging from the forbidden to the acceptable, a principled opposition to practices not associated with the Prophet remained an important element in Islamic discourse and had a profound effect in later centuries, as we shall see. On a political level, traditionalism emphasized the historical authority of the Muslim community *as it had taken shape*, affirming, for example, in the face of Shiᶜi claims, the legitimacy of the earliest caliphs and also their successors. Once the ᶜAbbasids had broken definitively with the Shiᶜa and the Muᶜtazila, the traditionalists, including the Hanbalis, became their staunchest supporters. And so it was Ahmad ibn Hanbal who insisted that anyone who crossed the authority of the caliph deserved exclusion from the ranks of the Muslims.

The pervasive influence of traditionalism returns us to the question of the role and authority of the ulama. In theory, the aim of traditionalism was to unify Muslim practice and to anchor Islam in unchanging Prophetic/scriptural precedent, rather than in the vagaries of human reason. In practice, what it did was to carve out a sphere of authority for a particular group of Muslims, the ulama, and in particular the jurists. It was not Muhammad himself who defined the *sunna*, but rather a memory of him, and that memory was embedded in certain texts, including the collections of hadith and especially the various legal books which made use of the Prophetic traditions. The *enactment* of those texts, and also their *replication*, required that they be transmitted and commented upon – in short, that the texts be mediated through a series of human relationships. And those relationships were under the control of the ulama. Scholars taught jurisprudence in informal teaching circles in mosques or houses, and later in institutions founded specifically for the transmission of religious and legal knowledge. Whatever the setting in which they taught and studied, the men (and occasionally women) responsible for transmitting the textual foundations of Islamic law from one generation to the next preferred oral modes of transmission. That is, even after a text was written down, a student did not simply read it and master its contents: rather, he read it aloud, or heard it read aloud, and commented upon it, all in the presence of his teacher, and so entered into a chain of authorities which linked him to the author of the book or, in the case of hadith, to the Prophet himself. What that meant is that the system of education was less one of the transmission of knowledge than it was one of the transmission of personal authority over the texts in which that knowledge was found, and also of socialization. The system was flexible and informal, but it also tended to confirm the authority of particular scholars, who commanded the respect of large numbers of students and their colleagues.[16]

In other words, the patterns of authority within Islamic law had a "genealogical" character – a pattern we will see reflected in other aspects of Muslim religious life. That is, religious authority was something that one claimed from one's intellectual forefathers. This pattern can be detected already in the process whereby the schools of law crystallized around the memories of particular scholars whose names were attached to the body of their followers – Abu Hanifa, al-Shafi^{c}i, etc.[17] Not infrequently, the "genealogical" pattern of transmitting authority manifested itself literally. One consequence of the system was that the social status which accrued to those who were recognized as outstanding scholars and transmitters of the religious authority embedded in texts tended to be concentrated in families, as fathers passed that status to their sons, to other family members, and to those students with whom they were most intimately associated. In other words, the social authority of the ulama tended to produce family dynasties of scholars, with all of a dynastic system's usual mechanisms for guarding the integrity and value of the family's authority, including nepotism (in which sons succeeded to the offices and privileges of their scholarly fathers) and intermarriage with other socially elite groups.[18]

The embodiment of religious authority in the persons and families of the ulama must be seen against the background of the radical social and political changes of the ninth and tenth centuries. The collapse of the *mihna* may have represented the failure of the caliphal institution to assert its primacy on religious matters – in other words, the surrender of the caliphs to the religious authority of the ulama. But it took place at the same moment that effective political power was passing from the hands of the caliphs into those of the predominantly Turkish military elite at the center and, in the provinces, of a variety of autonomous and semi-independent regimes which sprang up to fill the political vacuum. The ascendance of a traditionalist outlook and the crystallization of the social status and authority of the religious elite, the ulama, should be read in part as a response of disenfranchised social elites representing, or claiming to represent, the older traditions of Islam, to the fractured new political arrangements and (in some cases) alien political powers. At the center, the authority of the ulama continued, for the moment anyway, to bump up against the power of the caliphal state or the military regimes, which may be one reason why it sometimes manifested itself suddenly and violently, as in the crowds led by traditionalist followers of Ibn Hanbal. But

---

[16] Although it relates to a later period, a succinct summary of the traditional mode of transmission of religious knowledge in Islam can be found in Jonathan Berkey, *The Transmission of Knowledge in Medieval Cairo: A Social History of Islamic Education* (Princeton: Princeton University Press, 1992), 21–43. On the social and political consequences of the transmission of knowledge, see Bulliet, *Islam*, passim, esp. 9–22.

[17] A point made by Melchert, *Formation*, 38 and elsewhere.

[18] See for example Bulliet, *Patricians*, esp. 24–5 and 55–7.

elsewhere, as in the provinces, the authority of the ulama had clearer political implications. For example, the ulama families commanded a limited but effective authority through their control of the *qadis'* courts, and their status with the community at large could at moments of political crisis result in a city casting its support to one claimant to power or another. The ulama's authority, in other words, constituted one of the only effective checks to the potential tyranny of the alien military regimes which began to dominate the Muslim world in this period.[19] As a result, the history of the Islamic world in the ensuing centuries would be to a large degree the history of the accommodation between the alien military regimes and the local ulama elite.

---

[19] Bulliet, *Patricians*, 25–6 and 61–75.

CHAPTER 16

Asceticism and mysticism

The mystical tradition which came to be known as Sufism has always had a problematic relationship with certain elements within the Islamic religious community. On the one hand, those identified as Sufis have often come into conflict with both political authorities and some ulama, particularly the jurists, both on doctrinal grounds and because of the Sufis' embrace of practices which most jurists abhor. On the other hand, the Sufis themselves have traced, with sincere conviction, the intellectual descent of their principles and ideas back to the very earliest Muslims, including most importantly ʿAli ibn Abi Talib and the Prophet Muhammad himself. That claim is certainly a pious fiction, but the Koran does contain a number of verses which can legitimately be read as expressing support for certain principles, such as asceticism, which came to be hallmarks of the Sufi tradition. In any case, by the Middle Period of Islamic history Sufism had made its presence felt throughout the Muslim world, capturing in one form or another the allegiance of virtually the whole of the Islamic establishment, including representatives of the strictest juristic traditions.

Like Islam itself, Sufism took a considerable time to develop. The roots of what came to be known as Sufism can be traced back to ascetic and pietistic circles within the *umma* in its first two centuries. By the ninth century, the ascetic spirit was joined, not without difficulty, to mystical speculations expressed in a specifically Islamic idiom, and the term Sufi came to be applied to certain groups and individuals. Arguably, however, it was not until the tenth and eleventh centuries that Sufism as a distinctive movement within Islam took a form in which later observers would recognize it.

Discussions of the origins of Sufism have often been obscured by two interesting but ultimately unresolvable issues. The first concerns the movement's possible roots in pre-Islamic religious traditions. It was once argued, on the basis of theories and assumptions about racial identities which circulated widely in the late nineteenth and early twentieth centuries, that Islamic mysticism represented an alien, and especially Iranian or "Aryan," grafting onto the stark Semitic monotheism of Islam. This, of course, is a view which is now thoroughly discredited.[1]

---

[1] For an early refutation of it, see Louis Massignon, *Essai sur les origines du lexique technique mystique musulmane* (Paris: J. Vrin, 1954), 638.

Nonetheless, Sufism did not develop in a hermetically sealed environment, any more than did Islam as a whole, and its roots inevitably lie, at least in part, in the larger religious background of the late antique Near East. A number of Sufi ideas and practices, and even the very lexicon of Islamic mysticism, betray close parallels to earlier developments in other Near Eastern religious traditions, especially Christianity. Among various possibilities, for example, it is likely that the term "Sufi" itself derives from the Arabic *suf*, "wool," presumably because of a tendency among ascetics in the hot Near Eastern climate to wear wool – a practice common among Nestorian monks in the Islamic period. More significantly, the notion that certain individuals rank as the special "friends of God" (*awliya'*, sing. *wali*, their quality of special closeness to God being known as *walaya*), characteristic of Sufism in later centuries, bears a strong conceptual similarity to the idea and function of the "holy man" who had such a prominent role in the religious landscape of the late antique Near East. It is significant that early Sufi narratives should often include accounts of Muslim mystics encountering, and learning from, Christian ascetics and hermits – not that any particular story is necessarily historical, but the trope may suggest a common pattern of historical experience. Others have attempted to trace elements of Sufi mysticism to Buddhism or Hindu monism – for example, the doctrine of *fana'*, the annihilation of the self, which was central to the thinking and practice of mystics such as the Persian Abu Yazid al-Bistami (d. 874), from Khurasan on the eastern fringes of the Islamic world – although such efforts have been treated with some skepticism.

The second problematic issue concerns the relationship between Sufism and the Koran itself. Western scholars sympathetic to the project of mysticism, whether in its specifically Muslim guise or more generally, have been willing to affirm the Sufi position that Islamic mysticism grew organically, even inevitably, from the Koran and from the earliest Muslim community. So, for example, the great French scholar Louis Massignon concluded that "it is from the Koran, constantly recited, meditated upon, applied, that Islamic mysticism proceeds, in its origin and development."[2] There may be a certain truth in that observation. Leaving aside the claim that the Koranic message is fully consistent with the principles of Sufism as they were later articulated, a claim which can be accepted or rejected only on theological rather than historical grounds, it is certainly the case that the Koran itself, however it came to be collected and edited and preserved, was from the beginning *recited* by Muslims as an act of devotion, and that such recitation and repetition – of Koranic verses, of God's many names – constitute one of the central practices of later Sufism. That in itself, however, tells us little about the historical origins of the Sufi movement. And the Sufi claim that "Muhammad is the first link in the spiritual chain of Sufism,"[3] if interpreted literally, is surely a historical conceit.

---

[2] Massignon, *Essai*, 104. Cf. Annemarie Schimmel, *Mystical Dimensions of Islam* (Chapel Hill: University of North Carolina Press, 1975), 23f.
[3] Schimmel, *Mystical Dimensions*, 27.

The historical origins of Sufism within the larger Islamic tradition should be sought among those Muslims whose response to the crisis of the eighth century took the form of concentrated piety – among people such as Hasan al-Basri, whom in fact the later Sufis claim as one of their own. What is important for our purposes is the social form in which such piety was expressed, and its connection to larger developments within the *umma*. As should be expected at this relatively early stage of Islamic history, the terminology which the sources use to describe this concentrated piety and those who practiced it was fluid, but one term which appears regularly is *zuhd*. Sometimes this term is translated as "asceticism," but the inevitable comparison to the behavior of Christian ascetics such as Simeon Stylites or St Antony of Egypt is somewhat misleading. As a general rule, *zuhd* did not involve acts of extreme mortification such as those which enhanced the reputation of Simeon and others in Egypt, Syria, and Asia Minor in late antiquity. Rather, it was a more generalized personal orientation, through which the believer sought to shun the distractions of the world in favor of things divine – simply a vigorous response to the ethical claims of the faith.[4] To embrace it did not necessarily involve abandoning completely one's ties to the world, or one's responsibilities to society – it did not involve, that is, running away to the desert, or climbing a pillar to escape the world, or for most, embracing the celibate life. Several of the most celebrated of those pious individuals later identified as founders of the Sufi tradition, for example, participated actively in campaigns of *jihad* against the Byzantine Empire, including Ibrahim ibn Adham and ᶜAbdallah ibn al-Mubarak. But a studied indifference to wealth and renunciation of the delights of this world did come to characterize much of the early Sufi tradition, and remained a part of that tradition in its later guises. A Sufi was often identified as a *faqir*, meaning "poor," and the exaltation of poverty was one of the most familiar themes of Sufi exempla.[5]

Even if the Islamic tradition did not fully embrace the other-worldliness of the Christian – Sufis were not monks, isolated in remote areas behind imposing monastic walls – the spiritual impetus behind the notion of *zuhd* could move an individual in unpredictable and startling ways. Stories concerning those early figures which the Sufi tradition claims as its own are full of accounts of their spiritual exploits, which often focus on behavior which can only be labeled ascetic. So, for example, Ibrahim ibn Adham may have been a holy warrior, but he is also remembered for his acts of self-denial: his continual fasting, and wearing of coarse garments inhabited, to his delight, by hundreds of lice. The ascetic impulse had considerable momentum, and remained an element in the fully-formed Sufi tradition. Sahl al-Tustari (d. 896), for instance, developed a much fuller system of mystical thought than earlier figures such as Hasan or Ibrahim, but renunciation

---

[4] Leah Kinberg, "What is Meant by *Zuhd*?", *Studia Islamica* 61 (1985), 27–44.

[5] Michael Bonner, *Aristocratic Violence and Holy War: Studies in the Jihad and the Arab–Byzantine Frontier* (New Haven: American Oriental Society, 1996), 107–34; Christopher Melchert, "The Transition from Asceticism to Mysticism at the Middle of the Ninth Century C.E.," *Studia Islamica* 83 (1996), 51–70, esp. 52–5.

was still very much a part of his religious life: fasting in some ways constituted the central feature of his ritual practice, and he was remembered for living for a year on a single dirham's worth of barley.[6] Such asceticism led to a sort of competition among the spiritual athletes who embraced it. Judging by the popularity of such stories, renunciants who tested the limits of what was humanly possible and what the law allowed held for Muslim audiences a mesmerizing attraction similar to that which drew fourth-century Christians to Simeon's pillar and Antony's cave. What this represents is Islam's assimilation of the tendency, well-known from late antique Christianity and Judaism, to locate spiritual power in particular persons and places which then serve as objects of veneration, models for imitation, or intercessors with God.

The practices (whether historical or legendary) of the Muslim ascetics demonstrate once again that the developing Islamic tradition needs to be understood as the product of the same historical and religious forces that gave rise to the other Near Eastern traditions. For example, one common form which this concentrated piety took was that of weeping – shedding tears, that is, for one's sins, for the sins of the world, and the torments which await those who spurn God's mercy. "Those who weep," *al-bakkaʾun*, including the pious Hasan al-Basri, could find a Koranic basis for their practice: according to the holy book, the ancient prophets, upon encountering the signs of God's mercy, "fell down, prostrating themselves, weeping" (19.58). Eventually, weeping as a devotional exercise – in prayer, at graves, during the visitation of the Kaʿba, upon hearing a sermon or the recitation of the Koran – became one of the most common signs of Muslim piety, and a trope of the biographical literature of Muslim "saints." Weeping over the frailty of human nature, our tendency to sin and in despair over God's impending judgment, was something that Muslims shared with adherents of other Near Eastern faiths for whom it served as a mode of pious expression. The practice is attested in Judaism, for example in apocalyptic works from the early Roman period, such as Fourth Ezra and from a few references in the Talmud. But it was especially common among Syrian Christian ascetics, for example Isaac of Nineveh.[7] Drawing on the 58th verse of the 19th *sura* of the Koran, Muslims themselves made the connection: the so-called "stories of the prophets" dwell at some length on the weeping of various Old Testament figures, such as David, who wept in penance for his sins, and Noah, whose name itself was etymologically linked to the Arabic verb "to wail" (*n/w/h*). And it is telling that, according to some biographical dictionaries of prominent early Muslims, there was a significant rise in the number of figures identified as ascetics at precisely the moment (the ninth century) when the process of conversion was picking up speed, perhaps reflecting the expectations which converts from Christianity, Judaism, and other religious traditions brought with them to their new faith.[8]

---

[6] Gerhard Böwering, *The Mystical Vision of Existence in Classical Islam: The Qurʾānic Hermeneutics of the Ṣūfī Sahl Al-Tustarī (d. 283/896)* (Berlin: de Gruyter, 1980), 55–6.

[7] A. J. Wensinck, *Some Semitic Rites of Mourning and Religion: Studies on Their Origin and Mutual Relation* (Amsterdam: Johannes Müller, 1917), 78–95.

[8] Richard Bulliet, *Islam: The View from the Edge* (New York: Columbia University Press, 1994), 89. On weeping generally, see *EI²*, art. "Bakkāʾ" (by F. Meier).

Two further developments over the ninth and tenth centuries helped to lay the groundwork for the fully-formed Sufism which in the Middle Period played such an important role in Muslim religious experience. The first was the grafting onto the ascetic tradition of a mystical dimension. The full doctrinal history of Sufism lies well beyond the scope of this work, but it is clear that various elements of a distinctly mystical approach to religious understanding began to enter the Islamic mix at this time: for example, the emphasis on secret and intuitive knowledge (*maʿrifa*, as opposed to *ʿilm*) as a means of comprehending God's will which was first articulated in an Islamic guise by Dhuʾl-Nun al-Misri (d. 859), or the notion of the "annihilation" (*fanaʾ*) of the individual self, an idea with such a pregnant future in the Sufi tradition and which can be traced back at least to Abu Yazid al-Bistami. This development remained for centuries the source of much controversy, in part because of the conceptual and doctrinal parallels between Sufi mystical speculation and a variety of pre-Islamic religious systems. Dhuʿl-Nun, for example, was repeatedly associated with the Hermetic traditions of late antiquity and Hellenistic philosophy, while more than one Sufi found himself accused of being a *zindiq*, an "infidel" (the term originally meant Manichaean, but came to be used as a more generalized and derisive epithet).[9]

The second development was the initial steps toward the routinization of the mystical experience in the Islamic tradition. The full emergence of Sufi "brotherhoods" and of institutions devoted specifically to housing and supporting their members belonged to a later period, but the foundations of both were laid in the ninth, tenth, and early eleventh centuries. Asceticism and mysticism as distinctive strains of Islamic thought began as the teaching of particular individuals. There is a certain parallel here to the way in which the legal schools grew out of clusters of scholars who saw themselves as intellectually-related disciples of a common master. Sufism, like the law schools, has a kind of "genealogical" style. Just as jurists passed to their students less a body of knowledge than a public recognition of their personal authority over texts, so the social process through which an individual was exposed to and mastered the ascetic and mystical disciplines was an intensely personal one, in which adepts observed and imitated their masters and ultimately received from them some sort of overt recognition of their progress. In time, the most common form of this recognition was the bestowal by the master on his disciple of a *khirqa*, a worn and patched garment symbolic of the individual's indifference to worldly wealth, although in the ninth century the use of *khirqas* for this purpose was at most in only a rudimentary stage. It is still too early to speak of the *tariqas*, the orders through which later Sufis received a comprehensive discipline and participated in a larger, corporate identity, but by the early eleventh century certain spiritual masters were beginning to articulate specific rules to govern the behavior of their followers. Abu Saʿid ibn Abiʾl-Khayr (d. 1049), for instance, published a set of

---

[9] For one instance of a Muslim mystic of this period accused rather loosely of being a *zindiq*, see Carl Ernst, *Words of Ecstasy in Sufism* (Albany, NY: SUNY Press, 1985), 97–101.

rules to guide the comportment of his disciples, requiring that they keep their garments clean, welcome and extend hospitality to the poor, eat together as a community, and pray and read the Koran collectively.[10]

A similar story can be told concerning the settings in which Islamic mystics practiced their art. Originally, asceticism and mysticism flourished, like the transmission of juristic knowledge, independently of any institutional structure. One of the characteristic features of later medieval Sufism was the spread of institutions, variously known as *khanqahs* or *ribats*, complete with buildings and endowments which housed and supported the activities of the mystics. Their origins are quite obscure, but it is likely that their roots lie in ninth- and tenth-century Iran. There is some evidence that adherents of an Islamic sect known after their eponymous founder Ibn Karram (d. 896) as the Karramiyya, who were prominent in Khurasan and other eastern provinces in this period, operated *khanqahs* as centers of worship and instruction, and that they may have modeled their institutions on others operated by Manichaeans in Khurasan and Transoxania. The Karramiyya were rejected by many Sunni theologians as heretical and eventually disappeared, so later Sufis distanced themselves from them; but in fact there is much that is "Sufiish" about the Karramiyya, especially their pronounced asceticism. In any case, from the very end of the tenth century, institutions called *khanqahs* or *ribats* appear which are specifically associated with Sufi groups. And at roughly the same moment that Ibn Abiʾl-Khayr was outlining those collective activities which would distinguish his followers' religious experience, Abu Ishaq al-Kazaruni (d. 1033) was requiring that his disciples live and pray together in the *khanqahs* which he founded.[11]

The routinization of the ascetic-mystic tradition, with programs of spiritual discipline and institutions to house and support the adepts, may have guaranteed the tradition's survival by bringing it under some form of control. But the tension between Sufism and juristic Islam never disappeared, perhaps because the Sufi tradition is inherently subversive. Its dynamism could result in perfectly unobjectionable manifestations of Muslim piety and enthusiasm for the faith – Ibrahim ibn Adham's commitment to *jihad*, for example. Sufis ranked among Islam's most effective proselytizers: Abu Ishaq al-Kazaruni, for instance, is credited with a fruitful campaign of conversion in the province of Fars, in southwest Iran, which had remained a bastion of Zoroastrianism. But Sufism's disruptive potential was never far from the surface. It may be that the sharp contrast between Sufi poverty and the wealth of the court or (on a more limited scale) the urban bourgeoisie whose interests and values are reflected in the *shariᶜa* contributed to the underlying tension between Sufism and other elements of the Islamic traditions. Doctrinally, Sufi mysticism could wreak havoc on certain

---

[10] R. A. Nicholson, *Studies in Islamic Mysticism* (Cambridge: Cambridge University Press, 1921), 1–76, esp. 46.

[11] Wilferd Madelung, *Religious Trends in Early Islamic Iran* (Albany, NY: Bibliotheca Persica, 1988), 48–9. On the Karrāmiyya, see *ibid.*, 39–46. On the early history of Sufi institutions, see *EI*², arts. "Khānqāh" and especially "Ribāṭ" (by J. Chabbi).

foundational principles of Islam. For example, without delving too deeply into what are linguistically and theologically extraordinarily complex matters, the notion of *ittihad*, the mystic "union" of the lover (Sufi) and beloved (God), could be read as undermining the radical separation between God and his creation, including humanity. Thus, the famous mystic al-Hallaj (executed 922) found himself arrested, condemned, beaten, crucified, and finally decapitated for expressions such as *anaʾl-haqq*, "I am the Truth" (*al-haqq* being one of the names of God).[12] But it was not simply doctrinal idiosyncrasies for which al-Hallaj was condemned: indeed, some at the time expressed a reluctance to judge expressions of mystical insight which the uninitiated could not fathom.[13] There were more important issues of sectarian affiliation and religious authority at stake. So, for example, al-Hallaj's critics persistently associated him with the Qarmatians whose state in Bahrayn threatened ʿAbbasid authority in the early tenth century. That was no doubt in part a useful trick of political abuse, but it may also have reflected some basic sympathy between his ideas and those of the Ismaʿilis. More generally, while the precise historical connections between the origins of Sufism and Shiʿism are difficult to disentangle, there are plenty of parallels and indications of cross-fertilization between the two movements (for example, in the emphasis in both upon esoteric interpretation, *taʾwil*, of the Koran), connections which were perfectly obvious to a medieval Muslim observer such as Ibn Khaldun.[14] In some of its manifestations, Sufism posed a threat to the authority of the ulama, and so the mystics frequently found themselves accused of antinomianism, a hostility to Islamic law. Again, the example of al-Hallaj is instructive. He is reported to have made statements that could be read as subsuming the legal requirement that Muslims perform the *hajj* to Mecca in a more generalized and interiorized pilgrimage "of the heart." Such a position threatened to unravel the work of the jurists by shifting the locus of religious authority from the consensus of the community to the experience of the individual.[15]

---

[12] The classic and very sympathetic work on al-Hallaj is that of Louis Massignon, *The Passion of al-Hallaj: Mystic and Martyr of Islam*, trans. Herbert Mason, in 4 vols. (Princeton: Princeton University Press, 1982).

[13] See, for example, *ibid.*, 1:373–8.

[14] Ibn Khaldūn, *Muqaddimah*, ed. M. Quatremère (Paris: 1858), 2.164f, trans. Franz Rosenthal (Princeton: Princeton University Press, 1967), 2:186f; Seyyed Hossein Nasr, "Le shiʿisme et le soufisme: leurs relations principelles et historiques," in *Le Shiʿisme Imamite: Colloque de Strasbourg (6–9 mai 1968)* (Paris: Presses Universitaires de France, 1970), 215–33.

[15] Melchert, "The Transition from Asceticism to Mysticism," 64f.

CHAPTER 17

The non-Muslim communities

From the perspective of the non-Muslim communities of the Near East, the three centuries which followed the ᶜAbbasid revolution were decisive in two respects. In the first place, it was in this period that the non-Muslims were reduced to minority status in most areas. In the second, with the fuller articulation of Islamic law, the conventions and procedures which would govern relations between the non-Muslim communities and the Islamic state, and which would institutionalize the political and social inferiority of the former, took on a normative shape. Viewed from such a perspective, it is difficult to characterize the period as anything other than one of overall decline. That perspective and that characterization, however, can obscure a more complex reality. In the first place, non-Muslims experienced life under Muslim regimes in different ways: the Jewish experience, for example, was not exactly the same as the Zoroastrian, despite certain common patterns. Moreover, the *dhimmi* communities were hardly moribund, and in many instances responded vigorously to the challenges posed to them by the new dominant Muslim culture.

The Islamic societies of the Near East in this period were deeply multicultural, and so there were plenty of opportunities for significant contact and exchange across the sectarian divide. The Islamic world-view, in which Islam was simply one (albeit the final and most perfect) of many distinct faith traditions, perhaps inherently raised the question of what a conversation with those other traditions would produce. On occasion, Muslims, Jews, Christians and others pursued that conversation, on a variety of different levels. Intellectual exchanges among the philosophers were the most free, and Christians played a pre-eminent role in the transmission of classical science and philosophy in Baghdad and elsewhere. Among religious scholars, as might be expected, the "conversation" was more likely to be polemical. The similarities (and also the differences) between Koranic stories about Abraham, Moses, and others, and those recorded in the Hebrew Scriptures and the Christian Gospels, posed the question in starkly and un-comfortably comparative terms. As we have seen, the ulama grew skeptical about the value of texts such as the *isra'iliyyat* as a source of religious knowledge, and worried in particular that the uneducated – that is, the non-ulama – could be led astray by stories which were not, as it were, kosher. Despite the polemics, however,

Muslim, Jewish, and Christian scholars, in a variety of settings, in Baghdad, Cairo, and elsewhere, indulged in a dialogue that was essentially an exercise in comparative religion, meeting sometimes in the presence of caliphs, amirs, their viziers, and other leading officials, for the exchange of ideas, even (within limits) debates about the relative merits of the different faith traditions.[1]

On the level of common religious experience, there was also considerable exchange, although its precise mechanisms are naturally less visible to us. Some of this came about because of the conversion of Jews, Christians, and others to Islam, as the converts brought with them ideas, concerns, and practices which were shaped or informed by their previous religious allegiance. An even more important factor, however, was the relatively open character of life in medieval Islamic cities. As a general rule, non-Muslims were not systematically isolated as were, say, Jews in medieval European ghettos, and so there naturally developed a common vernacular of religious assumptions, expectations, and practices. So, for example, Muslims in Egypt and elsewhere shared with their non-Muslim neighbors the belief that the dead continued to "live" in a sense inside their graves, making it possible for the living to engage in continuous interaction with the dead. That assumption gave rise to a cult of saints which loomed large in the religious life of late antique and medieval Near Eastern Christians. It also became the basis for a parallel Muslim cult which, for all that it annoyed some of the ulama, constituted a significant component of the religious experience of many Muslims, as we shall see later in this book.[2] Muslims might even adopt as their own practices explicitly identified with their non-Muslim neighbors. So, for example, according to the tenth-century geographer al-Muqaddasi, the Muslims of Syria participated in the celebration of Easter, Christmas, and other Christian feast-days, in part because their more-or-less regular appearance according to the solar calendar helped to mark the agricultural seasons more accurately than the Muslim holidays, which of course moved forward each year according to the lunar Muslim

---

[1] See Hava Lazarus-Yafeh, *Intertwined Worlds: Medieval Islam and Bible Criticism* (Princeton: Princeton University Press, 1992), esp. 133–4; Joel Kraemer, *Humanism in the Renaissance of Islam: The Cultural Revival during the Buyid Age* (Leiden: E. J. Brill, 1986), 52–86, esp. 58–60, 76–7, 82; Wadi Z. Haddad, "Continuity and Change in Religious Adherence: Ninth-century Baghdad", in *Conversion and Continuity: Indigenous Christian Communities in Islamic Lands, Eighth to Eighteenth Centuries*, ed. Michael Gervers and Ramzi Jibran Bikhazi (Toronto: Pontifical Institute of Mediaeval Studies, 1990) (Papers in Mediaeval Studies 9), 34–53. For a fascinating account of one such session, presided over by Yaʿqub ibn Killis, the Jewish convert to Islam who served as vizier to the early Fatimid caliphs in Egypt, see Mark R. Cohen and Sasson Somekh, "In the Court of Yaʿqūb ibn Killis: A Fragment from the Cairo Genizah," *Jewish Quarterly Review* 80 (1990), 283–314. Of course, these "discussions" did not preclude sharper polemical exchange. See, for example, David Thomas, *Anti-Christian Polemic in Early Islam: Abū ʿĪsā Warrāq's "Against the Trinity"* (Cambridge: Cambridge University Press, 1992).

[2] The classic work on the Christian cult of the saints is Peter Brown, *The Cult of the Saints: Its Rise and Function in Latin Christianity* (Chicago: University of Chicago Press, 1982). On the popular Muslim understanding of communication between the living and the dead, see Leah Kinberg, *Morality in the Guise of Dreams: A Critical Edition of Kitāb al-Manām with Introduction* (Leiden: E. J. Brill, 1994), 18.

calendar.[3] The records of the Geniza, the storehouse for a vast miscellany of texts and documents produced by the Jewish community of Fustat (near Cairo), testify to the important role of magic, charms, incantations, and other attempts to manipulate the world of spirits (*jinn*) in the daily lives of the members of that community. Jewish scholars such as the famous Maimonedes often objected to such manifestations of popular religion, although their struggle seems to have been a losing one. Their concerns were shared by many of the Muslim ulama, and so it seems that the picture derived from the Geniza documents reflects Muslim realities as well.[4]

Conversation between Muslims and non-Muslims and a shared reservoir of assumptions and experience did not, of course, imply that non-Muslims had anything approaching equal status in Islamic societies. As *dhimmis*, that is, *ahl al-dhimma*, the "people of the covenant of protection," they enjoyed the protection and toleration of Muslim regimes. In general they were left to organize their internal communal affairs as they saw fit, and to apply their own laws to the members of their communities. In exchange, they submitted to a number of restrictions, not so much on their beliefs, as on their public behavior. So, for example, according to the terms of the so-called "Pact of 'Umar" and the various other legal texts which expand upon the status of the *dhimmis* according to Muslim law, non-Muslims were required to wear clothing of a certain color, to humiliate them and make their identification easier – a goal made more important, perhaps, in a world without ghettoization. On the whole, such restrictions were not terribly onerous. In some cases, however, the restrictions seriously circumscribed the *dhimmis'* religious lives. So, for example, the Pact of 'Umar stipulated that, while churches and synagogues in existence at the moment a town or territory was conquered by the Muslims could remain, they could not be repaired, and new buildings could not be constructed. This restriction on the activities of the *dhimmis* was one that the jurists took especially seriously, and they routinely repeated the prohibition in their lawbooks. On the other hand, it is also clear that the prohibition was frequently ignored – a fact attested by the number of churches, synagogues, and other *dhimmi* religious institutions in Baghdad, Fustat, and other towns founded after the Muslim conquest. More immediately galling was the requirement that adult, free, male *dhimmis* pay an annual poll tax, which the jurists referred to as the *jizya*. The origins of the *jizya* are extremely cloudy. The tax as it was described in Islamic legal texts in the ninth, tenth, and later centuries was

---

[3] Abu ʿAbd Allāh Muḥammad ibn Aḥmad al-Muqaddasī, *Aḥsān al-taqāsīm fī maʿrifat al-aqālīm*, ed. de Goeje (Leiden: E. J. Brill, 1906), 182–3; trans. André Miquel (Damascus: Institut Français de Damas, 1963), 223–4.

[4] Norman Golb, "Aspects of the Historical Background of Jewish Life in Medieval Egypt," in *Jewish Medieval and Renaissance Studies*, ed. Alexander Altmann (Cambridge, Massachusetts: Harvard University Press, 1967), 1–18, esp. 13–16. On the Geniza documents generally and the social world they describe, see S. D. Goitein, *A Mediterranean Society: The Jewish Communities of the Arab World as Portrayed in the Documents of the Cairo Geniza*, in 6 vols. (Berkeley: University of California Press, 1967–1993). On the Geniza as reflecting the experience of medieval Egyptians generally, and not simply that of the Jews, see 1.70–4.

probably different than any imposed at the time of the Prophet or in the first decades of the Islamic period. The payment of the *jizya* became, for ordinary *dhimmis*, a considerable burden, both psychologically and as a simple matter of payment. This was a requirement which Muslim governments were naturally more interested in enforcing. As a result, it was common for receipts to be given indicating an individual had paid his poll-tax. That receipt was necessary for *dhimmis* wishing to travel, as it could be demanded as proof that the tax had been paid; failure to produce it could result in severe punishment.[5]

Arguably the most pressing problem for the *dhimmi* communities was that of conversion. Unfortunately, the precise contours of the process by which the majority of the inhabitants of the Near East, who in 632 (or even 750) were not Muslim, shifted their religious allegiance are difficult to determine – although it is probably the case that the shift had occurred around the end of the tenth century. The uncertainty derives from the lack of detailed studies of the process of conversion, which in turn is fueled by the character of the surviving sources, which contain some impressionistic evidence but little in the way of easily accessible comprehensive empirical data. Nonetheless, we can tentatively hazard some general propositions about the experience of the *dhimmi* communities as they confronted the growing reality of conversion to Islam in the eighth through the early eleventh centuries.[6]

By the eighth and ninth centuries, the indifference to non-Arabs converting to Islam that had characterized Muslim governments and society in their early years had dissipated, although instances of forced conversion were still relatively rare. Where there was no issue of compulsion, people converted for a variety of over-lapping reasons. No doubt some individuals were driven principally by the conviction that the new religion possessed a firmer grasp on divine truth. For an individual, the actual steps to conversion were relatively few: the act of *islam*

---

[5] The literature on the status of the *dhimmis* is enormous. A good place to begin is with *EI*[2], art. "Dhimma" (by Claude Cahen), and Bernard Lewis, *The Jews of Islam* (Princeton: Princeton University Press, 1984), 3–66. A. S. Tritton's *The Caliphs and Their Non-Muslim Subjects*, 2nd edition (London: Frank Cass, 1970), is a thoroughly uncritical and at times ahistorical study, but still useful as a source of detail. Mark Cohen, *Under Crescent and Cross: The Jews in the Middle Ages* (Princeton: Princeton University Press, 1994), 58–60, surveys the literature on the issue of the construction of *dhimmi* houses of worship. On the complicated story of early Islamic taxation and the development of the *jizya*, see *EI*[2], art. "Djizya" (by Claude Cahen). On its actual application in the early Middle Period, and on the burden it could pose on ordinary *dhimmis*, see Goitein, *A Mediterranean Society*, vol. 2: *The Community*, 380–94, and idem, "Evidence on the Muslim Poll Tax from Non-Muslim Sources: A Geniza Study," *Journal of the Economic and Social History of the Orient* 6 (1963), 278–95.

[6] The effort of Richard Bulliet to trace the curve of conversion is the most sophisticated study to date, although the author himself acknowledged that it is difficult to know how readily we can generalize from his account, which is rooted most firmly in the experience of the urban elites, particularly those of northeastern Iran. Compare *Conversion to Islam in the Medieval Period* (Cambridge, Mass.: Harvard University Press, 1979), passim, and Michael G. Morony's critique, "The Age of Conversions: A Reassessment," in *Conversion and Continuity: Indigenous Christian Communities in Islamic Lands, Eighth to Eighteenth Centuries*, ed. Michael Gervers and Ramzi Jibran Bikhazi (Toronto: Pontifical Institute of Mediaeval Studies, 1990) (Papers in Mediaeval Studies 9), 135–50. Another useful study is that of Ira Lapidus, "The Conversion of Egypt to Islam," *Israel Oriental Studies* 2 (1972), 248–62.

involved on one level the simple doctrinal declaration that there is no god but God, and that Muhammad is his messenger. (For men, at least in theory, it also demanded circumcision, and, except for those such as Jews who were already circumcised, this must have represented a considerable impediment. On the other hand, we may wonder how frequently circumcision was actually imposed on adult converts. During his trial for apostasy, the Iranian prince and famous ᶜAbbasid general al-Afshin, a convert from Zoroastrianism or possibly Buddhism who served in the ᶜAbbasid army, admitted that he had not been circumcised, pleading that he had worried [not without reason?] that the operation could have proven detrimental to his health.)[7]

For others, however, social concerns were just as pressing as theological ones, and the convictions and hopes which led them to the act of *islam* were shaped by a variety of factors. This was natural, given the importance of religious affiliation to social status and experience: it could determine what one wore, and whom one married, and certainly whether one was governed by the *shariᶜa*'s law of personal status or that enforced by the rabbinical courts or the legal authorities of the other religious communities. But the nature of those social concerns varied widely. Once the nexus of legal restrictions on the *dhimmis'* behavior was fixed in the *shariᶜa*, and when those strictures were seriously enforced, non-Muslims could hardly experience them as anything other than a humiliation, and therefore an incentive to convert. Some responded to calculations of individual gain. For centuries, many Muslim governments relied on non-Muslim functionaries and bureaucrats – in Egypt, for example, Copts played an important role in government administration well into the later Middle Period – a situation which led to an ongoing discussion on the part of the jurists as to whether such reliance was acceptable. Especially at the higher reaches of government office, such individuals surely felt pressure, or perhaps incentive, to convert. And in fact, we can identify a number of prominent political and administrative figures who were themselves converts to Islam: Ibn al-al-Muqaffaᶜ, for example, secretary to imperial governors in Iran and Iraq under the later Umayyads and the first ᶜAbbasid caliphs, and Yaᶜqub b. Killis, a Jewish convert to Islam and vizier to the Fatimid caliphs in Egypt in the late tenth century.

For most, the social considerations were broader. For some, particularly those who were members of tribes, the decision was surely a matter for the group – as, indeed, it had been for some Arab tribes in the earliest days of Islam. But even when tribal structures and hierarchies were not an issue, the dynamics and pressures of larger social groups was usually critical. At times we can see the process at work in its broadest social outlines. So, for example, Egyptian peasants,

---

[7] See Muhammad ibn Jarīr al-Ṭabarī, *Tārīkh al-rusul waʾl-mulūk*, ed. M. J. De Goeje and others (Leiden: E. J. Brill, 1879–1901), 1/3.1312–13 = *The History of al-Ṭabari*, vol. 33, trans. C. E. Bosworth (Albany, NY: SUNY Press, 1991), 192. The story is a famous one, and frequently cited. But a few pages later, al-Tabari recounts a subsequent episode, which has attracted less attention, in which al-Afshin coyly implied, without directly claiming as much, that he was in fact circumcised, and that he had acknowledged the charge simply in order to avoid the humiliation of having to expose himself in public. *Tārīkh*, 1/3.1317 = *History*, 33.199. On al-Afshin's religion, see below.

still overwhelmingly Christian, staged a series of revolts during the eighth and early ninth centuries. These rebellions resulted from excessive taxation rather than religious oppression, and were brutally suppressed by the Muslim authorities (including al-Afshin). In their wake, however, the rural Coptic communities found their networks of social support disrupted; moreover, the rebellions prompted the Islamic authorities to enforce more strictly the *shariᶜa*'s sumptuary regulations. The assertion of the fifteenth-century historian al-Maqrizi that it was then, as a result of the rebellions and their aftermath, that Islam became a majority religion in the Egyptian countryside, may be somewhat premature, and a vigorous Coptic culture by no means disappeared in this period. But the suppression of the rebellions did undermine the social integrity of the Christian communities, and contributed significantly to the conversion of most Egyptians to Islam.[8]

The Near East was very much the demographic center of world Jewry in this period. Jews of course converted to Islam, as did the followers of other faith traditions, but the pronounced ethnic character of Judaism may have contributed to the cohesion of the community and, possibly, strengthened resistance to the lure of Islam.[9] Iraq had an especially large concentration of Jews, and it was there that one of the two principal Jewish academies was based, and where much of what we now know as Jewish law took shape. But Jewish communities could be found almost everywhere, even (still) in parts of Arabia.[10] This is not to say that, at least outside of Iraq, the Jews constituted a significant proportion of the population of any given place. Firm data are of course elusive, but in Egypt, for example, estimates for the number of Jews in this period do not exceed 40,000, and the actual figure was probably lower. The total population of Egypt probably did not exceed three or four million, and so the Jews made up only a tiny fraction of the overall population.[11] The Jewish population, or at least portions of it, was relatively mobile, and there was some degree of movement of Jews from Iraq to points west, such as Palestine and especially Egypt, as the situation in Iraq grew more unstable with the decline of ᶜAbbasid power and then with the flourishing of the Fatimid caliphate – anticipating, in a way, the shift of both people and the center of Muslim cultural activity from Iraq to Syria and Egypt at the time of the Crusades and the Mongol invasions. At the Muslim conquests, the Jews were not yet a predominantly urban, commercial community. In Iraq, the majority of the Jews were peasants and laborers. In Egypt, too, there were Jewish communities far from the

---

[8] Taqī ᵓl-Dīn al-Maqrīzī, *al-Mawāᶜiẓ waᵓl-iᶜtibār bi-dhikr al-khiṭaṭ waᵓl-athār*, 2 vols. (Bulaq: Dar al-Ṭibāᶜa al-Miṣriyya, 1853–4), 2:494; Lapidus, "Conversion of Egypt," 256–60.

[9] Cf. a point made by Patricia Crone and Michael Cook, *Hagarism: The Making of the Islamic World* (Cambridge: Cambridge University Press, 1977), 86.

[10] Gordon Newby, *A History of the Jews of Arabia from Ancient Times to Their Eclipse under Islam* (Columbia, SC: University of South Carolina Press, 1988), 97–100.

[11] Eliyahu Ashtor, "The Number of the Jews in Medieval Egypt," *Journal of Jewish Studies* 18 (1967), 9–42, and 19 (1968), 1–22; J. C. Russell, "The Population of Medieval Egypt," *Journal of the American Research Center in Egypt* 5 (1966), 69–82; and the cautions in David Ayalon, "Regarding Population Estimates in the Countries of Medieval Islam," *Journal of the Economic and Social History of the Orient* 28 (1985), 1–19.

major urban centers, including the Delta region, Upper Egypt, and the Fayyum oasis to the south and west of Fustat (modern Cairo), and as the Geniza attests, those non-metropolitan communities survived through this period. But it was in these centuries that the character of the Near Eastern Jewish communities changed, and the Jews became more firmly associated with urban artisnal activities and international commerce. The image that emerges from the records of the Geniza, so exhaustively studied by S. D. Goitein in his magisterial work on *A Mediterranean Society*, is one of a Jewish population intimately associated, almost defined by an international trade which linked separate communities in southern Europe, north Africa, the Near East, and south Asia. Not every Jew was a prosperous international merchant, but through a network of partnerships the benefits (and risks) of international commerce trickled down to Jews of different occupations and social status. Their commercial success was made possible by, and at the same time reinforced, feelings of international communal solidarity, and also by the far-flung nature of the Jewish population, with its outposts in virtually every Near Eastern region – as attested by the twelfth-century Rabbi Benjamin of Tudela, who left a description of the myriad Jewish communities he encountered on his journey through Syria, Iraq, and Egypt. Religious considerations played an important role in this feeling of international communal solidarity. The Talmudic academies in Palestine and especially Iraq and their heads (*geonim*) provided the disparate Jewish communities with both the intellectual and personal infrastructure which made possible their autonomous life under the terms of the Islamic *dhimma*, in the form of responsa to questions put to them by Jews in the various communities, and more immediately in the form of judges and other religious figures who supervised religious life at home. The disparate communities in turn supported the work of the academies through financial contributions.[12]

The period from the middle of the eighth to the start of the eleventh century saw significant developments in patterns of authority within the Jewish community, and also the emergence of a sectarian schism. In the very first years of the ʿAbbasid regime, a crisis of leadership developed within the Iraqi Jewish community which pitted ʿAnan ben David, a claimant to the exilarchate, against his brother, who was supported by the geonic community. ʿAnan sought the intervention of the caliph al-Mansur, who responded by throwing him into prison, where, according to one story, the advice of a fellow prisoner, a Muslim jurist who may have been Abu Hanifa, saved him from execution. The story is interesting in several respects. For one thing, it shows the caliph intervening directly in the internal affairs of the Iraqi Jewish community, and therefore can be read as a marker of a broader pattern, in which the non-Muslim religious communities settled into a symbiotic relationship to the Muslim state, one similar to that which had characterized relations between the Sasanian shahs and their non-Zoroastrian subjects. The ties were not so formalized as they were to become in later centuries, especially in the Ottoman period, but the autonomy granted to the *dhimmis* was

---

[12] See Goitein, *A Mediterranean Society*, vol. 2, passim, esp. 5–23 and 311–45.

subject to the changing needs of their relationship with the Islamic regimes under which they lived. So the election of an exilarch (or the religious and communal leaders of the Christians and other *dhimmis*) might be subject to the approval of the caliph or other Islamic ruler; and so they might be held responsible for the collection of the *jizya*, or the enforcement of the sumptuary restrictions required by Islamic law. Al-Mansur took an interest in the Jewish exilarch, because the exilarch, if he was not exactly an officer of the state, nonetheless had communal responsibilities which made him the principal channel through which the state and the *dhimmi* community negotiated their respective rights and responsibilities. The relationship was fully symbiotic, and when the leaders of the Jewish (and other *dhimmi*) communities participated in public processions on holidays or on state occasions, as was common in Egypt and elsewhere in the medieval period, they were making a public statement about both their community's importance and the claims which they made on the indulgence and protection of the ruler. The second aspect of ᶜAnan ben David's experience to claim our attention, and the more important from the perspective of the internal development of the Jewish community, is that it marks the beginning of the Karaite schism. What made ᶜAnan suspicious to the rabbis was his rejection of the notion of an oral Torah which formed the foundation of the Talmudic Judaism preached by the rabbis. The exclusive reliance on Biblical texts was the distinguishing characteristic of the Karaite sect as it evolved in the ninth and tenth centuries into a branch of Judaism, with its own synagogues and communal structure, to rival the Rabbanite community.[13]

In the common view, the Christian communities of the Islamic world began to experience an irreversible and ultimately paralyzing decline in the early medieval period. So, for example, the great Orientalist G. E. von Grunebaum remarked: "The intellectual life of the Christians in Syria, Egypt, and Mesopotamia was isolated from the centres of Christian thought and excluded from Muslim imperial policies, though not from imperial administration. The natural consequence was that it was gradually squeezed out of the broad intellectual currents as well."[14] To be sure, the Christians did suffer from conversion to Islam, and perhaps, for reasons adduced above, a higher proportion of them converted than did Jews.

---

[13] On Karaism and the ᶜAnan ben David affair, see Michael G. Morony, *Iraq After the Muslim Conquest* (Princeton: Princeton University Press, 1984), 329, and Salo W. Baron, *A Social and Religious History of the Jews*, second edition (New York: Columbia University Press, 1952), vol. 5: *Religious Controls and Dissensions*, 209–85, 388–9. It has been suggested that the Karaite aversion to the rabbis' oral traditions was possibly inspired by "scripturalist" opposition to the emphasis on hadith within the Muslim community – in other words, that it represents an instance of Muslim influence on one of the pre-Islamic religious traditions. See Crone and Cook, *Hagarism*, 38, and Michael Cook, "ᶜAnan and Islam: The Origins of Karaite Scripturalism," *Jerusalem Studies in Arabic and Islam* 9 (1987), 161–82.

[14] G. E. von Grunebaum, *Classical Islam: A History, 600–1258* (Chicago: Aldine Publishing Company, 1970), 64. For an even bleaker view, see Kenneth Cragg, *The Arab Christian: A History in the Middle East* (Louisville, KY: Westminster/John Knox Press, 1991), 57, where he remarks that the isolation of the Christian communities within the Islamic world led to their "irrelevance," and to "centuries of ghetto-style existence," condemning them to slow attrition.

There is evidence, too, that the pace of conversion, which picked up steam in the early ᶜAbbasid period, helped to shape the psychological profile of the world view of Christians living under Islamic rule. So, for example, Christian writers in the eighth and ninth centuries produced a slew of accounts extolling individuals who were martyred for their beliefs, for their steadfastness in the face of Muslim pressure to convert. The stories, which are generally not corroborated in Muslim sources, may or may not be historical; their significance lies in what they reveal about Christian perceptions, and in particular their apprehension of a need to reinforce the loyalty of wavering co-religionists.[15] And Christians, probably more than Jews, served as the targets of the periodic bouts of rigorous enforcement of the covenantal restrictions on *dhimmis* of which the medieval chronicles give ample testimony, such as that inflicted by the Fatimid caliph al-Hakim.

Here, too, however, there is evidence of ferment, adaptation, accommodation, and even growth beneath the surface. Active Christian missions did not end with the coming of Islam, and the Nestorian, Melkite, and Jacobite churches all made serious efforts to expand into northeastern Iran and central Asia in the wake of the Arab conquests. The forms in which Christians understood and expressed their faith shifted significantly in response to the altered world they confronted. Already by the ninth century, the Christians of Syria, such as Theodore Abu Qurrah, the Melkite bishop of Harran, were composing theological and liturgical tracts in Arabic, a phenomenon which suggests several things about the social and intellectual condition of the Christian community under early Islam. Certainly it reflects the astonishingly rapid progress of the adoption of Arabic by the inhabitants of the Near East, both those who converted to Islam as well as those who remained faithful to the older religious traditions. Christian writers wrote in Arabic, that is, because their audiences had come to speak the language. It also reflects a Christian tradition in intellectual transition, as writers such as Abu Qurrah adopted Muslim terminology to express their explicitly Christian theological positions – and so Christ, for example, could be identified with the Koranic epithet *rabb al-ᶜalamin*, "lord of the worlds." But that may in turn suggest not only that the Christian tradition accommodated itself to the new environment shaped by Islam, but also an awareness of the challenge posed to Christianity by the new religion. Much of the Christian literature of this period has a polemical nature, and its argumentative and apologetic edge betrays a tradition quite willing to compete with Islam for the allegiance of the inhabitants of the Near East. The polemic was waged at a high level of cultural discourse, but also informed hagiographical literature aimed at a much broader audience. Take, for example, a delightful story found in the *History of the Patriarchs of the Egyptian Church*, about a tenth-century Coptic patriarch who, challenged by the Fatimid caliph al-Muᶜizz and his vizier Ibn Killis to demonstrate the power of Christian faith by moving a mountain (cf. Matthew 17:20), managed (with the assistance of a one-eyed water carrier) to

---

[15] See Robert Schick, *The Christian Communities of Palestine from Byzantine to Islamic Rule: A Historical and Archaeological Study* (Princeton: Darwin, 1995), 171–7, and the sources cited there.

lift the hill outside Cairo known as al-Muqattam, not once, but three times. Yet different versions of the tale unconsciously reflect the ambiguity and precariousness of the Christian position. In one "popular" but hopelessly optimistic version, the miracle results in the conversion of the caliph, who then disappears to become a monk. The more sober version found in the *History of the Patriarchs* claims a more modest triumph: namely, that al-Mu^{c}izz permitted the reconstruction of several demolished churches.[16]

Egypt provides a useful example of the complex forces at work within Christian communities living under Islamic rule in the early medieval period. It serves, first of all, as a reminder that the Christian community itself was not united. Demographically, the so-called "Coptic" church – that is to say, the indigenous Egyptian church which embraced the Monophysite position on theological matters – claimed the allegiance of by far the lion's share of the Christian population of Egypt, but there were others churches, too, most notably the Melkite, representing the orthodox institution connected with the Byzantine Empire. The tension which had existed between Melkites and Monophysites in the pre-Islamic period did not dissipate once the Muslims were in control. The two churches maintained separate ecclesiastical organizations and structures of authority, and their leaders frequently sought to secure advantage from the rulers at the expense of their Christian rivals. Given the level of mutual suspicion between Copts and Melkites, reinforced by Muslim wariness toward a resurgent Byzantine Empire in this period, it is perhaps not surprising that there was little contact between the Egyptian church and the Church of Constantinople. But Copts were not entirely isolated, as sweeping conclusions like von Grunebaum's might suggest, and they maintained institutional and intellectual connections with other Christians living within the Muslim commonwealth, particularly with Syrian Monophysites. Still, the Coptic community retained certain distinctive features which maintained historical continuity with its pre-Islamic past and provided a line of defense against the increasingly powerful cultural gravity of Islam. The Coptic language was gradually replaced by Arabic as a medium of daily communication among most Christian Egyptians. The development was not sudden: the pace of Arabization differed from one place to another, and in certain remote areas Coptic probably survived as a spoken language through the end of the Middle Period. But Coptic survived longer as a liturgical language, and in the process acquired an iconic status which made it

---

[16] Johannes den Heijer, "Apologetic Elements in Coptic-Arabic Historiography: The Life of Afraham ibn Zur^{c}ah, 62nd Patriarch of Alexandria," in *Christian Arabic Apologetics During the Abbasid Period (750–1258)*, ed. Samir Khalil Samir and Jørgen S. Nielsen (Leiden: E. J. Brill, 1994), 192–202. The volume edited by Samir and Nielsen is a useful collection of essays on Christian polemics in a Muslim setting. On Christian expansion into central Asia, see J. Nasrallah, "L'Église melchite en Iraq, en Perse et dans l'Asie centrale," *Proche-Orient Chrétien*, 26 (1976), 16–33, and J. Dauvillier, "L'Expansion de l'Église syrienne en Asie Centrale," in *L'Orient Syrien* 1 (1956), 76–87. On Theodore Abu Qurrah and the earliest Arabic Christian writings, see the various studies by Sidney Griffith, many of them collected in *Arabic Christianity in the Monasteries of Ninth-Century Palestine* (London: Ashgate, 1992), and especially idem, "The View of Islam from the Monasteries of Palestine in the Early ^{c}Abbasid Period: Theodore Abu Qurrah and the *Summa Theologiae Arabica*," *Islam and Christian–Muslim Relations* 7 (1996), 9–28.

psychologically a potent vessel of Coptic identity – even if the churchmen who used it often required Arabic "cribs" to understand their texts. That it survived, and acquired new meaning as a marker of non-Muslim cultural identity, is thanks in large part to the activities of the Coptic monks. Egypt was of course one of the principal crucibles of late antique monasticism, and the monasteries survived the Muslim conquest as institutions critical to the on-going life of the Coptic church: as sites for the production of manuscripts, but also as the objects of pilgrimage which contributed to the cultivation and preservation of a Coptic identity among rural Egyptian Christians.[17]

Because they were not monotheists possessing a recognized revealed scripture, pagans and Manichaeans should in principle have had more trouble than Jews or Christians winning a protected place within the new Muslim societies. The historical record suggests that that was, in fact, the case, although again, the situation was more nuanced than one might expect. Pagan cults did not disappear overnight with the Arab invasions, despite the later juridical position that their practitioners were not entitled to the protection of the *dhimma*. In the remote and mountainous district of Ghur, for example, in what is now Afghanistan, Islam made few inroads and the older pagan religious traditions survived intact until the early eleventh century. In the tenth and eleventh centuries the region was ringed by *ribats*, fortresses from which Muslim warriors waged a constant low-level campaign of *jihad*, in the course of which they captured slaves to supply the markets of the Muslim cities of eastern Iran. It was only with the rise of the Ghaznavid dynasty that the region was conquered by a Muslim government and a systematic campaign of proselytization carried out in the early eleventh century.[18] But in areas under effective Muslim rule, pagans came under greater pressure. As we have seen, a few communities, most notably those belonging to the astral cult at Harran who claimed for themselves the Koranic name "Sabians," survived well into the medieval period. In the cosmopolitan atmosphere of the ʿAbbasid court, a mathematician and philosopher such as the Sabian Thabit ibn Qurra (d. 901) could play, alongside Christians such as the famous medical doctor Hunayn ibn Ishaq, a prominent role in the translation movement which grafted into Arabic culture the legacy of classical Greek science. Thabit's example is instructive for several reasons. In the first place, he came to Baghdad because of certain doctrinal disagreements with his own pagan community at Harran, as a result of which he was proscribed and forbidden entrance to their temples. This suggests that the Sabian community in Harran possessed something in the way of a clearly-defined doctrinal character. A passage in Ibn al-Nadim's *Fihrist*, in which he lists the

---

[17] An extremely useful survey of the sources on the Coptic experience in early Islamic Egypt can be found in Terry G. Wilfong, "The Non-Muslim Communities: Christian Communities," in *The Cambridge History of Egypt*, vol. 1: *Islamic Egypt, 640–1517*, ed. Carl Petry (Cambridge: Cambridge University Press, 1998), 175–97, esp. 188–91 on Coptic monasteries. For a catalogue of Coptic pilgrimages, see Gérard Viaud, *Les pèlerinages coptes en Égypte* (Cairo: IFAO, 1979).

[18] On the pagan enclave in Ghur, see C. E. Bosworth, "The Early Islamic History of Ghūr," *Central Asiatic Journal* 6 (1961), 116–33.

various "headmen" of the community under the caliphs, suggests that that doctrinal identity was accompanied by a structure of communal organization and authority that paralleled that of the *dhimmis* under Muslim rule. Secondly, after Thabit's removal to Baghdad, where he became an intimate of the caliph al-Muʿtadid, his descendants after him followed in his footsteps as scholars of the mathematical and philosophical sciences, and at least as far as his grandson, Thabit ibn Sinan, identified themselves as (pagan) "Sabians." In Harran itself, the Sabian community gradually withered. Ibn al-Nadim suggests that many there lived a shadowy religious life as crypto-pagans, formally identifying themselves as Muslims or Christians, while the last temple of the Sabians at Harran was finally closed in the early eleventh century.[19]

Manichaeism was more problematic for the Muslim authorities. In this, once again, Islam continued patterns of religious experience and interaction which had characterized the pre-Islamic Near East, since both the Roman and Sasanian empires had sought to suppress the sect. The Koran referred to Jews, Christians, Magians (Zoroastrians), and even (although ambiguously) to the religion of the "Sabians". Regarding Mani and his followers, however, it was silent. Earlier in this book, we noted that the religion had a strong intellectual appeal. The historian al-Tabari's account of a campaign launched by the ʿAbbasid caliph al-Mahdi in 779–80 to extirpate Manichaeism testifies to its allure even for those most deeply tied to the Arab-Islamic order. In 782–3, several sons of prominent figures in the ʿAbbasid regime were arrested. Their lenient treatment – after confessing their error, they were released to their families' care – contrasts with the torture and execution meted out to others, and must have resulted from their social prominence. Not even direct descent from the Prophet's paternal grandfather, however, nor membership in the caliphal family itself, could spare one who refused to recant his dualist conventions: a cousin of the first two ʿAbbasid caliphs died in prison awaiting execution, while an imprisoned and unrepentant member of the Hashimi family was smothered under a mattress at the orders of the caliph Musa al-Hadi – as, in fact, the caliph's first order of business after his accession to the throne.[20] It was not only the political authorities who persecuted the Manichaeans; on the contrary, they and their dualist doctrines seem to have provoked high levels of genuine hostility on the part of the Muslim *umma*. At one point, for example, al-Maʾmun invited a Manichaean named Yazdanbakht from Khurasan to Baghdad to engage in theological disputation. The caliph gave the wary scholar an assurance of his personal safety, but also found it necessary to set

---

[19] Ibn Khallikān, *Wafayāt al-aʿyān wa anbāʾ abnāʾ al-zamān* (Beirut: Dār al-Sādir, 1977), 1.313, trans. MacGuckin de Slane, *Ibn Khallikan's Biographical Dictionary*, in 4 vols. (Paris: Oriental Translation Fund of Great Britain and Ireland, 1842–3), 1.288–9; Ibn al-Nadīm, *Fihrist*, trans. Bayard Dodge, 2 vols. (New York: Columbia University Press, 1970), 2.745–72. On the Sabians of Harran, see Michel Tardieu, "Ṣābiens Coraniques et 'Sābiens' de Ḥarrān," *Journal asiatique* 274 (1986), 1–44.

[20] Al-Ṭabari, *Tārīkh*, 1/3.517, = *History*, vol. 29, trans. Hugh Kennedy (Albany, NY: SUNY Press, 1990), 234–5; idem, *Tārīkh*, 1/3.548–50, = *History*, vol. 30, trans. C. E. Bosworth (Albany, NY: SUNY Press, 1989), 10–13.

guards over his residence, as he feared the populace of the city might attack him. Manichaeism was less a religion of the masses than of the elites; nonetheless, there is evidence for their presence in various cities of Iraq, Syria, and Iran in this period. (It may be worth mentioning that a ninth-century polemic defending Christianity from Islam, composed in Arabic in Palestine, also includes rejoinders to Manichaean objections to Christian doctrine.)[21] But over time, their numbers dwindled. Ibn al-Nadim reports an incident from the reign of al-Muqtadir (early tenth century) in which the "king of China" intervened with the governor of Khurasan to prevent his massacre of Manichaeans there, threatening to retaliate against the much larger Muslim population in China. By the end of the tenth century, a few Manichaean outposts remained in the far east of Iran, but in Baghdad itself their numbers had dwindled to fewer than five.[22]

In the long run, Zoroastrianism suffered far more from the Arab conquests than did Judaism or Christianity. Jewish communities remained intact, if greatly reduced in number, throughout the Islamic world, while Copts and other Christians form significant minorities in the Near East down to the present day. The Zoroastrian community of Iran, however, is today minute and marginalized. The traditional explanation is that the religion was tied closely to the Sasanian regime, and that with the imperial apparatus destroyed, Zoroastrianism quickly withered. There is a certain truth in this picture – the Zoroastrian hierarchy was closely tied to and integrated with the imperial structure, and the loss of the state's patronage was, among other things, a serious financial blow to the Zoroastrian "church." This was especially true in Iraq, where Zoroastrianism in the Sasanian period was principally the religion of the ruling elite, and where the Muslim Arabs confiscated institutions and land belonging to the Sasanian royal family which had previously supported the work of the Zoroastrian priests. But in general, Zoroastrians, including their temples and property, were protected by the treaties of capitulation which they made with the conquerors, as were Jews, Christians, and others elsewhere. Once again, the overall process of Islamization was nuanced and uneven, and one which bound both Zoroastrianism and Islam in a complicated dialectic of interlocking identities.[23]

In the first place, as we have already noted, the Zoroastrian community was already suffering from the conversion of its members to other faiths, especially Christianity and Manichaeism, before the Muslim conquests. In that respect, once again, patterns established in late antiquity continued to guide the religious history of Iraq and Iran (the Zoroastrian sphere) into the early medieval period, albeit with a very changed dynamic. After the Muslim Arab conquests, the curve of

[21] Griffith, "The First Christian *Summa Theologiae*," 17.

[22] Ibn al-Nadīm, *Fihrist*, 2:773–805; Gholam Hossein Sadighi, *Les mouvements religieux iraniens au IIe et au IIIe siècle de l'hégire* (Paris: Les Presses Modernes, 1938), 83–107; G. Vajda, "Les zindīqs en pays d'Islam au debut de la période abbaside," *Rivista degli Studi Orientali* 17 (1937), 173–229.

[23] Morony, *Iraq*, 280–305, and especially Jamsheed K. Choksy, *Conflict and Cooperation: Zoroastrian Subalterns and Muslim Elites in Medieval Iranian Society* (New York: Columbia University Press, 1997), from which much of the following is drawn.

conversion may have been more accelerated here than elsewhere. Conversion to Islam was more rapid in the towns – that is, the urban centers from which the Arabs ruled – than in rural areas. Some regions, such as Fars in southwestern Iran, remained staunchly Zoroastrian: the tenth-century geographer al-Istakhri described it as a region in which Zoroastrians remained numerically strong and in which they preserved intact the institutional structure of their faith, including their fire temples, and also the "ancestral customs" through which they expressed it. The important point is that the pace of conversion differed significantly within the vast region in which Iranian culture predominated. It tended to be slower in regions such as Fars and more generally in western Iran, and much faster in urban centers and on the northeast frontier. Khurasan and surrounding regions, which had played an important role in Islam for some time, continued to do so under the early ʿAbbasids, as measured, for example, by the significant number of Muslim scholars who lived in, or came from, cities such as Nishapur, Samarqand, Balkh and Bukhara. That Islam finally made further headway into rural and western regions in the tenth and eleventh centuries was due not only to the process of "social conversion" which figured so prominently in the cities, but also to the new efforts of Sufi mystics and preachers, such as Abu Ishaq al-Kazaruni, to bring Iranians to Islam.[24]

The example of Shaykh al-Kazaruni is especially instructive, because it illustrates the degree to which some Zoroastrians resisted the incursions and pressures of Islam. Al-Kazaruni was perhaps fired by the zeal of a new Muslim – his grandfather had been a Zoroastrian, and it was only his father who had embraced Islam. In any case, he undertook to convert the people of his native town, who responded by stoning him and repeatedly attacking the mosque which he sought to construct. Despite the violence, al-Kazaruni persevered, and is credited with the conversion of 24,000 Zoroastrians (and Jews).[25] Resistance in Kazarun was sharpened by the fact that a considerable proportion of the population of the region of Fars had not previously converted, but it also reflected a pattern evident in other regions of Iran as well. A Zoroastrian named Sunbadh, for example, instigated a rebellion to avenge the murder of his friend the ʿAbbasid agent Abu Muslim by the caliph al-Mansur. His rebellion took on an explicitly anti-Arab and anti-Muslim coloring – Sunbadh is said to have anticipated reaching Mecca and destroying the Kaʿba – and drew on the support, not just of Zoroastrians, but of Khurramis (see below) and Muslims disaffected with the outcome of the ʿAbbasid revolution. The rebellion was crushed fairly quickly by an ʿAbbasid army, but for a brief moment it seriously threatened Muslim rule in Iran: his army is said to have numbered as

---

[24] On conversion in Iran, see of course Bulliet, *Conversion to Islam*, passim, esp. 33f on "social conversion"; Choksy, *Conflict and Cooperation*, esp. 69–109, and idem, "Conflict, Coexistence, and Cooperation: Muslims and Zoroastrians in Eastern Iran During the Medieval Period," *Muslim World* 80 (1990), 213–33; Richard Frye, *The Heritage of Central Asia* (Princeton: Markus Wiener, 1996), 221–32, esp. 228. On conversion in rural areas, see also the cautionary remarks of Morony, "Age of Conversions," 137 and 141–4.

[25] Choksy, *Conflict and Cooperation*, 81, and *EI*², art. "Al-Kāzarūnī" (by H. Algar).

many as 100,000, and Sunbadh drew on the support of local Zoroastrian rulers from Daylam and Tabaristan.[26] Indeed, Tabaristan and the mountainous regions to the south of the Caspian Sea, where caliphal authority was always tentative at best, experienced a series of rebellions, fomented by local rulers, against the remote authority of the Muslim caliphs. While the issues over which these rebellions were fought included broader problems of the regions' integration with the political structure of the caliphate (such as taxation), religious matters were never far below the surface, and the tensions sometimes boiled over into massacres of the Muslim population.[27] Zoroastrian resistance to the encroachment of Islam took less violent forms as well. Zoroastrian literature of the ninth and tenth centuries reveals a community quite conscious of its efforts to survive in the face of a Muslim juggernaut. Zoroastrian writers, for example, were able to draw on their own eschatological narratives and assumptions to cast the triumph of the Muslim Arabs in apocalyptic terms, as the harbinger of the final catastrophe and ultimate restoration of the proper order. Efforts to circumscribe and defend the Zoroastrian tradition sometimes took on the challenge of the new faith directly, in polemical works which refuted the claims of Islam (and of Judaism, Christianity, and other religions).[28]

Zoroastrianism drew on a specifically Iranian identity – Zoroastrian texts tended to describe apostasy by embracing Islam as becoming a "non-Iranian." Accordingly, the path to fuller conversion may have been smoothed (or Zoroastrian resistance undermined) by the Muslim elite's adoption of many aspects of Iranian culture and civilization – for example, in the court ceremonial of the caliphs, or the prominence of Iranian bureaucrats in the ᶜAbbasid administration. Islamic narratives about its own past developed in ways that merged Iranian and Islamic identities, despite their very different roots, and so encouraged Iranians to think of the religion as their own. One could mention most prominently the Persian companion of the Prophet, Salman al-Farsi, who acquired in the Sufi literary tradition an exalted status as one initiated into mystical knowledge, and as a figure who enabled medieval Persian mystics to link themselves directly to Muhammad and the origins of Islam.[29] Another figure of importance in this regard is Shahrbanu, a daughter of the last Sasanian emperor, who according to a legendary tale married the Prophet's grandson al-Husayn, and

---

[26] On Sunbadh, see Sadighi, *Les mouvements religieux*, 132–49; Elton Daniel, *The Political and Social History of Khurasan under Abbasid Rule, 747–820* (Minneapolis: Bibliotheca Islamica, 1979), 126–30.

[27] Choksy, *Conflict and Cooperation*, 40–2; M. Rekaya, "Māzyār: Résistance ou integration d'une province iranienne au monde musulman au milieu du ixᵉ siècle ap. J.C.," *Studia Iranica* 2 (1973), 143–92; idem, "La place des provinces sub-Caspiennes dans l'histoire de l'Iran de la conquête arabe à l'avènement des Zaydites (16–250 H/637–864 J.C.): Particularisme regional ou role 'national'?" *Rivista degli studi orientali* 48 (1974), 117–52; *EI²*, art. "Kārinids" (by M. Rekaya).

[28] Choksy, *Conflict and Cooperation*, 54–6, 88–9; Mary Boyce, *Zoroastrians: Their Religious Beliefs and Practices* (London: Routledge and Kegan Paul, 1979), 154–6; Jean de Menasce, "Problemes des Mazdéens dans l'Iran musulman," in *Festschrift für Wilhelm Eilers* (Wiesbaden: Otto Harrassowitz, 1967), 220–30.

[29] On Salman, see Louis Massignon, *Salmān Pāk et les prémices spirituelles de l'Islam iranien* (*Bulletin de la société des études iraniennes* no. 7 [1934]).

who gave birth to his son ᶜAli Zayn al-ᶜAbidin, the fourth in the line of Twelver Imams.

The history of the Islamization of Iran is further clouded by a series of syncretistic religious movements, which fused Islamic and older Iranian elements in ways which disturb the neat polarity which sets Islam against Zoroastrianism. The terminology employed by the later Muslim heresiographers indicates that there were a number of discrete groups, most of which fell under the general heading of the religious movement known as the Khurramiyya (or Khurramdiniyya). The Khurramiyya grew out of the Mazdaki religious movement which had roiled the Zoroastrian establishment during the sixth century. Doctrinally, the Khurrami groups drew on a potpourri of principles familiar to the Iranian religious landscape, including dualism, messianism, metempsychosis and continuing prophecy, and, perhaps, anti-nomianism. Many who were labelled "Khurramis" by the heresiographers were attracted by the clandestine call to arms of the ᶜAbbasids' agents in Khurasan. Some Khurramis became especially attached to Abu Muslim, the Iranian agent who organized the ᶜAbbasid revolution, and his execution at the hands of the caliph al-Mansur led to a series of rebellions which punctuated the religious history of Iran from the ᶜAbbasid revolution down to the middle of the ninth century. While there were a plethora of different groups, and not all of them are always called "Khurrami" by the sources, they took similar doctrinal positions drawing on the principles listed above. They tended to be further united by the memory of Abu Muslim, or by the anticipation of Abu Muslim's imminent return as a messianic restorer. The last major rebellion of Khurrami inspiration was that led by the Iranian Babak, which began in Azerbaijan around 816 or 817, and which was only crushed by the general al-Afshin in 837–8, although Khurrami communities continued to exist down to the twelfth century.[30]

The Khurramiyya constitute a reminder of the very slow and convoluted process of resolving Near Eastern religious identities which began in late antiquity but which continued well into the Islamic period. One marker of how complex this process could be is the figure of Abu Muslim himself: Iranian *mawla*, ᶜAbbasid agent and missionary, associate of the Zoroastrian rebel Sunbadh, and (at least in death) messianic redeemer for a variety of "Khurrami" or extremist Shiᶜi (*ghulat*) sects. Another intriguing marker is the nemesis of the Khurrami movement of Babak, al-Afshin. It is significant that al-Afshin, despite his service to the Muslim state, was tried and finally executed for *apostasy* – for which one of the proofs adduced was his failure to be circumcised. The historian al-Tabari's account of his

---

[30] On the Khurramiyya, see Sadighi, *Les mouvements religieux iraniens*, 150–280; Madelung, *Religious Trends*, 1–12; Ehsan Yarshater, "Mazdakism," in *The Cambridge History of Iran*, vol. 3: *The Seleucid, Parthian, and Sasanian Periods*, ed. Ehsan Yarshater (Cambridge: Cambridge University Press, 1983), 991–1024, esp. 1001–6; B. S. Amoretti, "Sects and Heresies," in *The Cambridge History of Iran*, vol. 4: *The Period from the Arab Invasions to the Saljuqs*, ed. Richard N. Frye (Cambridge: Cambridge University Press, 1975), 481–519, esp. 503–5; M. Rekaya, "Le H̲urram-Dīn et les mouvements h̲urramites sous les ᶜabbāsides: Rê-apparition du Mazdakisme ou manifestation des Ǧulāt-Musulmans dans l'ex-empire sassanide aux viiiᵉ et ixᵉ siècles ap. J. C.," *Studia Islamica* 60 (1984), 5–57; and *EI²*, art. "Khurramiyya" (by W. Madelung).

trial leaves a very confused image of the religious identities of the accused apostate. The charges arose from the fact that the ostensibly Muslim al-Afshin had apparently encouraged a rebellion in Tabaristan by a local Iranian prince, Mazyar, who may have sought the extirpation of Islam and the restoration of Zoroastrian primacy. That same Mazyar, however, testified against al-Afshin at the latter's trial, and hinted that the accused, through his brother, was linked to the Khurrami movement of Babak (which he had, of course, been instrumental in suppressing) and to what he ambiguously referred to as the "white religion." The religious background of al-Afshin's family was possibly Buddhist, rather than Zoroastrian, and it would appear from Tabari's account that there existed some tension between the Iranian prince and at least certain Zoroastrian priests.[31] On the whole, the al-Afshin episode and the fate of the memory of Abu Muslim leave the impression that the long term process of resolving religious identities was not over, that those identities were still elastic and susceptible to considerable flux, at least at the margins – the margins occupied by converts, by opportunistic politicians, and by religious movements which would eventually be squeezed out by the dominant traditions. On the other hand, the very possibility of a trial for apostasy or heresy presumes a sufficiently well defined sense of religious identity. Even if a few loose ends were left, the crystallization of religious identities, and their settling upon a fairly stable dynamic – through the conversion of the majority of the inhabitants of the Near East, and through the emergence of the ulama and their articulation of the doctrine of *ijma*[c] – was the primary religious development of the era which began with the [c]Abbasid revolution.

---

[31] The account of the trial can be found in al-Ṭabari, *Tārīkh*, 1/3.1304–13, and 1314–18, = *History*, vol. 33, trans. C. E. Bosworth (Albany, NY: SUNY Press, 1991), 180–93, 196–200. On the meaning of the phrase "white religion," see 190n. On al-Afshin's religion, see Sadighi, *Les mouvements religieux iraniens*, 287–305. On the religious element in Mazyar's rebellion, compare Sadighi, *Les mouvements religieux iraniens*, 218–29, with *EI*², art. "Kārinids" (by M. Rekaya).

CHAPTER 18

The medieval Islamic Near East

Some readers will take exception to the use of the term "medieval" to describe a phase of Islamic history. The term is borrowed from European history, where it signifies a period, the "Middle Ages," distinguished from the "classical" one that preceded it and the "Renaissance" by which it was followed. In European history the term originally had something of a pejorative connotation – that the Middle Ages constituted a sort of valley between the peaks of classical and Renaissance culture and learning – although most historians would today describe the Middle Ages as considerably less "dark" than was earlier thought. The risks of abstracting the term from the European context that produced it, and applying it to the wholly different circumstances of the Islamic Near East, are obvious.

On the other hand, there were peculiar characteristics of the Islamic society and its religious institutions that took shape in the period between the beginning of the eleventh and the end of the fifteenth centuries. In the "Islam" which emerged over the course of these centuries are to be found various patterns of religious authority, affiliation, and relationship which distinguish it from what came before, which laid the foundation for the Islamic societies (particularly in the form of the Ottoman and Safavid empires) that followed, and which shaped the Islamic identities of those Muslims who suddenly found themselves faced with the changed circumstances of the modern period. The phrase "Middle Ages" really does through usage seem tied to the peculiarities of European history, and so we shall instead refer to the five centuries between 1000 and 1500 as the "Middle Period." But since that phrase is not easily rendered in an adjectival form, we shall retain, with apologies, and with no pejorative implications, the term "medieval."[1]

---

[1] The phrase "Islamic Middle Period" is borrowed from Marshall Hodgson. See *The Venture of Islam: Conscience and History in a World Civilization*, in 3 vols. (Chicago: University of Chicago Press, 1974), vol. 2: *The Expansion of Islam in the Middle Periods*, esp. 3–11. For a pungent critique of the use of the term "medieval" in Islamic history, see Daniel J. Varisco, "Making 'Medieval' Yemen Meaningful," an unpublished paper delivered at the 1999 meetings of the Middle East Studies Association, available on-line at http://www.geocities.com/Athens/Oracle/9361/mesa99.html. The question of periodization is quite a serious and substantive one. S. D. Goitein, for example, approaching the question from an entirely different perspective, proposed a radically different way of conceptualizing the eras of Islamic history. See "A Plea for the Periodization of Islamic History," *Journal of the American Oriental Society* 88 (1968), 224–8.

The political narrative of the five centuries covered in this chapter was extraordinarily complex, and will be summarized only briefly here.[2] At the outset of the Middle Period, the Islamic Near East was politically fragmented. Egypt was separated from the caliphate, ruled by the Ismaᶜili Fatimids who also controlled parts of Syria and the Hijaz over the eleventh century. Baghdad and most of Iran and Iraq were under the control of various members of the Buyid family who, as we have seen, while Shiᶜis themselves, did not formally disrupt the continuity of ᶜAbbasid rule. Important changes, however, were afoot. In Afghanistan and eastern Iran, for example, a Turkish soldier named Mahmud ibn Sebuktegin had come to power at the very end of the tenth century. Mahmud presented himself, and was remembered by Islamic posterity, as a champion of Sunni Islam, zealously defending the honor (if not the actual power) of the ᶜAbbasid caliph and combating the Shiᶜism of which the Buyids had been the patrons. His pretensions brought him into conflict with the Buyids, and in the wake of his conquest of the Iranian town of Rayy (which had been an important locus of Buyid power) Mahmud, in collaboration with Sunni jurists, launched a public campaign to extirpate Shiᶜism and other "heresies," bringing to trial and executing or expelling a number of prominent Shiᶜis. The efforts of Mahmud's contemporary, the ᶜAbbasid caliph al-Qadir, to defend Sunnism and define its contours more narrowly and precisely did little to restore the effective authority of the caliph, but did contribute significantly to a sharpening of religious tensions.

By the middle of the eleventh century, the Buyids had been defeated by the Saljuq Turks, whose impact on the course of Islamic history over the rest of the Middle Period was enormous. The Saljuqs were the leading family of a confederation of Turkish tribes from Central Asia who had been converted to Islam by Sufi missionaries in the late tenth century, and who had then entered the Islamic world as mercenaries in the armies of various regimes in eastern Iran. By the early eleventh century, one of them, Toghril Beg, had conquered Nishapur and other cities, acquired from the caliph the title of *sultan*, and begun to construct an empire of his own. In 1055, he drove the Buyids from Baghdad, and under his reign and that of his first two successors, Alp Arslan and Malik Shah, the Saljuqs, ably assisted by their famous Persian vizier Nizam al-Mulk, brought a measure of political stability to the central Islamic world, including Iraq, much of Iran, as well as parts of Syria. It was a fruitful moment, and much that was characteristic of medieval Islam flourished first under Saljuq rule. But the moment was also a brief one, and by the early twelfth century political authority had once again fragmented, especially in the western portions of the Saljuq realm, as several Crusader states were established in Syria and the surviving Saljuq princes there lost power to various *atabegs* (roughly, military tutors or guardians).

---

[2] For narrative histories of the period, see P. M. Holt, *The Age of the Crusades: The Near East from the Eleventh Century to 1517* (London: Longman, 1986), and David Morgan, *Medieval Persia, 1040–1797* (London: Longman, 1988).

Most of the regimes established in the western regions of the Near East in the ensuing centuries were in one way or another successor states of the Saljuqs, heirs to the political and religious patterns which took root during their rule. In the Fertile Crescent, some of the *atabegs* managed to establish dynastic regimes of their own, most notably Zangi, a Turkish soldier appointed by a Saljuq sultan as governor of Mosul in northern Mesopotamia and *atabeg* for his two sons. Zangi's own son, Nur al-Din, was the first Muslim ruler to organize an effective response to the challenge of the Crusaders, while Nur al-Din's successor, his sometime lieutenant, sometime rival Salah al-Din al-Ayyubi (known in the West as Saladin) extinguished the Fatimid caliphate, thereby restoring Egypt to Sunni rule. Saladin's own heirs, known collectively as the Ayyubids, ruled over Egypt and the western Fertile Crescent from Cairo, Damascus, and other urban centers until they were supplanted by a group of soldiers known as the Mamluks.

The Mamluk regime, the most powerful in the Near East until it was conquered by the Ottomans in 1516–7, was one of the most fascinating in all of Islamic history, and it embodies especially clearly many of the tensions underlying Near Eastern political arrangements in the Middle Period, arrangements which had considerable impact on religious developments. The Mamluks were the slave (the term *mamluk* means "one who is owned") soldiers who formed the heart of the army of al-Malik al-Salih, the last effective Ayyubid sultan in Egypt. Slave soldiers (or more precisely, soldiers whose *origins* were servile, since they were routinely manumitted) had for centuries had a dominant military role, but al-Malik al-Salih's actually established a regime of their own. For two and a half centuries, that regime perpetuated itself not principally through family dynasties, but rather through the constant replenishing of the ruling elite's ranks by the importation of new *mamluk* soldiers. As a result, Mamluk society was characterized by a constant tension between its ruling elite, which was largely (although not exclusively) Turkish in language and cultural orientation, and the Arabic-speaking population over whom they ruled. On an individual level that tension could be mitigated by intermarriage and conversion, among other things, but it could never be eliminated, since the ethnic and cultural "otherness" of the elite was renewed each generation. That "otherness" was especially pronounced under the Mamluks, but it was not atypical of other regimes. The Saljuqs, for example, emerged from a tribal confederation of Turks, while most of the other regimes represented the interests of various social or ethnic groups which were foreign to the peoples over whom they ruled. The tension generated by that "otherness" encouraged the regimes to accommodate themselves to the religious structures of the local Muslim population, and so the rulers and the ruled entered into a symbiotic relationship which, as we shall see, proved fertile ground for the spread of religious institutions and especially for deepening the authority of the ulama.

Elsewhere in the Near East, the situation was more confused. This was especially so in northwest Iran and Anatolia. By at least the middle of the eleventh century, groups of Turkmen nomads and warriors were penetrating the region, a process which picked up speed after the Saljuqs decisively defeated a Byzantine army at Manzikert in 1071. In the decades that followed, a number of states with roots among the nomadic Turkmen were established, including that of the Saljuqs of Rum (Konya) and, later, the principality of the Ottomans which eventually grew into the greatest of the medieval Turkish empires. From the standpoint of religion, this was important for several reasons, not least because it resulted in the Islamization of Asia Minor, which until this point had remained predominantly Christian. In the ensuing years, Anatolia proved to be a hotbed of religious enthusiasm. That enthusiasm took the form of a militant *ghazi* spirit among the Turkmen, who inexorably expanded the borders of the *dar al-islam* at the expense of the Christian Byzantine empire. It also took the form of heterodox and syncretistic mystical movements among those same Turkmen, movements that ultimately produced the Safavid order which, at the beginning of the sixteenth century, conquered Iran.

In the central province of the old Islamic empire, Iraq, political disintegration offered remarkable opportunities for religious development. For example, the waning of Saljuq power gave rise to an effort on the part of the ⁽Abbasid caliphs, especially al-Nasir (r. 1180–1225), to restore their effective as well as nominal authority over matters both religious and political. Those efforts were cut short by the devastating Mongol invasions of the thirteenth century. In 1258, an army led by Hulegu, a grandson of Chingiz Khan, destroyed Baghdad and put an end to the ⁽Abbasid caliphate there. (Some refugees claiming to be members of the ⁽Abbasid family arrived in Cairo and were installed as "caliphs" there by the Mamluk sultan Baybars, but their position was not widely recognized outside the Mamluk realm.) The Mongols were finally stopped in Syria by a Mamluk army, an accomplishment which added considerably to the Mamluks' prestige – the great historian and jurist Ibn Khaldun credited them with saving Islam – but much of Iran remained for some time under the rule of Hulegu's successors, known as the Ilkhanids. When they arrived in the Near East, the Mongols practiced a religion which is commonly labelled "shamanism," which is to say they did not embrace any of the universalist, and generally monotheistic faiths which had emerged from the ancient Near East. (When Hulegu died in 1265, his funeral was conducted with traditional Mongol rites, including human sacrifice.) On religious matters the Mongols were quite tolerant: Christians, Nestorians especially, actively proselytized among them (and European Christians sought an alliance with them against the Muslims), while Buddhism too had significant numbers of Mongol adherents, including at least one of the Ilkhanid rulers. But from the end of the thirteenth century, the Mongol rulers of Iran embraced Islam, formally at least, although their conversion did not mean that they suddenly rejected entirely their Mongol and shamanistic heritage.[3] Perhaps because of their shamanistic backgrounds, the Mongols proved to be especially respectful and supportive of Sufi *shaykhs*, among them Safi al-Din

---

[3] See now Charles Melville, "*Pādshāh-i Islām*: The Conversion of Sultan Maḥmūd Ghāzān Khān," *Pembroke Papers* 1 (1990), 159–77; and Reuven Amita-Preiss, "Ghazan, Islam and Mongol Tradition: A View from the Mamlūk Sultanate," *Bulletin of the School of Oriental and African Studies* 59 (1996), 1–10.

of Ardabil in northwest Iran, the leader of a mystical order, the Safawiyya, which in mutated form would transform the religious history of Iran in the sixteenth century.

Around the turn of the fifteenth century, the pattern repeated itself when another warlord with roots among the Central Asian nomads invaded the Near East and advanced as far as Damascus. Timur (to give the conqueror the Persian form of his name; he was known in the West as Tamerlane) was of mixed Mongol and Turkish background, although unlike his Mongol predecessors, he was already a Muslim. But while he displayed remarkable military talent, he showed little interest in building a lasting regime. After his death in 1405, political fragmentation again ruled the day, with the territories under his control in Iran, Iraq, and eastern Anatolia coming under the dominion of a variety of Mongol (Timurid) and Turkish regimes. Despite the occasional presence of strong and stable regimes such as that of the Mamluks, and of militarily awesome but institutionally evanescent ones such as that of Timur, political power in the Near East during the Middle Period was generally decentralized and splintered. That political fragmentation forms the background to the religious development of the period.

CHAPTER 19

Characteristics of the medieval Islamic world

Despite the importance of the preceding centuries, the medieval period was a creative one for Islam. Political theory and structure provide an instructive example. Most discussions of Islamic political thought begin with and focus on the office of the caliph. It is easy to see why this should be the case, given the struggles over leadership within the early Islamic community. But the result is often to measure later developments against standards of legitimacy based on events and decisions of that early period. And so, for instance, when viewed from this perspective, the extinction of the ʿAbbasid caliphate in Baghdad by the Mongols in the mid-thirteenth century appears to mark the end of a normative institution and phase of Islamic history. In fact, however, far from marking an end, the Mongol invasions provided an opportunity for solidifying and extending the social, political, and religious developments of the previous two centuries.

For all of their differences, the Islamic societies of the Middle Period shared certain common patterns – for example, that of political dominance by alien, mostly Turkish or Mongol military elites, or the social and institutional forms in which religious learning was transmitted from one generation to the next. More-over, those patterns had long-term effects that stretched down to the modern period. It is in these centuries that Islamic society takes a form which we can almost literally *feel*, since a city like Cairo, which loomed so large in both late medieval Islamic history and in the modern European encounter with the Islamic Near East, is architecturally largely a product of the Middle Period. There is admittedly a certain myopic quality to this perspective. The vision is narrowed by the vagaries of historical survival: that, for example, Baghdad was destroyed by the Mongols while Cairo was not, or that the textual legacy for the region stretching from Iran to Egypt in the Middle Period is generally so rich, in comparison to that of earlier centuries. But Islam, like any other historical abstraction, is a construct, and must be reconstructed from the materials available.

One central feature of Islamic history in the Middle Period is a creative tension – sometimes symbiotic, sometimes competitive – between religious and political authority. Religion and politics were closely intertwined, but religious and political authority were never identical: in general the religious establishment was not an arm of the state, nor was the political power subservient to the religious scholars.

It is misleading to think of the period as one in which religious develc
shaped by "inquisitions" supported by the apparatus of a militantly S
There was a brief effort to fuse politics and religion, under the calir
Al-Nasir's program was an ambitious one, which in some ways ran
principal currents flowing through Sunni Islam; had it succeeded, S..... ....
would have evolved in a very different direction. Al-Nasir and his Sufi propagandist, Abu Hafs ʿUmar al-Suhrawardi, sought not only to restore effective
political power to the caliph, but to make him the locus of religious authority as
well. There was more than a whiff of Shiʿism in al-Nasir's program; as some
medieval Muslims observed, his idealized caliph would function rather like a Shiʿi
Imam.[2] In effect, that threatened to undermine the role of the ulama in defining
Islam which had, in the previous centuries, been central to the evolution of a Sunni
identity. That is not to say that al-Nasir was hostile to the ulama; on the contrary,
his policy was to try to bring all Islamic factions together under his leadership. To
that end he stressed his personal credentials as a transmitter of ʿilm, a scholar
of hadith, compiling a collection of Prophetic traditions which he transmitted
to "kings" (muluk) as well as to "scholars" (ʿulamaʾ), and having the collection
published and publicly recited in various parts of the Muslim world. But that
project may obscure the fundamental differences between al-Nasir's goals and
those of the ulama, and some religious scholars saw through the charade. Looking
back on al-Nasir's work of hadith scholarship from three centuries' perspective,
the Egyptian scholar Jalal al-Din al-Suyuti (d. 1505) remarked that those who
cited it did so for reasons of vainglory (fakhr), that is, in an effort to please the
prince, rather than out of a recognition of the work's scholarly merits.[3]

Another common feature of medieval Islam in the Near East is a curious
disjuncture between political and social realities. On the one hand, the political
framework was a fragmented one. The Sunni caliphate survived, at least until
1258, and in attenuated fashion even longer, but its authority was eclipsed by the
rise of autonomous regimes in virtually all regions of the Near East, extending a
pattern that as we have seen had begun well before the year 1000. Within that
framework, Muslim regimes jockeyed with each other, with the residual (and
occasionally renascent) caliphate at the center, and with non-Muslim regimes and
armies that in this period had a significant impact on developments within the
Islamic world. On the other hand, the historical cosmopolitanism of the region
persisted, at least at certain social and cultural levels. Certain common patterns
prevailed in Muslim religious life, for example in the transmission of religious
knowledge, and in the development of the institutional structures within which
mystical life transpired. Islamic law provided a unifying force, too, so that, for

---

[1] As did, for example, Eliyahu Ashtor, "L'inquisition dans l'état mamlouk," *Rivista degli studi
orientali* 25 (1950), 11–26.
[2] Jalāl al-Dīn al-Suyūṭī, *Tārīkh al-khulafāʾ* (Cairo, 1964), 451.
[3] Al-Suyūṭī, *Tārīkh al-khulafāʾ*, 448, 451. The standard work on al-Nasir and his program is that of
Angelika Hartmann, *al-Nāṣir li-Dīn Allāh: Politik, Religion, Kultur in dem späten ʿAbbāsidenzeit*
(Berlin: de Gruyter, 1975); and *EI²*, "al-Nāṣir li-dīn allāh" (by A. Hartmann).

example, a Shafiᶜi student from Baghdad could move to Damascus or Cairo and study and be judged according to the standards of the same juristic tradition. This no doubt encouraged a lingering feeling of unity in an *umma* now broken into dozens of political pieces. In some cases, the non-Muslim communities also participated in cultural patterns that united the different regions of the Near East. While a large but localized community such as that of Coptic Christians in Egypt was understandably defined in part by place, others, especially the Jews, with their scattered settlements and genuinely international network of scholars who defined Jewish law and regulated communal life, transcended the borders of any one regime or homeland. The political fragmentation did not in most cases inhibit long-distance travel: even at the height of the Crusades, in 1183, as the Muslim warrior and ruler Saladin marshalled his forces for the campaign which four years later resulted in the reconquest of Jerusalem, the Spanish Muslim traveller Ibn Jubayr was able to travel from Acre in Palestine to Sicily, and thence to Spain, on Christian-owned ships. And even if the political scene was fragmented, the various pieces of the puzzle, though of different sizes, shared a number of common ethnic and social characteristics. As a result the alien ruling elites tended to interact with local peoples in similar fashion, developing a common political system within the larger Islamic framework. It was against this background that distinctive patterns of Islamic religious life developed during the Middle Period.[4]

Still, even on the level of religious life, there was probably considerable variation in local experience, although the state of the sources and the absence of focused regional studies makes the situation uncertain.[5] But we can chart a sort of geographical trajectory to the religious history of the Islamic Near East in this period. At the outset, Baghdad still loomed large as a center of Islamic religious culture, despite the decline in the political fortunes of the caliphate. From the time of the civil war between the caliphs al-Amin and al-Maʾmun in the early ninth century, down to the devastation of the Mongol invasion in the mid-thirteenth, the city suffered repeated waves of physical destruction, sometimes at the hands of external enemies, but also as a result of social disturbances involving crowds of local toughs (ᶜ*ayyarun*) and also mobs motivated by religious passions. Even so, al-Khatib al-Baghdadi, in his monumental history of the city, written during the eleventh century, situated Baghdad at the center of the world.[6] This was more

---

[4] On the unity of the Islamic world, at least in southwest Asia and the Mediterranean regions, see S. D. Goitein, "The Unity of the Mediterranean World in the 'Middle' Middle Ages," in *Studies in Islamic History and Institutions* (Leiden: E. J. Brill, 1966), 296–307. Michael Chamberlain, one of the few historians of the medieval Islamic world since Marshall Hodgson who has consciously approached the subject from a genuinely comparative perspective, also makes a number of extremely cogent remarks in *Knowledge and Social Practice in Medieval Damascus, 1190–1350* (Cambridge: Cambridge University Press, 1994), 28–37.

[5] A point made by Richard Bulliet, *Islam: The View from the Edge* (New York: Columbia University Press, 1994), passim, esp. 124–5.

[6] Al-Khatīb al-Baghdadī, *Tārīkh baghdād* (Beirut: Dār al-Kitāb al-ᶜArabī, 1966), 1.22–3; Jacob Lassner, *The Topography of Baghdad in the Early Middle Ages* (Detroit: Wayne State University Press, 1970), 25. So, too, did Ibn al-Jawzī, in his panegyric to the city: *Manāqib baghdād* (Baghdad: Matbaᶜat Dār al-Salām, 1342 AH), 4.

than a hollow statement of civic pride. Baghdad was still a major center of religious learning, especially for traditionists and jurists of the Hanbali school, which had a solid social base among the city's inhabitants. The cultural gravity of Baghdad is illustrated in an interesting anecdote about an altercation that took place in Cairo, at the very end of the Fatimid era. By this point, as we shall see, the Sunni majority in Egypt had already been flexing its political muscle and reinvigorating its cultural life at the expense of the Isma'ili regime for some time. Even so, when a dispute arose as to whether human activities were uncreated and pre-existent – a perpetually thorny theological problem for a religion such as Islam, with its emphasis on God's omniscience and omnipotence – it was felt necessary to send to Baghdad for guidance in the form of *fatwas* from the city's leading ulama.[7]

Baghdad's pre-eminence was not permanent, and one of the hallmarks of the Middle Period is the rise of alternative centers of political and cultural gravity. This was particularly true in the Persian-speaking region, and it is significant that this is the period in which Iranian culture made its greatest contributions to Muslim religious life more generally. Sufism, for example, was not an explicitly Iranian manifestation of Islam, as was once widely thought; nonetheless, the Iranian contribution to Sufism looms large in this period, in its literature and its institutional structure. So, too, with another institution which figures prominently in the history of Islam in the Middle Period – the *madrasa*, devoted to instruction in jurisprudence, which probably first made its appearance in Khurasan before becoming perhaps the most characteristic religious institution of the medieval Near Eastern urban landscape, most notably as a result of the efforts of the Saljuqs' vizier Nizam al-Mulk, an ardent patron of the Shafi'i *madhhab*.[8] By the end of the period, however, the center of cultural gravity had shifted to the west. In part this resulted from the catastrophe of the Mongol and then the Timurid invasions, but it was also a result of the Crusades. The Crusaders, in comparison to the Central Asian warriors, constituted a considerably less significant military threat. However, their presence in Syria and Egypt and the challenge they posed did foster the emergence of new and dynamic Sunni regimes in the lands of the eastern Mediterranean region.

The basic questions concerning religious identities which had emerged from late antiquity and continued to inform the history of the first few Islamic centuries were, by the Middle Period, more or less resolved: the dividing lines between Muslim, Christian, and Jew, and even between Sunni and Shi'i, or Isma'ili and Twelver, were fairly distinct. (There were some exceptions to this, which will be

---

[7] Ibn Rajab, *al-Dhayl 'alā ṭabaqāt al-ḥanābila*, 2 vols. (Cairo: Maṭab'at al-Sunna al-Muḥammadiya), 1.309; Gary L. Leiser, "Ḥanbalism in Egypt before the Mamlūks," *Studia Islamica* 54 (1981), 166.

[8] The centrality of the Iranian contribution to Islam in the Middle Period is one of the central themes of Bulliet, *Islam*; see esp. 146–7. Bulliet's analysis differs in fundamental ways from that of Marshall Hodgson, but on this point – that of the centrality of the Iranian contribution to Islam in this period – they are in fact in close agreement. See, for example, *The Venture of Islam: Conscience and History in a World Civilization*, in 3 vols. (Chicago: University of Chicago Press, 1974), vol. 2: *The Expansion of Islam in the Middle Periods*, 70.

discussed below.) Within the Muslim community, however, a number of fundamental questions concerning *how* those religious identities were to be understood and experienced remained open. On a political level, for example, there was the question of how the ruling elites would relate to the local population. Those elites shared certain common characteristics: they were predominantly Turkish, meaning that the ethnic identities of many of them were rooted in nomadic groups from Central Asia, who spoke a Turkic language, and who had come into the Islamic world either as mercenary soldiers, as slaves, or as part of a larger tribal movement (for more on their ethnic identity and its significance, see below, pp. 205f.); they were *military* elites, in that their status rested on their monopoly of military power; and they, or their forebears, were relatively recent converts to Islam. Some of them were very enthusiastic converts indeed, although others (especially the Mamluks) often embraced Islam somewhat less than wholeheartedly. In any case, their status and identity marked them out as distinct from the local, now predominantly Muslim populations, and the patterns by which they accommodated themselves to Near Eastern Muslim culture constitute a central theme of the history of this period. If the basic building blocks of Islam were in place by the start of the Middle Period, there remained considerable scope for their further development. The *madhahib*, for example, had crystallized around teaching traditions resting on the authority of particular legal scholars; but what would it mean to identify oneself as a Shafiᶜi or a Hanafi, and how would those *madhahib* relate to each other and to the state? How would Sufi mysticism respond to its phenomenal growth in popularity?

CHAPTER 20

A Sunni "revival"?

It is conventional to speak of a "Sunni revival" in the eleventh and twelfth centuries. According to this view, militantly Sunni regimes such as that of the Saljuqs responded to the challenge of the "Shi°i century," that period between the mid-tenth and mid-eleventh centuries when much of the central Muslim world was dominated by Shi°i regimes (the Fatimids, the Buyids) of varying stripes, by vigorously re-asserting – reviving – Sunni identity and claims to dominance. Like many grand historical themes, this one is perhaps a bit too neat and simple. On a political level, for example, the Saljuq seizure of power in Baghdad was not a *restoration* of pre-Buyid political patterns. It is true that the Buyid amirs, whom the Saljuqs replaced, were Shi°is, but their power had been in decline for some time previously. Moreover, relations between them and the °Abbasid caliphs, still the symbol of Sunni legitimacy, were often cordial; indeed, as the Saljuq armies approached Baghdad in 1055, the caliph intervened with the Saljuq leader, Toghril Beg, seeking protection for the Buyid amir al-Malik al-Rahim. Relations between the Saljuq leader and the °Abbasid caliph were hardly warm at the outset: Toghril Beg had been in Baghdad for thirteen months before he met the caliph.[1]

If the notion of a Sunni "revival" is in some ways misleading, there were nonetheless extremely important developments at work that shaped the character that Sunni Islam would carry into the modern period. One recent study has proposed that the notion of a Sunni "recentering" is a more accurate description of the process than the more dramatic terms "revival" or "renaissance."[2] The phrase "Sunni recentering" is especially useful in that it calls attention to developments not only in relations between Sunni and Shi°i Islam, but also *within* Sunni Islam itself. Indeed, one of the most important characteristics of the period was a tendency toward the *homogenization* of religious life, a process through which Muslim scholars and others strove (not always with success) to eliminate various sources of contention within the Islamic community. The process was one whereby

---

[1] George Makdisi, *Ibn °Aqīl et la résurgence de l'Islam traditionaliste au xie siècle (ve siècle de l'Hégire)* (Damascus: Institut Français de Damas, 1963), 77–88, and idem, "The Marriage of Tughril Beg," *International Journal of Middle East Studies* 1 (1970), 259–75.
[2] Richard Bulliet, *Islam: The View from the Edge* (New York: Columbia University Press, 1994), passim.

the tradition attempted to work out the practical implications of the doctrine of "consensus."

A central issue concerns the relationship of Shiᶜi and Sunni Islam in this period. Shiᶜism represented an ideological challenge to the basic principles of Sunni Islam, but the degree to which it posed an immediate and serious existential threat in the early Middle Period is harder to judge. In particular places, Shiᶜism had a marked demographic presence. Baghdad, Kufa, and Qum are obvious examples, but there were others, such as the city of Aleppo in northern Syria, where local rulers of the Hamdanid dynasty such as the famous Sayf al-Dawla (d. 967) had patronized Shiᶜism and encouraged Shiᶜi scholars from Qum to settle there, and so the local Shiᶜi community had grown in size and self-confidence. In most places, however, a sectarian Shiᶜism did not claim the adherence of overwhelming numbers of Muslims – as it has, for instance, in Iran since the early modern period.

Moreover, with the clearer articulation of Sunni Islam and especially Sunni jurisprudence in the ninth and tenth centuries, some Shiᶜis now found it necessary or advantageous to reformulate the doctrinal contours of their own version of the faith. For example, if the Sunnis rejected Shiᶜism as violating the consensus of the community, some Shiᶜi scholars responded by trying to repackage Shiᶜism in a form more acceptable to Sunnis. Hence the development, possibly as early as the late tenth century but with greater clarity by the eleventh, of a specifically Shiᶜi jurisprudential system (identified by some as the Imami *madhhab*) and mechanism for the training of Shiᶜi jurists. Many of the Shiᶜi scholars involved in this process benefited from the patronage of the Buyid amirs, including the Baghdadi al-Sharif al-Murtada (d. 1044), who embraced a specifically Shiᶜi doctrine of *ijmaᶜ* which could locate authority in the consensus of the community – when, that is, that consensus included the will of the infallible Imam.[3] A Shiᶜi doctrine of *ijmaᶜ* may seem contradictory, and many have treated the doctrine of al-Sharif al-Murtada and other Shiᶜi jurists as mere "window dressing," but its significance lies in the degree to which the growing force of Sunni traditionalism and jurisprudence drove even committed Shiᶜis to reformulating their understanding of religious authority.

The ambivalent position of Shiᶜism within the larger Muslim world is important in assessing one putative aspect of the Sunni "revival" (or whatever we wish to call the process of development that defined the Sunni community in this period): namely, its response to the Shiᶜi "challenge." There were certainly points of conflict between Sunnis and Shiᶜis. Baghdad in the early eleventh century was the scene of repeated communal violence, as partisan crowds of Sunnis and Shiᶜis traded attacks on people and institutions associated with the different religious communities, in part as a result of a more strident Sunni traditionalism promoted by the ᶜAbbasid caliph al-Qadir and others. Mahmud ibn Sebuktegin, as we have seen, consciously donned the mantle of militant defender of Sunnism, a role which brought him into direct conflict with both Twelver and Ismaᶜili Shiᶜis in

---

[3] Devin Stewart, *Islamic Legal Orthodoxy: Twelver Shiite Reponses to the Sunni Legal System* (Salt Lake City: University of Utah Press, 1998), esp. 111–73.

the Iranian city of Rayy. In the middle of the twelfth century, with political conditions in Crusader-era Syria in flux, the Sunni ruler Nur al-Din ibn Zangi restricted the freedom of Aleppan Shiᶜis to practice their religion, and violently suppressed a Shiᶜi revolt in 1157, in the process significantly reducing the size of the community.[4]

But the regimes most closely associated with Sunni Islam did not always adopt the fundamental and implacable opposition to Shiᶜism, at least in its Twelver guise, to which some of the ulama subscribed. Opposition to Shiᶜism among the Saljuqs, for example, who in many ways served as a model for later Sunni regimes, did not prevent either the sultan Malik Shah or his famous vizier Nizam al-Mulk from giving their daughters in marriage to Shiᶜi notables, nor did it prevent the appointment of several Shiᶜis as viziers.[5] In the face of a common enemy, Sunnis and Shiᶜis could find common ground, at least at first: so, for example, in the very early twelfth century Ibn al-Khashshab, head of the Shiᶜi faction in Aleppo, led a delegation to Baghdad – that is, to the seat of the caliphate and of Saljuq power – to complain about the inaction of local Muslim leaders in the face of the threat posed by the newly-arrived European Crusaders.[6] When Sunni governments did pursue policies designed to suppress or at least restrict public manifestations of Shiᶜism, it was usually in response to some particular political problem. On several occasions, for instance, the Mamluks did launch campaigns against non-Sunni communities, including the Druze, Nusayris, and Twelver Shiᶜis in parts of Syria in the late thirteenth and fourteenth centuries. To some extent, these campaigns were made possible by developments in the Muslim understanding of the doctrine of *jihad* and a willingness on the part of some of the ulama to take a more intolerant stand against beliefs and practices which they considered inconsistent with Islam – a point to which we will return. But a critical factor in each case was the political circumstances: for example, accusations that the non-Sunni communities had been in alliance with either the Crusaders or the Mongols, or a revolt led by a self-proclaimed *mahdi* (that is, a messianic savior) among the Nusayri peasants and laborers in the Jabala region in 1317, or the willingness of some radical Shiᶜis to indulge in the public cursing of the first three caliphs, which constituted a threat to the historical foundations of any explicitly Sunni regime. One place where the Mamluks did make consistent efforts to constrain Shiᶜism was in Mecca, where the leading family of *sharifs*, the Banu Hasan, who exercised a local pre-eminence while formally recognizing Mamluk sovereignty, maintained

---

[4] Stewart, *Islamic Legal Orthodoxy*, 121–25; Makdisi, *Ibn ᶜAqīl*, 310–27; Emmanuel Sivan, *L'Islam et la croisade: Idéologie et propagande dans les réactions musulmane aux croisades* (Paris, 1968), 71; Henri Laoust, "Les agitations religieuses à Baghdād aux ivᵉ et vᵉ siècles de l'hégire," in *Islamic Civilisation, 950–1150*, ed. D. S. Richards (Oxford: Cassirer, 1973), 169–85; Simha Sabari, *Mouvements populaires à Bagdad à l'époque ᶜabbaside, ixᵉ – xiᵉ siècles* (Paris: Librairie d'Amérique de l'Orient, 1981), 106–12; C. E. Bosworth, *The Ghaznavids: Their Empire in Afghanistan and Eastern Iran, 994–1040* (Edinburgh: Edinburgh University Press, 1963), 53–4.

[5] Bulliet, *Islam*, 148.

[6] Claude Cahen, *La Syrie du nord à l'époque des croisades et la principauté franque d'Antioche* (Paris: R. Geunther, 1940), 261.

a Zaydi Shi^ci identity until the early fifteenth century. There is a certain irony here, since the Hasanids' moderate Shi^cism was not so scrupulous as to prevent their recognizing the ^cAbbasid caliph or the nominal authority of the Sunni Mamluk sultan. But again, political circumstances drove Mamluks' policy, since their formal suzerainty over the holy cities of the Hijaz constituted one of the most prestigious bases of their claims to political legitimacy.[7]

On the other hand, there was considerably less ambivalence about the challenge posed to the new Sunni international order by developments within the Isma^cili Shi^ci community at the end of the eleventh century, and, as a result, much cooperation between the Sunni ulama and the political authorities in responding to that challenge. At the outset of the Middle Period, as the Buyid regimes disintegrated in the first half of the eleventh century, the Fatimids continued to pose a substantial challenge to the legitimacy of the ^cAbbasid caliphate and of all the local regimes which wielded effective power while formally acknowledging ^cAbbasid authority. The Fatimids actively promoted a campaign to win the allegiance of the people and rulers of those portions of Syria, Iraq, and other places which remained officially in the ^cAbbasid orbit, and for a moment, in 1059, succeeded in having the *khutba* read in the name of the Isma^cili Imam in Baghdad itself.

Beginning in the 1060s, however, the Fatimid regime was undermined by famines, military insubordination, and administrative chaos. Its equilibrium was temporarily restored under the careful rule of the Armenian vizier Badr al-Jamali, but a dispute over the succession to the imamate following the death of the caliph al-Mustansir in 1094 split the movement in two. The regime was not formally extinguished until Saladin dismissed the last Fatimid caliph in 1171, but by then it had ceased to pose a serious threat to the Sunni regimes of the Near East. Even in Egypt itself, despite the presence of an organized Isma^cili mission (*da^cwa*) under the patronage of the state, two centuries of Fatimid rule apparently left relatively few Isma^cili Shi^cis among the Egyptian population. (There was a fairly sizeable Shi^ci population in the towns and villages of Upper Egypt, one that remained active and provoked efforts to suppress it by Sunni ulama well into the Mamluk period; but it probably predated the arrival of the Fatimids, and was not for the most part the product of Isma^cili mission work.)[8] In 1188, just a few years after

---

[7] Richard T. Mortel, "Zaydi Shi^cism and the Hasanid Sharifs of Mecca", *International Journal of Middle East Studies* 19 (1987), 455–72. On the Mamluks' campaigns against Shi^cis and others in Syria, see Henri Laoust, "Remarques sur les expéditions du Kasrawan sous les premiers Mamluks," *Bulletin du Musée de Beyrouth* 4 (1940), 93–115; Urbain Vermeulen, "Some Remarks on a Rescript of al-Nāṣir Muḥammad b. Qalā'ūn on the Abolition of Taxes and the Nuṣayris (Mamlaka of Tripoli, 717/1317)," *Orientalis Lovaniensia Periodica* 1 (1970), 195–201; idem, "The Rescript against the Shi^cites and Rafiḍites of Beirut, Ṣaidā and District (746 A.H./1363 A.D.)", *Orientalia Lovaniensia Periodica* 4 (1973), 169–75; and especially now Stefan Winter, "Shams al-Dīn Muḥammad ibn Makkī 'al-Shahīd al-Awwal' (d.1384) and the Shi^cah of Syria," *Mamlūk Studies Review*, 3 (1999), 149–182.

[8] Jean-Claude Garcin, *Un Centre Musulman de la Haute-Égypte Médiévale: Qūṣ* (Cairo: Institut Français d'Archéologie Orientale, 1976), 71, 128–31; cf. Devin Stewart, "Popular Shiism in Medieval Egypt: Vestiges of Islamic Sectarian Polemics in Egyptian Arabic," *Studia Islamica* 84 (1996), 35–66, esp. 52–61.

Saladin's coup, a group of Shiᶜis rebelled in Cairo, running through the streets and calling for the restoration of the Fatimid state. They numbered all of twelve.[9] Ismaᶜili supporters of the Fatimids were exiled to Upper Egypt where they survived for some time, but aside from a few abortive rebellions posed little threat.

The end of the Fatimids did not, however, spell the end of an Ismaᶜili challenge to Sunni Islam. Ismaᶜilism had since the ninth century attracted a small but committed following in the towns and cities of the Fertile Crescent and the Iranian world. For the first century or so of Fatimid rule, many of those Ismaᶜili communities had followed the *daᶜwa* emanating from Cairo – that is, they submitted to the authority of the Fatimid Imams. Developments in the second half of the eleventh century, and in particular the crisis of leadership within the Fatimid family, encouraged Iranian Ismaᶜilis to cultivate more local sources of authority. Under the leadership of the *daᶜi* Hasan-i Sabbah (d. 1124), Iranian Ismaᶜilis acknowledged the imamate of al-Mustansir's eldest son Nizar, but the dynastic struggle in Egypt resulted in Nizar's brother's accession to the imamate, while Nizar himself was captured and eventually died. In the absence of a recognized and accessible Imam, Hasan took for himself the title of *hujja* ("proof") and so effectively staked a personal claim to final religious authority. At the direction of Hasan, the Ismaᶜilis of Iran launched a scattered but vigorous revolt against the Saljuq regimes that dominated the Iranian world in the late eleventh and early twelfth centuries. Ismaᶜilis seized and held a series of fortresses, especially in Quhistan and in the mountainous region to the south of the Caspian Sea, in particular Hasan's inaccessible redoubt at Alamut; but Ismaᶜili cells were active in the cities as well. Together these communities, though geographically fragmented, constituted a remarkably close-knit polity.

The "Ismaᶜili revolt" was dramatic and, for a time, posed a serious challenge to the Sunni political order, and especially to the various Saljuq regimes. In the fragmented political circumstances of the time, in which local political authority was often highly personal, that is, adhering in some individual (usually a military leader), assassination was a common instrument of political action; but the Ismaᶜilis developed it more systematically than most, training and dispatching individuals who would insinuate themselves into the retinue of leading men and, if their targets proved threatening to Isma'ili interests, dispatch them at appropriate moments. (Lurid accounts of how the Ismaᶜilis drugged these disguised warriors, known as *fidaʾis* ["those willing to sacrifice themselves"] with hashish and plied them with visions of the sexual favors which awaited martyrs in paradise are, however, the product of hostile Sunni fabrication and the seemingly insatiable Western appetite for tales of the exotic East.)[10] The Ismaᶜili reputation for assassination understandably stoked fear among Sunnis, and their response was

---

[9] Ibn al-Athīr, *al-Kāmil fi'l-tārīkh*, 10 vols. (Beirut: Dār al-Kutub al-ᶜIlmiyya, 1995), 10: 177–8; Taqī ʾl-Dīn Ahmad al-Maqrīzī, *Kitāb al-sulūk*, 4 vols. (Cairo: Lajnat al-Taʾlīf waʾl-Tarjama, 1956–73), 1:127–8.

[10] On these colorful tales, see Farhad Daftary, *The Assassin Legends: Myths of the Ismaᶜilis* (New York: I. B. Tauris, 1995).

sometimes vituperative. Isma°ilis were accused of anti-nomianism (not entirely without cause, particularly in the later years of the revolt), and Nizam al-Mulk and others tried to link them to older Iranian religious movements such as the Khurramdiniyya. The effect of such slander was to mark the Isma'ilis as apostates, with the practical consequence that, from a Sunni legal perspective, their blood could licitly be shed. Even al-Ghazali, the Sunni theologian whose own interests and inclinations ranged rather broadly, was of the opinion that, unless they repented, Isma°ilis were to be regarded as having abjured the faith and that they should therefore suffer the consequences.[11] Such talk had practical consequences, including a series of massacres of Isma'ilis, particularly in the towns of Iran, some of them spurred on by Sunni ulama.[12] But it was not simply the drama and violence of the Isma°ili revolt that agitated the Sunni imagination. On an intellectual level, there was a profound suspicion of the Isma°ili doctrine of *ta°lim*, which asserted the absolute authority of the Imam or, in his absence, of the *hujja*. A similar doctrine formed a part of Twelver Shi°i teaching as well, but under Hasan and his successors the doctrine of *ta°lim* was joined to a present and dangerous threat. *Ta°lim* contradicted the Sunni doctrine of consensus (and by extension the religious authority of the ulama). As such, Nizari Isma°ilism really did pose a fundamental challenge to Sunni Islam, to the emerging political order but even more importantly to the doctrinal and intellectual foundations of Sunnism, and so it has been suggested that the response of the Sunni ulama, led by al-Ghazali, was central to the entire "self-definition of Islam" in the Middle Period.[13]

Hemmed in by implacably hostile Sunni regimes, the Nizari Isma°ilis in their Iranian fortresses evolved in increasingly bizarre directions. In the month of Ramadan in the year 1164, the Isma°ili leader at Alamut, at the instruction, he said, of the (hidden) Imam, proclaimed the arrival of the day of resurrection (*qiyama*), and the resulting abolition of the *shari°a*. Accordingly, the month-long fast required by the law was abandoned, replaced by a celebratory feast. Soon thereafter, the Isma'ilis of Alamut claimed that their leaders were in fact the Imams, the descendants of Nizar through a son who had been smuggled out of Egypt. The doctrine of *qiyama* involved an even further elevation of the figure of the Imam, from one of authority to one in which the entire cosmic order – the divinity, it seems – could be glimpsed. Then in the early thirteenth century, during the reign of the °Abbasid caliph al-Nasir, an Imam at Alamut rejected Isma'ilism, proclaimed the reinstallation of the *shari°a* (in Shafi°i form, this time), had the caliph's name recognized in the Friday *khutba*, and, to further establish his Sunni *bona fides*, sent his mother on the *hajj*. From an Isma'ili perspective, this was certainly an odd development, unless it was an act of defensive dissimulation

---

[11] See now Farouk Mitha, *al-Ghazālī and the Ismailis: A Debate on Reason and Authority in Medieval Islam* (London: I. B. Tauris, 2001), esp. 67–70.

[12] See, for example, Ibn al-Athīr, *al-Kāmil fiʾl-tārīkh*, 9:107–9; Farhad Daftary, *The Isma°ilis: Their History and Doctrines* (Cambridge: Cambridge University Press, 1990), 354–6.

[13] Marshall Hodgson, *The Order of Assassins: The Struggle of the Early Nizārī Ismā°īlīs Against the Islamic World* (The Hague: Mouton, 1955), 124.

(*taqiyya*), and in any case his reforms were later abandoned. Finally, like many others, including the caliph in Baghdad, the Nizaris succumbed to the onslaught of the Mongols. Their surviving followers in Iran continued in the form of a Sufi *tariqa*, lead by a *pir* (shaykh), and may have contributed to the volatile mixture of Sufism and Shiʿism in northwestern Iran and eastern Anatolia from which, later, emerged the Safavids.[14] (Small communities of Ismaʿilis, adhering to various lines of Imams descending from Muhammad b. Ismaʿil, remain scattered throughout the Muslim world today, in Iran, Syria, Yemen, India, and elsewhere.)

Beyond opposition to Ismaʿilism, especially in its radical Nizari form, what can we identify as characteristic features of Sunni Islam as it developed during the Middle Period? Certainly it experienced a deepening of the hold which traditionalists had placed on Islamic identities and principles in the preceding centuries. Hanbalism, not simply as a recognized legal school but as a social movement with a conservative, traditionalist orientation, played an important role, at least on the Baghdadi scene, in the eleventh century. We noted in the last chapter how, once the *mihna* had been suspended, the traditionalists allied themselves closely with the ʿAbbasid caliphs. That alliance can be clearly seen in a series of public statements and proclamations of faith issued under the name of the caliph al-Qadir in the early eleventh century. Al-Qadir's pronouncements were directed against political threats to the ʿAbbasid regime, such as the Shiʿis, but they also condemned and sought to prevent the public preaching of rationalist theological doctrines, including Muʿtazilism but also the more moderate theological specu-lations of the Ashʿaris. The real strength of the traditionalist movement lay in its espousal, not simply by scholars, but by significant portions of the city's populace. Chronicles describing Baghdadi life in the eleventh century reveal instances in which Hanbali crowds reacted violently to, say, the preaching of a sermon rife with rationalist theology.[15]

The traditionalism propounded by al-Qadir and many ulama wielded con-siderable force, intellectual, social, and political. Traditionalist pressure, for example, convinced the Hanbali scholar Ibn ʿAqil in 1072 to renounce publically the Muʿtazili principles with which he had earlier toyed. But traditionalism did not earn an unqualified victory, in part because of the fractured and complex political background. The ʿAbbasid caliph's authority remained limited by that

---

[14] On the Nizari Ismaʿilis and their "revolt," see Hodgson, *Order of Assassins*, and idem, "The Ismaʿili State," in *The Cambridge History of Iran*, vol. 5: *The Saljuq and Mongol Periods*, ed. J. A. Boyle (Cambridge: Cambridge University Press, 1968), 422–82. See also Bernard Lewis, *The Assassins: A Radical Sect in Islam* (New York: Basic Books, 1968); Wilferd Madelung, *Religious Trends in Early Islamic Iran* (Albany: Bibliotheca Persica, 1988), 101–5; Farhad Daftary, "Hasan-i Sabbāh and the Origins of the Nizārī Ismaʿili movement," in *Mediaeval Ismaʿili History and Thought*, ed. Farhad Daftary (Cambridge: Cambridge University Press, 1996), 181–204, and idem, *The Ismaʿilis*, 324–434. On the temporary abrogation of the *shariʿa* in 1164, see Jorunn J. Buckley, "The Nizārī Ismaʿilites' Abolishment of the Sharīʿa During the 'Great Resurrection' of 1164 AD/559AH," *Studia Islamica* 60 (1984), 137–65.

[15] The most important work on this topic is that of George Makdisi, especially, *Ibn ʿAqil et la résurgence de l'Islam*. See also idem, "The Sunni Revival", in *Islamic Civilisation, 950–1150*, ed. D. S. Richards (Oxford: Cassirer, 1973), 155–68, and Laoust, "Les agitations religieuses," 178f.

of the Buyid amirs and then the Saljuq sultans, and al-Qadir's very public traditionalism, directed at both Shiᶜism and the rationalist theologians who were prominent in Baghdadi cultural life in this period, could be read tactically as part of an effort on the part of the caliphs to reassert their authority by reaching out to the traditionalist population. But for all their efforts, the caliphs were no longer the only source of political power or even legitimacy, and so their traditionalism had its challengers, too. For example, the great Nizam al-Mulk (d. 1092), powerful vizier to the Saljuq sultans in the second half of the eleventh century, encouraged Ashᶜari theologians as a counter-weight to caliphal traditionalism, inviting over the years a number of them to publically preach their doctrines in Baghdad. One such occasion, in 1077, led to five months of rioting in the city, but did not result in the elimination of the underlying tensions between traditionalists, Ashᶜaris, and others.

Moreover, while the most strident traditionalists, the Hanbalis, were strong in Baghdad, they were less so elsewhere, and one of the characteristic features of Islamic history in the Middle Period is that Baghdad grew less important as a center of Muslim religious life – especially, of course, after its sacking by the Mongols in the mid-thirteenth century. As a result, traditionalism was one aspect, but only one, of a broader process of homogenizing Sunni religious life during this era. That process had an institutional dimension, as particular forms of institutional organization and authority spread throughout the Islamic Near East – for example, the *madrasa*, or college of law, and the Sufi convents under the various names by which they were known. On this level it is important to stress the Iranian contribution, as institutions "rooted in the urban Muslim communities of eleventh-century Iran, communities that evolved from the local consolidation of societal edges rather than from a centralized religious tradition or authority symbolized by the caliphate," spread throughout the Near East, to Iraq, Syria, Egypt and Anatolia.[16] Both the *madrasa* and the *khanqah*, it appears, had their origins in the Iranian east, in Khurasan. That it was these institutions which came to have such an impact on the Islamic experience in the later Middle Period (and also, through a process of institutionalization in the Ottoman Empire, on the shape that Islam took on the cusp of the modern period) was in part a consequence of an "Iranian diaspora" whereby Muslims scholars and mystics of Iranian origin took up residence and achieved prominence in Iraq, Syria, Egypt and especially Anatolia, even before the Mongol invasions. It also, however, reflected the value of this new institutional "idiom" to the various Sunni regimes which dominated the Near East in this period.

In Egypt, for example, circumstances were quite different, but the institutional idiom of a rejuvenated Sunnism as developed in the east proved valuable none-theless. After two centuries of Ismaᶜili rule, Shiᶜism had failed to supplant the Sunni Islam of most Muslims, but the *dhimmi* populations were perceived by some as posing a reinvigorated challenge. Except for a brief period of persecution

---

[16] Bulliet, *Islam*, 146.

under the caliph al-Hakim, the *dhimmi* communities in general flourished under Fatimid rule.[17] Ibn Killis (see above, p. 163) was not the only Jew, or Jewish convert, to serve the Fatimids in high position; their success prompted a poet to exclaim,

> The Jews of this time have attained their uttermost hopes, and have come to rule.
> Glory is upon them, money is with them, and from among them come the counselor and the ruler.
> O people of Egypt, I advise you, turn Jew, for the heavens have turned Jew![18]

But the most pronounced change in status occurred with the Christian community. By this point Muslims were likely a majority, but there remained nonetheless a sizeable Coptic population in Egypt. Moreover, over the last century of Fatimid rule, Christians had reached positions of considerable authority within the regime and its armed forces. The Armenian soldier and vizier Badr al-Jamali (d. 1094) and his son and successor al-Afdal (assassinated 1121) may have been Muslims – the latter in fact played a critical role in the succession dispute which resulted in the Nizari schism within the Ismaʿili movement – but they nonetheless surrounded themselves with Christians in high office, and relied to a great extent on Armenian Christian soldiers. One of these, Bahram (d. 1140), served as vizier to the caliph al-Hafiz, and while he held the customary title "Sword of Islam," he patronized Christians (especially Armenians, who immigrated to Egypt in large numbers) and Christian churches to the extent that a Muslim source claimed that Egyptian Muslims feared that the country was about to leave the Muslim orbit forever. Hyperbole aside, Christian sources, such as the *History of the Patriarchs of the Egyptian Church* and the description of Egyptian churches and monasteries by Abu Salih the Armenian, confirm that Christians benefitted from the benevolence and patronage of the Fatimids and their leading officers of state.

Under these circumstances, the institutional developments which began in the Persian east, in particular the rise of the *madrasa*, served the Sunni population of Egypt as a means of strengthening the Muslim community in the face of what was perceived to be a Christian challenge. The first Egyptian *madrasas* were founded in Alexandria, the port city which became a hotbed of Sunni militancy during the final century of Fatimid rule. The very first may have been that founded on the ground floor of his house by Abu Bakr al-Turtushi (d. 1126), a Spanish Muslim who settled in Egypt. Al-Turtushi is especially interesting in the present context, as he was the author of an important treatise condemning "innovations," of a type which became characteristic of medieval Sunni polemical discourse. One the themes of that discourse (to which we will return below) is that Muslims were

---

[17] On al-Hakim's persecution and conversion to Islam in the early eleventh century, see Yaacov Lev, "Persecutions and Conversion to Islam in Eleventh-Century Egypt," *Asian and African Studies* 22 (1988), 73–91.

[18] Jalāl al-Dīn al-Suyūṭī, *Ḥusn al-muḥāḍara fī tārīkh miṣr wa'l-qāhira*, 2 vols. (Cairo: al-Ḥalabī, 1968), 2:201; cited in Bernard Lewis, *Islam from the Prophet Muhammad to the Capture of Constantinople* (New York: Oxford University Press, 1987), 2:227.

flagrantly borrowing a variety of religious practices from the *dhimmis* – al-Turtushi, for instance, mentions particular styles of chanting the verses of the Koran which imitate Christian practice, or the decoration of mosques so that they resemble churches and synagogues. One of the first in Egypt to construct a building specifically designed as a *madrasa* was Ridwan al-Walakhshi, a militantly Sunni opponent of Bahram who, as vizier, was remembered in the *History of the Patriarchs* for his assault on the churches of Cairo, for doubling the *jizya* imposed on the *dhimmis*, and for prohibiting the employment of *dhimmis* in important positions in government. Significantly, Ridwan appointed as the *madrasa*'s first professor the Maliki jurist Abu Tahir Ibn ʿAwf (d. 1185–6), who engaged in inter-confessional polemic by writing a treatise refuting an attack on the *shariʿa* by a Muslim who had converted to Christianity.[19]

What gave further impetus to concerns over the threat posed by Christianity was the Crusades, and the development of Sunni Islam in this period was in part a response to the challenge of the European Crusaders. There were three developments which, within the context of the "recentering" of Sunni Islam in this period, we can identify as resulting from that challenge. The first has to do with a certain reorientation in the mental compass of Near Eastern Muslims, at least those living in greater Syria and Egypt. For several centuries before the arrival of the first Crusaders in the Near East in 1098, the center of Muslim cultural gravity (or at least Sunni cultural gravity, Cairo being the center of an Ismaʿili state) lay to the east, in Iraq and Iran, in the seat of the caliphate and in the various Iranian states which contributed so much to the early development of Islamic mysticism, jurisprudence, etc. The Muslim east did not suddenly cease to be important in the later Middle Period, even after the Mongol conquests; once the various Mongol regimes had converted to Islam, they became important patrons of Muslim culture. But the sudden appearance of the Crusaders, and the attention which their presence demanded from the Muslims who confronted them, made the western half of the Near East more important. From a long-term perspective, we might identify this as the first step in a much longer process, as the growing power and reach of western Europe from the later Middle Period posed ever greater threats to Islam, threats which culminated in colonialism and the challenge of secular modernity. At the time, however, the immediate consequence was the rise to power of various regimes, first that of the Ayyubids and then the even greater empire of the

[19] Abū Bakr al-Ṭurṭūshī, *Kitāb al-ḥawādith waʾl-bidaʿ* (Beirut: Dār al-Gharb al-Islāmī, 1990), 188–9, 220–1, and cf. Maribel Fierro, "The Treatises Against Innovations (*kutub al-bidʿa*)," *Der Islam* 69 (1992), 204–46; Sawīrus ibn al-Muqaffaʿ, *Tārīkh baṭārika al-kanīsa al-miṣriyya* (*History of the Patriarchs of the Egyptian Church*), ed. and trans. Antoine Khater and O. H. E. Khs-Burmester (Cairo: Société d'Archéologie Copte, 1968), 3/1:31 (Eng. trans., 50) (on Ridwan and the *dhimmis*); Ibn Farhūn al-Mālikī, *al-Dībāj al-mudhhab fī maʿrifat aʿyān ʿulamāʾ al-madhhab*, 2 vols. (Cairo: Dār al-Turāth, 1972), 1:294 (on Ibn ʿAwf); Gary Leiser, "The Madrasa and the Islamization of the Middle East: The Case of Egypt," *Journal of the American Research Center in Egypt* 22 (1985), 29–47; Marius Canard, "Un vizir chrétien à l'époque fatimide: l'Arménien Bahrām," *Annales de l'Institut d'Études Orientales* 12 (1954), 84–113; idem, "Notes sur les Arméniens en Égypte à l'époque fatimite," *Annales de l'Institut d'Études Orientales* 14 (1956) 147–57.

Mamluks, which drew on the new Sunni idioms first articulated in the east and spread and refined them, building up a vibrant Sunni Muslim culture in Egypt and Syria which was the principal legacy of medieval Islam to the modern world.

The Crusades also encouraged among Muslims a renewed focus on the city of Jerusalem. A growing preoccupation with Jerusalem as a locus of holiness was already underway before the Crusaders arrived, thanks in part to the mystics. It may be significant that al-Ghazali, a few years before the Crusaders arrived and during that period of his life in which he renounced his scholarly activities in favor of spiritual retreat and introspection, took up residence in Jerusalem, and wrote there a part of his classic work, *Ihyaʾ ʿulum al-din* ("The Revival of the Religious Sciences"). But the obsession with the holy city on the part of European pilgrims and the Crusaders, who established the capital of their principal state in it, stimulated further Muslim interest in it, an interest which revealed itself on many levels. As so often in Islamic history, the development finds a reflection in words attributed to the Prophet, to the effect that, save for his own death, the worst thing that could happen to Islam would be the fall of Jerusalem to infidels.[20] More generally, the genre of the *fadaʾil al-quds*, treatises recounting the splendors of the city, flourished in the wake of the Crusaders. Muslim leaders such as Nur al-Din ibn Zangi (d. 1174) encouraged scholars to produce them as a propaganda device to encourage the faithful to support efforts to drive out the Franks and re-take the city. As Saladin led his army in a successful attack on the city in 1187, one such treatise was read aloud to his troops. Strategically, Jerusalem remained a fairly remote and insignificant town: one of Saladin's successors, his nephew al-Malik al-Kamil, was willing to cede the city to the German emperor Frederick II in 1229, in a treaty through which he hoped to consolidate his position vis-à-vis his Ayyubid rivals. But the *idea* of Jerusalem, and the prestige which its conquest and control afforded Muslim rulers, was firmly established. So deeply was the idea of Jerusalem now rooted in the Muslim imagination that al-Kamil's surrender of the city to the Christians provoked an outcry among ulama and common Muslims alike. Driven on by preachers, a group of Muslim peasants from the hill country around Jerusalem temporarily occupied the city before being driven out by the Franks, while al-Kamil, taken aback by the ferocity of the protests, was forced to cultivate an extensive campaign of propaganda to re-establish his bona fides as a respectable Sunni ruler. And Jerusalem has remained fixed as a locus of Muslim veneration and pilgrimage down to the present day.[21]

A final development driven by the Crusades was the reinvigoration of a militant spirit expressed in the ideology and practice of *jihad*, or holy war. This is a

[20] Ibn ʿAsakir, *Tārīkh madīnat dimashq*, ed. Ṣalāḥ al-Dīn al-Munajjid (Damascus: Maṭbaʿat al-Majmaʿ al-ʿIlm al-ʿArabī, 1951), 1.223.

[21] The most important work on Muslim attitudes toward Jerusalem is that of Emmanuel Sivan, "The Sanctity of Jerusalem in Islam," in *Interpretations of Islam* (Princeton: The Darwin Press, 1985), 75–106, and idem, *L'Islam et la croisade*, esp. 46–9 and 62–3. See also S. D. Goitein, "The Sanctity of Jerusalem and Palestine in Early Islam," in *Studies in Islamic History and Institutions* (Leiden: E. J. Brill, 1966), 135–48, and Carole Hillenbrand, *The Crusades: Islamic Perspectives* (Chicago: Fitzroy Dearborn, 1999), 141–50 and 188–92.

perpetually thorny topic for Western audiences, encumbered as they so often are by assumptions about the inherent militancy of the Islamic religion. *Jihad*, "struggle [in the path of God]," is in fact a complex idea in Islamic discourse, a principle which has many different meanings – among them, of course, the waging of war against infidels, but also the interior struggle to make one's will conform to the divine. In the Middle Period, however, the challenge posed by what amounted to a Christian *jihad* did stimulate a renewal of interest in armed warfare against infidels, an interest which had broader and long-lasting ramifications for the Sunni Muslim outlook.[22]

In the centuries since the original Arab conquests, the spirit of *jihad* had, in places like southern Syria, become somewhat dulled by time and the relative stability of distant frontiers. A militant spirit had survived in some border regions, particularly in Central Asia, and was given fresh life by particular Muslim regimes, such as that of the Hamdanids in northern Mesopotamia and Syria in the tenth century, patrons of the preacher Ibn Nubata (d. 984/5) whose sermons extolling the duty of *jihad* remained a paragon of Muslim predication throughout the Middle Period. But elsewhere the ideal of *jihad*, pitting the "House of Islam" against the "House of War" in a struggle whose end could only be reached by extending Muslim rule over the entire world, was muted by the realities of cross-border and inter-confessional exchange. Most jurists thought of *jihad* as a *fard kifaya*, that is, as a religious obligation incumbent on the community of Muslims, rather than on individuals, its exercise by some Muslims somewhere relieving others of the duty.

But the militant spirit of a universalist faith was always there as a latent force, and the circumstances of the Middle Period encouraged Near Eastern Muslims to embrace it. Jurists and scholars were among the first to understand the new threat posed by the Crusaders. A chronicle written in Aleppo in the mid-twelfth century reveals they understood that the Crusades constituted only a part of a larger Christian movement which included the budding *reconquista* in Spain and the Norman attack on North Africa in 1086, and so that they posed a new level of challenge to the Muslim world. Already within just a few years of the arrival of the Crusaders in Syria, a treatise was published in Damascus on the requirements and merits of *jihad*, arguing that the circumstances faced by the Muslims of a country attacked and occupied by infidel forces transformed *jihad* from a *fard kifaya* to a *fard ᶜayn*, that is, a duty incumbent on Muslims individually. But the more profound changes were psychological, spurred on perhaps by the actions of the Christian warriors. The Crusaders raised the stakes considerably through measures calculated to offend Muslim sensibilities: for example, the appropriation of Muslim religious structures, including the conversion of the Dome of the Rock into a church and the turning over of the al-Aqsa mosque to the Knights Templar, and later an abortive effort to sack the Muslim holy cities in the Hijaz. Such actions inflamed tensions between the religious communities, and Muslims, working with the notion of *jihad* as a religious ideal and obligation, enthusiastically embraced

[22] On this topic generally, see Sivan, *L'Islam et la croisade*, and Hillenbrand, *The Crusades*, passim.

the struggle. For example, in Aleppo in the early twelfth-century, the *qadi* and preacher Ibn al-Khashshab, after delivering a sermon extolling *jihad*, led a crowd to convert by force a number of churches into mosques, in retaliation for the Franks' desecration of Muslim shrines in Jerusalem.[23] Both scholars and increasingly rulers, acting in tandem, raised the profile of the doctrine and ideal of *jihad*. Along with the recrudescence of literature on the splendors of Jerusalem came a flurry of texts extolling *jihad*, such as a collection of forty hadith on the subject compiled by Ibn ᶜAsakir (d. 1176), a prominent jurist, historian, and confidant of the sultan Nur al-Din. Nur al-Din and other contemporary rulers made practical use of such works, which might be read aloud in public fora in order to stimulate both enthusiasm for *jihad* and support for their regimes among the Sunni Muslims of Syria.

More generally, such acts of cooperation between rulers and the ulama reflect one of the most important characteristics of the new Muslim polities shaped by the experience of the Crusades: namely, a sometimes tense but deep and symbiotic relationship between the ruling military elites and the religious scholars and functionaries who constituted the closest thing to an indigenous political class in the Muslim cities of the medieval Near East. From the rulers' perspective, this alliance provided a critical validating function. In the face of enemies such as the infidel Crusaders, preachers might accompany the troops to battle, urging them on with sermons extolling the value of *jihad* and stressing the qualities of rulers such as Nur al-Din and Saladin, in particular their accomplishments as *mujahids*, practitioners of the art of holy war. From the standpoint of the ulama, the relationship was equally valuable. Sunni rulers cultivated the support of the ulama by funding an expansive program to construct and endow *madrasas* and *khanqahs*, thereby providing the religious classes with an institutional and financial structure supportive of their activities.[24] The religious elite did not become an arm of the state, as they did later in the Ottoman period, but the new Sunni regimes did frequently align themselves with the ideology and interests of the ulama. So, for example, a ruler might crack down on practices which contravened the spirit and letter of Islamic law, such as the sale of wine or the playing of musical instruments. Even more, they embraced the ulama's increasingly restrictive definitions of what constituted acceptable Muslim identity and behavior, as when Nur al-Din in the mid-twelfth century made efforts to suppress the Shiᶜism which was common among the population of Aleppo.[25]

It is here that the "Sunni re-centering" had its greatest impact. The history of Sunni Islam in the Middle Period is not so much one of new developments as it is one which brought a sharper resolution to identities and principles which had crystallized earlier. The spread of institutions devoted to the transmission of

---

[23] Sivan, *L'Islam et la croisade*, 41–3; Hillenbrand, *The Crusades*, 108–10.

[24] For a systematic treatment of one Sunni ruler's program for the construction of religious monuments, see Nikita Elisséeff, *Nūr ad-Dīn, un grand prince musulman de Syrie au temps des Croisades (511–569 h./1118–1174)* (Damascus: Institut Français, 1967), 750–79.

[25] Cahen, *La Syrie du nord*, 377; Elisséeff, *Nūr al-Dīn*, 428–30.

religious knowledge or to the mystical devotions which were becoming central to the Sunni experience were important, and we shall have much to say about that phenomenon in what follows. But the more profound developments were psychological and intellectual. Among the most important was a sharpening of the Islamic doctrine of *bidᶜa*, "innovation," according to which "every innovation is an error, and every error leads to hell," in words attributed to the Prophet.[26] Such is the logical extenuation of the doctrine of *sunna*, the opposite of *bidᶜa*, whereby the practice of the Prophet and his companions established a permanent normative framework. Human experience being what it is, innovation could not be avoided, and the tradition made the necessary adjustments; so, for example, some jurists came to rate innovations on a sliding scale, from reprehensible to obligatory. But a fervent opposition to innovations was one element in a discourse through which the ulama sought to rein in the Islamic tradition, to assert control over a religious community which lacked a centralized and institutionalized locus of authority – which lacked, that is, a church. Treatises hostile to innovations went back a long way, but a number of highly influential works condemning deviations from the path of the *sunna* were written in the period, and constituted a distinct theme of medieval Islamic religious writing.[27]

This sharpened opposition to innovations was simply one aspect of what Emmanuel Sivan called the "moral rearmament" of Sunni Islam in the wake of challenges such as the Crusades. That moral rearmament drew on the language and enthusiasm of the Muslims' response to the Crusades to articulate more precisely what it meant to be a (Sunni) Muslim. *Jihad* became an instrument, not only of resistance to infidels, but of the enforcement of standards of proper belief and behavior, particularly in the ulama's struggle against various elements of "popular religion" (see below, pp. 248–57). So, for example, when ᶜAli ibn Maymun al-Idrisi, a Maghribi Sufi who settled in Damascus in the late fifteenth and early sixteenth centuries, wrote a treatise condemning practices of Syrian Muslims of which he disapproved, he drew naturally on the language of holy war. According to him, waging *jihad* against these miscreant Muslims (he was condemning in particular popular raconteurs of religious tales) "is preferable to doing so against the infidels of the House of War, as the damage [which they inflict on Islam] is more severe and more significant than that of the infidels."[28]

---

[26] Cited in Ibn al-Ḥājj, *Madkhal al-sharᶜ al-sharīf*, 4 vols. (Cairo: al-Maṭbaᶜa al-Miṣriyya, 1929), 1.79.

[27] Fierro, "The Treatises Against Innovations"; and Jonathan P. Berkey, "Tradition, Innovation, and the Social Construction of Knowledge in the Medieval Islamic Near East," *Past & Present* 146 (1995), 38–65.

[28] ᶜAlī ibn Maymūn al-Idrīsī, *Bayān ghurbat al-islām*, Princeton Garrett Ms. 828H, fol. 64v; cf. Sivan, *L'Islam et la croisade*, 70–3.

CHAPTER 21

Common patterns in social and political organization

There were two basic patterns in medieval political life which had a profound impact on the religious life of the Muslim communities of the Near East. The first was a persistent and constantly shifting diffusion of power away from the center and towards more local and limited regimes. The central fact here was the decline in the power and authority of the ᶜAbbasid caliphs. So much of early Islamic discourse and conflict had focused on the institution of the caliphate, yet in the Middle Period, despite moments of resurgence, its authority flickered and finally died. The jurists held a deep attachment to the office of the caliph as an integral part of the *shariᶜa*; nonetheless they too were forced to confront the political realities. Toward the end of the Buyid period, the Baghdadi Shafiᶜi *qadi* al-Mawardi (d. 1058) wrote a treatise on the law of government, in the first chapter of which he outlined the position and powers of the caliph. His famous description is a classic treatment of the caliph as an active centerpiece of the unity of the Islamic *umma*, as the cornerstone of the administration of God's law, in the face of the growing political fragmentation of the medieval period. There is a certain irony here, as al-Mawardi wrote his treatise at a time when the caliphate had ceased to wield effective authority. His portrait is one of a very active caliph, taking charge of *jihad*, collecting taxes in accordance with the law, making sure that the precepts of the *shariᶜa* are effectively imposed. It was incumbent on the caliph, he wrote, that he "personally supervise the direction of affairs [of state] and the examination of circumstances, and undertake the administration of the community and the guarding of religion, and not delegate his authority to others." That may have been an effort to prop up the reputation of the caliphs at a moment when the Fatimids posed a major ideological threat and the Buyid amirs had usurped much of what was left of the caliphs' authority in Iraq. But the real juridical problem was that the caliph's powers had in fact been usurped by other forces for over a century before al-Mawardi wrote. How was that fact to be reconciled with the responsibility of the caliph, the highest authority in the Islamic state and the "successor to the prophet of God," to implement the *shariᶜa*?[1]

---

[1] Abūʾl-Ḥasan ᶜAlī al-Māwardī, *al-Aḥkām al-sulṭāniyya waʾl-wilāya al-dīniyya* (Beirut: Dār al-Kutub al-ᶜIlmiyya, 1985), 18. This is now available in an English translation: *The Ordinances of*

The tension between theory and reality only grew worse. The Saljuqs, as Sunnis, might in theory have been expected to restore to the caliph the powers intendant on his position as the head of the Islamic *umma*, but in fact the Saljuq sultans did nothing of the sort. In the growing political chaos which followed the assassination of Nizam al-Mulk and the death (possibly also by assassination) of the sultan Malik Shah in 1092, the caliphs made efforts to re-establish their authority, efforts which culminated in al-Nasir's program in the late twelfth and early thirteenth centuries. Those efforts were doomed by the arrival of the Mongols, and the larger pattern of medieval political history is one in which effective power passed into the hands of the (mostly-Turkish) military regimes, from the Saljuqs to the Mamluks and, ultimately, the Ottomans who dominated the Near East in the early modern period. Writing two generations after al-Mawardi, the theologian al-Ghazali (d. 1111) represents a marker of how far the religious establishment was willing to compromise on the basic political principles developed in earlier centuries. As a jurist, al-Ghazali naturally expressed considerable concern for the institution of the caliphate, but he also acknowledged the *de facto* importance of the alien soldiers to the survival of Islam. And so he accepted the fracturing of political authority under the numerous (and sometimes competing) Sunni sultans who cluttered the medieval political landscape, even those who had seized power by force, as long as they recognized the nominal primacy of the caliph, for example, by having the Friday *khutba* recited in his name.[2] With the extinction of the caliphate in Baghdad, the jurists pursued this model to its logical conclusions and shaped a political theory which undergirded the various regimes of the medieval Near East. Among them were Badr al-Din ibn Jamaᶜa (d. 1333) and his more famous and controversial contemporary, Ibn Taymiyya (d. 1328), both of whom wrote when the only caliphate was the "shadow" institution installed in Cairo by the Mamluk sultans. For Ibn Jamaᶜa, the "imamate" remained the central and necessary political institution, whose responsibilities included the protection of religion, the administration of justice, the defense of the *dar al-islam* against its enemies, and the preservation of the order and stability which a properly functioning Islamic society required. But the "imam" was, in fact, the sultan, the military ruler whose path to power, the jurist admitted, was frequently that of violence. For Ibn Taymiyya, too, social stability was the key to his acknowledgment of the rule of the Mamluks and other military regimes – sixty years with an unjust imam, he said, quoting a well-known maxim, was preferable to one night without an effective sultan – because social chaos inhibited the administration of the *shariᶜa* which was, in his view, the fundamental purpose of the Islamic state.[3]

Government, trans. Wafaa Wahba (London: Garnet, 1996). See also Ann K. S. Lambton, *State and Government in Medieval Islam. An Introduction to the Study of Islamic Political Theory: The Jurists* (Oxford University Press, 1981), 83–102.

[2] Carole Hillenbrand, "Islamic Orthodoxy or Realpolitik? Al-Ghazali's Views on Government," *Iran: Journal of the British Institute of Persian Studies* 26 (1988), 81–94.

[3] Lambton, *State and Government*, 138–51; Henri Laoust, *Essai sur les doctrines sociales et politiques de Takī-d-dīn Aḥmad b. Taimīya* (Cairo: Institut Français d'Archéologie Orientale, 1939), 310–15.

The devolution of political power to local centers had profound consequences: it contributed, for example, to the relative ease with which the Crusaders first established a presence in the Near East, and then frustrated Muslim efforts to respond to the Crusaders' challenge. However, it did not necessarily mean that religious experience was similarly fragmented. A number of factors helped to maintain centripetal pressures in the cultural arena, not least the international networks through which the ulama transmitted religious knowledge. Moreover, not all of the military regimes were of limited geographical reach. Some of them built strong, centralized, and large states: Saladin temporarily brought under his rule Egypt and all of Syria, minus what was left of the Crusader states, while the Mamluk regime for over two centuries controlled the whole of the territory from the Nile valley to Upper Mesopotamia, and (more tentatively) the Hijaz including Mecca and Medina as well. The clearer distinction between Sunni and Shiʿi, coupled with the "moral rearmament" fueled by the challenge of the Crusades, may also have encouraged the feeling among Muslims, whether in Egypt, Syria, or elsewhere, that they participated in a common historical project. Nonetheless, it was the smaller, more localized military regimes which dominated the political history of the Near East in the Middle Period until the rise of a more ecumenical Ottoman Empire, and it was in interaction with them, and in response to their needs, that local Muslims developed the contours and the institutions of medieval Islam.

The second basic pattern of political life in the medieval Near East was that the ruling elites were in various ways outsiders, bound to each other through ties of blood or comradeship but lacking organic bonds to the local peoples over whom they ruled. This too had a profound impact on religious developments. These elites took different forms. In some cases, they represented entire tribes or tribal confederations. So, for example, the power of the Saljuq family rested at first on a confederation of recently-Islamized Turkish tribes whom they led out of Central Asia and into Iran, and thence to further regions of the Near East. At the other extreme stood the Mamluks, who, as their name suggests, were in origin slaves, imported into the Muslim world and then trained for the express purpose of constituting a distinct social group possessing a monopoly on military (and thus political) power. Whether these elites were in origin tribes, slaves, or simply hired as mercenaries, they possessed, broadly speaking, a Turkish ethnic character. For centuries, Turks had formed a critical component of the armed forces of many Near Eastern Muslim states: already in the ninth century al-Jahiz had extolled the martial qualities of the Turks in a famous essay.[4] By the Middle Period the association of Turks with military skills and political power was a commonplace: the regime of the Mamluks, for instance, was known simply as *dawlat al-atrak*, the "state of the Turks." The term must be understood broadly, and not all members of the military elites were Turkish. They included Circassians, Georgians, Armenians, and others; the great Saladin, for example, was a Kurd. But the regimes and the

---

[4] Charles Pellat, *The Life and Works of Jāḥiẓ*. (Berkeley: University of California Press, 1969), 92–7.

warriors who constituted their social base marked themselves off as distinct, through claims of kinship or ethnicity, but also through language – Turkish dialects often served as the lingua franca of the ruling military elites during the Middle Period, even in places such as Egypt and Syria where the native population consisted almost entirely of Arabic speakers – and through a shared martial culture from which locals were deliberately excluded. That sense of distinctness was sometimes cultivated through an artificially constructed sense of social solidarity which the great medieval historian Ibn Khaldun (d. 1406) recognized could constitute a secure foundation for political power.[5] Under the Mamluks, that social solidarity took the form of a comradeship (*khushdashiyya*) which bound the client-soldiers of a military officer to themselves and to their patron. As a result, politics was often less a matter of exercising power through formal institutions than it was of competition among households of client soldiers linked to a common patron.[6]

On the other hand, the very "otherness" of the rulers meant that their successful exercise of authority had to be negotiated through local channels, and this proved critical to the development of religious institutions and patterns in the medieval Near East. These societies, like their predecessors, were dominated by cities: it was in them for the most part that the soldiers settled, and the most active and important social group they encountered there were the ulama. Much of what follows will describe the tense but symbiotic relationship which evolved between soldiers and ulama over this period. In effect they developed a complex con-dominium, through which secular and religious authority grew even further apart than they had been in the days of a functioning caliphate, but in which neither political nor religious elites could function in isolation from the other.[7] In the long run, however, it was Islam, and the scholars who constituted its most obvious and widely-accepted spokesmen, whose gravitational force proved more compelling. Not surprisingly, Islam pulled into its orbit the alien soldiers themselves. For all their self-conscious otherness, the military elites adopted Islam, sometimes with a passion. Turkish dialects usually remained the lingua franca of the elite, but the soldiers were also instructed in Arabic, and exposure to religious texts (and not simply the Koran) often formed an important component of their training. Some of the soldiers were only superficially Islamized, and their behavior on occasion scandalized their Muslim subjects. But many others were deeply pious – the piety of the Kurdish sultan Saladin was legendary, even in his own day, but he was

---

[5] Ibn Khaldūn, *al-Muqaddima*, ed. M. Quatremère in 3 vols. (Paris: Didot, 1858), 1.332; trans. Franz Rosenthal, 2nd edition (Princeton: Princeton University Press, 1967), 1.374. Cf. Charles Issawi, *An Arab Philosophy of History* (London: John Murray, 1950), 105, and David Ayalon, "The Mamluks and Ibn Xaldun," *Israel Oriental Studies* 10 (1980), 11–13.

[6] For a stimulating discussion of the politics of households in the medieval Near East and its relationship to broader cultural patterns, see Michael Chamberlain, *Knowledge and Social Practice in Medieval Damascus, 1190–1350* (Cambridge: Cambridge University Press, 1994), esp. 44–7.

[7] The phrase "condominium" is Ira Lapidus': *Muslim Cities in the Later Middle Ages* (Cambridge, Mass.: Harvard University Press, 1967), 116. Marshall Hodgson, in the second volume of his *Venture of Islam*, described this arrangement in some detail, labeling it the "amir-aʿyan" system. For a nuanced study of its operation in one particular society, see Chamberlain, *Knowledge and Social Practice*.

hardly alone – and quite a few became accomplished scholars of the religious sciences.[8] (To be sure, some of his contemporaries, as well as later biographers, viewed Saladin's well-publicized piety as a cynical ploy. That hardly matters, however, from a historical if not a biographical perspective: the point is that it was *useful* to Saladin, for political purposes, to make a public show of his embrace of Islam.) Above all, as we shall see, Islam became an integral component of the ideological universe through which the soldiers justified their rule.

Other than the military elites, in the cities the dominant local group was almost uniformly the ulama. For the last several decades, much Western scholarship on the medieval Islamic Near East has focused on their role and the critical social functions performed by them. For all their importance to medieval and post-medieval Muslim self-definitions, the ulama were not present from the beginning, and their emergence as a recognizable group was a product of the struggles over the office of the caliph and the locus of religious authority in the seventh through tenth centuries. It was in the Middle Period, however, under the conditions outlined above, and as a part of the process of Sunni "re-centering" which characterized the period, that the ulama came to play a critical social and political role, the closest thing to an indigenous political class representing the interests of the local Muslim population. They accomplished this through the variety of their social functions. Educating their successors and transmitting religious knowledge in more diffuse form to the Muslim population at large was perhaps their principal responsibility. But they also supervised charitable activities, served as intermediaries with the various military regimes (or, in some cases, as instruments of challenge to them, articulating the interests and concerns of the local populations), and at least occasionally helped to produce a cadre of scribes and bureaucrats who assisted in the management of the affairs of the state and the soldiers who controlled it.[9]

As a counterweight to centrifugal tendencies, the ulama represented a force promoting the cultural unity of the politically fragmented Sunni world. Traveling in search of knowledge had become a trope of Islamic biographical literature well before the Middle Period, and the image of students and scholars wandering from city to city studying hadith with local religious dignitaries is frequently encountered both in the modern studies and in the original sources on which they are based.[10] The image is misleading if it suggests a deracinated elite: the power

---

[8] See Barbara Flemming, "Literary Activities in Mamluk Halls and Barracks," in *Studies in Memory of Gaston Wiet*, ed. Myriam Rosen-Ayalon (Jerusalem, 1977), 249–260; Ulrich Haarmann, "Arabic in Speech, Turkish in Lineage: Mamluks and their Sons in the Intellectual Life of Fourteenth-Century Egypt and Syria," *Journal of Semitic Studies* 33 (1988), 81–114; Jonathan Berkey, "Mamluks and the World of Higher Education in Medieval Cairo, 1250–1517," in *Modes de transmission de la culture religieuse en Islam* (Cairo: Institut Français d'Archéologie Orientale au Caire, 1993), 93–116; and idem, " 'Silver Threads Among the Coal': A Well-Educated Mamluk of the Ninth/Fifteenth Century," *Studia Islamica* 73 (1991), 109–25.

[9] Studies on the ulama and their social and political functions are numerous. The best place to start is with Lapidus' seminal work, *Muslim Cities in the Later Middle Ages*, and R. Stephen Humphreys' survey of the literature, in *Islamic History: A Framework for Inquiry* (Princeton: Princeton University Press, 1991), 187–208.

[10] Sam Gellens, "The Search for Knowledge in Medieval Muslim Societies: A Comparative Approach," in *Muslim Travellers: Pilgrimage, Migration, and the Religious Imagination*, ed. Dale F. Eickelman and James Piscatori (Berkeley: University of California Press, 1990), 50–65.

of the ulama derived principally from their rootedness in local societies. But the frequent movement of religious scholars from one locale to another did serve to cultivate a common religious culture and also, in some cases, to increase the prestige of some ulama. A city such as Cairo, with its extensive network of religious institutions patronized by the Mamluk elite, attracted scholars from throughout the Sunni Muslim world, so much so that particular *madrasas* might be associated in the popular mind with Maghribis, Syrians, or Iranians.[11] Jalal al-Din al-Suyuti, the prominent but controversial Egyptian polymath of the fifteenth century, described in his autobiography how his books (he was, or claimed to be, the author of more than 500) were purchased and copied by students and others visiting Cairo from abroad, and how they spread from there to shape intellectual trends in various corners of the Muslim world.[12] The disruptions of the Mongol and later the Timurid invasions wreaked havoc in many parts of south-west Asia, but the resulting flood of scholars seeking refuge in Syria, Egypt, and other places enriched the fabric of cultural life in their cities. The movement of scholars often carried political implications, as well. The influx of Persian scholars into Anatolia in the twelfth and thirteenth centuries, for example, contributed to the Islamization of the region and to the development there of a sophisticated urban Sunni culture which ultimately fostered the triumph of the imperial Ottoman state over other Turkish (and sometimes religiously-suspect) political groups. In the later Middle Period, Turkish-speaking scholars from that region moved in the other direction as well, and contributed to the integration of the military elites into the fabric of native Muslim social and cultural life.[13] The contacts and networks fostered by peripatetic scholars also served to diffuse cultural patterns developed in the major cities to the less urbanized hinterland, and in the process reinforced the moral and social authority of the ulama.[14]

It is easy, however, to lose sight of the fact that the ulama as a group are in fact difficult to define. They were not a "class" in Marxist or economic terms: the wealth and social status of those who could be classified as ulama in fact varied widely, and they overlapped with virtually all other identifiable social groups. It is true (as we have noted) that many of the leading religious scholars were from or related to wealthy merchant families, or even engaged in commercial activities themselves, so that connections between the urban bourgeoisie and the religious scholars were especially close. Moreover, some scholars indulged in a perhaps natural inclination to arrange for their sons to inherit their remunerative offices and professorships in various institutions, while some ulama families, through the

---

[11] Carl Petry, *The Civilian Elite of Cairo in the Later Middle Ages* (Princeton: Princeton University Press, 1981), 161.

[12] Elizabeth Sartain, *Jalāl-Dīn al-Suyūṭī*, vol. 1: *Biography and Background* (Cambridge: Cambridge University Press, 1975), 46–9.

[13] A classic example is the Turkish-speaking fifteenth-century jurist and historian Badr al-Din al-ʿAyni, originally from ʿAyntab, north of Aleppo, a close friend and confidant of several Mamluk sultans; Petry, *Civilian Elite*, 69–70.

[14] See, for example, Jean-Claude Garcin, *Un centre musulman de la haute-égypte médiévale: Qūṣ* (Cairo: Institut Français d'Archéologie Orientale, 1976), 344–57.

careful cultivation in their members of the "cultural capital" their learning represented, were able to establish veritable dynasties of scholars.[15] At the same time,
religious scholarship could be a channel of social mobility, particularly under the
conditions of the Middle Period, when the widespread creation and endowment of
institutions such as *madrasas* provided scholarships to support students who might
otherwise have lacked the financial resources to devote themselves to full-time
study in preparation for a religious or legal career. It was even possible for
individuals to *acquire* wealth through a career in religious scholarship, for example
through a practice common in Mamluk times of particular scholars holding paying
professorships at several institutions simultaneously.[16] As a result, the ulama never
constituted a closed profession, let alone a sacramentally distinct group (i.e., a
clergy). Above all, individuals of vastly different socio-economic rank and of
professional function participated in diverse ways in the transmission of religious
knowledge which, in the end, is the only real marker of those who constituted the
ulama. For every scholar who held a prestigious professorship or whose learning
earned him appointment as a *qadi* or as a preacher in a large congregational
mosque, there were dozens of lower-ranking religious functionaries – muezzins,
Koran readers, prayer leaders, Sufi adepts, etc. – who also commanded at least a
limited status by virtue of their roles in the social networks through which Islamic
religious knowledge was passed on from one generation to the next and diffused
throughout society. The very heterogeneity of the ulama worked to accentuate the
political power of particularly prominent scholars, since the breadth and depth of
the ulama's networks fostered a widespread sense of identity and loyalty to those
most closely associated with the Islamic ideal.[17]

The consequence of the deeply rooted social status of the ulama was that
politics took the form of a constantly shifting pattern of accommodation between
them and the military elites. For all their otherness, the ruling powers found it
necessary to articulate an ideal which was framed in very religious terms. Military
rulers assiduously sought to cultivate images of themselves as models of piety and
of devotion to the Muslim cause. The first Muslim ruler to successfully challenge
the Crusaders, the *atabeg* ʿImad al-Din Zangi (d. 1146), was apparently a ruthless
and at times tyrannical ruler, assassinated by a group of slaves who caught him
in a drunken stupor. But a very different picture emerges from the account left
by the historian Ibn al-Athir, who came from a family which for several generations served the Zangid dynasty, and who depicted the *atabeg* as a *mujahid* (holy
warrior) and *shahid* (martyr) whose relatively limited successes against the Franks
he compared to the victories won by the early Muslims.[18] Zangi's successors, his

[15] Jonathan Berkey, *The Transmission of Knowledge in Medieval Cairo: A Social History of Islamic Education* (Princeton: Princeton University Press, 1992), 123–7; Chamberlain, *Knowledge and Social Practice*, 62–8; Kamal S. Salibi, "The Banū Jamāʿa: A Dynasty of Shāfiʿite Jurists," *Studia Islamica* 9 (1958), 97–109.
[16] Berkey, *The Transmission of Knowledge*, 112–16.
[17] Berkey, *The Transmission of Knowledge*, 182–218.
[18] ʿIzz al-Dīn ibn al-Athīr, *al-Tārīkh al-bāhir fiʾl-dawla al-atabakiyya* (Cairo: Dār al-Kutub al-Ḥadītha, 1963), 66–7.

son Nur al-Din and his rival Saladin, cultivated (and perhaps also deserved) even more a religious image: of the ruler as *mujahid*, but also as friend and patron of the ulama, indeed as a religious scholar himself.[19]

The Muslim-ness of the military regimes extended well beyond the cultivated public images of their rulers to inform their purposes and policies more broadly. With their destruction of the caliphate in Baghdad, the Mongol invasions posed a significant challenge to traditional formulations of the religious character of Muslim governments. Several individuals who claimed to be members of the ʿAbbasid family escaped the carnage and made their way to Egypt, where the Mamluk soldiers installed them as "caliphs." This, however, was a mere feint, a gesture to past political realities: their caliphate was not widely recognized as legitimate outside the Mamluk realm, and even within played at best a marginal political role. Rather, it was the regimes of the sultans who ruled from Cairo and elsewhere who articulated and realized the meaning of an Islamic polity in the transformed circumstances of the Middle Period. So, for example, the Mamluk sultan al-Zahir Baybars came to power under difficult circumstances which cast a shadow on the legitimacy of his rule – his immediate predecessor had been assassinated through a conspiracy in which Baybars had taken part, and the Mamluks themselves still operated under the pall of having overthrown and murdered the son of their former master, the Ayyubid sultan and grand nephew of Saladin, al-Malik al-Salih – a position not entirely unfamiliar to other Near Eastern rulers of this period. Although it was Baybars who recognized the ʿAbbasid refugees' claims and installed them as caliphs in Cairo, his efforts to legitimize his regime focused less on restoring the caliphate than it did on a conscious policy of cultivating the support of the ulama and reconstituting the social and institutional basis of Muslim life: restoring Islamic monuments such as the Dome of the Rock in Jerusalem and the Prophet's mosque in Medina, constructing and endowing new institutions such as an important *madrasa* and the large congregational mosque in Cairo which bear his name, and enforcing *shariʿa* rules more vigorously. The titulature by which they were known in inscriptions on the monuments they established and in official documents demonstrates that the Mamluks understood their rule to have a religious basis. The public image of the ruler, as presented in these inscriptions and documents, described him as (for example) "the learned [in the religious sciences], the one who dispenses justice, the foundation [of the state], the warrior of *jihad*, … the sultan of Islam and [all] the Muslims, the reviver of justice among the inhabitants of the world, the one who dispenses righteousness to those who have been wronged, … the servant of the two noble sanctuaries [i.e., Mecca and Medina], the shadow of God on earth,

---

[19] Carole Hillenbrand surveys the images of these rulers, both in the original sources and in modern scholarship, in *The Crusades: Islamic Perspectives* (Chicago: Fitzroy Dearborn, 1999), 112–16 (on Zangi), 119–41 (on Nur al-Din), and 171–95 (on Saladin). The central work on Nur al-Din is Nikita Elisséeff, *Nūr al-Dīn, un grand prince musulman de Syrie au temps des Croisades (511–569 h./1118–1174)* (Damascus: Institut Français, 1967). The scholarly view of Saladin is much more complex. H. A. R. Gibb gave the most favorable account in "The Achievement of Saladin," in *Studies on the Civilization of Islam* (Princeton: Princeton University Press, 1962), 89–107.

... the one who is close to the commander of the faithful [i.e., the caliph]."[20] The Mamluk sultans' political and military responsibilities were conceived and expressed in an explicitly Islamic idiom: that they shouldered the burden of waging *jihad*, of defending the two holy places of Mecca and Medina, of ensuring the effective application of the *shariʿa*. There was a caliph in the Islamic world after the devastation of the Mongol invasions, in the person of the ʿAbbasid sitting in Cairo, but the full scope of his authority had been swallowed up by the military rulers.[21]

The military rulers' ideological reliance on Islam gave the ulama an opening, and they exercised their political power in a variety of ways. Some members of the ulama served the military regimes directly, although the extent of their participation in the affairs of government was limited. Some historians have assumed that one of the driving forces behind the spread of *madrasas* in Near Eastern cities in the Middle Period was the preparation of a class of scholars trained in the religious sciences, who served the military regimes as bureaucrats and functionaries. For these historians, the state's growing administrative reliance on men with a religious education and outlook constituted a central accomplishment of the putative "Sunni revival."[22] The military regimes did of course require a considerable number of civilian agents to collect taxes, publish decrees, and perform various other administrative functions. For the most part, however, regimes such as those of the Saljuqs and the Mamluks were able to rely on old and established bureaucratic traditions and on families of scribes trained in those traditions. Bureaucratic and religious functions and professions did to some degree overlap – in the Mamluk period, individuals who served in religious posts and in bureaucratic ones were sometimes known collectively as "men of the turban" or "men of the pen," to distinguish them from the "men of the sword" who actually ruled. In most cases, however, there remained fairly clear distinctions, of family background, identity and of training, between those who served the state or its ruling elite in an administrative capacity, and those who were recognized for the extent of their religious learning. Bureaucrats might have some minimal training in the religious sciences, but that did not mean that, in either status or outlook, the pools of civilian administrators and of ulama were coterminous.[23] Significantly, one area in which the interests and concerns of the ulama and the military rulers did overlap

---

[20] Aḥmad ibn ʿAlī al-Qalqashandī, *Ṣubḥ al-aʿshā fī ṣināʿat al-inshāʾ*, 14 vols. (Cairo: al-Muʾassasa al-Miṣriyya al-ʿĀmma liʾl-Taʾlīf waʾl-Tarjama, 1964), 7.378–9. On Muslim titulature and its religious message, see Hillenbrand, *The Crusades*, 230–5.

[21] A point made explicitly in documents in which the caliph formally conveyed to the sultan his responsibility for, among other things, waging *jihad* and protecting the Muslim community. See, for example, al-Qalqashandī, *Ṣubḥ al-aʿshāʾ*, 10.116–20, in which the ʿAbbasid caliph al-Hakim bi-amr allah commits his responsibilities to the Mamluk al-Mansur Qalawun. Cf. Lambton, *State and Government in Medieval Islam*, 141–3. See also Linda Northrup, *From Slave to Sultan: The Career of al-Manṣūr Qalāwūn and the Consolidation of Mamluk Rule in Egypt and Syria (678–689 A.H./1279–1290 A.D.)* (Stuttgart: Franz Steiner Verlag, 1998), 166–176.

[22] See, for example, Hodgson, *The Venture of Islam*, 2.46f.

[23] See Petry, *The Civilian Elite of Cairo*, 202–20, 312–25; Richard Bulliet, *Islam: The View from the Edge* (New York: Columbia University Press, 1994), 148; Daphna Ephrat, *A Learned Society in Transition: The Sunni ʿUlamāʾ of Eleventh-Century Baghdad* (Albany, NY: SUNY Press, 2000),

to a considerable degree, and in which the ulama served the rulers directly, was in the administration of the law. In some cases, for example under the Saljuqs, *qadis* could be found serving the rulers as viziers or in the state's administrative bureaucracy, a combination of religious and administrative function which foreshadows the full bureaucratization of the judiciary in the Ottoman period.[24] Under the Mamluks, the chief *qadis*, appointed by the sultans, administered a vast juridical bureaucracy, and also supported the state through their participation in an elaborate public ceremonial, sitting with the sultan and leading amirs on holidays and on solemn state occasions.

But the ulama also possessed a reservoir of political power which drew on their moral authority as religious leaders, and which was reinforced by the centrality of the *shariᶜa*, of which they were the guardians and the administrators, to the ideology of medieval Muslims states and to the self-identity of individual Muslims. The decentralized political structures of the times gave them the opportunity to flex their political muscle. In circumstances of political chaos, the ulama could take a very active political role indeed, as they did in the Iranian city of Nishapur in the eleventh century, when they collectively determined to hand the city over to the Saljuq leader Toghril Beg and recognize his rule.[25] We have already encountered the Aleppan *qadi* Ibn al-Khashshab as a proponent of *jihad* who organized a public and violent response to the challenge of the Crusaders. More generally, however, in the confused political conditions of the early twelfth century, characterized by the bewildering spectacle of European Christian invaders, the disintegration of Saljuq rule, and persistent threats from Ismaᶜilis, it was Ibn al-Khashshab who rallied the population of Aleppo (to, among other things, a massacre of Ismaᶜilis) and oversaw its administration until stable Muslim rule was restored under the Zangids and then the Ayyubids.[26] When the political authority of the military rulers momentarily collapsed, it was often the ulama who filled the breach. In the thirteenth and fourteenth centuries, the religious elite of Damascus repeatedly found themselves faced with the necessity of undertaking the difficult task of negotiating with Mongol invaders, when the Mamluks, to avoid destruction, tactically withdrew their forces towards Egypt: in 1260, when the Mongol leader Hulegu reached Damascus, and again in 1299–1300, when Ibn Taymiyya was among among the ulama of different *madhahib* who sought to persuade the Ilkhanid ruler Ghazan to restrain his marauding troops.[27] Similarly, when Timur

131; R. Stephen Humphreys, *From Saladin to the Mongols: The Ayyubids of Damascus* (Albany, NY: SUNY Press, 1977), 377–80; Joan Gilbert, "Institutionalization of Muslim Scholarship and Professionalization of the ᶜUlamāᵓ in Medieval Damascus," *Studia Islamica* 52 (1980), 105–35, esp. 122; Bernadette Martel-Thoumian, *Les civils et l'administration dans l'état militaire mamlīk (ixᵉ/xvᵉ siècle)* (Damascus: Institut Français de Damas, 1991), esp. 59–64, 177–9.

[24] Ephrat, *A Learned Society in Transition*, 131.

[25] Richard Bulliet, *The Patricians of Nishapur: A Study in Medieval Islamic Social History* (Cambridge, Massachusetts: Harvard University Press, 1972), 69–70.

[26] Jean Sauvaget, *Alep: Essai sur le développement d'une grande ville syrienne, des origines au milieu du xixᵉ siècle* (Paris: Librairie Orientaliste Paul Geuthner, 1941), 98–9n.

[27] Humphreys, *From Saladin to the Mongols*, 353; Joseph Somogyi, "Adh-Dhababi's Record of the Destruction of Damascus by the Mongols in 699–700/1299–1301," *Ignace Goldziher Memorial Volume*, ed. Samuel Löwinger and Joseph Somogyi (Budapest, 1948), 353–86.

invested the city of Damascus a century later and the Mamluk sultan Faraj ibn Barquq fled to Cairo, it was a Hanbali *qadi*, Ibn Muflih, who represented the Damascene population in negotiations to surrender the city, and who then supervised the collection of money from the population to pay as tribute.[28]

The ulama's political power did not only manifest itself on those occasions when, for various reasons, the military rulers momentarily disappeared from the scene. The ulama did not directly challenge the military's collective monopoly on the mechanisms of coercive power and of government, but the dynamics of the situation could make the rulers vulnerable to pressure, prudently applied. This resulted not simply from the rulers' foreign origin and their subsequent need to negotiate their rule through the local elite, but also from the medieval jurists' understanding of the nature of authority in an Islamic state. As we have seen, those jurists (such as Ibn Taymiyya) enjoined on Muslims obedience to the state, in order to avoid social chaos, but they also stressed the rulers' duty to implement the *shariʿa* – of which they were the guardians and the spokesmen. The need to satisfy the claims of the *shariʿa* and those who represented it moderated the rulers' exercise of power in a number of ways. A sultan might, for instance, be reluctant to impose taxes above and beyond those stipulated by the *shariʿa* without the consent of the *qadis* or of the leading legal scholars, even in circumstances of dire necessity.[29] Even in the arena of their own internal politics, to which as a rule the ulama were studiously indifferent, the military rulers sometimes made overtures to the scholars to seek their cooperation in support of one political faction or another – as did, for example, those Mamluks who overthrew Sultan Barquq in 1389, when they sought a decree (*fatwa*) from the leading *qadis* justifying their coup d'état.[30]

On the other hand, the rulers had mechanisms through which they sought to control the ulama. Interestingly, these mechanisms relied for the most part not on their monopoly on coercive instruments of power, but rather on their access (considerable, although hardly exclusive) to wealth: they were, in other words, principally carrots rather than sticks. And it was here that the complex "condominium" of power involving soldiers and scholars had the greatest impact on the religious scene. From the days of Nizam al-Mulk down through the regime of the Mamluks, it was the rulers and the members of the ruling elite who were responsible for the construction and provisioning of the institutional structure of religious life. They did so by means of endowments (*awqaf*, sing. *waqf*) that,

---

[28] Muḥammad ibn ʿAbd al-Raḥmān al-Sakhāwī, *al-Ḍawʾ al-lāmiʿ li-ahl al-qarn al-tāsiʿ*, 12 vols. (Cairo: Maktabat al-Qudsī, 1934), 1.167–8; ʿAbd al-Ḥayy ibn al-ʿImād, *Shadharāt al-dhahab fī akhbār man dhahab*, 8 vols. (Cairo: Maktabat al-Qudsī, 1931–3), 7.22–3; Lapidus, *Muslim Cities*, 131–3; Walter Fischel, *Ibn Khaldun and Tamerlane: Their Historic Meeting in Damascus, 1401 A.D. (803 A.H.)* (Berkeley: University of California Press, 1952).

[29] Sherman A. Jackson, *Islamic Law and the State: The Constitutional Jurisprudence of Shihāb al-Dīn al-Qarāfī* (Leiden: E. J. Brill, 1996), 10–11; cf. Lapidus, *Muslim Cities*, 135.

[30] For a discussion of this episode, see Walter J. Fischel, *Ibn Khaldūn in Egypt: His Public Functions and His Historical Research (1382–1406): A Study in Islamic Historiography* (Berkeley: University of California Press, 1967), 34–39.

under Islamic law, allowed individuals to set aside property the income from which could be used for a mix of charitable and private purposes. In this way, the rulers built and funded by far the greater number of mosques, *madrasas*, and other institutions of religious life.

This development served to bind the ulama and the military elites together in an ever more complicated relationship. From the standpoint of the ulama, the proliferation of religious institutions had great advantages, although it was not an unmitigated blessing. It did of course provide them with considerable resources to support their scholarly and other religious activities, in the form of stipends, the provision of food and accommodations, and other forms of payment, not to mention a plethora of imposing urban spaces in which those activities could transpire. The question of who was to oversee the distribution of these resources was obviously crucial, and often highly-regarded scholars could secure effective control over them to ensure that they could pass them on to their sons or preferred students. But frequently the endowments were structured in such a way that those who established them (or their political heirs) retained some degree of control over appointments to them, and the natural tendency of rival scholars to compete for those appointments reinforced the leverage which control of appointments afforded the ruling elite.[31]

Under the political conditions of the medieval period, however, the rulers proved themselves unable to make full use of this mechanism of control – that is, of the endowment of institutions and control of appointments to them. The endowments created to support these institutions were, under the terms of the *shari*ᶜ*a*, the private actions of the individuals who chose to establish them. That is, a sultan who built a *madrasa* and endowed it did so as a private individual, rather than in his official capacity as sultan. To be sure, the creation of such an institution and an endowment to support it had a very public and political dimension – indeed, from the standpoint of the ruling elite, one of the major points of undertaking such a task was to make a very public display of piety, and thus to stake a claim to the goodwill it engendered among the Muslim population and in particular among the ulama. But the essentially private character of the action reflected several important factors, including, in the first place, the values of the *shari*ᶜ*a*, which privileged individual rights and responsibilities. Secondly, and far more importantly, the private nature of the act reflected the character of the political systems of the medieval Islamic Near East, in which power rested less in abstractions like the "state" than it did in the extended households of the leading figures of the military elites.[32]

---

[31] For an interesting and early example of a struggle among the ulama for control of an institution's endowment, and one which provided an opportunity for intervention by a political figure, see Jacqueline Chabbi, "La fonction du ribat à Bagdad du vᵉ siècle au début du viiᵉ siècle," *Revue des études islamiques*, 42 (1974), 116. The question of appointments to remunerative positions in *madrasas* and other institutions is discussed at some length in Berkey, *The Transmission of Knowledge*, and Chamberlain, *Knowledge and Social Practice*.

[32] On the private nature of the establishment and endowment of such institutions, see George Makdisi, *The Rise of Colleges: Institutions of Learning in Islam and the West* (Edinburgh: Edinburgh University Press, 1981), 35–74, and the criticisms in Chamberlain, *Knowledge and Social Practice*, 51–4.

The result was what has been called a "maladroit patrimonialism,"[33] in which neither the religious nor the political elite was able to exercise unchallenged hegemony. Both groups relied upon each other, the ulama needing the financial support provided by the soldiers, the latter benefitting from the ideological legitimation which only the former could supply. Competition, both between the ulama and the military elite and also between members of each group, provided the system with its dynamic and at the same time placed limits on the authority which any individual, or group of individuals, could wield.

[33] Chamberlain, *Knowledge and Social Practice*, 8.

CHAPTER 22

Modes of justice

Islamic law, both as a general ideal and as a body of concrete guidelines for social behavior, functioned as a powerful "glue" in the Islamic societies of the medieval Near East. The importance of the law was a product of a number of the developments which we have been tracing – for example, the evolution of Islam in a world of multiple faith traditions and through a sometimes tense, sometimes creative dialogue with them, since law was understood to be something which attached to the individual, not from social rank or place of habitation, but through his or her membership in one religious community or another. Even more important was the emergence of the ulama as the principal locus of Muslim religious authority. The political fragmentation of the *umma* may actually have fostered a fixation on the *shariᶜa* as a focal point of Muslim identity, since the cosmopolitan ulama constituted the most immediate and visible reminder of the persistently compelling ideal of Muslim unity.

Even so, the changed circumstances of the Middle Period saw significant developments in the social experience of Islamic law. By the beginning of the Middle Period, after several centuries of development, the Sunni *madhahib* were fairly well established – the four which have survived into modern times (the Shafiᶜi, Hanafi, Hanbali, and Maliki), as well as a number of others which petered out at various times. Most notable among these was the Zahiri school, which had something of a minor flowering in the Maghrib in the eleventh century, through the works of the Spanish scholar Ibn Hazm (d. 1065), but which, by the time Ibn Khaldun wrote in the fourteenth century, had ceased to function because of the extinction of the personal chains of authority, linking teacher to pupil, through which status as a scholar of the law was transmitted. Ibn Khaldun's famous comment is worth quoting at some length, for the light it sheds on both the process through which learned status was transmitted and on the role of consensus in the crystallization of the *madhahib* and in the broader intellectual discourse of medieval Islam:

> The Zahiri school has become extinct today as the result of the extinction of their religious leaders and disapproval of their adherents by the great mass of Muslims. It has survived only in books, which have eternal life. Worthless persons occasionally feel obliged to follow this school and study these books in the desire to learn the (Zahiri)

system of jurisprudence from them, but they get nowhere and encounter the opposition and disapproval of the great mass of Muslims. In doing so, they often are considered innovators, as they accept knowledge from books for which no key is provided by teachers.[1]

But what exactly did the *madhahib*, and membership in them, signify? As we saw above, the various *madhahib* at times served as focal points for intense rivalries between different groups of Muslims, rivalries which may have been grounded in interests and issues that had little to do with juristic questions. The city of Nishapur, for example, was convulsed in the early Middle Period by civic disturbances pitting "Hanafis" against "Shafiᶜis," where it is pos-sible that the *madhhab* labels served as a screen for underlying social compe-tition or even theological disagreements. Under Saljuq rule more generally, and especially in Baghdad, the various *madhahib* became associated with particular political factions and interests. The sultans Toghril Beg and Alp Arslan, for example, patronized the Hanafi school, appointing Hanafi scholars as *qadis* and preachers. On the other hand, the Saljuqs' Persian vizier Nizam al-Mulk cultivated the Shafiᶜis, including the famous scholars Abu Hamid al-Ghazali and Abu Ishaq al-Shirazi (d. 1083), particularly in the *madrasas* which he built and endowed for them in Baghdad and elsewhere. It is tempting to trace the rivalry between Shafiᶜis and Hanafis to underlying differences in their juristic orientation, in particular the Shafiᶜi emphasis on upon tradition, expressed in their privileging of *hadith* reports, against a greater willingness on the part of Hanafis to sanction the use of human reason in jurisprudential argument. There are also some indications that the growing appeal of Islamic mysticism was a factor bubbling under the surface of the *madhhab* differences, as very few Hanafi jurists in the early Middle Period can be identified as having been associated with Sufism. On the other hand, it is also clear that *madhhab* rivalry transcended any intellectual differences, and became enmeshed in a complex web of social and political competition.[2]

For all the importance of Islamic law generally, however, it is difficult to make further generalizations about the broader communal significance of *madhhab* identification. Geographically, the schools were not evenly distributed: Malikis, for example, were barely present in Baghdad or, for that matter, in the larger Iranian world, in which Hanafis and Shafiᶜis predominated. Malikis were strong in North Africa, and also in Egypt, at least until the restoration of Sunni rule

---

[1] Ibn Khaldūn, *al-Muqaddima*, ed. M. Quatremère in 3 vols. (Paris: Didot, 1858), 3.3–4; trans. Franz Rosenthal, 2nd edition (Princeton: Princeton University Press, 1967), 3.5–6.

[2] On the situation in Nishapur, see Richard Bulliet, *The Patricians of Nishapur: A Study in Medieval Islamic Social History* (Cambridge, Massachusetts: Harvard University Press, 1972), especially 28–46, and idem, *Islam: The View from the Edge* (New York: Columbia University Press, 1994), 110–13. On the rivalry of Hanafis and Shafiᶜis under the Saljuqs, see the various works of George Makdisi, in particular *Ibn ᶜAqīl et la résurgence de l'Islam traditionaliste au xiᵉ siècle (vᵉ siècle de l'Hégire)* (Damascus: Institut Français de Damas, 1963), and *EI²*, art. "Saldjūḳids" (by C. E. Bosworth), § IV.1. A more recent study is that of Daphna Ephrat, *A Learned Society in Transition: The Sunni ᶜUlamāʾ of Eleventh-Century Baghdad* (Albany, NY: SUNY Press, 2000), esp. 85–93.

under Saladin, who strongly favored the Shafi^{c}is.[3] And the degree to which the *madhahib* served as focal points of religious identity for Muslims other than the religious elite and their political patrons is very difficult to determine, and must have varied considerably from one time and place to another.[4] One possible exception is that of the Hanbalis, whose importance in Islamic history, and in particular in the shaping of the contours of Islam during the medieval "recentering," has often been overlooked. Hanbalis were especially numerous in Baghdad, with significant communities also in Harran, in the Salihiyya suburb of Damascus, and various other Syrian and Palestinian locales, and more limited presences elsewhere.[5] More than any other *madhhab*, Hanbalism (like Shi^{c}ism) represented a relatively broad-based social movement, one with which common people as well as scholars might readily identify. In Baghdad, for example, particular mosques were associated with the Hanbali movement, while particular quarters of the city acquired a reputation as Hanbali strongholds. The school had its prominent intellectuals, such as Ibn ^{c}Aqil, but also a broader following. Above all, it was Hanbali preachers and others who were most active in mobilizing crowds to oppose, vociferously and sometimes violently, the public expression of religious ideas which ran counter to the strict traditionalism which was popular with the Baghdadi populace. The Hanbalis did not always act alone; in Baghdad, for instance, some Shafi^{c}i scholars and preachers were also active in the traditionalist movement and in stirring up protest against exponents of rationalist Ash^{c}ari theology or Shi^{c}i partisanship. But identification with the Hanbali school does seem to have reached further down the social ladder, and in some cases provided a channel for dissemination of the principles and rulings of juristic Islam to Muslims living at some distance from the urban centers of legal education and discourse.[6]

During the course of the Middle Period, the *madhahib* themselves evolved into intellectual communities whose impact on the understanding and enactment of

---

[3] Sherman Jackson, *Islamic Law and the State: The Constitutional Jurisprudence of Shihāb al-Dīn al-Qarāfī* (Leiden: E. J. Brill, 1996), 53–5; Ira M. Lapidus, "Ayyūbid Religious Policy and the Development of the Schools of Law in Cairo," *Colloque internationale sur l'histoire du caire* (Cairo, 1969), 279–86.

[4] See the very cogent remarks of Roy Mottahedeh in his review of Bulliet's *The Patricians of Nishapur,* in the *Journal of the American Oriental Society* 95 (1975), 491–5, and Ephrat, *A Learned Society,* 137f.

[5] See, for example, Henri Laoust, "Le hanbalisme sous le califat de Bagdad," *Revue des études islamiques* 27 (1959), 67–128; Dominique Sourdel, "Deux documents relatifs à la communauté hanbalite de Damas," *Bulletin d'études orientales* 25 (1972), 141–6; Gary L. Leiser, "Hanbalism in Egypt before the Mamlūks," *Studia Islamica* 54 (1981), 155–81, correcting Laoust, "Le hanbalisme sous les Mamlouks bahrides (658–784/1260–1382)," *Revue des études islamiques* 28 (1960), 1–71.

[6] On the latter point, see Daniella Talmon Heller, "The Shaykh and the Community: Popular Hanbalite Islam in 12th–13th Century Jabal Nablus and Jabal Qaysūn," *Studia Islamica* 79 (1994), 103–120. On the reasons why Western historians have often overlooked the contribution of Hanbalism to medieval Islam, see George Makdisi, "Hanbalite Islam," in *Studies on Islam* ed. Merlin Swartz, (New York: Oxford University Press, 1981), 216–74. On the broad social base of Hanbalism and the ability of Hanbalis to mobilize crowds, see idem, *Ibn ^{c}Aqīl et la résurgence de l'islam traditionaliste,* 317–27, 337–40, and 340–75.

religious authority was profound. Over time, the intense and sometimes violent rivalries which had enveloped, for example, the Shafiʿis and Hanafis of Nishapur diminished, and the four surviving Sunni schools generally regarded their mutual orthodoxy as axiomatic. At the same time, what we might call the collective "consciousness" of the different schools of law grew increasingly well-developed and precise. In some places this was in part the result of a deliberate policy on the part of the ruling authorities. After Saladin had restored Egypt to Sunni rule by deposing the last Fatimid caliph, for example, he and his successors appointed a series of Shafiʿi jurists as chief *qadis*, and routinely nominated as judges scholars who taught in the *madrasas* which under Ayyubid and then Mamluk rule were established and endowed at a quickening pace, tying the administration of justice more firmly to the academic institutions and networks in which legal and religious learning was transmitted and *madhhab*-identity fostered. Under the Mamluk Baybars and successive sultans, the pattern was extended to the other schools, as it became routine to appoint four chief judges, one from each of the recognized Sunni schools, and also for benefactors to endow their *madrasas* and other institutions with funds to support professors and students in the four schools. There were moments when boundaries between the schools were crossed: an individual scholar might leave one *madhhab* for another, on intellectual grounds or for more mundane reasons, as when a group of Shafiʿi students in Cairo became Hanafis in the mid-fourteenth century in order to take advantage of especially lucrative stipends for which a new endowment provided. But in general the emergence of what amounted to a *cursus honorum* contributed to a feeling of solidarity among scholars belonging to a single school of law.[7]

The question of the role and function of the *madhahib* is closely linked to the controversial issue of the persistence of what the lawyers referred to as *ijtihad*, usually translated as "independent reasoning." The older interpretation, associated especially with the pioneering Western historian of Islamic law, Joseph Schacht, is that at some point around the tenth century, the jurists reached a consensus that the *bab al-ijtihad*, or "gates of independent reasoning," had closed. Schacht in fact defined *ijtihad* more precisely as indicating "the drawing of valid conclusions from the Koran, the *sunna* of the Prophet, and the consensus, by analogy (*kiyās*) or systematic reasoning."[8] The presumed consequence of this development was that Islamic lawyers of the Middle and later periods were required to exercise *taqlid*, "imitation": that is, they were expected to follow their intellectual forebears in their legal judgments.

The historical controversy over the doctrines of *ijtihad* and *taqlid* has been as much about contemporary perceptions of Islam as anything else. Some have

---

[7] The incident from Cairo is described in Taqī ʾl-Dīn Ahmad al-Maqrīzī, *al-Mawāʿiẓ waʾl-iʿtibār bi-dhikr al-khiṭaṭ waʾl-athār*, 2 vols. (Bulaq, A.H. 1270), 2.269. On developments in the *madhahib* and the connection to the office of the *qadi*, see Ephrat, *A Learned Society*, 95–124; Lapidus, "Ayyūbid Religious Policy"; Jackson, *Islamic Law and the State*, 53–68; and Joseph Escovitz, *The Office of Qāḍī al-Quḍāt in Cairo under the Baḥrī Mamlūks* (Berlin: Klaus Schwarz Verlag, 1984).

[8] Joseph Schacht, *An Introduction to Islamic Law* (Oxford: Clarendon Press, 1964), 69f, esp. 70.

viewed the "closing of the *bab al-ijtihad*" as in effect the end of creative legal development in Islam. It is of course highly unlikely that a legal system as complex as that of Islam could simply cease to evolve, even if its proponents wanted it to. Recently, historians have demonstrated that *ijtihad* continued as both a theoretical possibility and a practical necessity throughout the Middle Period.[9] The problem is complicated by the fact that *ijtihad* can have different meanings, but proponents of its continuance and, indeed, the *necessity* of its continuance can be found across the spectrum of medieval Islamic thought, from cantankerous jurists such as Jalal al-Din al-Suyuti (d. 1505) to the controversial mystic Ibn al-ʿArabi (d. 1240), for whom *ijtihad* was a necessary component of his theology of continual revelation.[10]

But the arguments of some jurists for the persistence of *ijtihad* should not obscure the intellectual and social impact of the doctrine of *taqlid*, which came to vest in the collective opinion of the *madhhab* the authority to insist that its adherents accept both the basic methods of deriving the law from its foundations, and also limits to the range of substantive legal rules which were acceptable. The point is not that change and development were impossible, but rather that, at least in theory, they were now only possible within the framework of opinion established by the consensus of the four *madhahib*. Intellectually this reflects an unspoken effort on the part of the jurists to develop a more rational and predictable system of law, in which future rulings would be tied more closely to precedent as expressed through a *madhhab*'s consensus. One practical expression of that effort was the growing importance in legal education of *mukhtasars*, abridged collections of the most commonly accepted rules within a given school of law. The growing popularity and use of *mukhtasars* paralleled efforts within the *madhahib* to restrict the degree to which members of the school, and in particular its lower-ranking members, might freely select from among divergent opinions accepted by the school's consensus.[11] In social and structural terms, all this constitutes an element in the broader pattern of the "homogenization" of Sunni religious life and thought which was characteristic of the period. The jurists had no church, no institutional structure through which to realize their authority. In the absence of such structures, the doctrine of *taqlid* as expressed by the *madhahib* served to make the authority of the ulama, and in particular the leading and most prestigious legal scholars, more real.

In practice, the legal sphere was even more fractured and fluid than the doctrines of the jurists might suggest. One reason is that, for all the importance of the *shariʿa* to Islam and to Muslim self-definition, the jurisdiction of the *qadis* competed with others as well. On various administrative and political matters,

[9] Wael Hallaq, "Was the Gate of *Ijtihād* Closed?," *International Journal of Middle East Studies* 16 (1984), 3–41; idem, *A History of Islamic Legal Theories* (Cambridge: Cambridge University Press, 1997), 143–61, 199–205; and idem, *Authority, Continuity, and Change in Islamic Law* (Cambridge: Cambridge University Press, 2001).
[10] See Sartain, *Jalāl al-dīn al-Suyūṭī*, 1.61–72; and Michel Chodkiewicz, *An Ocean Without Shore: Ibn Arabi, the Book, and the Law* (Albany, NY: SUNY Press, 1993), 54–7.
[11] Jackson, *Islamic Law and the State*, xxv–xxxv; Mohammad Fadel, "The Social Logic of *Taqlīd* and the Rise of the *Mukhtaṣar*," *Islamic Law and Society* 3 (1996), 193–233.

Muslim jurists had at least since the early °Abbasid period deferred to the rulers and their bureaucrats. Under the military regimes which dominated the Near East in the Middle Period, the encroachment of the political sphere on the administration of justice became more firmly entrenched. The Mongols had a body of customary laws, the *yasa*, which represented the normative practice of their ancestors and which they applied to themselves, independently of the *shari°a* which governed the lives of their subjects. This pattern, of a separate legal system applying to the ruling elite and helping to distinguish them from the local population, became a model of sorts. The Mamluks, for example, came to believe that they too possessed a *yasa*, modeled on that of the Mongols, which governed relations among themselves. The direct dependence of Mamluk customs on those of the Mongols is unlikely, but the more important phenomenon is the perception that a separate and independent body of laws applied to the ruling elite, to their military organization and political administration.[12]

On a wholly different level, the jurisdiction of the *muhtasib* supplemented that of the *qadis*, especially in regulating the lives of urban populations. The *muhtasib* was a common figure in the urban landscape of the medieval Islamic Near East, and in some places the office acquired a sophisticated bureaucratic apparatus. Under the Mamluks, for example, the *muhtasib* of Cairo was assisted by a number of deputies, as well as *muhtasibs* based in other Egyptian towns who reported to him. As we have already seen (above, pp. 121–2), the *muhtasib*'s authority had diverse roots, both in a Koranic injunction to "command what is right and forbid what is wrong" and in a common need for the informed supervision of commercial transactions and customary exchanges in urban marketplaces. Over time, the character of the office evolved. Muslim writers on political matters routinely described the *muhtasib* as the holder of a "religious office" (*wazifa diniyya*), and included among his responsibilities various matters attendant upon the *shari°a*, such as making sure that public prayers and fasting during Ramadan were observed, that openly-displayed containers of wine be destroyed, and that restrictions on *dhimmis* be enforced. But the *muhtasib*'s association with the marketplace, the site of commercial activity and therefore a source of renewable wealth, raised the profile of the office in the eyes of the rulers. The Mamluk sultans in their early years appointed reputable religious scholars to the post, but over time amirs and others who directly represented the ruler's interest came to predominate. As a result, the *muhtasib* came more and more to act as an agent of royal coercion, collecting taxes or setting prices for wheat and other staples.[13]

---

[12] On the *yasa* and its influence on medieval Near Eastern regimes, see David Ayalon, "The Great *Yasa* of Chingiz Khan: A Re-examination," *Studia Islamica* 33 (1971), 97–140; 34 (1971), 151–80; 36 (1972), 113–58; 38 (1973), 107–56; Jørgen Nielsen, *Secular Justice in an Islamic State: Maẓālim under the Baḥrī Mamlūks, 662/1264–789/1387* (Istanbul: Nederlands Historisch-Archaeologisch Instituut, 1985), 104–9; and David O. Morgan, "The 'Great *Yāsā* of Chingiz Khān' and Mongol Law in the Īlkhānate," *Bulletin of the School of Oriental and African Studies* 49 (1986), 163–76.

[13] See Jonathan P. Berkey, "The Muḥtasibs of Cairo Under the Mamluks: Toward an Understanding of an Islamic Institution," in *The Mamluks in Egyptian and Syrian Politics and Society*, ed. Amalia Levanoni and Michael Winter (Brighton: Sussex Academic Press, 2002). Several treatises describing

The ruling elites became directly involved in the adjudication of legal matters among their subjects as well through the jurisdiction known as *mazalim*, "wrongs." The earliest Islamic regimes had inherited from previous empires the custom of the ruler periodically sitting in a public forum to adjudicate disputes and to right "wrongs" suffered by his subjects. There were many reasons why an individual might seek out the jurisdiction of the *mazalim* court, in which the ruler himself or his designated lieutenant would settle disputes, in particular since it was supported by the full power of the state and was not restrained by sometimes cumbersome *shari*ᶜ*a* rules regarding evidence and procedure. The practice was common among the ᶜAbbasids and other early Islamic rulers, and received a definitive theoretical formulation from the eleventh-century jurist al-Mawardi, who identified it as a fundamental duty of the caliph or "imam." The Saljuqs, too, conducted *mazalim* sessions, which their vizier Nizam al-Mulk portrayed as deriving from both Sasanian and Islamic practice. Under the regimes of the Ayyubids and then the Mamluks, the sultans' *mazalim* jurisdiction became a central administrative and ideological pillar of their regimes. An extensive bureaucratic apparatus took shape through which the aggrieved submitted petitions for redress, while an elaborate ceremonial developed which involved the public procession of the sultan and his subordinates to the site of the *mazalim* session and the careful arrangement of the leading *qadis* and *amirs* around the ruler. Nur al-Din ibn Zangi was apparently the first sultan to construct a *dar al-*ᶜ*adl*, a "house of justice," as a center for the administration of the *mazalim* jurisdiction, but the practice was repeated by several Ayyubid and Mamluk sultans. Under the Mamluks, the *dar al-*ᶜ*adl* was used for a variety of other purposes as well, such as the reception of foreign ambassadors and the formal gathering of the *jizya*, and so became an important architectural manifestation of the sultan's authority.

The connections between the *mazalim* jurisdiction and the religious sphere, that is the sphere in which the authority of the ulama was paramount, were complex. In general *mazalim* judgments were based on custom (ᶜ*urf*) or general principles of equity. There were occasions when the *mazalim* courts encroached on matters of direct pertinence to the *shari*ᶜ*a* which were in theory reserved for the jurisdiction of the *qadis*, especially when circumstances gave a highly public or political profile to a case. Under the Mamluks, for example, the sultan's court often dealt with cases involving pious foundations (*awqaf*), particularly when the increase in the number of such foundations threatened to tie up a significant share of the country's resources or to eat into the fisc. They also attended to notorious and politically sensitive cases of blasphemy, and, in one famous case involving Ibn Taymiyya, even the Islamic law of divorce. The authority of the *mazalim* court might be sought to overturn a *qadi*'s decision; on the other hand, it might also be invoked in order to enforce a *qadi*'s decree, since the *qadis* had few enforcement

the *muhtasib*'s duties have been published; the most accessible is that of Ibn al-Ukhuwwa, *Ma*ᶜ*ālim al-qurba fī aḥkām al-ḥisba*, ed. and trans. Reuben Levy (Cambridge: Cambridge University Press, 1938) (E. J. W. Gibb Memorial Trust, vol. 12).

mechanisms of their own. Jurists might even serve in an advisory capacity to the administrator of the *mazalim* session, the ruler or his deputy. The *mazalim* jurisdiction thereby competed with that of the *shariᶜa*, but at the same time could function as an instrument of its application. Whether or not the *mazalim* courts played an important role in the actual administration of justice was also a function of location: *qadis* in remote towns may have felt less infringement on their jurisdiction than their colleagues in centers of political power, such as Baghdad under the Saljuqs or Cairo under the Mamluk sultans.[14]

What all this represents is the complex and shifting character of the relationship between political and religious authority in the medieval Islamic world, one in which the *qadis* oversaw their own system of justice but also made public appearances in the *mazalim* courts and thereby lent the weight of their authority to the ruler (or his representative) who presided over it. It suggests the importance of the law and of the notion of justice, whether grounded in the *shariᶜa* or in more general principles of equity, to medieval Islamic rulership. The choreography of *mazalim* sessions stressed that connection: for example, Ibn Shaddad, court biographer of Saladin, portrayed the sultan actively administering justice "attended by the jurists, *qadis*, and *ulama*," while a fourteenth-century description of Mamluk-era sessions had the four chief *qadis*, each representing one of the Sunni *madhahib*, lined up in order of rank on the right hand of the sultan.[15] In the Mamluk state, before the construction of a separate *dar al-ᶜadl*, *mazalim* sessions were held in the Salihiyya *madrasa* in Cairo, one of the most prominent centers of religious learning in the realm, as if to ground the authority of the supervisor of the sessions in the larger religious authority of the *shariᶜa*. The *mazalim* sessions were the most direct way in which medieval sultans discharged a duty which the jurist Badr al-Din ibn Jamaᶜa (d. 1333), himself a *qadi*, identified in his important treatise on political authority as a duty second only to that of waging *jihad* and defending Islam: namely, the administration of justice.[16]

[14] A point made by Bulliet, *Patricians of Nishapur*, 25–6. On the relation of the *mazalim* to the administration of the *shariᶜa* more generally, see Nielsen, *Secular Justice in an Islamic State*, esp. 95–104, 114–121.

[15] Bahāʾ al-Dīn ibn Shaddād, *al-Nawādir al-sulṭāniyya waʾl-maḥāsin al-yūsufiyya*, trans. D. S. Richards, *The Rare and Excellent History of Saladin* (Aldershot: Ashgate, 2001), 23; Ibn Faḍl Allāh al-ᶜUmarī, *Masālik al-abṣār fī mamālik al-amṣār* (Cairo: Institut Français d'Archéologie Orientale, 1985), 36–7.

[16] Hans Kofler, "Handbuch des islamischen Staats- und Verwaltungsrechtes von Badr-al-dīn ibn Djamāᶜah," *Islamica* 6 (1933), 6:361. On the *mazalim*, see Nielsen, *Secular Justice in an Islamic State*, passim; Nasser O. Rabbat, "The Ideological Significance of the Dār al-Adl in the Medieval Islamic Orient," *International Journal of Middle East Studies* 27 (1995), 3–28; and *EI*², art. "Maẓālim" (by J. S. Nielsen).

CHAPTER 23

The transmission of religious knowledge

Religious knowledge (*ʿilm*) was perhaps the central cultural lynchpin of the Islamic tradition and of the social patterns in which that tradition was experienced in the Middle Period. This knowledge was embedded in the rich and inter-related body of texts – principally the Koran, collections of hadith, legal treatises and textbooks, and commentaries on them – which formed the substantive basis for the training of those scholars who were known as the ulama. Our principal concern here, however, is less with the intellectual parameters of this *ʿilm* than with the social uses to which it was put, and with the way in which these uses helped to define Muslim identities and the nature of the ulama's authority.

For the ulama, it was the active process of transmitting religious knowledge that was critical. As we have seen, the ulama were in fact socially quite diverse, and the only thing that marked them as a distinctive group was their command of these highly valued texts, and their control of access to them. In part this was simply a matter of education, that is, of transmitting to students a familiarity with essential texts which was necessary to the proper discharge of the responsibilities they might incur upon appointment to a range of offices – for example, that of the *qadi*, or that of professor (*mudarris*) in the myriad religious institutions which sprang up in medieval Islamic cities. But more importantly, *ʿilm* constituted a kind of "cultural capital," which those who possessed it could employ in a variety of strategies to ensure the public recognition of their status and secure for themselves appointment to remunerative positions, and, if possible, to guarantee that their heirs, whether their sons or their students, would inherit and benefit from their status. To put the matter another way, the whole process by which one became recognized as an *ʿalim*, a "learned" person, and then parlayed that status into a career as a professor, judge, or whatever, involved much more than the simple acquisition of knowledge. It was, first and foremost, a process of socialization, in which students developed close relationships with older scholars who served as mentors as well as teachers, and so developed those "social contacts necessary for a successful career."[1]

---

[1] Richard Bulliet, *The Patricians of Nishapur: A Study in Medieval Islamic Social History* (Cambridge, Massachusetts: Harvard University Press, 1972), 47. More generally, these issues are discussed in Jonathan Berkey, *The Transmission of Knowledge: A Social History of Islamic Education* (Princeton:

The forms and channels through which religious knowledge was transmitted were highly articulated, but they were also quite fluid, and their persistent informality and flexibility made the system open and contributed to its ability to draw into the cultural center Muslims from diverse social groups. The transmission of knowledge relied fundamentally on close personal relationships between teachers and students, and on what we have called a "genealogical" style of authority. The Middle Period saw a significant expansion in the number of institutions established to promote the transmission of *ʿilm*, to which we will return in a moment; for all of that, however, institutions never replaced persons as the focus of academic life and of the reputations which gave a scholar his professional identity. The copious compendia of collective biography which constitute the most important source for the social history of the medieval Near East routinely tell us with whom a scholar studied, but almost never where he studied. Teaching took place in "circles" (*halaq*, sing. *halqa*) centered on a particular shaykh, circles which might be held in institutions established for the purpose, but which also might transpire almost anywhere else. What mattered was not the venue but the close personal bond between teacher and student, a relationship which carried reciprocal obligations and which was known as *suhba*. As it is used in texts describing the transmission of knowledge in medieval Islam, *suhba* can indicate both the concepts of "companionship" and "discipleship," and thus presumed both an almost familial intimacy (teachers were often likened to a father) and also hierarchy, the hierarchy of age and status as well as expertise. Through it a teacher transmitted less a body of knowledge than a very personalized authority over the texts in which *ʿilm* was embedded. There was nothing like an institutional diploma; the formal attestation of achievement was called an *ijaza*, a certification that an individual had studied (in some fashion) a particular text (or in some cases a wider body of knowledge) with a particular shaykh. By acquiring *ijazas* from reputable shaykhs, a student would himself become a link in the chains of personal authority which tied a pupil to his teacher and to the teacher's teacher on back to the author of a text, an accomplishment which could then be parlayed into the pupil's own status in the social networks of religious scholars.[2]

The persistence of this informal and personalized system was especially notable because it transcended a veritable explosion in the number of religious institutions in Near Eastern cities in the Middle Period. As we have already seen, the construction and endowment of these institutions was one of the principal means by

Princeton University Press, 1992), and Michael Chamberlain, *Knowledge and Social Practice in Medieval Damascus, 1190–1350* (Cambridge: Cambridge University Press, 1994), who dwells at some length on the notion of *ʿilm* as "cultural capital."

[2] George Makdisi, *The Rise of Colleges: Institutions of Learning in Islam and the West* (Edinburgh: Edinburgh University Press, 1981), 128–9; idem, "Ṣuḥba et riyāsa dans l'enseignement médiéval," in *Recherches d'Islamologie: Recueil d'articles offerts à Georges Anawati et Louis Gardet par leurs collègues et amis* (Louvain: Editions Peeters, 1978), 207–21; Berkey, *Transmission of Knowledge*, 21–43; Chamberlain; *Knowledge and Social Practice*, 69–90, 108–25; Daphna Ephrat, *A Learned Society in Transition: The Sunni ʿUlamāʾ of Eleventh-Century Baghdad* (Albany, NY: SUNY Press, 2000), 75–85, 101–4.

which the ruling military elites established their legitimacy. Many of these institutions were *madrasas*, which typically would provide space for a shaykh and his students to conduct their lessons, and also stipends to support their activities and sometimes food and accommodations as well. The principal subjects supported by the terms of the *madrasas'* endowments were jurisprudence (*fiqh*) according to one or more of the four *madhahib*, and sometimes "ancillary" sciences such as Koranic exegesis or the study of hadith. The *madrasa* had its origins in Khurasan in the tenth century. By the eleventh, the institution had become a fixture in the principal cities of the Iranian world – the Saljuq vizier Nizam al-Mulk, for example, established a series of *madrasas* in Baghdad and various other towns under Saljuq rule. Over the ensuing centuries, as the fulcrum of Sunni religious culture moved westward, so too did the *madrasa*, and the Ayyubid and Mamluk sultans and their amirs were responsible for the construction of those institutions, such as the enormous *madrasa* of Sultan Hasan (r. 1347–51 and 1354–61) in Cairo, which are still architecturally prominent in the older portions of the cities of Egypt and Syria. But what is most notable is the degree to which the social and religious functions of the *madrasa* merged with those of other institutions, such as mosques and Sufi convents, and in the process contributed to a social broadening of intellectual life. *Madrasas* were not closed institutions, set up for the benefit of the relatively small number of teachers and students their endowments supported. Rather, they were deeply embedded in the religious life of the urban milieu: they were frequently open for prayer and worship by Muslims who had no formal connection to the institution, and as such functioned as mosques as well as schools. Institutions formally known as mosques, too, often came to resemble *madrasas*, as their endowments sometimes provided stipends and other material support for shaykhs and students as well. And by the end of the Middle Period, there was little to distinguish either *madrasa* or mosque from a Sufi *khanqah*. In Cairo, for example, any number of institutions established over the last century and a half of Mamluk rule included stipends for both Sufi adepts and for studies in jurisprudence or its ancillary subjects, and their deeds of endowments frequently assumed that the Sufis and the students would, in fact, be the same people. The transmission of knowledge, in other words, was not so much a specialized profession as it was one component of a broader range of activities which marked out the social parameters of Muslim piety.[3]

As such, the transmission of religious knowledge had a claim on virtually all Muslims, and so, even beyond the ranks of well-known scholars, it helped to forge and make permanent a common Sunni identity – even more, perhaps, than the widespread commitment to Islamic law. The means by which *ᶜilm* was transmitted, and also the standards by which that transmission was measured, helped to draw towards the center social groups which in other circumstances, such as those of medieval Europe, were marginalized by the expectations and demands of religious education. A woman, for example, might not be able to serve as a *qadi*, but as a

---

[3] Berkey, *Transmission of Knowledge*, 44–94.

Muslim she might nonetheless have a personal interest in *ᶜilm* and its transmission, and in acquiring for herself some of the spiritual blessing or power (*baraka*) with which the activity was believed to be endowed. Consequently, quite a few girls studied with and received *ijazas* from experts in various disciplines, especially hadith, and later themselves issued *ijazas* in turn to students who sought out their authority over some particular text – they became, in other words, valued links in the chains of personal authority through which religious knowledge was passed on. The transmission of knowledge did not exactly undermine the gender boundary and hierarchy which cut across the medieval Islamic world, but it did, at least in this limited sense, soften it, and gave some women a stake in the learning which was so central to Muslim identity.[4] The very procedures by which *ᶜilm* was transmitted, since they constituted an expression and enactment of Muslim piety, helped to broaden the appeal of "education" and to make it more accessible. The books in which *ᶜilm* was embedded, for example, were typically read aloud, sometimes in very public places so that, as one historian has observed, books were in a way "performed" rather than "read."[5] The endowments which supported religious institutions such as *madrasas* routinely made provisions for the constant public chanting of the Koran, sometimes from windows overlooking the streets outside, so that the recitation could benefit passers-by as well as students and others housed in the institution, while grand public readings of the principal collections of hadith during Ramadan were a popular feature of urban religious life. Those who attended such sessions, including Mamluk amirs as well as average citizens who would not normally be considered ulama, might themselves be issued *ijazas* in recognition of their participation in them, and thus acquire some symbolic but nonetheless valued stake in the social process by which religious knowledge was transmitted and replicated.[6]

And so both the forms and processes of the transmission of religious knowledge, and even the institutions established to support it, served to broaden the social base of those committed to it. At the same time, however, a countervailing trend worked to define more precisely and narrowly the character of Sunni Islam and the circle of those recognized as authoritative on questions of religious knowledge. Institutional developments contributed to this trend. An earlier generation of Western historians understood this process in a narrow political sense, seeing the proliferation of *madrasas* during the Middle Period as a direct response to the challenge of Shiᶜism, as a way for new and newly militant Sunni rulers, in particular Nizam al-Mulk and his Saljuq patrons, to cultivate a cadre of jurists and bureaucrats who would help construct a deliberately Sunni society and government in the wake of the threat posed by Ismaᶜilism and Fatimid claims to the caliphate. This interpretation must now be modified, in part because,

---

[4] Berkey, *Transmission of Knowledge*, 161–81; and idem, "Women and Education in the Mamluk Period," in *Women in Middle Eastern History: Shifting Boundaries in Sex and Gender*, ed. Nikki Keddie and Beth Baron (New Haven: Yale University Press, 1992), 143–57.

[5] Chamberlain, *Knowledge and Social Practice*, 135–48.

[6] Berkey, *Transmission of Knowledge*, 142–60, 182–218.

as we have already seen, there remained fairly clear personal and professional distinctions between the ulama and the bureaucratic servants of the state, and in part because, by the time the *madrasa* became so common in places like Egypt, the threat from Shiᶜism was, for all intents and purposes, vestigial and remote.[7] But the spread of *madrasas* did contribute more generally to a sharpening of a specifically Sunni identity, and so could help to fashion a response to particular circumstances and immediate threats – as in, for example, the perceived threat of a resurgent Christianity in the late Fatimid period (above, pp. 196–8). If the spread of *madrasas* and other institutions supporting the organized transmission of religious knowledge broadened the social base of that pious activity, the increasing availability of remunerative posts for the teaching of jurisprudence and related subjects encouraged a kind of professionalization within the higher ranks of the ulama. In some cases that professionalization served to restrict the circle of those achieving public recognition as scholars. So, for example, in Cairo as well as elsewhere, a scholar who held rights to a teaching post in one *madrasa* or another might take exceptional steps to ensure that the position was inherited by his sons, or by his favored pupils.[8]

This trend was reinforced intellectually by developments in an internal Muslim debate over how religious knowledge could most reliably be passed down. A certain tension between the written and spoken word underlay the transmission of knowledge in the medieval Islamic world. On the one hand, as has been widely recognized, oral transmission was always preferred, so that even written texts, including texts whose written form had been fixed for centuries (such as the principal collections of hadith, let alone the Koran itself), would generally be "read" out loud – hence the "performative" aspect of their transmission referred to above.[9] At the same time, written texts – actual, physical written books – played by the Middle Period a critical role in the education of young scholars, forming the centerpiece of their studies. *Madrasas* and other religious institutions amassed considerable libraries of books, libraries which attracted scholars from all over the Muslim world who came to copy texts and so spread ᶜilm in its written form – as, for example, those scholars from the Maghrib, West Africa, Anatolia, Syria, and Muslim lands even further afield whose dedication to copying his (many!) books so pleased the Egyptian jurist and historian al-Suyuti. The treatise of a thirteenth-century jurist on the acquisition of knowledge embodies the tension between the two modes of transmission. On the one hand, Ibn Jamaᶜa observed that, unless a student really mastered a text through memorization, a feat which was to be

---

[7] There are, of course, exceptions; in Upper Egypt, for example, the network of religious and educational institutions founded by the Mamluks and others helped to mobilize resistance to the persistent Shiᶜism of the local population. Jean-Claude Garcin, *Un Centre Musulman de la Haute-Égypte Médiévale: Qūṣ* (Cairo: Institut Français d'Archéologie Orientale, 1976), passim.

[8] Berkey, *Transmission of Knowledge*, 95–127. For a slightly different view, see Chamberlain, *Knowledge and Social Practice*, 91–107.

[9] The orality of the transmission of texts is a dominant theme in virtually all studies of Islamic religious knowledge and education; see, for example, Chamberlain, *Knowledge and Social Practice*, esp. 133–51, and Berkey, *Transmission of Knowledge*, 24–31.

achieved principally through the oral recitation of the text, "accumulating [written] books will do you no good." At the same time, he urged students to "strive to acquire those books he needs however possible – by purchasing, renting, or borrowing [them]," for books are the "instruments of knowledge."[10]

The tension between oral transmission and the written text was never resolved. On the one hand, the persistently oral nature of reading and of the transmission of texts, combined with the emphasis upon personal connections between shaykh and pupil described above, contributed to broadening the social base of this religious activity, since it made the "reading" of texts (of which, in the manuscript age, physical copies were expensive) more widely accessible. On the other, the growing importance of books – that is, of clearly defined texts – contributed to what we might call the increasing "inscription" and "circumscription" of religious authority. In the eleventh century, the scholar and historian al-Khatib al-Baghdadi devoted an entire treatise to the competing claims of oral transmission and the written word in religious education, and while acknowledging the importance of the "heart" in the study and passing on of the religious sciences, in the end came down firmly in favor of the importance of the written word and of its greater reliability as a medium of transmission.[11] Consequently, as one historian has put it, the Islamic Middle Period saw "the development of a homogeneous corpus of authoritative Islamic texts that contributed greatly to a growing uniformity of Islamic belief and practice throughout the vast area in which Muslims lived," that is, to the "Sunni recentering."[12]

This inscription and circumscription of religious authority constituted a part of the "homogenization" of religious life which we have identified as one of the dominant motifs of medieval Islamic history. The phenomenon manifested itself in a variety of ways, including the growing role in legal discourse and education of *mukhtasars* and the doctrine of *taqlid*. The hostility to innovations which was a recurrent theme in medieval Islamic polemic was another. The inscription of religious authority took very precise forms as well. The ulama, for example, sought to restrict the ability of individuals who possessed only a modicum of intellectual training, or who might even be illiterate, but who nonetheless claimed considerable religious authority among the uneducated masses, to define for their audiences what was properly Islamic, an issue to which we will return in the chapter on "popular religion." Moreover, the "growing uniformity of Islamic belief and practice" may have helped to marginalize the so-called "rational" sciences – philosophy, logic, the natural sciences and the like – from the Sunni intellectual mainstream. Here we must be careful. This point has been much over-stressed and mis-construed by previous historians pre-disposed to find signs of "decline"

[10] Ibn Jamāʿa, *Tadhkirat al-sāmiʿ waʾl-mutakallim fī adab al-ʿālim waʾl-mutaʿallim* (Hyderabad: Dāʾirat al-Maʿārif al-ʿUthmāniyya, 1935), 163–7.
[11] Al-Khatīb al-Baghdādī, *Taqyīd al-ʿilm*, 2nd edition (n.p.p.: Dār Iḥyā' al-Sunna al-Nabawiya, 1974).
[12] Richard Bulliet, *Islam: The View from the Edge* (New York: Columbia University Press, 1994), 21.

in medieval Islamic civilization.[13] A number of major Muslim philosophers and scientists lived and wrote during the Middle Period, among them Ibn Sina (d. 1037) and Ibn Rushd (d. 1198). The most current research has demonstrated how in certain fields, such as astronomy, Muslim scientists pursued creative lines of research through the end of the Middle Period and into the early modern.[14] There is nothing inherently anti-rational about Islam, and some important Islamic communities and traditions have continued to be nourished by a continuous and vigorous philosophical discourse down to the present day. On the other hand, many medieval ulama and their supporters harbored a suspicion of intellectual traditions whose roots lay in a pre-Islamic discourse independent of any base in revealed sources of knowledge (the Koran, *sunna*). The Ayyubid sultan al-Malik al-Kamil, for instance, in the early thirteenth century prohibited the ulama of Damascus from studying or teaching any but the religious sciences (hadith, jurisprudence, and Koranic exegesis), and expelled students of logic and the "sciences of the ancients" from the town. The relationship of the ongoing study and transmission of the "rational sciences" to that of religious *°ilm* in the Middle Period is still badly understood, but there is evidence that the two drifted apart over the Middle Period, as part of the process whereby the Sunni ulama, or at least some of them, sought to define the parameters of their religious authority in more exclusive terms.[15]

---

[13] Norman Daniel, *Islam and the West: The Making of an Image* (Edinburgh: Edinburgh University Press, 1960).

[14] See, for example, George Saliba, *A History of Arabic Astronomy: Planetary Theories During the Golden Age of Islam* (New York: New York University Press, 1994). Cf. Sonja Brentjes, *"Orthodoxy," Ancient Sciences, Power, and the Madrasa ("College") in Ayyubid and Early Mamluk Damascus* (Berlin: Max-Planck-Institut für Wissenschaftsgeschichte, Preprint 77, 1997).

[15] Ibn Kathīr, *al-Bidāya waʾl-nihāya* in 14 vols. (Cairo: Matbaʿat al-Saʿāda, 1932–9), 13:148. Chamberlain, *Knowledge and Social Practice*, 83–4, comes to a slightly different conclusion. The evidence he cites, however, can also be read as reflecting the tension between the rational and religious sciences, and the marginalization (as opposed to the eclipse) of the former.

CHAPTER 24

Sufism

Surveys of Islam frequently present the history of Sufism in the Middle Period as a process of reconciliation between the mystical and juristic sides of Islam, the one shedding the more extreme and outlandish forms in which its practitioners (such as al-Hallaj) had expressed their mystical insights, the other reconciling itself to the claims of the mystics to a special experience of the divine. The jurist and theologian Abu Hamid al-Ghazali – who famously renounced his position as teacher of jurisprudence in the Nizamiyya *madrasa*, wandered through the Near East for several years subjecting himself to Sufi discipline, and finally composed a book which aimed, as its title suggested, at "the revivification of the religious sciences" – al-Ghazali is generally named as the pivotal figure in this drama.[1] There is something to this argument, and in so far as it is true, the rapprochement of juristic and mystical Islam was characteristic of the Middle Period. But there is a countervailing side to this story. At best, this viewpoint constitutes an over-simplification, in part because it is in fact difficult to specify what precisely the term "Sufism" (most often a translation of the Arabic *tasawwuf*) indicates. Phenomena which are conventionally labeled "Sufi," either by medieval observers or contemporary historians, are extraordinarily diverse, and as a religious movement Sufism often pulled medieval Islam in opposite directions. In the Middle Period, however, we can at least begin to identify the parameters of the confusion: we can be more precise, that is, about the points of complexity and about the contradictory impulses and effects of the beliefs and actions of those who are known as Sufis.

In the first place, despite the enormous reputation and influence of al-Ghazali, juristic Islam did not abandon its objections to at least some principles and practices which lay at the center of medieval Sufism. Individuals with a deep personal commitment to the legal sciences and to the rigorous transmission of their text-based knowledge could still feel an instinctive aversion to mysticism, and a decision to embrace the mystical path continued to be described as a kind of

---

[1] For classic statements of this viewpoint, see Fazlur Rahman *Islam*, 2nd edition (Chicago: University of Chicago Press, 1979), 137–40, and W. Montgomery Watt, *The Faith and Practice of al-Ghazālī* (London: George Allen and Unwin, 1953), 11–15. For a critique of the traditional view, see George Makdisi, "Hanbalite Islam," in *Studies on Islam*, ed. Merlin Swartz (New York: Oxford University Press, 1981), 242–6.

conversion. The example of Ibn ᶜAta Allah al-Iskandari (d. 1309) is instructive in this regard. Ibn ᶜAta Allah eventually became one of the most prominent and popular mystics in medieval Cairo, a vigorous defender of Sufism, and a professor of both Shafiᶜi *fiqh* and *tasawwuf* at the mosque of al-Azhar; but coming as he did from a family of Alexandrian jurists, he absorbed from his pious father and grandfather a suspicion of the Sufi path which he jettisoned only after coming under the influence of the Andalusian mystic Abuᵓl-ᶜAbbas al-Mursi (d. 1287).[2]

On a doctrinal level, there remained plenty of fuel to stoke the fires of the ulama's suspicions. The great Andalusian mystic Ibn al-ᶜArabi is only the most obvious example of medieval Sufis whose ideas aroused considerable controversy. We cannot here resolve the controversy over Ibn al-ᶜArabi's extraordinarily complex mystical theology, and over the question of whether his metaphysical doctrines such as that of *wahdat al-wujud* (very inadequately translated as the "oneness of being") constituted a pantheism at odds with the basic Muslim understanding of the distinction between a creator God and his creation. It is enough to note that his ideas stirred up considerable opposition among the ulama, his critics having included jurists of widely different outlook and temperament, such as, most famously, the astringent Ibn Taymiyya, but also the well-known scholars Taqiᵓl-Din al-Subki (d. 1344), Badr al-Din ibn Jamaᶜa, Ibn Khaldun, and Shams al-Din al-Sakhawi (d. 1497). Ibn al-ᶜArabi himself did not deny the claims of the *shariᶜa* or the value of jurisprudence as a means to acquire legitimate religious knowledge, but he did understand the depth of the tension between his approach to God and the outlook of many of the *fuqahaᵓ*, at one point likening them to the "pharaoh" who, in the Koran, represents the archetypal enemy of God and of his prophets. And it is important to stress, too, that for all their complexity, his ideas were popular, that the very vocabulary in which he outlined his mystical approach to religious knowledge had an enormous impact on the medieval Sufi experience at all social and intellectual levels. One of his later defenders, the Egyptian mystic al-Shaᶜrani (d. 1565), wrote a treatise summarizing and simplifying Ibn al-ᶜArabi's most ambitious work, *al-Futuhat al-makkiyya* ("The Meccan Revelations"), and it was popularizations such as this which most worried the skeptical ulama.[3]

One of the things which disturbed the Sunni ulama, whose intellectual identity and social power was grounded in the particularity of the Islamic revelation and the traditions derived from it, was Sufism's tendency to blur the distinction

---

[2] Paul Nwyia, *Ibn ᶜAṭāᵓ Allāh (m. 709/1309) et la naissance de la confrérie šāḏilite* (Beirut, 1972).

[3] Georges C. Anawati, "Un aspect de la lutte contre l'hérésie au XVème siècle d'après un inédit attribué à Maqrīzī," *Colloque internationale sur l'histoire du caire* (Cairo, 1969), 23–36, and Michael Winter, *Society and Religion in Early Ottoman Egypt: Studies in the Writings of ᶜAbd al-Wahhāb al-Shaᶜrānī* (New Brunswick, NJ: Transaction Books, 1982), 165–7. For a full discussion of the controversy over Ibn al-ᶜArabi in the later Middle Period, see Eric Geoffroy, *Le soufisme en Égypte et en Syrie sous les derniers Mamelouks et les premiers Ottomanes: orientations spirituelles et enjeux culturelles* (Damascus: Institut Français, 1995), 451–76, and Alexander Knysh, *Ibn ᶜArabi in the Later Islamic Tradition: The Making of a Polemical Image in Medieval Islam* (Albany, NY: SUNY Press, 1999). The contemporary literature on Ibn al-ᶜArabi, much of it sympathetic in nature, is enormous. A good place to start is with Michel Chodkiewicz, *An Ocean Without Shore: Ibn ᶜArabī, The Book, and the Law*, trans. David Streight (Albany, NY: SUNY Press, 1993).

between Islam and other religious traditions. The famous couplet of Jalal al-Din Rumi (d. 1273), "What is to be done, O Muslims? for I do not recognize myself. / I am neither Christian, nor Jew, nor Gabr [i.e., Zoroastrian], nor Muslim" expresses a sentiment found frequently in mystical writing, as in the following verses by Ibn al-ᶜArabi: "My heart has become capable of every form: it is a pasture for gazelles and a convent for Christian monks, / And a temple for idols, and the pilgrim's Kaᶜba, and the tables of the Torah and the book of the Koran."[4] It may be that the universalism, or at least the indifference to sectarian labels implicit in those verses is characteristic of mystical strands in most religious traditions, and some have suggested that the flowering of Sufism in the Islamic Middle Period was part of a larger fluorescence of mysticism throughout the region stretching from western Europe to south and east Asia.[5] As we saw in the previous chapter, possible connections between Sufism and mystical developments in Christianity and other religions have constituted a persistent theme of much earlier research. Whatever the doctrinal connections and influences between the mystical traditions of Islam and other religions, it is clear from the historical evidence that Sufism in the Middle Period provided a meeting ground for mystically-inclined followers of different faiths, especially Christianity and Judaism. At the popular level, where Muslims and non-Muslims might inter-mingle relatively free from supervision by the ulama, this could be especially troubling, and formed the basis for strident criticism on the part of zealous defenders of Islamic law, as we shall see. But in fact it was common among Sufis at all social and cultural levels, from ᶜAbd al-Rahim al-Qushayri (d. 1120), a Shafiᶜi jurist and mystic from Nishapur, on down.[6] Anatolia, where Rumi lived and wrote in the city of Konya, boasted an ethnically and culturally mixed population and a dynamic religious scene for some time after the Turkish invasions beginning in the late eleventh century, and there, perhaps, Sufi ecumenism reached its high point. As with most hagiographies, it is difficult to be certain of the historicity of episodes in the accounts of Rumi's life written by his followers, but it is significant that his interaction with Christian priests, monks, and others constitutes an important trope of those stories. Indeed, according to an account of the Sufi's funeral, the Jews and Christians of Konya publicly displayed their grief alongside the town's Muslims, holding aloft their holy books, chanting their lamentations, and proclaiming that

---

[4] R. A. Nicholson, *Selected Poems from the Dīvāni Shamsi Tabrīz* (Cambridge: Cambridge University Press, 1898), 125; idem, *The Mystics of Islam* (London: Routledge & Kegan Paul, 1963), 105, 161.

[5] Marshall Hodgson, *The Venture of Islam: Conscience and History in a World Civilization*, in 3 vols. (Chicago: University of Chicago Press, 1974), vol. 2: *The Expansion of Islam in the Middle Periods*, 201–4.

[6] Tāj al-Dīn al-Subkī, *Ṭabaqāt al-shāfiᶜiyya al-kubrā*, 2nd edition, in 10 vols. (Cairo: Hajar, 1992), 7.161. See also S. D. Goitein, "A Jewish Addict to Sufism in the Time of the Nagid David II Maimonides," *Jewish Quarterly Review*, n.s. 44 (1953–4), 37–49, and idem, "Abraham Maimonides and his Pietist Circle," in *Jewish Medieval and Renaissance Studies*, ed. Alexander Altmann (Cambridge, Mass.: Harvard University Press, 1967), 145–64.

"in seeing him [Rumi], we have comprehended the true nature of Jesus, of Moses, and of all the prophets."[7]

Of equal concern to the ulama may have been the persistent and puzzling connections between Sufism and Shi°ism. This is a complex question, one to which very different answers have been given.[8] Certainly there are parallels of a doctrinal nature: the Sufi emphasis upon a special "knowledge" (*ma°rifa*) acquired through intuitive insight, which is distinct from the exoteric "knowledge" (*°ilm*) represented by the law, for example, recalls the Shi°i doctrine of the hidden meaning (*batin*) which lies behind, and is superior to, the external sense (*zahir*) of, say, a Koranic verse. The terminology in which Shi°is and Sufis express their ideals – the Shi°i doctrine of the "sovereignty" (*wilaya*) of the Imams, for example, and the Sufi notion that some are graced with a special "closeness" to or "friendship" with God (for which the same Arabic term served) – may also betray common origins, although the meanings of those terms in their fully-developed form were obviously quite different. It is striking, too, that the Sufi orders almost invariably trace their chains of authority (*silsila*) back to the Prophet through °Ali ibn Abi Talib. Whatever the answer to the question of their origins, however, in the Middle Period the connections between Sufism and Shi°ism constituted at most a latent problem which would only acquire significance under particular circumstances. Given the widespread veneration of the Prophet's family among Sunnis as well as Shi°is, the tracing of *silsilas* back through °Ali did not necessarily have any sectarian significance. One order of Sufis, for example, the Wafa°iyya, served in Egypt down into the modern period as the corporation of those claiming descent from the Prophet's cousin, but that dual function apparently implied no explicitly Shi°i identity.[9] But political circumstances could make an alleged connection between Sufism and Shi°ism much more incendiary, especially in the early Middle Period, when Isma°ilism still posed a threat in the form of the Fatimid caliphate or the Assassins of Iran and Syria, as can be seen from the case of the controversial theosophist Shihab al-Din Yahya al-Suhrawardi (executed 1191 at the orders of Saladin). Al-Suhrawardi is perhaps the critical figure of the Middle Period on the subject of links between Sufism and Shi°ism; his "philosophy of illumination," which drew heavily on neo-Platonic speculation and Zoroastrian imagery, had considerable influence on later Twelver Shi°ism. But the philosophical subtlety of al-Suhrawardi's epistemology was probably of less concern to Saladin than the political threat which he perceived in his teaching about authoritative instruction (what the Isma°ilis called *ta°lim*) and its potential to help some enlightened ruler (himself, or someone instructed by him) establish a more perfect state, all of which

---

[7] Speros Vryonis, Jr., *The Decline of Medieval Hellenism in Asia Minor and the Process of Islamization from the Eleventh through the Fifteenth Century* (Berkeley: University of California Press, 1971), 386–91.

[8] Compare J. S. Trimingham, *The Sufi Orders in Islam* (Oxford: Clarendon Press, 1971), 133–7, with Seyyed Hossein Nasr, "Le shi°isme et le soufisme: leurs relations principelles et historiques," in *Le Shi'isme Imamite: Colloque de Strasbourg (6–9 mai 1968)* (Paris: Presses Universitaires de France, 1970), 215–33.

[9] F. de Jong, *Turuq and Turuq-linked Institutions in Nineteenth-Century Egypt: A Historical Study in Organizational Dimensions of Islamic Mysticism* (Leiden: E. J. Brill, 1978), 76–7.

may well, under the circumstances, have sounded to Saladin and others very much like Isma^cilism.[10] One place where there certainly was an important connection between Sufism and Shi^cism, and one with major political ramifications, was in Anatolia and northwest Iran, where the confused political and cultural scene, and the destruction of the Isma^cili networks in the thirteenth century in the wake of the Mongol conquests, left room for considerable religious ferment – a point to which we will return shortly.

In general, however, Sufism, unlike Shi^cism, was never truly sectarian. From a relatively early period, Sufis referred to themselves as a *ta^ɔifa*, a "group" – that is, a group of believers distinguished by some particular trait or conviction – a term which appears frequently in the Koran and which was also used in a more general sense to denote some particular party or religious or political sect. For all of the tension over points of doctrine and practice between some jurists and some of the Sufis, whether early figures such as al-Hallaj or later ones such as Ibn al-^cArabi, Sufism did not constitute a form of Islam completely distinct from that which was grounded in the *shari^ca*. Nor was it persistently associated specifically with one *madhhab* or another. In places such as Nishapur and Baghdad, there is some indication of tension, in the early stages of Sufism's development, between the mystics and members of the Hanafi *madhhab*. Over time, however, any tension must have dissipated: by the early fourteenth century, institutions were being founded in Cairo specifically for Sufi scholars who were students of Hanafi law.[11] The connection between Sufism and Hanbalism is more complicated. The hostility to many Sufi ideals and practices of the Wahhabi sect, in which Hanbalism survives in the modern world, may have encouraged the view that Hanbali traditionalism and Sufism were intrinsically hostile. Some Hanbalis have at times come to that conclusion. The son of a Hanbali *faqih* in Baghdad in the twelfth century, having buried his deceased father in a cemetery attached to a Sufi *ribat*, was subject to the reproach of the dead man's colleagues, who asked, "What is a Hanbali doing among the Sufis?"[12] The fervent commitment to Hanbali traditionalism of a number of prominent medieval critics of particular practices associated with some levels of Sufi experience, such as Ibn al-Jawzi (d. 1200) and Ibn Taymiyya, has served to strengthen the perception. But in fact there has never been any widespread and categorical rupture between traditionalism and Sufi

---

[10] John Walbridge, *The Leaven of the Ancients: Suhrawardī and the Heritage of the Greeks* (Albany, NY: SUNY Press, 2000), 201–10. Cf. the case of the Sufi ^cAyn al-Qudat, also executed in circumstances which suggest a suspicion on the part of the political authorities that his mystical ideas constituted a expression of Isma^cilism and thus a political threat. Carl Ernst, *Words of Ecstasy in Sufism* (Albany, NY: SUNY Press, 1985), 110–15.

[11] Richard Bulliet, *The Patricians of Nishapur: A Study in Medieval Islamic Social History* (Cambridge, Massachusetts: Harvard University Press, 1972), 41–3; Daphna Ephrat, *A Learned Society in Transition: The Sunni ^cUlamā^ɔ of Eleventh-Century Baghdad* (Albany, NY: SUNY Press, 2000), 48–9; Jonathan Berkey, *The Transmission of Knowledge in Medieval Cairo: A Social History of Islamic Education* (Princeton: Princeton University Press, 1992), 57.

[12] ^cAbd al-Raḥmān ibn Rajab, *al-Dhayl ^calā ṭabaqāt al-ḥanābila*, 2 vols. (Cairo: Maṭba^cat al-Sunna al-Muḥammadiyya, 1952-3), 1.303–5; Jacqueline Chabbi, "La fonction du ribat à Bagdad du ve siècle au début du viie siècle," *Revue des études islamiques*, 42 (1974), 113.

mysticism, and by the Middle Period many prominent Hanbalis were themselves initiated into Sufi chains of authority – most notably, perhaps, Ibn al-Jawzi and Ibn Taymiyya themselves.[13] Over the course of the Middle Period, Sufi affiliations became *de rigeur* among the ulama, so much so that, as we have seen, it became increasingly difficult to distinguish the institutions which supported the activities of the jurists and mystics.

Two developments in the Middle Period gave more structure to the Sufi experience. In the first place, the *ta²ifa* of those pursuing a mystical path to God took a more precise shape as particular "groups" of Sufis began to identify themselves by the "way" or "path" (*tariqa*) which they followed in their journey. The process was not uniform, but we can identify certain common patterns among the *turuq* (the plural of *tariqa*). Typically, a *tariqa* took the form of an order of mystics linked via a spiritual genealogy to some revered *shaykh*, and through him and his own masters back, in theory, to the Prophet himself – the Qadiriyya of ᶜAbd al-Qadir al-Jilani (d. 1166), for example, or the Shadhiliyya of Abu²l-Hasan al-Shadhili (d. 1258), to name two of the most important medieval orders. As with the *madhahib*, it was usually his disciples and followers, rather than the eponym himself, who were responsible for the crystallization of a *tariqa*'s identity. The eponym's role was a retrospective one, that of model and patron saint, as expressed in the hagiographical accounts which constituted a distinctive genre of medieval Sufi literature. As with the transmission of juristic knowledge, it was the personal connection which was critical, a connection realized through some initiatory experience, and formalized in the bestowal of a *khirqa*, a "cloak" whose rough and tattered character symbolized the adept's embrace of material poverty in favor of spiritual riches. Admission to a *tariqa* was tantamount to admission into a chain of spiritual authority (*silsila*) stretching back to the order's putative founder. Here we encounter again the "genealogical style" which was characteristic of much medieval Islamic religious culture, the *silsila* functioning in a similar fashion to the *isnads* through which hadith and other religious texts were transmitted. And that genealogical mode of reproduction was intrinsically hierarchical, binding disciple to master in a vertical chain of dependence – a point which the common translation of *tariqa* as "fraternity" or "brotherhood" misses.[14]

In this respect, the growth of the *turuq* contributed to clarifying the forms and loci of religious authority, a process which included the "inscription" of the ulama's authority described above. Submission to the authority of a *shaykh* and of that *shaykh*'s "spiritual genealogy," and thus pursuing the "way" represented by the *tariqa*, might involve not only entering into a personal chain of authority and

---

[13] George Makdisi, "Hanbalite Islam," in *Studies on Islam*, ed. Merlin Swartz (New York: Oxford University Press, 1981), 246–51; idem, "Ibn Taimīya: A Ṣūfī of the Qādirīya Order," *American Journal of Arabic Studies* 1 (1974), 118–29. On the more complex question of relations between Hanbalis and the very early mystics, see Christopher Melchert, "The Ḥanābila and the Early Sufis," *Arabica* 48 (2001), 352–67.

[14] The forms and styles of the *turuq* are described in Trimingham, *The Sufi Orders in Islam*, 1–66, and especially now *EI²*, art. "Tarīka" and "Tā'ifa" (both by E. Geoffroy).

acknowledging the spiritual supervision of a *shaykh*, but also the adoption of various practices and rituals which together constituted a sort of spiritual method. Chief among these practices was the *dhikr*, the "recollection" of God's presence. *Dhikr* as a spiritual exercise could take different forms, but typically consisted of the repetition, either individually or in a group, of God's name, a portion of the Koran, or some other litany. Sufis understood the *dhikr* to be their response to the Koranic command to "remember God with much remembrance" (33.41), and Abu Hamid al-Ghazali characteristically saw it as a means of inscribing on the heart of the believer a constant reminder of God's presence. Sufi manuals elaborated the prescribed methods and procedures of the *dhikr* in some detail, and stressed the importance of undertaking this spiritual discipline under the direction of a *shaykh*.[15]

But here the process of the "inscription" of authority bumped up against the intrinsic anarchism of the mystical life. *Dhikr*, for example, could become a means to a wild and ecstatic religious experience, such as that suggested by the "howling" of the dervishes of the Rifaᶜiyya order, which became especially popular over the course of the Middle Period, in Egypt, Syria, and Iraq. Other Sufi practices complicated further the matter of religious authority, and so aroused more controversy, especially the *samaᶜ*, the spiritual "hearing" or "concert" (itself closely related to *dhikr*) in which adepts listened to music or the singing of various poems, and often supplemented the auditory experience with dances designed to invoke an experience of spiritual ecstasy. Ritualized music and dance were a part of the Sufi experience from a very early point, but became especially popular in the Middle Period with Sufis in Iran, India, and Anatolia, where they reached their highest expression among the dervishes of the Mevlevi *tariqa* who followed their shaykh, the poet Jalal al-Din Rumi (d. 1273). Nonetheless, criticism of the practice was extensive. It came from both juristic (especially Hanbali) and "sober" mystic circles. Behind the dispute lay basic theological questions about the nature of the human soul and its relationship to the divine: whether, for example, the soul itself had a divine character, and whether listening to music could induce an erotic longing for and remembrance of God. But there was a social and ethical dimension to the debate that was at least as important. The danger was that practitioners of the *samaᶜ* in their ecstatic state might transgress the authority of the law and of their masters. Much of the critics' concern focused on the sexual licentiousness that the activity was alleged to induce. Ibn Taymiyya, for example, likened the effects of the *samaᶜ* to those of wine, and worried about the moral dangers of listening to musical instruments such as the flute, which a hadith identified as "the muezzin of Satan."[16] Critics believed that the music, let alone the rhythmical swaying of the dance, would excite the passions of the participants, and scathingly condemned the

---

[15] There are good general discussions of the development of *dhikr* practices in Annemarie Schimmel, *Mystical Dimensions of Islam* (Chapel Hill: University of North Carolina Press, 1975), 167–78; L. Gardet, "La mention du nom divin dans la mystique musulmane," *Revue thomiste* 52 (1952), 641–79 and 53 (1953), 197–216; and *EI*², art. "Dhikr" (by L. Gardet).

[16] Jean Michot, *Musiqe et danse selon Ibn Taymiyya: Le Livre du Samāᶜ et de la Danse (Kitāb al-Samāᶜ waʾl-Raqṣ)* (Paris: J. Vrin, 1991), 82–3, 126.

practice as a screen for illicit, sometimes homoerotic behavior. So, for example, Ibn al-Jawzi condemned the "singing of a handsome beardless boy [accompanied] by delightful instruments, and a craft which excites the appetite and erotic odes which mention the gazelle, male and female, the beauty mark, the cheek, the body, and the well-proportioned form."[17] Even al-Ghazali, while generally approving of the *sama*, would restrict it to individuals who had learned to control their youthful lusts.[18] At the very least, the controversy over the *sama* demonstrates how the *turuq*, while on the one hand serving to inscribe religious authority in the person of the *shaykh*, at the same moment contributed to the diversification of the Muslim religious experience through the methods they embraced for the Sufis' expression of their devotion.

The *turuq* were themselves diverse in character and in style, and reflected again the contradictory religious pressures at work: on the one hand, serving to concentrate authority in particular persons and institutions, on the other working to diffuse that authority more broadly among the population. One of the most popular *tariqas*, the Shadhiliyya, was also one of the most moderate in tone. This *tariqa* traced its spiritual lineage back to Abu'l-Hasan al-Shadhili, one of many Maghribi mystics who, over the course of the Middle Period and for various reasons, migrated to the eastern Mediterranean and profoundly influenced the course of Sufism there. Its lasting place in the spiritual life of medieval Egypt and Syria, however, was due to the efforts of al-Shadhili's successors, Abu'l-ʿAbbas al-Mursi and above all his own pupil, the great Egyptian mystical preacher and writer Ibn ʿAta Allah. The *tariqa*'s popularity stemmed in part from its aversion to the antinomian behavior and doctrinal irregularities which characterized some mystics. The Shadhiliyya eschewed mendicancy, for example, insisting that its members lead socially normal and economically productive lives. More importantly, they embraced and affirmed the exoteric traditions of juristic Islam, including the *shariʿa* and the usual forms of public Muslim worship, thereby attracting to their ranks a number of *fuqahaʾ*, while many of the Shadhiliyya themselves developed a reputation for public preaching and pious exhortation. But other orders were equally popular, such as the Rifaʿiyya, whose bizarre and extravagant practices (including fire-walking and fire-swallowing, as well as their trademark "howling" during the *dhikr*) scandalized more sober Muslims. The Malamatiyya, while skeptical of mendicancy like the Shadhiliyya, adopted a very different public posture, avoiding any open demonstration of piety, including prayer and *dhikr*, out of fear of hypocrisy and spiritual ostentation. The Malamatiyya, who were especially strong in Khurasan, were perhaps not strictly

[17] Ibn al-Jawzī, *Talbīs iblīs* (Beirut: Dār al-Rāʾid al-ʿArabī, n.d.), 238.
[18] Abū Ḥāmid al-Ghazālī, *Iḥyāʾ ʿulūm al-dīn*, 5 vols. (Cairo: al-Ḥalabī, 1967), 2.385, 390. On the *samāʿ* and criticism of it, see: Michot, *Musique et danse*; Louis Pouzet, "Prises de position autour du *samāʿ* en Orient musulman au VIIᵉ/XIIIᵉ siècle," *Studia Islamica* 57 (1983), 119–34; Arthur Gribetz, "The *Samāʿ* Controversy: Sufi vs. Legalist," *Studia Islamica* 74 (1991), 43–62; Jean During, *Musique et extase: L'audition spirituelle dans la tradition soufie* (Paris: Albin Michel, 1988); *EI²*, art. "Samāʿ" (by J. During); Geoffroy, *Le soufisme en Égypte et en Syrie*, 411–22.

speaking a Sufi *tariqa*, but they did earn the admiration of a number of important medieval Sufis, including Ibn al-ᶜArabi and the Egyptian *shaykh* al-Shaᶜrani. Moreover, their example inspired several Sufi orders, including the Naqshbandiyya who played an important role in the Ottoman Empire from the fifteenth century right down to the twentieth, and the Qalandariyya, the antinomian dervishes who lent such religious color to the medieval urban scene, who shared the Malamatis' fear of hypocrisy in open demonstrations of piety but who responded to those concerns by ostentatiously flouting the religious law. What this range of attitude and behavior demonstrates is the diversity of Sufism in its *tariqa* form. And individuals could capitalize on that diversity to enrich their religious lives. The crystallization of the spiritual genealogies of the *silsilas* did not imply the isolation of those in one chain from those in another, or from other forms and expressions of Islam: if all Sufis sought the same goal (God), they could pursue that goal along several different paths. Just as students might seek *ijazas* from multiple teachers for the same text, mystics might secure initiation into several different *turuq*. Al-Shaᶜrani was a member of the Shadhili *tariqa*, but he also formally belonged to twenty-five others.[19]

The competing pressures of the centralization and diffusion of authority can also be seen at work in the service the *turuq* provided for the popularization and geographical spread of Sufi affiliation. The Sufi *turuq* became a link binding the religious experience of rural areas to that more common in the cities. The Shadhiliyya, for example, although principally an urban phenomenon, established a strong presence in Upper Egypt through *shaykhs* who had been initiated into the Shadhili *silsila*. Even more important in the countryside was the order associated with Ahmad al-Badawi (d. 1276), already as popular among Egyptians in the Middle Period as it is today, which reached deeply into the rural scene, the annual birthday celebration held at the saint's shrine in Tanta drawing visitors not only from Cairo but from all over the Nile Delta.[20] But the growing popularity of the *turuq* also brought under the penumbra of Sufism many who were only tangentially tied to a course of mystic discipline. The routinization the *turuq* represented invested Sufism with a more catholic appeal, and helped to make Sufism a form of "institutionalized mass religion" in the medieval Islamic world.[21] Many Muslims who had not undergone a full initiatory experience might nonetheless feel themselves attached to a Sufi order, or more frequently perhaps to a particular *shaykh*. Lavish public festivals, such as the *mawlids* (birthday celebrations) held to honor either the Prophet or some revered *shaykh*, became popular especially from the

---

[19] Michael Winter, *Society and Religion in Early Ottoman Egypt: Studies in the Writings of ᶜAbd al-Wahhāb al-Shaᶜrānī* (New Brunswick, NJ: Transaction Books, 1982), 90.

[20] Jean-Claude Garcin, *Un Centre Musulman de la Haute-Égypte Médiévale: Qūṣ* (Cairo: Institut Français d'Archéologie Orientale, 1976), 213–21; idem, "Histoire et hagiographie de l'Égypte musulmane à la fin de l'époque mamelouke et au début de l'époque ottomane," in *Hommages à la mémoire de Serge Sauneron*, vol. 2: *Égypte post-pharaonique* (Cairo: IFAO, 1979), 287–316; Catherine Mayeur-Jaouen, *al-Sayyid Aḥmad al-Badawī: un grand saint de l'islam égyptien* (Cairo: Institut Français d'Archéologie Orientale, 1994).

[21] Hodgson, *The Venture of Islam*, 2.210–22.

thirteenth century, often in association with one *tariqa* or another; they became, in fact, a central manifestation of a more popular side of Islam, and so we will return to them in the following section. But their very public character appealed to and invited the participation – limited and peripheral, perhaps, from the standpoint of a Sufi order, but nonetheless potentially meaningful from the standpoint of the individual concerned – of large numbers of people who in other respects lived their lives with little attention to Sufi discipline. An emphasis on experience, such as *dhikr* and *sama*[^c], provided an opportunity for a wide variety of people to participate in Sufi rites, even if they did not systematically subject themselves to a more rigorous spiritual curriculum. As early a Sufi as al-Hujwiri (d. 1072 or 1077) had recognized the seductive appeal of the *sama*[^c] and its accompanying dance, and their tendency to draw into Sufi ranks hangers-on who were less than fully committed to the path. "I have met with a number of common people who adopted Sufism in the belief that it is this (dancing) and nothing more," he wrote.[22] In Egypt in the early fourteenth century, the jurist and acerbic social critic Ibn al-Hajj, in his long treatise describing religious behavior of which he did not approve, claimed that most of those who identified themselves as Sufis did so simply in order to participate in the *sama'* and its titillating dance.[23]

A second medieval development shaping the Sufi experience was the spread of institutions designed to support the mystics and their rituals. As we have seen, these institutions had their origins in an earlier period, and probably first arose in the stimulating and diverse religious milieu of eastern Iran. But in the Middle Period they became a characteristic feature of the Near Eastern urban scene. The nomenclature by which these institutions were known was varied and imprecise. The use of the term *ribat*, especially in Iraq, is suggestive, since in other contexts a *ribat* was a fortified station for holy warriors on the frontier. Some, including the Sufi ally of the caliph al-Nasir, Abu Hafs ᶜUmar al-Suhrawardi (d. 1234), in his treatise on the mystic life, *ᶜAwarif al-maᶜarif*, suggested that the connection reflected the *jihad* which Sufis waged against base instincts and temptation, and in this respect it is tempting to recall the commitment of early "Sufis" such as Ibrahim ibn Adham to *jihad* as "holy war." But this is pure speculation, and any *historical* connections between the *ribats* of the frontier and medieval urban institutions housing Sufis is obscure.[24] Other terms predominated elsewhere, especially the Persian word *khanqah*, which the twelfth-century traveler Ibn Jubayr famously remarked was used in Syria to describe institutions known elsewhere as *ribats*, and also *zawiya*, which could have a number of different meanings but which frequently was used for smaller convents, very often established specifically by or for the benefit of some particular *shaykh*. Like *madrasas*, these Sufi convents were typically founded as the result of an act of private charity,

[^c]:

---

[22] Al-Hujwīrī, *Kashf al-Maḥjūb*, trans. R. A. Nicholson (London: Luzac & Co., 1936) (E. J. W. Gibb Memorial Series, 17), 416.

[23] Ibn al-Ḥājj, *Madkhal al-sharᶜ al-sharīf*, 4 vols. (Cairo: al-Maṭbaᶜa al-Miṣriyya, 1929), 3.93.

[24] Abū Ḥafṣ ᶜUmar al-Suhrawardī, *Kitāb ᶜawārif al-maᶜārif* (Cairo: al-Ḥalabī, 1968), 5.115–17; Chabbi, "La fonction du ribat," 102.

by a sultan, amir, or other wealthy individual, sometimes also by prominent Sufi *shaykhs* themselves, and as such were supported by endowments (*awqaf*) which the founders set aside for their maintenance and upkeep.[25]

Over the course of the Middle Period, these institutions proliferated throughout the Islamic Near East. On one level, their popularity constitutes a marker of the assimilation of mystical to juristic Islam. Increasingly, *madrasas* and Sufi convents, by whatever name they were called, came to resemble each other in terms of the activities which took place in them and which their endowments supported. This was already true in Baghdad in the twelfth and thirteenth centuries, where *ribats* housed lessons in jurisprudence and were frequently headed by jurists.[26] But the process of assimilation reached its peak in the cities of the Mamluk empire. There, institutions known as *madrasas* frequently housed Sufis and their rituals, while the endowments of *khanqahs* made provisions for the support of lessons in jurisprudence according to one or more of the *madhahib*. It was not simply a question of close spatial proximity, but rather of the fusion of function and outlook. At an institution established on Cairo's main thoroughfare by sultan al-Ashraf Barsbay (d. 1437), for example, whose endowment provided for both Sufi rituals and lessons in jurisprudence, the *dhikr* and other mystical devotions were actually to be led by the resident instructor in Hanafi law. The process was so complete that, by the end of the fifteenth century, the terms *madrasa, khanqah*, and "mosque" were often used interchangeably.[27] Here we encounter the institutional consequence of the full integration of Sufism into Muslim religious life, a process which, even if we discard the melodrama of accounts which focus on the famous conversion of al-Ghazali and accept that opposition to particular Sufi ideas and practices continued, was nonetheless central to the religious history of the Middle Period.

Given the growing prominence of Sufis and of Sufi modes of piety, it is not surprising that Islamic mysticism began to have an impact on political life. The most striking manifestation of this development came in the late twelfth and early thirteenth centuries, with the political and religious reforms led by the caliph al-Nasir and his ally, the Sufi Abu Hafs al-Suhrawardi. As a part of his program to (re-)unite the Islamic world under his authority, al-Nasir relied upon organized brotherhoods known as *futuwwa*. The *futuwwa*, which were common in Baghdad and the other towns of Iraq, originated as urban fraternities of mostly young men which sometimes functioned as quasi-militias, with apparently little or no religious significance; but from the eleventh century they began to acquire a Sufi cast. Al-Nasir had himself initiated into a branch of the *futuwwa*, and then began a systematic reformation of the different orders which sought to locate the caliph as their head and the font of authority over them. As articulated by al-Suhrawardi, the caliph's authority as leader of the *umma* and as mediator between it and God was conceived in terms parallel to that of the Sufi *shaykh* over his disciples – and

---

[25] Leonor Fernandes, *The Evolution of a Sufi Institution in Egypt: The Khanqah* (Berlin: Klaus Schwarz Verlag, 1988).
[26] Chabbi, "La fonction du ribat," esp. 111–12, 114–20.
[27] Berkey, *The Transmission of Knowledge*, 47–50 and 56–60.

indeed, at this time, the term *khalifa*, "caliph," came also to be used to described the leaders of the Sufi *turuq*.[28] Since Sufism played a critical role in al-Nasir's program, the caliph devoted considerable resources to the establishment and control of those Sufi institutions which, like the *turuq* themselves, were becoming more common. He himself founded at least six *ribats* in Baghdad at the end of the twelfth century; in addition, he named al-Suhrawardi director of several spiritual hospices founded by others, and in general sought to control the appointment of the spiritual directors of the city's Sufi institutions.[29]

Al-Nasir's program of reform eventually came to nought. But Sufism having moved to center stage, later Muslim rulers had to grapple with the movement's political force as well, and the proliferation of Sufi institutions served in part to further the centralization of religious authority and the subordination of that authority to the political. In general, as with the growth of other religious institutions, the foundation of *khanqahs* and their endowment, especially by individuals from the military elites, served to strengthen the ties between the religious and the ruling classes, and to bind the authority wielded by Sufis and their institutions to the political power. At certain points, that relationship took on a more formal guise. For example, the *shaykh* of the *khanqah* known as Saʿid al-Suʿadaʾ, founded by Saladin in Cairo in 1173–4, came to be known by the title *shaykh al-shuyukh*, "master of the masters," and the holder of that office had some sort of supervisory authority over the Sufis of Egypt and Syria under the Mamluk sultans, until sultan al-Nasir Muhammad (d. 1340) transferred the title and office to the *shaykh* of a new *khanqah* he established at Siryaqus outside the city. The *shaykh al-shuyukh* became in effect an officer of the Mamluk state, and it may be possible to see in his office the roots of the official heads of the Sufi orders which, in the Ottoman period, served to bind the mystics' syndicates to the state.[30]

But the relation of mystical to political authority was a complex *pas de deux*, and Sufi *shaykhs* possessed, and sometimes wielded, a reservoir of political power of their own. That power could derive from their status as leaders of well-established and well-respected orders such as the Shadhiliyya, but it could also emerge from their very rejection of wealth and worldly status, from their express contempt for those who wielded political power, or even from the reputation of some who operated at the boundaries of Islamic propriety. The Mamluks, for example, developed a well-deserved reputation for honoring and respecting Sufi *shaykhs*, despite (or perhaps because of) the fact that these *shaykhs* were willing to confront them with reminders of the ephemeral character of their status and authority. Zakariyya al-Ansari (d. 1520), an influential *shaykh* and preacher, developed a reputation for delivering stern sermons to those in power. Some

---

[28] On the *futuwwa* and al-Nasir's reform of them and their subsequent role in his political program, see Claude Cahen, "Mouvements populaires et autonomisme urbain dans l'Asie musulmane de Moyen ge," *Arabica* 5 (1958), 225–50 and 6 (1959), 25–56, 233–65; *EI²*, art. "Futuwwa" (by Claude Cahen and Fr. Taeschner) and "al-Nāṣir li-Dīn Allāh" (by Angelika Hartmann).

[29] Chabbi, "La fonction du ribat," 116f.

[30] For a cursory study of this office, see Fernandes, *The Evolution of a Sufi Institution*, 51–4.

envious officials sought to persuade the sultan Qaytbay to reprimand the *shaykh* for his temerity, but he refused: "What [would you have me] say," he asked, "to someone who has opened my eyes to my own faults and has given me good advice?"[31] The rulers were not necessarily discriminating in their respect for the mystics. It was not at all unusual for members of the ruling military elites, sultans included, to come under the influence of some Rasputin-like *shaykh* less reputable than Zakariyya al-Ansari. The Mamluk sultan al-Zahir Baybars for years lived under the tutelage of a *shaykh* named Khadir al-Mihrani. It appears that the sultan stood in awe of the *shaykh* less for his spiritual discipline or piety – the *shaykh* had, in fact, originally fled his home in Upper Mesopotamia out of fear of being castrated for sleeping with the daughter of a local amir, and accusations of sexual impropriety continued to dog him – than for the mysterious powers of prognostication with which he was credited. In any event, Baybars was impressed, and, until the *shaykh*'s reputation was undone by a cabal of his enemies, regularly met with him, performed with him the Sufi *dhikr*, and constructed for him a number of *zawiyas* in Cairo and elsewhere.[32] Later Mamluk sultans and amirs had similar relationships with Sufis of varying reputations. Qansuh al-Ghuri (d. 1516) the last effective Mamluk sultan, had a fairly low opinion of the ulama, at one point offering a prize for every drunken *faqih* his police could find, but a great respect for Sufi *shaykhs*, and took the *khalifa* of the Badawi order along with him to Syria on his last, ill-fated campaign against the Ottomans. According to the chronicler Ibn Iyas, when that campaign resulted in al-Ghuri's death, it was another popular *shaykh* who was instrumental in the naming of his successor, in the process extracting from the leading Mamluks a promise to do justice to the population and, in particular, to revoke certain oppressive taxes which the dead sultan had imposed.[33]

The complex nexus of political power in which Sufi *shaykhs* operated is demonstrated clearly in a controversy which erupted in Cairo in 1469–70 over the verse of the Sufi poet Ibn al-Farid (d. 1235). The controversy had at its root certain doctrinal issues which paralleled those raised by the teaching of Ibn al-ʿArabi, but it also involved the legitimacy of the popular cult of visitation which had grown up around Ibn al-Farid's tomb in the enormous cemetery outside the city. In the first place, the parameters of this controversy demonstrate how thoroughly Sufism had penetrated Egyptian society, and so how the controversies which it continued to stir up can hardly be analyzed in terms of a simple dichotomy between juristic and mystical Islam. Ibn al-Farid's detractors included a number of jurists, but also some very popular mystics, including an illiterate chickpea seller named Ibrahim

---

[31] ʿAbd al-Wahhāb al-Shaʿrānī, *al-Ṭabaqāt al-ṣughrā* (Cairo: Maktabat al-Qāhira, 1970), 42.

[32] Louis Pouzet, "Ḥadir ibn Abī Bakr al-Mihrānī (m. 7 muḥ. 676/11 juin 1277), ṣayḥ du sultan mamelouk Al-Malik az-Ẓāhir Baïbars," *Bulletin d'études orientales* 30 (1978), 173–83.

[33] Ibn Iyās, *Badāʾiʿ al-zuhūr fi waqāʾiʿ al-duhūr*, 3rd edition (Cairo: al-Hayʾa al-Miṣriyya al-ʿĀmma liʾl-Kitāb, 1984), 5.85–6; Jean-Claude Garcin, "Deux saints populaires du Caire au début du xviᵉ siècle," *Bulletin d'études orientales* 29 (1977), 131–43; Winter, *Society and Religion in Early Ottoman Egypt*, 19, 100. On Sufi *shaykhs* and the ruling elites more generally, see Geoffroy, *Le soufisme en Égypte et en Syrie*, 120–8.

al-Matbuli. By the same token, the poet's defenders (who ultimately prevailed) included not only those swayed by the mystical force of his verse, but also some very sober-minded members of the ulama. But the dispute also had a clearly political dimension, first, because the poetry of Ibn al-Farid had grown so enormously popular among the population of the city, and second because several leading Mamluks had invested their own reputations in that of the poet by very publicly establishing endowments to support his tomb shrine and the cult of visitation to it. In the end, with Zakariyya al-Ansari issuing a *fatwa* defending Ibn al-Farid, the reigning sultan Qaytbay seized the opportunity to reshuffle the judiciary and replace Ibn al-Farid's opponents with a younger generation of scholars more sympathetic both to him and to the mystical ideas of Ibn al-Farid.[34]

The Ibn al-Farid controversy also recalls the point from which this discussion of Sufism started – namely, that it is difficult to define precisely what it meant to be "Sufi" in the Islamic Middle Period, or more precisely, how wide was the range of attitudes and behavior to which the term could reasonably be attached. On the one hand, Sufism certainly did grow ever closer to juristic Islam, a development which can be measured in any number of ways – in the convergence of curriculum and purpose in the different institutions, and in the increasingly common *tariqa* affiliations of Muslim scholars, including strident opponents of some Sufi practices. But other manifestations of Sufism served to resist the "Sunni recentering" which in other respects characterized the period, and contributed to the diversity, rather than the homogenization, of the Muslim experience.[35] One Sufi figure who clearly complicated the religious experience of medieval Islam and the authority of jurists and the more learned Sufi masters was the *shaykh ummi*, the "unlettered [Sufi] master." Ibn al-Farid's defender Ibrahim al-Matbuli fell into this category, but he was not alone. Typically, the *shaykh ummi* came from a humble social background, and so had not had access to much in the way of education. The attitude of such figures toward books and the "inscripted" culture of the ulama was, at least on the surface, dismissive: the Sufi master prevailing upon a learned disciple to dispose of all his books was a trope of Sufi literature. The *shaykh ummi* might or might not be *literally* illiterate, but he claimed a kind of "knowledge" that he had acquired, not from books, but from dreams, or visions of the Prophet, or more vaguely from his "heart." The *shaykh ummi* might seek to transmit that knowledge to his pupils, but in a language or style which itself was alien to the discourse of the jurists and more learned Sufis. So, for example, Muhammad Wafa, founder of a branch of the Shadhiliyya in Egypt in the fourteenth century, composed a number of works in verse and prose; according to his Sufi biographer, however, his was a "strange tongue" (*lisan gharib*) and his literary works remained "cryptically sealed" (*multasama*).[36]

---

[34] Geoffroy, *Le soufisme en Égypte et en Syrie*, 439–43; Th. Emil Homerin, *From Arab Poet to Muslim Saint: Ibn al-Fārid, His Verse, and His Shrine* (Columbia, South Carolina: University of South Carolina Press, 1994), 55–75.

[35] Cf. the cogent comments in Bulliet, *Islam*, 173–4.

[36] ʿAbd al-Wahhāb al-Shaʿrānī, *al-Ṭabaqāt al-kubrā*, 2 vols. (Cairo: Muhammad ʿAlī Ṣubayḥ, 1965), 2.19. On the *shaykh ummi*, see Geoffroy, *Le soufisme en Égypte et en Syrie*, 299–307, and Winter, *Society and Religion*, 192–5.

Nowhere was the multifaceted character and disruptive potential of Sufism clearer than with various *turuq* which flouted social and legal conventions and which flourished in the Near East from the thirteenth century, chief among them the Qalandariyya. The movement may have had its origins (as did so much else in Islamic history) in eastern Iran, in Khurasan, among unorganized ascetics of the Malamati type, but it blossomed as a *tariqa* in Egypt and especially Syria over the later Middle Period, where a number of *zawiyas* were established for them. In Damascus and elsewhere, radical dervishes ostentatiously flouted social and religious norms: dressing in rags or (in some cases) not at all; shaving off hair, beard, moustache, and eyebrows, in violation of conventions rooted in the *sunna*; deliberately disregarding cultic practices such as prayer; publically indulging in the use of hashish and other intoxicants; and, according to numerous reports, piercing various bodily parts, including their genitals. Inevitably their flamboyance attracted hostile attention: Ibn Taymiyya, of course, disapproved of them, while in 1360 the Mamluk sultan Hasan forbade them to shave their beards.[37] But these flamboyant ascetics and mendicants also attracted the patronage of the powerful, including several Mamluk sultans, among them al-Zahir Baybars. Religious movements such as that represented by the Qalandariyya are susceptible to various explanations, but for all their extravagance, their basic impulses and motivations are not altogether inconsistent with basic Sufi themes – asceticism, and the individual's utter devotion to God – while many of their practices, such as dressing in ragged garments and their enthusiastic embrace of music and dance, mark them as operating within the broader penumbra of Sufism. Abu Hafs al-Suhrawardi sought to distinguish the Qaladariyya from "real" Sufis, but he described the Qalandariyya as those who "refuse to be bound by social conventions," and who "are not attached to anything but the contentment of [their] hearts" – words which could well describe many mystics.[38]

The example of the Qalandariyya suggests that Islam was capable in the Middle Period of manifesting itself in a brilliant complexity of forms, even at the center – even, that is, in major centers of juristic culture such as Cairo and Damascus – and that Sufism, broadly conceived, constituted one of the principal sources of that complexity. On the frontier, Sufism was, if anything, even more fertile. In Anatolia over the course of the later Middle Period, a heady mix of Sufism and Shiᶜism contributed both to the Islamization of the region and to the articulation of religious and political movements which would have a tremendous impact on the form in which Islam would encounter the modern world. In the wake of the influx of Turkmen nomads into Anatolia from the eleventh and twelfth centuries,

---

[37] Taqī ᵓl-Dīn Aḥmad al-Maqrīzī, *al-Mawāᶜiẓ waᵓl-iᶜtibār bi-dhikr al-khiṭaṭ waᵓl-athār*, 2 vols. (Bulaq, A.H. 1270), 2.432–3.

[38] al-Suhrawardī, *ᶜAwārif al-maᶜārif*, 100, 101. The most comprehensive study of the Qalandariyya and similar movements is that of Ahmet Karamustafa, *God's Unruly Friends: Dervish Groups in the Later Islamic Middle Period*, 1200–1500 (Salt Lake City: University of Utah Press, 1994). Karamustafa argues vigorously for seeing these phenomena as perfectly continuous with basic Islamic and Sufi principles. He discusses the passage from Suhrawardi on pp. 34–6.

Sufism proved a dominant mode of Islamic piety. It took quite a range of forms. In cities such as Konya, Sufism was closely interwoven with juristic Islam – Rumi himself lived and taught in a *madrasa* in that town – and was supported by the ruling elites, in *khanqahs* and other institutions established and endowed by rulers and ruling elites. In rural and nomadic settings, however, Sufi *turuq* provided cover for an astonishing range of religious beliefs and practices. Among the Turkmen, comparatively recent immigrants from Central Asia and converts to Islam, a variety of shamanistic elements survived and flourished in Sufi guise: belief in the transmigration of souls, for example, or the possibility of ecstatic contact with the divine (induced by the dance associated with the *sama'*, which mirrored the dances which played an important role in Turco-Mongol shamanism). The dervishes known among the Turkmen as *babas* were essentially the Islamized successors of the Central Asian shamans.[39]

Even more importantly, this popular Sufism was colored by a pronounced Shi^{c}i tint. Shi^{c}i leanings among the Turkmen and their Sufi orders did not usually take a regular sectarian form – they were not, for example, explicitly Twelver in orientation, centered on expectations of the imminent return of the Hidden Twelfth Imam. Rather, they took the form of a less disciplined attachment to the figure and family of ^{c}Ali ibn Abi Talib, and so proved influential even on *turuq* which were, at least formally, "Sunni." As such, they represented what has been called "une sorte de shi^{c}itisation intérieure du sunnisme" – a perhaps vague formulation which nonetheless captures well the heterogeneity of these religious movements. Some of these orders, such as the Kubrawiyya, gradually embraced a more explicitly Shi^{c}i identity. The persistent heterogeneity of religious belief and practice among them, however, could take surprising forms. Among the Turkmen, for example, they were sometimes expressed in ways that Twelver Shi^{c}is would reject – for example, a belief in the divinity of ^{c}Ali. These vaguely Shi^{c}i movements could also serve as the religio-political expression of the social tensions between the Turkmen nomads and the more centralized governments which operated from Anatolian towns, such as the Saljuqs of Rum. Hence, for example, an important but badly understood rebellion led by a charismatic popular preacher, Baba Ishaq, who just before the middle of the thirteenth century claimed for himself prophetic powers and drew in some poorly-defined way on the unstable Sufi-Shi^{c}i mix which characterized the Turkmen's Islam. The Anatolian Saljuqs were finally able to suppress the Baba'i revolt with the assistance of Frankish mercenaries, but the religio-political potential of Baba'i-style syncretism was not extinguished. At this very moment, the Mongols destroyed the Sunni caliphate in Baghdad, and so helped to make the late thirteenth and fourteenth centuries a propitious moment for Shi^{c}ism. In the confused circumstances of eastern Anatolia and northwest Iran, the

---

[39] M. Fuad Köprülü, *Influence du chamanisme turco-mongol sur les ordres mystiques musulmans* (Istanbul: Mémoires de l'Institute de Turcologie de l'Université de Stamboul, 1929), and idem, *Islam in Anatolia After the Turkish Invasion*, trans. Gary Leiser (Salt Lake City: University of Utah Press, 1993); Irène Mélikoff, "Les origines centre-asiatiques du soufisme anatolien," *Turcica* 20 (1988), 7–18.

"Shiᶜitisation" of Anatolian Sufism paved the way for the emergence of the Safawiyya, a millenarian Sufi order which, under the leadership of their *pir* Shah Ismaᶜil, conquered Iran and ultimately established an explicitly Shiᶜi regime, under whose auspices Twelver Shiᶜism became established in Iran as it was nowhere else in the Islamic world.[40]

---

[40] On the "Shiᶜitisation" of Anatolian Sufism in the Middle Period, see Claude Cahen, "Le problème du Shiᶜisme dans l'asie mineure turque préottomane," in *Le Shiᶜisme Imamite: Colloque de Strasbourg (6–9 mai 1968)* (Paris: Presses Universitaires de France, 1970), 115–29; Marijan Molé, "Les kubrawiya entre sunnisme et shiᶜisme aux huitième et neuvième siècles de l'hégire," *Revue des études islamiques* (1961), 61–142; and the sources cited in the previous note.

CHAPTER 25

Popular religion

In the medieval Islamic Near East, did "popular religion" constitute a distinctive phenomenon susceptible to analysis as such? Certainly "religion" was quite "popular," in at least two socially significant senses: first, that religious structures and patterns such as those we have been investigating contributed decisively to shaping the social identities of the population; and second, that religious concerns permeated daily life and religious hopes provided the first line of defense against crisis. No doubt, individuals sincerely turned to God for help in times of trouble, but of greater interest were the public manifestations of pious expectations which reflect a society in which religion constituted the central organizational principle. In a typical entry, for example, the chronicler al-Dhahabi described the reaction of the population of Damascus to the approach of the Ilkhanid ruler Ghazan in 1299. While the Mamluks, the ruling elite, prepared (ineffectually, as it turned out) for war, the Muslims of the city, led by the *qadis* and leading ulama, made a public procession, at the head of which strode a *shaykh* carrying a copy of al-Bukhari's collection of Prophetic hadith – and in a fit of ecumenism, they were joined by the Jews carrying the Torah and the Christians with the Gospels, invoking the mercy of the Almighty.[1] But the phrase "popular religion" invokes something different: namely, a level of religious belief and experience distinct from, if not in opposition to, that defined by scholars, jurists, and well-respected mystics, and one shaped by the concerns and priorities of the mass (and especially the lower social ranks) of the population.

A preliminary answer to this question must be a cautious "yes." There was certainly a category of religious experiences which some scholars *at the time* perceived as deriving their inspiration and legitimacy from the people generally, that is, from those not widely recognized as members of the ulama qualified to participate in the informal but critical process of establishing the parameters of what constituted "Islam" through *ijma'*, "consensus." Opposition to these practices was expressed in various ways, most commonly in the language of "innovation":

---

[1] Joseph Somogyi, "Adh-Dhahabi's Record of the Destruction of Damascus by the Mongols in 699–700/1299–1301," *Ignace Goldziher Memorial Volume*, ed. Samuel Löwinger and Joseph Somogyi (Budapest, 1948), 361.

that one thing or another constituted an unacceptable *bid^{c}a*, something for which no recognized precedent could be found in the Prophetic *sunna*. A hostility to innovations was a long-standing element of Islamic discourse, and a nuanced one as well – many scholars would distinguish, for example, between innovations that were acceptable or even praiseworthy – but it was a theme developed with some stridency, even ferocity, in the Middle Period. That opposition was ideological – that is to say, it reflected one particular understanding or construct of what constituted Islam – but the practices against which it inveighed were quite real. Many of these religious experiences took the form of or occurred during public festivals and celebrations. Some, such as the festival known as Nawruz, were not specifically Islamic. Nawruz was in origin a Persian celebration of the new year, but became popular among the Muslims and Christians of Syria, Egypt, and elsewhere over the course of late antiquity and the medieval period. Its popularity no doubt stemmed from the practices associated with it – excessive consumption of food and drink, the exchange of gifts, masquerades and sexual games, the donning of new clothes and burlesque transvestism – practices reminiscent of the Saturnalia of antiquity and the carnivals of medieval and early modern Europe and which, it has been reasonably suggested, acted as a safety valve for various social pressures. But the festival understandably drew fire from religious scholars (who, in Cairo in the fourteenth and fifteenth centuries, worked with the military authorities to suppress it, with some success), whose opposition made the festival an issue of Islamic identity and legitimacy.[2]

What were some of the characteristic features of this "popular religion"? First of all, while it was not identical to Sufism, it was very closely identified with it. We have already seen how the routinization of Sufism, including the crystallization of various orders and the popularization of various practices associated with mystical experience, contributed to the spread of at least nominal Sufi identifications among the population. Some have argued that the *turuq*, by attracting less disciplined adherents to the Sufi path, may have encouraged the use of charms, magic, incense, and even chemical stimulants among the mystics – easier paths than rigorous spiritual discipline to mystical ecstasy.[3] Be that as it may, the spread of Sufi institutions was both a reflection of and catalyst for the broad-based popularity of Sufism, or at least of individuals identified as Sufis. Not all of these were the well-endowed *khanqahs* established in the cities by the rulers and other wealthy people. In Egypt and Syria especially, both the cities and smaller towns and villages were littered with other foundations of varying size, often called *zawiyas*. Many of these amounted to little more than a small mosque or hospice which had been built for, or by, or had become associated with some particular

---

[2] See Boaz Shoshan, *Popular Culture in Medieval Cairo* (Cambridge: Cambridge University Press, 1993), esp. 6–8 (on the category of "popular religion"), 40–51 (on Nawruz); Jonathan P. Berkey, "Tradition, Innovation, and the Social Construction of Knowledge in the Medieval Islamic Near East," *Past & Present* 146 (1995), 38–65 (on the discourse over innovations).

[3] The argument of J. S. Trimingham, *The Sufi Orders in Islam* (Oxford: Clarendon Press, 1971), 199–200.

shaykh; they were not necessarily attached to any particular *tariqa*. These institutions, or rather the *shaykhs* who led them, were intimately tied to the communities that surrounded them. Sometimes, for example, they were financed not by endowments but through the contributions of those who frequented them. Their *shaykhs* had important religious and social functions among the common people; in addition to leading prayers, or delivering sermons, or performing *dhikr*, they sometimes provided basic education to the people of their neighborhoods, or served as scribes and legal witnesses. In other words, they constituted the most accessible source of religious knowledge for their followers.[4]

A second characteristic of the religious experiences and expectations of the common people is that they tended to focus on particular individuals who were revered for their saintly character or great learning. In part, this reflects a larger pattern in Islamic culture, the personal and "genealogical" construction of authority, which we have seen elsewhere: in the emphasis placed upon close relationships between teachers and pupils, or in the role which Sufi *shaykhs* played as spiritual masters. Particularly popular preachers, for example, could acquire a significant following among the Muslim population of a given city, and the chronicles and biographical dictionaries of the period are replete with the mention of preachers who attracted enormous crowds, or in whom the "people" had great "confidence."[5] Some of these venerated figures were perfectly respectable scholars – Ibn Taymiyya, for instance, whose arrest on several occasions prompted riots and street disturbances, or al-Suyuti, who despite the bitterness of his relations with other ulama acquired a lasting reputation among the common people, who after his death quickly transformed his tomb into an object of veneration and visitation.[6] Other widely-respected religious figures, however, operated outside the institutional and social channels through which the ulama attempted to control the dissemination of religious knowledge, and this was a matter of some significance and concern.

But the common people's veneration of individuals was also a reflection of the social role which venerated religious figures could play. It was to these holy men that many Muslims, of all social ranks, looked for intercession and mediation, both with God and with established authorities. Despite some Koranic verses which seemed to reject the possibility (for example, 2.48), the anticipation that pious individuals might successfully plead with God on behalf of another became a

---

[4] Jean-Claude Garcin, "Histoire et hagiographie de l'Égypte musulmane à la fin de l'époque mamelouke et au début de l'époque ottomane," in *Hommages à la mémoire de Serge Sauneron*, vol. 2: *Égypte post-pharaonique* (Cairo: IFAO, 1979), 287–316; Leonor Fernandes, "Some aspects of the *zāwiya* in Egypt at the eve of the Ottoman conquest," *Annales islamologiques* 19 (1983), 9–17; Eric Geoffroy, *Le soufisme en Égypte et en Syrie sous les derniers Mamelouks et les premiers Ottomanes: orientations spirituelles et enjeux culturelles* (Damascus: Institut Français, 1995), 166–75.

[5] For some examples, see Jonathan P. Berkey, *Popular Preaching and Religious Authority in the Medieval Islamic Near East* (Seattle: University of Washington Press, 2001), 24–6.

[6] Jean-Claude Garcin, "Histoire, opposition politique et piétisme traditionaliste dans le *Ḥusn al-Muḥādarat* de Suyūṭī," *Annales islamologiques* 7 (1967), 39–40; Elizabeth Sartain, *Jalāl-Dīn al-Suyūṭī*, vol. 1: Biography and Background (Cambridge: Cambridge University Press, 1975), 109–12.

ubiquitous feature of medieval Muslim piety. Naturally, Muhammad was the principal figure whose intercession (*shafaᶜa*) was sought, particularly on eschatological concerns. But a more local, and thus more immediate and accessible figure, might also attract pious interest and hopeful expectation. It is this, for example, which lay behind the common practice (one shared by Near Eastern Jews and Christians as well as Muslims) of visiting the tombs of those revered for their own piety, learning, or religious accomplishment, to seek their intercession with God to cure an illness, or ensure the safe delivery of a child, or alleviate a debt.[7] But living scholars and "saints" might prove equally efficacious, perhaps even more so if the intercession was sought to settle some immediate social conflict. A popular Sufi mystic of late fifteenth- and early sixteenth-century Egypt once complained that, in almost four decades of living a life of pious renunciation, no one had ever come to him asking guidance on how to reach God, or how to repent properly of sins. However, they *did*, he said, seek him out for remedies for more worldly complaints: that their slaves had fled, or their master was unjust, or their friends and neighbors had deceived or harmed them. The *shaykh*'s admirers included common people but also a number of the ruling Mamluk elite, including Sultan Qansuh al-Ghuri, so that, as one historian has put it, "he who had quit the world saw it flow back towards him."[8]

Third, syncretistic elements and patterns tended to be more pronounced among the religious practices and expectations of the common people. Reports of Muslims participating in the religious festivals of their Jewish and Christian neighbors, such as those we encountered above (pp. 160–1), remained common in the Middle Period, and provided the foundation for a sustained polemic on the part of Muslim scholars. Jurists such as the Syrian Hanbali Ibn Taymiyya and his contemporary Ibn al-Hajj, a Maliki scholar of Maghribi origin living in Egypt, excoriated Muslims who indulged in Christian festivals such as Palm Sunday or Easter, or rested on Fridays in imitation of the Jewish practice of keeping the Sabbath. Many of the practices borrowed by Muslims from their *dhimmi* neighbors amounted to what we would call superstition – for example, driving away illness and the "evil eye" by washing themselves on Easter Saturday in a potion concocted of water and herbal leaves, or preparing certain foods on Christmas day in the hope that it would ensure that they would remain warm for the coming year, or purchasing amulets whose supposed power derived from scraps of paper with Hebrew characters on them[9] – although the distinction between "religion" and

---

[7] On the pious visitation of tombs for purposes of intercession, see Christopher S. Taylor, *In the Vicinity of the Righteous: Ziyārā and the Veneration of Muslim Saints in Late Medieval Egypt* (Leiden: E. J. Brill, 1999), esp. 127–67. On Muhammad as intercessor, the standard work is that of Annemarie Schimmel, *And Muhammad is His Prophet: Veneration of the Prophet in Islamic Piety* (Chapel Hill: University of North Carolina Press, 1985), 1985. There is also a good brief account in *EI²*, art. "Shafāᶜa" (in two parts, by A. J. Wensinck and D. Gimaret, and Annemarie Schimmel).

[8] Jean-Claude Garcin, "Deux saints populaires du Caire au début du xviᵉ siècle," *Bulletin d'études orientales* 29 (1977), 134–5; see also Daniella Talmon Heller, "The Shaykh and the Community: Popular Hanbalite Islam in 12th–13th Century Jabal Nablus and Jabal Qaysūn," *Studia Islamica* 79 (1994), 111–15.

[9] Ibn al-Ḥājj, *Madkhal al-sharᶜ al-sharīf*, 4 vols. (Cairo: al-Matbaᶜa al-Misriyya, 1929), 2.56, 58–9, 323.

"superstition" would no doubt have been lost on many of those who practiced such things. Moreover, even as acerbic a critic as Ibn Taymiyya acknowledged that some Muslims would indulge in such things simply because they were fun. "The nature of women, children, and most men particularly looks forward with eager fondness to the day which they celebrate as a holiday for idling and sport," he mused, "with the result that often many a king and leader has failed in altering the customs of a people in respect of their festivals, owing to a compelling inner need of people for them and the customary rallying of the masses for celebration."[10] But from the standpoint of the stricter jurists, frivolity was no excuse. Since the conditions of medieval Muslim life, which included a reduced but still significant *dhimmi* presence in most places, made the physical separation of Muslims and non-Muslims impossible, it was all the more important, Ibn Taymiyya reasoned, to insist on differentiating the religious communities, both psychologically and in their social intercourse. And to that end, the very public nature of religious festivals made them especially problematic. "Participation with [the *dhimmis*] in their festivals wholly or partly is synonymous with participation with them in unbelief wholly or partly," he said. Indeed, "festivals are that which most particularly serves to differentiate one religious law from another and constitute their most prominent symbols." Such behavior, the jurist worried, might lead ignorant and gullible Muslims to seeking blessing from the cross, or even baptism.[11] Were such concerns, even if exaggerated, completely unfounded? Not in some places, at least, since there are reports from the same period of Muslim Anatolians engaging in precisely such behavior.[12]

In these ways, it may perhaps be possible to locate a stratum of religious belief and practice which was in some sense "popular." Certainly many medieval Muslim scholars perceived the distinct character of popular religion, and believed that it constituted a threat to the edifice of Islam which they had constructed. Ibn Taymiyya and Ibn al-Hajj are among the most colorful examples, but a polemic against popular religion was in fact a staple of medieval Islamic scholarly discourse. The language of that polemic usually labeled popular practices of which the scholars disapproved as "innovation" (*bidʿa*). The distinction between that which was an innovation and that which was acceptable practice (*sunna*) was an old one, and many discussions of it were quite nuanced, characterized by a willingness to distinguish between innovations that were acceptable, or even praiseworthy, and those that were not. But the number of treatises by Ibn Taymiyya and others condemning both particular practices and the very idea of innovations,

---

[10] Muhammad Umar Memon, *Ibn Taimiya's Struggle Against Popular Religion* (The Hague: Mouton, 1976), 195.

[11] Memon, *Ibn Taimiya's Struggle*, 206, 213.

[12] Speros Vryonis, Jr., *The Decline of Medieval Hellenism in Asia Minor and the Process of Islamization from the Eleventh through the Fifteenth Century* (Berkeley: University of California Press, 1971), 487–9, and idem, "The Experience of Christians under Seljuk and Ottoman Domination, Eleventh to Sixteenth Century," in *Conversion and Continuity: Indigenous Christian Communities in Islamic Lands, Eighth to Eighteenth Centuries*, ed. Michael Gervers and Ramzi Jibran Bikhazi (Toronto: Pontifical Institute of Mediaeval Studies, 1990) (Papers in Mediaeval Studies 9), 195.

and the shrill tone in which they condemned the perceived assault on Islamic *sunna*, suggest that the struggle between these scholars and the behavior they condemned may reflect something important and characteristic about medieval Islam.[13]

From the scholars' standpoint, the danger of popular religion is that it constituted a challenge to the authority of the ulama. In the first place, popular religious festivals and practices often were associated with behavior that transgressed the *shari'a*, and so undermined the legal and ethical system which lay at the base of the ulama's authority. Ibn al-Hajj's description of people's behavior during the celebration of the Prophet's birthday (*mawlid*, or colloquially *mulid*), a festival of dubious origin which nonetheless became in the Middle Period one of the most popular in the Muslim calendar, is lurid in its detail. The noisy and frolicsome festivities, he said, became the cause of "the greatest temptation and most serious scandal." During them, men and women mixed freely, so that their hearts were "bewitched" and they indulged in practices "unbecoming to believers."[14] Concerns over sexual impropriety in fact are a common theme of the scholars' polemic, as for example in a treatise by Ibn al-Jawzi. In this work, he criticized the activities of popular preachers and storytellers who, on street-corners as well as in mosques, exhorted their audiences and entertained them with religious tales. From his remarks, it is clear that women regularly attended such sessions, and that the storytellers failed to insist that they separate themselves from the men. With men and women mixing relatively freely, the occasions might attract audiences for reasons that were not entirely pious, or so Ibn al-Jawzi seems to suggest: the storytellers, he insisted, "should prohibit [women who attend] from dressing in such a way so as to excite the lusts of men."[15]

Secondly, popular religion threatened the gender hierarchy in this patriarchal society, a hierarchy which was endemic in the *shari'a* and in the character of the ulama's authority. We have seen how women could participate, in some limited but meaningful way, in the transmission of religious knowledge, but their participation hardly threatened the near monopoly of men on positions of religious authority within the ulama elite. The world of popular religion, however, was a radically different place. From Ibn al-Hajj's detailed account, it is clear that it was women who were often responsible for absorbing the customs and rituals of their Jewish and Christian neighbors. Here, the prominence of Sufism in the religious life of the common people is probably significant: we know, for example, of *shaykhas* (the feminine form of the word *shaykh*) who led groups of female mystics in publicly performing the *dhikr*, especially on popular festivals such as the Prophet's

---

[13] On that polemic, see Berkey, "Tradition, Innovation, and the Social Construction of Knowledge."

[14] Ibn al-Hājj, *Madkhal*, 2.11, 16. On the *mulid* and the process by which it became widely celebrated in the medieval Near East, see N. J. G. Kaptein, *Muhammad's Birthday Festival: Early History in the Central Muslim Lands and Development in the Muslim West until the 10th/16th Century* (Leiden: E. J. Brill, 1993).

[15] Ibn al-Jawzī, *Kitāb al-quṣṣāṣ waʾl-mudhakkirīn*, ed. and trans. Merlin Swartz (Beirut: Dar al-Machreq, 1986), 142 (Eng. trans., 226).

mawlid. Moreover, the ranks of popular preachers and storytellers included numerous women, who would recite hadith and religious tales and expound on them to audiences of women, or even to mixed groups of men and women. Ibn al-Hajj, of course, condemned them. Even male scholars, he observed, frequently make mistakes; how much more dangerous is it when women, who are "crooked, root and branch" and unable to tell the difference between what is "sound" and "corrupt," try to elucidate matters of religion?[16]

A third problem concerned the character and training of those whom the common people sometimes looked up to as religious leaders. The ulama of course were not a closed elite, a clergy consecrated and set apart from the ordinary run of humans. This was arguably a source of great social strength for medieval Islam. But it also left the door open to the participation in the transmission of religious knowledge, at least to the common people, by those whom most scholars would regard as unfit. And it seems that the common people (*ʿamma*) did on occasion place considerable confidence in religious figures whose authority emerged from channels and "texts" quite different than those which produced an *ʿalim* ("scholar"). Sometimes these figures deliberately and explicitly parodied the pretensions of the ulama. In thirteenth- and fourteenth-century Damascus, for example, the *ʿamma* placed great stock in the religious authority of marginal holy men known as the *muwallahun*. This term did not signify a *tariqa* such as the Qalandariyya, despite certain similarities between the two groups, but simply indicated a group of "eccentric mystics" who lived antinomian and somewhat bizarre lives (inhabiting garbage heaps, for example, or wearing clothing polluted with ritually unclean things, or deliberately refusing to pray or to fast) and who through various public spectacles mimicked and mocked the learning of the ulama.[17] In other cases, however, the religious figures who earned the confidence of the common people did not parody the ulama so much as they claimed (falsely, in the scholars' eyes) to *be* such: that is, they claimed access to *ʿilm*, to religious knowledge, without sufficient training and preparation. The ranks of the storytellers and popular preachers, for example, were made up largely of individuals who (according to their ulama critics) transmitted to the indiscriminating masses dubious material: unsubstantiated hadith, or the popular but suspect tales of the pre-Islamic prophets known as the *israʾiliyyat*, or things that they had read in books but without the supervision of recognized scholars, or even things which the Prophet had relayed to them in their dreams. In short, they transmitted religious knowledge which they had acquired outside the channels (such as

---

[16] Ibn al-Ḥājj, *Madkhal*, 2:14; Berkey, *Popular Preaching*, 31–2; and cf. Huda Lutfi, "Manners and Customs of Fourteenth-Century Cairene Women: Female Anarchy versus Male Sharʿī Order in Muslim Prescriptive Treatises," in *Women in Middle Eastern History: Shifting Boundaries in Sex and Gender*, ed. Nikki R. Keddie and Beth Baron (New Haven: Yale University Press, 1991), 99–121.

[17] Louis Pouzet, *Damas au viiᵉ/xiiiᵉ siècle: vie et structures religieuses d'une métropole islamique* (Beirut: Dar al-Machreq, 1988), 222–26; Chamberlain, *Knowledge and Social Practice*, 130–3.

personal training with a reputable teacher, attested by an *ijaza*) which normally defined the parameters of the ulama's authority.[18]

Finally and most importantly, the danger of popular religion lay in its potential to shape what people understood "Islam" itself to be. Tolerating Muslim participation in *dhimmi* festivals, in Ibn Taymiyya's view, could lead to much more. "There is the further danger that once the practice spreads common people too would participate in it, forgetting all too soon its origin and letting it become their habit, nay their own festival, which festival would then be set up as a rival to, or might even suppress, the festival granted by God."[19] Even superorogatory acts of piety, harmless in themselves, could be dangerous if, through their repetition, people came to assume that they were Islamic, that is, that they constituted a requirement of the faith, that they were *sunna*. So, for example, jurists worried about the popular practice of fasting during the month of Rajab, and the possibility that the *ᶜamma* might come to believe that it was required by the *shariᶜa*.[20]

To make matters worse, the *ᶜamma* themselves might contribute to the shaping – from the scholars' perspective, the mis-shaping – of the faith. The posture which non-ulama took to their religious tradition was not a passive one. The nature of the surviving source material (most of it compiled by the ulama) makes it difficult to reconstruct their contribution to the shaping of Islam, but our understanding of the social history of the religion would be incomplete if we did not at least acknowledge the possibility that they did contribute to the process. Preachers, for example, might be peppered with questions from their audiences, and forced to spend hours explaining or defending their positions.[21] The common people were in fact capable of expressing their opinions on religious matters in a variety of ways. Some of them were no doubt crude, as a Maliki *qadi* in Aleppo in the late fifteenth century discovered: the jurist was accused by a popular Sufi *shaykh* of being an infidel, and the extent of the *shaykh*'s following among the people convinced the authorities to respond to the charge by having the *qadi* beaten and paraded through the town in disgrace.[22] (Ironically, the strict Ibn Taymiyya himself had a large following among the *ᶜamma*; according to the medieval traveller Ibn Battuta, when a Maliki jurist once interrupted a sermon of his to denounce him for anthropomorphism, the crowd turned on the critic and beat him.)[23] The potential of popular opinion to shape the common understanding of Islam is reflected in the explanation of the fifteenth-century scholar al-Suyuti as to why he had written a treatise condemning popular preachers and the reciters of religious tales. A storyteller, he said, had been

[18] Berkey, *Popular Preaching*, 70–87.
[19] Memon, *Ibn Taimiya's Struggle*, 207–8.
[20] Abū Bakr al-Ṭurṭūshī, *Kitāb al-Ḥawādith waʾl-bidaᶜ* (Beirut: Dār al-Gharb al-Islāmī, 1990), 276–84, esp. 282.
[21] Berkey, *Popular Preaching*, 54–5.
[22] Ira Lapidus, *Muslim Cities in the Later Middle Ages* (Cambridge, Mass.: Harvard University Press, 1967), 104.
[23] Ibn Baṭṭuṭa, *Travels*, trans. H. A. R. Gibb (Publications of the Hakluyt Society, v. 110) (Cambridge: Cambridge University Press, 1958), 1.135–5; but see on the incident Donald P. Little, "Did Ibn Taymiyya Have a Screw Loose?" *Studia Islamica* 41 (1975), 93–111.

reciting to his audiences hadith that were not genuine; al-Suyuti announced in a *fatwa* that it was the man's responsibility to confirm the authenticity of such hadith with reputable scholars like himself. The storyteller's reaction was visceral. "You expect the likes of me to verify my hadith with the scholars?" he fumed. "Rather," he said, "I will verify them with the people!" And to that end, he spurred his audience on, until they turned on al-Suyuti and threatened to stone him.[24]

The practices and expectations of the common people shaped their understanding and experience of Islam in important ways. One of the most popular practices for Muslims in many parts of the Near East was the visitation of tombs (*ziyarat al-qubur*), in particular those of individuals renowned for their piety or learning. Visitors sought such tombs in the belief that prayer there would benefit from the spiritual blessing or power (*baraka*) of the departed saint, and so be more likely to prove efficacious. In the later Middle Period, the practice was so common in Cairo that it spawned a veritable industry, with *shaykhs* leading organized groups of visitors to the cemeteries that lay outside the city walls, and published guidebooks cataloguing the hallowed tombs and the manifestations of their occupants' power. There was considerable opposition to the practice among the ulama, including Ibn Taymiyya, but that opposition did not prevail. On the contrary, the popularity of the practice among Near Eastern Muslims compelled the ulama, or at least some of them, to accept and approve it. In lamenting that fact, Ibn al-Hajj observed wryly that, while it used to be the case that the common people imitated the scholars on religious matters, it now appeared instead that the ulama imitated the people.[25]

Ibn al-Hajj found the fact that some scholars bowed to the popularity of practices such as the visitation of tombs and gave them their *imprimatur* disturbing, but to the historian his observation serves as a reminder that the construction of Islam by the full range of those who experienced it was a complicated, sometimes even contradictory phenomenon. On the one hand, the popular religious practices against which Ibn Taymiyya, Ibn al-Hajj and others fulminated constituted a challenge to the religious authority of the ulama and to the integrity of the Islam they championed. If we have been correct in seeing a process of "re-centering" as a dominant theme of the development of Islam in the Middle Period, then the persistence of practices such as the *ziyarat al-qubur*, and their acceptance (grudging or otherwise) by many ulama, constitute a countervailing tendency, a mode of resistance to the centripetal and homogenizing pressures of the ulama's Islam.[26] Put another way, those who participated in this "popular" religious life, such as the illiterate Ibrahim al-Matbuli, or those storytellers who recited pious but suspect tales frowned upon by the ulama and their texts, acted in opposition to the process of "inscripting" the ulama's authority. On the other hand, the ulama's

---

[24] See Berkey, *Popular Preaching*, 24–5; and on this point generally, idem, "Tradition, Innovation."

[25] Ibn al-Ḥājj, *Madkhal*, 2.23. On the visitation of tombs generally and the debate over it among the ulama, see Taylor, *In the Vicinity of the Righteous*.

[26] Cf. the remarks of Richard Bulliet, *Islam: The View from the Edge* (New York: Columbia University Press, 1994), 173–4.

acceptance of religious practices springing from or championed by the common people constitute a warning not to assume that what we have been calling "popular religion" and that of the jurists and scholars – "low" culture and "high" culture – constituted hermetically isolated categories of cultural life. It was not simply the *ᶜamma* who participated in *dhimmi* festivals and in raucous celebrations of the Prophet's birthday; Ibn al-Hajj remarked that one could find "those who claim to possess religious knowledge" indulging in them as well. After decrying those *shaykhas* who dress in wool like Sufis, and lead *dhikr* sessions and public chanting of the Koran, he commented that modest and respectable *shaykhs*, who would never be caught dead with a disreputable "singing-girl," will nonetheless attend religious performances led by women.[27] The concept of "popular religion" remains a useful analytical tool for understanding a certain stratum of medieval Islamic religious culture; but that stratum *was* Islamic – that is, it was just as much a part of "Islam" as was the textually-based authority of the ulama.[28]

What we are left with, then, is a complex and fluid model of religious culture in the medieval Islamic Near East. The struggle over what we have called "popular religion" was central to the whole identity of Sunni Islam in this period. At root, the question was one of authority: who would be privileged to speak for "Islam"? The ulama certainly had a strong claim, and in the sometimes chaotic political conditions of the Middle Period, they emerged with a privileged social role. But since there was no mechanism for establishing what was acceptably Islamic other than *ijmaᶜ*, or consensus, there was no foolproof way at this stage to institutionalize their authority. The polemic against innovations, against popular preachers and storytellers, against the careless adoption of *dhimmi* festivals, against the visitation of tombs and the unrestrained celebration of the Prophet's birthday – all this constituted an effort on the part of the ulama to make their authority more real. But it was simply one voice in a sea of others, and it was not always articulated consistently. As a result, the category of what was "acceptable" proved to be open and porous, more so than many of the ulama would have liked. And that contributed significantly to the diversity of religious life in medieval Islam.

---

[27] Ibn al-Hājj, *Madkhal*, 2.4-7ff and 141-3.
[28] As argued for different circumstances by Karamustafa, *God's Unruly Friends*; Berkey, *Popular Preaching*; and Taylor, *In the Vicinity of the Righteous*.

Epilogue

CHAPTER 26

From medieval to modern Islam

In a book entitled *Medieval Islam: A Study in Cultural Orientation*, the Orientalist G. E. von Grunebaum asserted that the difference between medieval and modern societies, in the Islamic Near East as well as in Christian Europe, could be located most clearly in the shift in the locus of social identity. In the "Middle Ages," he said, religious affiliation was the fundamental component of an individual's outlook, and of his and others' understanding of his place in the world. Only on a secondary level would he think of himself as rooted in a local society, or bound to some local center of political power. And only as an afterthought might he think of himself as part of a larger national or ethnic community. "The gradual reversal of the strength of these loyalties," von Grunebaum argued, "marks the close of the Middle Ages."[1] Like many grand themes of Orientalist scholarship, von Grunebaum's observation perhaps contains a certain truth. But it also obscures a great deal through over-simplification. As we have seen, the question of religious identity, even as late as what we have called the "Middle Period," was in fact a complex matter, and its complexity did not evaporate in the years after its close. Moreover, as anyone who reads a newspaper in the early twenty-first century knows, it is by no means clear that, of religious, local, and national identities, the former has been relegated to a place of insignificance.

In this epilogue, we will explore very briefly certain developments in the area of religious identity and authority in the Near East in the years between 1500 and 1800. The beginning of the sixteenth century had epochal significance for Muslims in the Near East, since it saw two transforming events: first, the conquest of Iran by the Safavids (from 1501–2) and the eventual conversion of its people to Twelver Shiʿism; and second, the Ottomans' defeat of the Mamluks (1516–17), the subsequent absorption into their empire of Syria, Egypt, and the Hijaz, and their emergence as the pre-eminent Sunni state in the region. There were certain structural similarities between these two states, but they came over time to represent significantly different understandings of what it meant to be Islamic. Both of them drew in important ways on religious developments of the preceding

---

[1] G. E. von Grunebaum, *Medieval Islam: A Study in Cultural Orientation* (Chicago: University of Chicago Press, 1953), 1–2.

centuries, on the patterns and institutions characteristic of medieval Islam, but also worked out new structures of religious authority that would shape the ways in which modern Muslims have experienced their faith. What exactly the "modern period" is, and when it begins, is a matter of some debate. For our purposes, however, 1800 is as good a date as any in which to bring this discussion to a close.

The Ottoman empire was probably the most ambitious effort to give political expression to the ideal of a united Muslim *umma* since the early ʿAbbasid period. It is significant that this should be the case, as in some ways the Ottomans at first constituted simply another of the Turkish military regimes which dominated a fractured and fragmented Islamic polity in the Middle Period. The geographical scope of at least nominal Ottoman authority was enormous: by the late sixteenth century, the name of the Ottoman sultan was mentioned in the *khutba* in the Turkish heartlands of Anatolia, in the Ottoman provinces in south-eastern Europe, and in almost all of the Arab lands, including the Maghrib in the far west. But Ottoman ambitions extended even further. Their strategic vision led them to make efforts to counter European military and commercial activity in the Indian Ocean region – in the late sixteenth century, an Ottoman naval expedition provided assistance to a Muslim ruler as far away as Sumatra, in the Indonesian archipelago. Military campaigns for the Ottomans were integrally related to their understanding of their religious identity and mission. The Ottomans' roots lay amongst the nomadic Turkish principalities which had arisen in Anatolia following the battle of Manzikert, and which vigorously pursued a campaign of holy war against the Byzantine Empire. It was the Ottomans who finally put an end to the Christian Roman Empire with their capture of Constantinople in 1453, and their campaign carried them into Europe and into a long series of wars with the Christian powers there. As a result, their reputations as *ghazis* ("holy warriors"), committed to the expansion of the borders of the *dar al-islam*, constituted one of the fundamental ideological building blocks of the Ottoman state.[2]

In many ways religious life in the Ottoman period owed much to developments in the centuries which had preceded it. In Istanbul, and in both Anatolia and in the empire's Arab provinces, the institutional structure of religious life was dominated by *madrasas* and Sufi convents similar to those which medieval rulers had constructed and endowed for the benefit of the ulama. Naturally there were some changes: the Ottomans, for example, were partisans of the Hanafi *madhhab*, which was raised to a pre-eminent position within the empire, and the imperial capital of Istanbul began to eclipse medieval centers of Muslim intellectual life such as Cairo. But the pattern whereby members of the ruling establishment supplied the financial and institutional framework for Muslim religious life continued, and cities in the Arab provinces, such as Cairo and Jerusalem, continued to benefit from institutions founded by sultans, other members of the Ottoman family, or

---

[2] The connections between the Ottomans and frontier holy war has been much debated; see now Cemal Kafadar, *Between Two Worlds: The Construction of the Ottoman State* (Berkeley: University of California Press, 1995).

provincial governors. As in the preceding centuries, Sufism continued to play a dominant role, although it continued to take radically different forms. One order popular in the Ottoman period was the Naqshbandiyya, whose sober outlook, which included a profound respect for Islamic law, made them popular among the ulama. The Khalwatiyya had roots in the turbulent religious atmosphere of late medieval Anatolia and Azerbaijan which also produced the Kubrawiyya and the Safawiyya, but whereas the Kubrawiyya drifted toward Shi°ism and millenarian expectations, and the Safawiyya finally and explicitly embraced Twelver Shi°ism, the Khalwatiyya in the Ottoman domains, both in Istanbul and in the provinces, attracted the support of many within the ruling establishment. Even so, particular practices among the Sufi orders continued to raise doubts of some of the religious scholars: the Khalwatiyya's embrace of coffee as a stimulant, for example. At the other extreme, an order such as the Bektashiyya appears to have retained many suspect doctrines and syncretistic practices; nonetheless, the order was tolerated because of its popularity, especially among the Janissary soldiers who formed the core of the Ottoman armies.

But the Ottoman period also saw significant changes in the structure of religious life. In particular, the religious establishment grew much more closely tied to the state. In the previous chapter we identified a pattern of "accommodation" between the rulers and the ulama as characteristic of medieval Islam in the Near East. Under the Ottomans, the higher-ranking ulama became part of an elaborate hierarchy, closely tied to the state, which administered and supervised the religious affairs of the empire. The Ottomans referred to those trained in the religious and legal sciences and professionally involved in their transmission and application as the °ilmiyye, or "learned establishment." That group included a carefully graded network of qadis, paid by the state, who not only rendered judgements according to the shari°a but also attended to a variety of purely administrative responsibilities. Qadis were appointed from among the graduates and professors at the principal Ottoman madrasas, according to a precise hierarchy. At the top of the religious institution stood (at least from the sixteenth century) the shaykh al-islam, whose position originally was simply that of mufti (i.e., one who issued fatwas) but who eventually acquired responsibilities for the supervision of the entire °ilmiyye and also a significant voice in the formulation of state policy. The pivotal figure in the rise to prominence of the shaykh al-islam, and in fixing the structure of the °ilmiyye as it would remain down into the modern period, was Abu'l-Su°ud Efendi (d. 1574), an Ottoman jurist who held the post for almost thirty years in the mid-sixteenth century.[3]

The changing pattern of relations between the ulama and the state was uneven. On the one hand, the Ottoman state became perhaps more clearly tied to the shari°a than any previous Muslim regime. Implementation of the Muslim holy

[3] R. C. Repp, *The Mufti of Istanbul: A Study in the Development of the Ottoman Learned Hierarchy* (London: Ithaca Press, 1986); Colin Imber: *Ebu'-s-su°ud: The Islamic Legal Tradition* (Stanford: Stanford University Press, 1997).

law became one of the central ideological pillars of the Ottomans' claim to rule. On the other hand, the "bureaucratization" of the ulama inevitably involved some restriction on their independence by making many of them in effect employees of the state. Moreover, the institutional intertwining of the sultan's state and the ulama was coupled with a limited but significant expansion in the ruler's prerogatives in relation to the *shari*ᶜ*a*. This involved the tentative claim of the Ottoman sultan to the office of the caliph. Since the Mongols destroyed Baghdad and the last ᶜAbbasid caliph there in 1258, the status of the caliphate had been somewhat uncertain. The Mamluks had established an 'Abbasid line as caliphs in Cairo, but as we have seen, that institution had little practical effect, except that Muslim rulers (including the Ottomans) on occasion sought the caliph's formal confirmation of their rule. Muslim rulers (including the Ottomans, from the early fifteenth century) on occasion used the title of caliph as a kind of august honorific, without necessarily any implication that the *nature* of their authority was greater than that of other Muslim rulers. But sultan Suleyman "the law-giver" (r. 1520–1566), guided by the *shaykh al-islam* Abuᵓl-Suᶜud, began to take in a more systematic fashion the title "caliph of the prophet of the Lord of the worlds" (as on the inscription above the portal of his great mosque in Istanbul) or even the more controversial "caliph of God." This assertion was accompanied, it appears, by efforts on the part of Abuᵓl-Suᶜud to use the sultan's authority to limit the range of accepted opinions within the Hanafi *madhhab* which the *qadis* appointed by the state could enforce in their courts. This did not involve an expansive claim that the sultan (as caliph) could *determine* what was genuinely Islamic as some pre-*mihna* caliphs may have done. But it did constitute a further narrowing of the scope of what was considered acceptable, a process which had been characteristic of medieval Islam, and it accorded the Ottoman sultan a role in that process alongside, and in some ways above, that of the ulama.[4]

At the same time, the closer symbiosis of secular and religious authority did not involve the wholesale subordination of the ulama to the authority of the sultan. There were occasions in the seventeenth century, for example, when the *shaykh al-islam* participated in the deposition of sultans, by issuing *fatwas* approving of their removal. Moreover, the Ottoman ulama were by no means a united bloc, either intellectually or socially. Not all members of the ulama were so closely tied to the state as the *shaykh al-islam*, the *qadis*, and the professors in the Istanbul *madrasas*. The older, more informal organization of the religious establishment prevailed especially in the Arab provinces, where the ulama depended more on income from pious endowments than on governmental stipends. These ulama retained their role as mediators between rulers and ruled, and at times came into conflict with *qadis* and other religious functionaries sent out by the Ottoman state. Even in Istanbul, the ulama in its broadest sense remained a diverse body, composed of disparate groups with sometimes competing interests. Indeed, as the hierarchy became more established, the social lines distinguishing one grade of ulama from another

---

[4] Imber, *Ebuᵓs-suᶜud*, 98–111.

hardened, as, for example, the leading *qadis* and professors sought to ensure that their sons could follow in their own career footsteps. In a reflection of the resulting social and professional frustrations, the lower-ranking students in the carefully graded hierarchy of religious and legal education, known as *softas*, frequently appear in the sources as a kind of unruly urban mob, with a generally reactionary character, participating in rebellions on behalf of one political faction or another.[5]

The centuries leading up to the modern era also saw significant changes in the religious lives of Near Eastern *dhimmis*, changes which laid the groundwork for even more radical transformations in the nineteenth and twentieth centuries. As in early centuries, religion remained for most the principal marker of social identity. The fundamental distinction was that between Muslim and non-Muslim. For some Ottoman jurists and officials, that was the only distinction that mattered, in accordance with the principle that "unbelief [*kufr*] constitutes a single religious community [*milla*]." As in earlier centuries, the psychological and social divisions between Muslims and non-Muslims might be greater or lesser, depending on circumstances. *Dhimmi* populations in the cities of the Near East remained largely integrated into urban life, although in some places there was a tendency toward separation of the communities over time. Restrictions such as those in the so-called "Pact of ʿUmar" were probably enforced especially strictly in the cities, where non-Muslims might be required, for example, to identify themselves by particular forms of dress, or by other special markers in spaces (such as bathhouses) where sartorial markers of identity were shed. The need to maintain unambiguous distinctions between religious identities is reflected clearly in records from Muslim courts (which have survived from the Ottoman era in significantly larger quantities than for earlier periods), in which Muslims and non-Muslims with the same name might find those names spelled differently, according to their confessional identity. On the other hand, the barriers between the communities remained porous in places. Sufism continued to offer a forum for relatively open exchange. ʿAbd al-Ghani al-Nabulusi (d. 1731), for example, a partisan of Ibn al-ʿArabi but also a jurist and for a time *mufti* in Damascus, defended the Sufis' tolerant attitude toward non-Muslims, including Ibn al-ʿArabi's speculation that Jews and Christians might enter paradise, and in his account of his travels through the Near East reverentially described a number of Christian shrines which he had visited.[6]

---

[5] For an example of the complex tensions at work among the Ottoman-era ulama, see Rudolph Peters, "The Battered Dervishes of Bab Zuwayla: A Religious Riot in Eighteenth-Century Cairo," in *Eighteenth-Century Renewal and Reform in Islam*, ed. Nehemia Levtzion and John O. Voll (Syracuse: Syracuse University Press, 1987), 93–115. On differences between the ulama in Istanbul and in the Arab provinces, compare R. C. Repp, "Some Observations on the Development of the Ottoman Learned Hierarchy," in *Scholars, Saints, and Sufis: Muslim Religious Institutions in the Middle East Since 1500*, ed. Nikki R. Keddie (Berkeley: University of California Press, 1972), 17–32, and Afaf Lutfi al-Sayyid Marsot, "The Ulama of Cairo in the Eighteenth and Nineteenth Centuries," in *ibid.*, 149–65.

[6] Michael Winter, "A Polemical Treatise by ʿAbd al-Ghānī al-Nabulusī against a Turkish Scholar on the Religious Status of the *Dhimmīs*," Arabica 35 (1988), 92–103; Abraham Marcus, *The Middle East on the Eve of Modernity: Aleppo in the Eighteenth Century* (New York: Columbia University Press, 1989), 39–48; Bruce Masters, *Christians and Jews in the Ottoman Arab World: The Roots of Sectarianism* (Cambridge: Cambridge University Press, 2001).

Dhimmis had traditionally been accorded a fair degree of internal autonomy over the organization of their communities, and that practice continued under the Ottoman sultans. Once the communities were organized and properly registered with the *qadis*, their leaders became on one level an administrative arm of the state, responsible for example for the collection of the *jizya*, and able to call upon the state's coercive instruments to enforce order within their communities. In this sense, the *dhimmis* experienced an integration of religious into political authority similar to that which characterized the Ottoman *ᶜilmiyye*. The non-Muslims of the empire are often described as having been organized into *millets*, from an Arabic word (*milla*) which in earlier usage (e.g., in the Koran) had meant simply "religion." By the late eighteenth or early nineteenth century, the Ottoman government had indeed recognized three principal *millets* – the Greek Orthodox, the Armenian, and the Jewish – as constituting the organized and semi-autonomous communities of non-Muslims within the Empire. Both the Ottomans and the *dhimmis* themselves projected this system backwards, and presented it as having been fully formed already by the sixteenth century. But in fact, the process took considerably longer than has traditionally been thought.[7] Ironically, the *millet* system was not fully in place until the moment in the late eighteenth and early nineteenth centuries when economic and cultural developments – in particular, the deeper penetration of the Near East by European economic interests and the activities of European (and later American) missionaries – undermined traditional patterns of relations between Muslims and non-Muslims in the region. Eventually, the traditional system would break down completely, as different *dhimmi* communities drifted into sharper competition and mutual suspicion (e.g., pitting Greek Orthodox against Uniate Catholic communities), and some of them developed proto-national identities.

Across the border in Iran, very different developments were underway. The roots of the Safavid dynasty lie in the radical Sufi orders popular among the Turkmen of northwestern Iran and eastern Anatolia in the later Middle Period. During the fifteenth century, the Safawiyya order of mystics took on an increasingly chiliastic and political form, embracing a militant commitment to holy war and also a potent mix of Sufi and shamanistic doctrine. Through their combination of militancy and Sufi extremism they acquired a loyal following among the Turkmen, who came to be known as the *qızılbash* ("red heads") because of their distinctive headgear. The future shah Ismaᶜil, who became leader of the order in 1493 at the age of six or seven, expressed his claims to leadership in different forms, including assertions that are astonishing by any common Islamic standards: for example, that he was the agent of the Hidden Imam heralding his imminent arrival, or that he was himself the Imam returned, or even that he was

---

[7] Masters, *Christians and Jews*, 61–5; Benjamin Braude, "Foundation Myths of the *Millet* System," in *Christians and Jews in the Ottoman Empire: The Functioning of a Plural Society*, ed. Benjamin Braude and Bernard Lewis (New York: Holmes and Meier, 1982), 1:69–88; Amnon Cohen, "On the Realities of the *Millet* System: Jerusalem in the Sixteenth Century," in *ibid.*, 2:7–18; and *EI²*, art. "Millet" (by M. O. H. Ursinus).

an incarnation of the deity. Inspired by these claims, the *qızılbash* conquered much of Iran and Iraq in the first decade of the sixteenth century, in the process establishing the Safavids as rulers with the capacity to challenge the supremacy of the Ottomans in the Islamic Near East.[8]

In the longer term, the rise of the Safavids is important for its impact on the religious identity of the Iranians. Having come to rule over a large territory with ancient political traditions, the Safavids found it necessary to tone down the extremist religious ideas which had motivated their original followers. Their abandonment of chiliastic expectations did not occur all at once: even towards the end of the period of Safavid rule, the shahs are reported to have kept a bevy of horses in the "stable of the Imam of the Age," two of which were kept saddled for the use of the Imam and the Messiah, Jesus son of Mary, upon their re-appearance. But gradually the religious extremism which had propelled the movement forward in the late fifteenth and early sixteenth centuries was replaced by the Safavids' embrace of orthodox Twelver Shiʿism. This was a development of major significance, since most Iranians were in the early sixteenth century Sunnis. The process by which Iran became overwhelmingly Shiʿi took longer than has sometimes been thought, and the precise religious commitments of the Safavid shahs themselves remained for some time ambiguous. There was some suspicion among Shiʿi ulama over the sincerity of Ismaʿil's embrace of Twelver Shiʿism and the lingering claims of the Safavid shahs to the authority of the Imam. Over time, however, the Safavid state successfully cultivated the support of Shiʿi scholars, many of them eventually induced to move to Iran from centers of Shiʿi learning in Lebanon, Bahrayn, and elsewhere. Shah ʿAbbas I (r. 1588–1629), for example, undertook a substantial program of constructing and endowing mosques and schools for the support of Shiʿi scholars in the Safavid capital of Isfahan, in the ancient center of Shiʿi scholarship Qum, and elsewhere. Above all, the Safavids entrusted to the Shiʿi religious establishment a campaign to persuade and coerce the population of Iran to embrace Twelver Shiʿism – hence, for example, a decree in 1532 placing the religious affairs of the kingdom in the hands of ʿAli al-Karaki, a Shiʿi jurist originally from Jabal ʿAmil in Lebanon, and authorizing him to expel Sunni ulama from Safavid territory and to deputize Shiʿi prayer leaders to Iranian villages to instruct their inhabitants in Twelver doctrine.[9]

If the Safavid regime resulted eventually in the reorientation of Iranians' religious identity, it also set the stage for the resolution of certain outstanding issues concerning religious authority in Shiʿi Islam. The shifting character of the

[8] On the origins of the Safavids, see Michel M. Mazzaoui, *The Origin of the Ṣafawids: Shīʿism, Ṣūfism, and the Gulāt* (Wiesbaden: Franz Steiner, 1972); Said Arjomand, *The Shadow of God and the Hidden Imam: Religion, Political Order and Societal Change in Shiʿite Iran from the Beginning to 1890* (Chicago: University of Chicago Press, 1984), 66–84.

[9] Andrew J. Newman, "The Myth of the Clerical Migration to Safawid Iran: Arab Shiite Opposition to ʿAlī al-Karakī and Safawid Shiʿism," *Die Welt des Islams* 33 (1993), 66–112; Devin Stewart, "Notes on the Migration of ʿĀmili Scholars to Safavid Iran," *Journal of Near East Studies* 55 (1996), 81–103; Kathryn Babayan, "The Safavid Synthesis: From Qizilbash Islam to Imamite Shiʿism," *Iranian Studies* 27 (1994), 135–61.

Safavids' claims to authority, and the development of an extensive network of religious institutions in Iran, formed the background to a doctrinal dispute among the Twelver ulama over the nature of religious authority in the absence of the Imam. Al-Karaki drew on doctrines stressing the religious authority of the properly-trained scholar or *faqih* and his ability to interpret for "common" (*ʿammi*) Twelvers the will of the Hidden Imam. This position, which grew out of the principles articulated by Imami scholars beginning in the tenth and eleventh centuries, became known as that of the "Usuli" school, because of its emphasis on certain rationalist "principles" or "foundations" (*usul*) of jurisprudence, and in general the ulama associated with the Safavid court and with the principal Iranian religious institutions followed the Usuli line. An alternative approach, stressing the authority of traditions (*akhbar*) from the Imams and rejecting the use of human reasoning and in particular the leading scholars' exercise of *ijtihad* (and known therefore as the "Akhbari" school), was hardly new in Safavid Iran, but it experienced a revival during the seventeenth and eighteenth centuries, especially in institutions and networks at some remove from the centers of Safavid power – in schools in smaller towns, for example, and in the Shiʿi shrine cities in southern Iraq. The debate was a nuanced one. It was perhaps inevitable that the Akhbaris in particular would represent a fairly broad spectrum of opinion – after all, it is easy enough to say in principle that the traditions of the (now hidden) Imams are authoritative, but inevitably problems or questions arise for which there was no clear guidance in the Imams' recorded statements. With the decline and finally the disappearance of the Safavids and their ambiguous claims in the eighteenth century, the Usuli ulama eventually overcame Akhbari opposition, confirming their own position as authoritative interpreters of the will of the Imam and laying the groundwork for the emergence of the doctrine of *vilayat-i faqih*, the "guardianship" or "governance of the jurist" – the doctrine which informed the revolution in Iran in the 1970s and the regime established by the Ayatollah Khomeini.[10]

On the Sunni side, too, the eighteenth century saw developments which foreshadowed conflict and controversy in the modern period. In much of the Islamic world, the eighteenth century was a period of decay in the authority of the principal states. But it also saw the flourishing of a number of movements of religious reform and revivalism. The sect which took its name from Muhammad ibn ʿAbd al-Wahhab, a Hanbali teacher from Najd in central Arabia, is the best known of these movements, largely because of its alliance with the Arabian family

---

[10] On the Akhbari/Usuli dispute, see Arjomand, *The Shadow of God*, 122–59; Andrew J. Newman, "The Nature of the Akhbārī/Uṣūlī Dispute in Late Ṣafawid Iran. Part 1: ʿAbdallāh al-Samāhījī's *'Munyat al-Mumārisīn'*," *Bulletin of the School of Oriental and African Studies* 55 (1991), 22–51, 250–61; Etan Kohlberg, "Aspects of Akhbari Thought in the Seventeenth and Eighteenth Centuries," in *Eighteenth-Century Renewal and Reform in Islam*, 133–60; Juan Cole, "Shīʿī Clerics in Iraq and Iran, 1722–1780: The Akhbārī-Uṣūlī Conflict Reconsidered," in *Iranian Studies* 18 (1985), 3–34; Devin Stewart, *Islamic Legal Orthodoxy: Twelver Shiite Reponses to the Sunni Legal System* (Salt Lake City: University of Utah Press, 1998), esp. 179–89; and *EI²*, art. "Ṣafawids," part IV: "Religion, Philosophy, and Science" (by Andrew Newman).

of Saᶜud which, in the twentieth century, led to the establishment of the Saᶜudi state in most of the peninsula. But the Wahhabis were only one of a number of similar revivalist movements, in Arabia, in the Ottoman Empire, in India and elsewhere. There were plenty of differences between these movements: the Wahhabis were Hanbalis, but others grew out of the other *madhahib*; the Wahhabis tended to be hostile to Sufism, but others took root within and were cultivated by Sufi *turuq*. But the disparate movements also shared much in common: a respect for Ibn Taymiyya and his ideas, for example, and consequently a simultaneous exaltation of Prophetic *sunna* and also a willingness not to bind themselves too closely to previous constructions of Islamic identity and authority. Many of them sought to purge Islam of what they considered accretions, alien ideas or practices which had been grafted onto a presumably "pure" and "original" Islam, and in this respect they carried over the homogenizing tendency which had been one of the principal characteristics of Islam in the Middle Period.[11] Above all, these movements were, by and large, activist: that is, they looked for the reformation of Islam, a reformation to be brought about through the action and preaching of properly informed religious scholars, rather than to any expectation of the imminent final intervention of God in history.

After 1800, the inhabitants of the Near East entered a new and different world. As a result of European imperial penetration and the broader reconfiguration of the global political order, traditional religious identities were subject to extraordinary and unforeseen pressures. For *dhimmis*, the new world order brought opportunities, sometimes in the form of claims to separate political identities (as for Maronite Christians in Lebanon, and later for Jews in the form of Zionism), sometimes as the possibility of subsuming religious differences in broader constructions of ethnic or national identity. By the end of the twentieth century, however, the modern period had brought with it considerably sharpened pressures for cultural homogeneity, with the result that non-Muslim populations in many places found themselves increasingly marginalized. Since much that was "modern" was Western in origin, the evolution of religious identity and authority in the modern period was probably even more traumatic for Near Eastern Muslims. The troubles encountered by the Tanzimat reformers in the Ottoman Empire in the middle of the nineteenth century, to reconfigure the legal order and in some cases the *shariᶜa* itself, are only one example of the dislocations brought about by the encounter between Islam and Muslim societies, on the one hand, and the enhanced political, economic, and intellectual power of non-Muslim Europeans on the other. From the late eighteenth century forward, the construction of religious identity and authority in the Near East would have to take place in a much larger, global context.

---

[11] Cf. Richard Bulliet, *Islam: The View from the Edge* (Columbia University Press, 1994), 185f.

Suggested reading

Note: This is not intended to be either a full bibliography or a complete list of works cited. Rather, it seeks to provide the general reader with a limited list of bibliographic references that might serve as a basis for further reading. More extensive citations will be found in the notes.

Part I: The Near East before Islam

Bagnall, Roger S., *Egypt in Late Antiquity* (Princeton: Princeton University Press, 1993)

Bowersock, Glen, *Hellenism in Late Antiquity* (Ann Arbor: University of Michigan Press, 1990)

Brown, Peter, *The World of Late Antiquity, AD 150–750* (New York: Harcourt Brace Jovanovich, 1976)

The Cambridge History of Iran, vol. 3: *The Seleucid, Parthian and Sasanian Periods*, ed. Ehsan Yarshater (Cambridge: Cambridge University Press, 1983)

Feldman, Louis H., *Jew and Gentile in the Ancient World: Attitudes and Interactions from Alexander to Justinian* (Princeton: Princeton University Press, 1993)

Fowden, Garth, *Empire to Commonwealth: Consequences of Monotheism in Late Antiquity* (Princeton: Princeton University Press, 1993)

Frankfurter, David, *Religion in Greco-Roman Egypt: Assimilation and Resistance* (Princeton: Princeton University Press, 1999)

Haldon, J. F., *Byzantium in the Seventh Century: The Transformation of a Culture* (Cambridge: Cambridge University Press, 1990)

Herrin, Judith, *The Formation of Christendom* (Princeton: Princeton University Press, 1987)

Kaegi, Walter, *Byzantium and the Early Islamic Conquests* (Cambridge: Cambridge University Press, 1992)

Lane Fox, Robin, *Pagans and Christians* (New York: Knopf, 1987)

Lieu, Samuel N. C., *Manichaeism in Mesopotamia and the Roman East* (Leiden: E. J. Brill, 1994)

Lieu, Samuel N. C., *Manichaeism in the Later Roman Empire and Medieval China*, 2nd edition (Tubingen: J. C. P. Mohr, 1992)

Morony, Michael G., *Iraq after the Muslim Conquest* (Princeton: Princeton University Press, 1984)

Neusner, Jacob, *Talmudic Judaism in Sasanian Babylonia* (Leiden: E. J. Brill, 1976)

Newby, Gordon Darnell, *A History of the Jews of Arabia from Ancient Times to Their Eclipse under Islam* (Columbia, South Carolina: University of South Carolina Press, 1988)

Schäfer, Peter, *Judeophobia: Attitudes Towards Jews in the Ancient World* (Cambridge, Massachusetts: Harvard University Press, 1997)

Sharf, Andrew, *Byzantine Jewry from Justinian to the Fourth Crusade* (New York: Schocken Books, 1971)

Widengren, Geo, *Mani and Manichaeism* (New York: Holt, Rinehart, and Winston, 1965)

Part II: The Rise of Islam, 600–750

Choksy, Jamsheed K., *Conflict and Cooperation: Zoroastrian Subalterns and Muslim Elites in Medieval Iranian Society* (New York: Columbia University Press, 1997)

Crone, Patricia, *Meccan Trade and the Rise of Islam* (Oxford: Blackwell, 1987)

Crone, Patricia, *Slaves on Horses: The Evolution of the Islamic Polity* (Cambridge: Cambridge University Press, 1980)

Crone, Patricia, and Michael Cook, *Hagarism: The Making of the Islamic World* (Cambridge: Cambridge University Press, 1977)

Crone, Patricia, and Martin Hinds, *God's Caliph: Religious Authority in the First Centuries of Islam* (Cambridge: Cambridge University Press, 1986)

Donner, Fred, *The Early Islamic Conquests* (Princeton: Princeton University Press, 1981)

Donner, Fred, *Narratives of Islamic Origins: The Beginnings of Islamic Historical Writing* (Princeton: Darwin Press, 1998).

Grabar, Oleg, *The Formation of Islamic Art* (New Haven: Yale University Press, 1973)

Hawting, G. R., *The First Dynasty of Islam: The Umayyad Caliphate AD 661–750* (Carbondale and Edwardsville: Southern Illinois University Press, 1987)

Hawting, G. R., *The Idea of Idolatry and the Emergence of Islam: From Polemic to History* (Cambridge: Cambridge University Press, 1999)

Hodgson, Marshall, *The Venture of Islam: Conscience and History in a World Civilization*, in 3 volumes (Chicago: University of Chicago Press, 1974)

Hoyland, Robert G., *Seeing Islam as Others Saw It: A Survey and Evaluation of Christian, Jewish and Zoroastrian Writings on Early Islam* (Princeton: Darwin Press, 1997)

Humphreys, R. Stephen, *Islamic History: A Framework for History*, revised edition (Princeton: Princeton University Press, 1991)

Madelung, Wilferd, *Religious Trends in Early Islamic Iran* (Albany: Bibliotheca Persica, 1988)

Madelung, Wilferd, *The Succession to Muhammad: A Study of the Early Caliphate* (Cambridge: Cambridge University Press, 1997)

Morony, Michael G., *Iraq after the Muslim Conquest* (Princeton: Princeton University Press, 1984)

Newby, Gordon Darnell, *A History of the Jews of Arabia from Ancient Times to Their Eclipse under Islam* (Columbia, South Carolina: University of South Carolina Press, 1988)

Shaban, M. A., *Islamic History, A.D. 600–750 (A.H. 132): A New Interpretation* (Cambridge: Cambridge University Press, 1971)

Sharon, Moshe, *Black Banners from the East* (Jerusalem: Magnes Press, 1983)

Watt, W. Montgomery, *The Formative Period of Islamic Thought* (Edinburgh: Edinburgh University Press, 1973)

Watt, W. Montgomery, *Muhammad at Mecca* (Oxford: Clarendon Press, 1953)

Watt, W. Montgomery, *Muhammad at Medina* (Oxford: Clarendon Press, 1956)

Part III: The Emergence of Islam, 750–1000

Bulliet, Richard, *Conversion to Islam in the Medieval Period* (Cambridge, Massachusetts: Harvard University Press, 1979)

Bulliet, Richard, *The Patricians of Nishapur: A Study in Medieval Islamic Social History* (Cambridge, Massachusetts: Harvard University Press, 1972)

Calder, Norman, *Studies in Early Muslim Jurisprudence* (Oxford: Clarendon Press, 1993)

The Cambridge History of Egypt, vol. 1: *Islamic Egypt, 640–1517*, ed. Carl Petry (Cambridge: Cambridge University Press, 1998)

The Cambridge History of Iran, vol. 4: *The Period from the Arab Invasions to the Saljuqs*, ed. Richard N. Frye (Cambridge: Cambridge University Press, 1975)

Cooperson, Michael, *Classical Arabic Biography: The Heirs of the Prophet in the Age of al-Ma'mūn* (Cambridge: Cambridge University Press, 2000)

Daftary, Farhad, *The Isma'ilis: Their History and Doctrines* (Cambridge: Cambridge University Press, 1990)

Daniel, Elton, *The Political and Social History of Khurasan under Abbasid Rule, 747–820* (Minneapolis: Bibliotheca Islamica, 1979)

Kennedy, Hugh, *The Prophet and the Age of the Caliphate* (London: Longman, 1986)

Kraemer, Joel, *Humanism in the Renaissance of Islam: The Cultural Revival during the Buyid Age* (Leiden: E. J. Brill, 1986)

Lambton, A. K. S., *State and Government in Medieval Islam: An Introduction to the Study of Islamic Political Theory: The Jurists* (Oxford: Oxford University Press, 1981)

Madelung, Wilferd, *Religious Trends in Early Islamic Iran* (Albany, NY: Bibliotheca Persica, 1988)

Mediaeval Isma'ili History and Thought, ed. Farhad Daftary (Cambridge: Cambridge University Press, 1996)

Melchert, Christopher, *The Formation of the Sunni Schools of Law, 9th and 10th Centuries C.E.* (Leiden: E. J. Brill, 1997)

Momen, Moojan, *An Introduction to Shi^{c}i Islam: The History and Doctrines of Twelver Shi^{c}ism* (New Haven: Yale University Press, 1985)

Mottahedeh, Roy, *Loyalty and Leadership in an Early Islamic Society* (Princeton: Princeton University Press, 1980)

Newman, Andrew J., *The Formative Period of Twelve Shī^{c}ism: Ḥadīth as Discourse Between Qum and Baghdad* (London: Curzon, 2000)

Sabari, Simha, *Mouvements populaires à Bagdad à l'époque ^{c}abbaside, ixe–xie siècles* (Paris: Librairie d'Amérique et d'Orient, 1981)

Schacht, Joseph, *An Introduction to Islamic Law* (Oxford: Clarendon Press, 1964)

Schacht, Joseph, *On the Origins of Muhammadan Jurisprudence* (Oxford: Clarendon Press, 1950)

Sadighi, Gholam Hossein, *Les mouvements religieux iraniens au IIe et au IIIe siècle de l'hégire* (Paris: Les Presses Modernes, 1938)

Stewart, Devin, *Islamic Legal Orthodoxy: Twelver Shiite Reponses to the Sunni Legal System* (Salt Lake City: University of Utah Press, 1998)

Wheatley, Paul, *The Places Where Men Pray Together: Cities in Islamic Lands, Seventh Through the Tenth Centuries* (Chicago: University of Chicago Press, 2001)

Zaman, Muhammad Qasim, *Religion and Politics under the Early ^{c}Abbasids: The Emergence of the Proto-Sunni Elite* (Leiden: Brill, 1997)

Part IV: Medieval Islam, 1000–1500

Berkey, Jonathan, *Popular Preaching and Religious Authority in the Medieval Islamic Near East* (Seattle: University of Washington Press, 2001)

Berkey, Jonathan, *The Transmission of Knowledge: A Social History of Islamic Education* (Princeton: Princeton University Press, 1992)

Bulliet, Richard, *Islam: The View from the Edge* (New York: Columbia University Press, 1994)

Cahen, Claude, *Pre-Ottoman Turkey* (New York: Taplinger, 1968)

The Cambridge History of Iran, vol. 5: *The Saljuq and Mongol Periods*, ed. J. A. Boyle (Cambridge: Cambridge University Press, 1968)

Chamberlain, Michael, *Knowledge and Social Practice in Medieval Damascus, 1190–1350* (Cambridge: Cambridge University Press, 1994)

Ephrat, Daphna, *A Learned Society in Transition: The Sunni ^{c}Ulamā$^{\,\ni}$ of Eleventh-Century Baghdad* (Albany, NY: SUNY Press, 2000)

Geoffroy, Eric, *Le soufisme en Égypte et en Syrie sous les derniers Mamelouks et les premiers Ottomanes: orientations spirituelles et enjeux culturelles* (Damascus: Institut Français, 1995)

Hodgson, Marshall, *The Order of Assassins: The Struggle of the Early Nizārī Ismā^{c}īlīs Against the Islamic World* (The Hague: Mouton, 1955)

Holt, P. M., *The Age of the Crusades: The Near East from the Eleventh Century to 1517* (London: Longman, 1986)

Humphreys, R. Stephen, *From Saladin to the Mongols: The Ayyubids of Damascus* (Albany, NY: SUNY Press, 1977)

Islamic Civilisation, 950–1150, ed. D. S. Richards (Oxford: Cassirer, 1973)

Karamustafa, Ahmet, *God's Unruly Friends: Dervish Groups in the Later Islamic Middle Period, 1200–1500* (Salt Lake City: University of Utah Press, 1994)

Laoust, Henri, *Essai sur les doctrines sociales et politiques de Takī-d-dīn Aḥmad b. Taimīya* (Cairo: Institut Français d'Archéologie Orientale, 1939)

Lapidus, Ira, *Muslim Cities in the Later Middle Ages* (Cambridge, Massachusetts: Harvard University Press, 1967)

Makdisi, George, *Ibn ʿAqīl et la résurgence de l'Islam traditionaliste au xie siècle (ve siècle de l'Hégire)* (Damascus: Institut Français de Damas, 1963)

Makdisi, George, *The Rise of Colleges: Institutions of Learning in Islam and the West* (Edinburgh: Edinburgh University Press, 1981)

Mediaeval Ismaʿili History and Thought, ed. Farhad Daftary (Cambridge: Cambridge University Press, 1996)

Morgan, David, *Medieval Persia, 1040–1797* (London: Longman, 1988)

Petry, Carl, *The Civilian Elite of Cairo in the Later Middle Ages* (Princeton: Princeton University Press, 1981)

Pouzet, Louis, *Damas au viie/xiiie siècle: vie et structures religieuses d'une métropole islamique* (Beirut: Dar al-Machreq, 1988)

Sartain, Elizabeth, *Jalā al-Dīn al-Suyūṭī*, 2 vols. (Cambridge: Cambridge University Press, 1975)

Shoshan, Boaz, *Popular Culture in Medieval Cairo* (Cambridge: Cambridge University Press, 1993)

Sivan, Emmanuel, *L'Islam et la croisade: Idéologie et propagande dans les réactions musulmane aux croisades* (Paris: Librairie d'Amérique, 1968)

Stewart, Devin, *Islamic Legal Orthodoxy: Twelve Shiite Reponses to the Sunni Legal System* (Salt Lake City: University of Utah Press, 1998)

Trimingham, J. S., *The Sufi Orders in Islam* (Oxford: Clarendon Press, 1971)

Winter, Michael, *Society and Religion in Early Ottoman Egypt: Studies in the Writings of 'Abd al-Wahhāb al-Shaʿrānī* (New Brunswick, NJ: Transaction Books, 1982)

Epilogue: From Medieval to Modern Islam

Arjomand, Said, *The Shadow of God and the Hidden Imam: Religion, Political Order and Societal Change in Shiʿite Iran from the Beginning to 1890* (Chicago: University of Chicago Press, 1984)

Christians and Jews in the Ottoman Empire: The Functioning of a Plural Society, ed. Benjamin Braude and Bernard Lewis (New York: Holmes and Meier, 1982)

Eighteenth-Century Renewal and Reform in Islam, ed. Nehemia Levtzion and John O. Voll (Syracuse: Syracuse University Press, 1987)

Imber, Colin, *Ebuʾs-Suʿud: The Islamic Legal Tradition* (Stanford: Stanford University Press, 1997)

Itzkowitz, Norman, *Ottoman Empire and Islamic Tradition* (Chicago: University of Chicago Press, 1980)

Kafadar, Cemal, *Between Two Worlds: The Construction of the Ottoman State* (Berkeley: University of California Press, 1995)

Marcus, Abraham, *The Middle East on the Eve of Modernity: Aleppo in the Eighteenth Century* (New York: Columbia University Press, 1989

Mazzaoui, Michel, *The Origin of the Ṣafawids: Shīʿism, Ṣūfism, and the Ġulāt* (Wiesbaden: Franz Steiner, 1972)

Masters, Bruce, *Christians and Jews in the Ottoman Arab World: The Roots of Sectarianism* (Cambridge: Cambridge University Press, 2001)

Repp, R. C., *The Mufti of Istanbul: A Study in the Development of the Ottoman Learned Hierarchy* (London: Ithaca Press, 1986)

Safavid Persia: The History and Politics of an Islamic Society, ed. Charles Melville (London: I. B. Tauris, 1996)

Savory, Roger, *Iran Under the Safavids* (Cambridge: Cambridge University Press, 1980)

Scholars, Saints, and Sufis: Muslim Religious Institutions in the Middle East Since 1500, ed. Nikki R. Keddie (Berkeley: University of California Press, 1972)

Shaw, Stanford, *History of the Ottoman Empire and Modern Turkey*, vol. 1: *Empire of the Gazis: Rise and Decline of the Ottoman Empire, 1280–1808* (Cambridge: Cambridge University Press, 1977)

Index